The Return of Oral Hermeneutics

"I welcome this provocative book. Steffen and Bjoraker rightly challenge Christians to embrace a more balanced approach to interpreting the Bible and applying it faithfully to daily life. They offer a lengthy defense of oral hermeneutics, of course, but they also show how to guide ordinary men and women to use oral hermeneutical processes to dig deeply into God's word and open themselves to its transforming power."

—**Grant Lovejoy**, International Mission Board, SBC

"Whatever you've thought about understanding the Bible, think again. Whatever you said in Bible studies, sermons, or wrote in commentaries, think again. Most of us were schooled only in textual ways to read Scripture. But that's a serious neglect of how to listen to God's voice, especially if we want to understand the Bible the way original hearers did. All of us need to enter into the world of oral culture, and Steffen and Bjoraker do a masterful job of showing the way. You owe it to yourself and to God to read this groundbreaking, hermeneutics-altering work."

—**D. Brent Sandy**, co-author of *The Lost World of Scripture: Ancient Literary Culture and Biblical Authority*

"Steffen and Bjoraker reestablish the place and power of *experiencing the word in community*."

—**Regina Manley**, author of *StoryFire*

"This book is a must-read for any Bible teacher who wants to understand how to effectively teach the Bible because all Bible teachers engage in oral communication of the Bible message at some point. Anyone interested in effective communication of the message of the Bible will benefit greatly from learning how oral hermeneutics works. This book is engaging enough for the scholar and yet accessible to the newcomer to this subject because of the 'handles' the authors include in the book. Readers can actually see how this works. I highly recommend this book to all Bible teachers and serious students of the Bible."

—**Bulus Y. Galadima**, Cook School of Intercultural Studies, Biola University

"Steffen and Bjoraker bravely go where few have dared to venture."

—**Larry W. Caldwell**, Sioux Falls Seminary

"Nearly erased or forgotten, oral hermeneutics is rediscovered, re-robed, and renewed. Steffen and Bjoraker are passionate academicians with the heart and hands of experienced practitioners. Elegantly written through storytelling, calmly articulated with a sense of urgency, compellingly illuminating the vivid oral voices of communities, the authors propose and provide ways and means forward. A must-read for anyone who is serious about the Bible and engagement in this century."

—**Samuel E. Chiang**, The Wycliffe Seed Company

"Steffen and Bjoraker have written an important book that, used properly, can revitalize the use of the Bible—bringing passion, life, and interaction. The book sets out a program for interaction and transformation that can be very powerful in so many ways. It is important to note that an ancient Hebraic way of thinking (not always the Greek influenced Rabbinic way) was based on engaging truth on a personal level. This book shows how that way of approach to the Scriptures can be made available to the modern reader—Jew and Gentile. . . . I hope that many small groups embrace the methods provided here. It will revitalize all who desire to see the success of small groups as essential to the life of congregations."

—**Daniel Juster**, Union of Messianic Jewish Congregations; Tikkun International

"Tom Steffen and William Bjoraker make a convincing case that interpreting the Bible orally has been neglected too long, both in the West and the majority world. They not only lay out the importance of oral hermeneutics, but they also illustrate it practically from their own extensive experience. I only wish I had encountered this book when I began teaching the Bible. Carefully researched and passionately argued, this book will help you see biblical narratives through a fresh and exciting lens."

—**Dean Flemming**, MidAmerica Nazarene University

"May well lead to a counterrevolution in the way we read, witness, write, and share God's story!"

—**John Cheong**, Asian Centre for Mission

"I have wanted a book like this to exist for a long time! Tom Steffen and William Bjoraker give us a glimpse into what it could look like to interpret the Bible in light of its oral background. Rather than merely identify the limitations to textual interpretation, they make a positive contribution. The book weaves together insights from multiple disciplines. It draws from their experience and the best of academic scholarship. The authors challenge readers to consider how ancient oral practices can inform contemporary ministry strategies. This book deserves a slow, careful read. I expect *The Return of Oral Hermeneutics* will have long-lasting influence among missionaries as it should for anyone who cares about biblical interpretation."

—Jackson Wu, author of *Reading Romans with Eastern Eyes*

"Whatever we want to call walking through God's great book with adults with limited formal education or any adult who prefers a non-reading experience, we must find a learning approach that works for this population—the majority of those on our planet. Like Steffen and Bjoraker, I have lived through the failure of textual hermeneutics with my own national partners. Something must change in the way Westerners attempt to do Bible study with the rest of the world—especially with our non-reading friends. I pray and believe this resource and others sure to follow will help along those lines."

—Lynn Thigpen, IMB missionary, Southeast Asia

"The early church's authoritative sacred text was less about physical and material texts as it was the stories they told from their respective memories of texts. Their disciples were hearers, for the most part, and not readers. Passed on through worship services were oral stories and reflections that contained memory of that which they held to be experientially sacred. In *The Return of Oral Hermeneutics*, professors Steffen and Bjoraker introduce readers to the church's ancient word as it sounded in the ancient world, all the while speaking to, for, and about the essence and substance of (re)discovering storytelling—to help us recover the lost art for our own. I commend this book."

—Jeffrey Seif, King's University-Houston

"A long overdue contribution for training pastors and teachers."

—Chuck Madinger, International Orality Network, Manila

The Return of Oral Hermeneutics

*As Good Today as it Was for the Hebrew Bible
and First-Century Christianity*

Tom Steffen
AND
William Bjoraker

FOREWORD BY
R. Daniel Shaw

WIPF & STOCK · Eugene, Oregon

THE RETURN OF ORAL HERMENEUTICS
As Good Today as it Was for the Hebrew Bible and First-Century Christianity

Copyright © 2020 Tom Steffen and William Bjoraker. All rights reserved. Except for brief quotations in critical publications or reviews, no part of this book may be reproduced in any manner without prior written permission from the publisher. Write: Permissions, Wipf and Stock Publishers, 199 W. 8th Ave., Suite 3, Eugene, OR 97401.

Wipf & Stock
An Imprint of Wipf and Stock Publishers
199 W. 8th Ave., Suite 3
Eugene, OR 97401

www.wipfandstock.com

PAPERBACK ISBN: 978-1-5326-8480-7
HARDCOVER ISBN: 978-1-5326-8481-4
EBOOK ISBN: 978-1-5326-8482-1

Copyright © 2011 by the Common English Bible. Used by permission. All rights reserved.

Copyright © 1998 by the Complete Jewish Bible: David H. Stern. Jewish New Testament Publications, Inc. Used by permission. All rights reserved.

Scripture quotations marked "Darby" are taken from the Darby Translation Bible (Public Domain).

Copyright © 2001 by the ESV® Bible (The Holy Bible, English Standard Version®): Crossway. Used by permission. All rights reserved.

Scripture quotations marked KJV are from the King James Version of the Bible (Public Domain).

Copyright © 1993, 2002, 2018 by *The Message* by Eugene H. Peterson: NavPress. Used by permission. All rights reserved.

Copyright © 1960, 1962, 1963, 1968, 1971, 1972, 1973, 1975, 1977, 1995 by the NEW AMERICAN STANDARD BIBLE®: The Lockman Foundation. Used by permission. All rights reserved.

Copyright © 1982 by the New King James Version®: Thomas Nelson, Inc. Used by permission. All rights reserved.

Copyright © 1973, 1978, 1984, 2011 by the New International Version®, NIV®: Biblica, Inc.TM Used by permission. All rights reserved.

Copyright © 1996, 2004, 2015 by the New Living Translation: Tyndale House Foundation. Used by permission. All rights reserved.

Copyright © 2014, 2016 by the Tree of Life Version: Tree of Life Bible Society. Used by permission. All rights reserved.

Copyright © 2012 by The Voice Bible: Thomas Nelson, Inc. Used by permission. All rights reserved.

Manufactured in the U.S.A.   08/16/22

Contents

Lists of Illustrations: Figures and Tables | ix
Foreword by R. Daniel Shaw | xi
Preface | xvii
Abbreviations | xxix

Setting the Stage | 1

Part 1: Demonstrations
1 Elisha and the Widow's Oil | 23
2 Reflections on the Elisha Story | 46

Part 2: Propositions
3 Orality's Influence on Text and Teaching | 63
4 Oral Hermeneutics | 103
5 Hebrew Hermeneutics | 135
6 Character Theology | 164
7 Questioning Our Questions | 196
8 Reflections | 230

Part 3: Echoes
9 Elisha and General Naaman | 247
10 Reflections on the Elisha Story | 274

Concluding Reflections | 292

Glossary | 315

Appendix A: Three Communication Eras | 320

Appendix B: The Continuum between Reading and Listening | 321

Appendix C: Alter's Oral-Textual Parameters | 322

Appendix D: The Quintessential Characters, Stories, and Texts of the Old Testament | 325

Appendix E: The Wise Counselor Story | 335

Bibliography | 339

Illustrations

Figures

3.1. First-Century Interfacing Dynamics within the Biblical Text | 66
3.2. Dominant Genres of Scripture Percentages | 96
4.1. The Robust Role of Oral Hermeneutics | 105
4.2. From Oral Hermeneutics to Creative-Correct Theology | 130
6.1. Character Theology Extends Existing Theologies | 165
7.1. Discovering Meaning through Literary-Based Questions | 202
7.2. Four Components of Oral Hermeneutics | 216
7.3. Questions for the Storying Process | 220
11.1 Oral Hermeneutics Summarized in a Wagon Wheel | 309

Tables

5.1 Four P's and Four D's | 161
6.1. Strategies for Biblical Criticism | 169
7.1. Character Explicitness Scale | 205
11.1. Oral Hermeneutic-Textual Hermeneutic Continuum | 307

Foreword

THE POWER OF STORY! I can recall good stories and their tellers: my granddad, eyes twinkling as he told of homesteading in Prineville, Oregon; a Sunday school teacher who captivated my attention as she narrated the story of Abraham taking his son up the mountain thinking he was about to offer his "boy" to God; stories of cannibal raids told by aging Samo men deep in the jungles of Papua New Guinea on a longhouse porch. I sat in awe of each one. But then I put away "childish" things and became a "man," got a PhD in anthropology, and became a professor at Fuller Seminary—propositions, didactic teaching with a logical argument, and publishing became the hallmarks of my existence. What happened to a good story? Is it a thing of the past or are we rediscovering the power of story to move human beings to reflect on what they can learn about God and about themselves as Tom Steffen and Bill Bjoraker maintain?

We give our grateful thanks to Moses, the prophets, the translators of the Septuagint, and even the scribes who gave Jesus such a difficult time, for the long tradition of writing God's word down, and preserving what was an even longer oral tradition. I recall my awe in looking at squiggles on papyrus a few years ago at the Dead Sea Scrolls expedition in Los Angeles. I experienced the same wonder when looking at an original of the Gutenberg Bible when it came to the Huntington Library. I felt like I was actually looking at history—wow. But that history, despite its value for us who live with the power of the written word, is based on a much longer oral tradition—stories passed from generation to generation, preserving over time the essence of what God intended us to understand about himself. And that oral style was thankfully preserved in the transcriptions of oral text, a close proximity of how the story was presented when the amanuensis put the oral style into writing.

Often when we from the West read the Bible, especially the Old Testament, we get a bit bored because stories are frequently repeated. That repetition reflects the oral style that cognitive psychologists Robert McCauley and Thomas Lawson note enhances memory.[1] A story told in great detail, later in the context of another story and then referenced repeatedly thereafter, gives credence to the impact of retelling on memory. Stories like the Israelites crossing the Jordan River and setting up a monument of twelve stones at their camp that first night in the land God was in the process of giving them. The stones, we are told, were a monument of remembrance for that momentous river crossing. Later we learn that the monument also provided an opportunity for people to tell the story in order to remind their children what happened there, and later still the monument is incorporated into other stories as a reminder of God's faithfulness to Israel (Josh 3–5 and following). Oral repetition reinforces the message behind the story but also provides opportunity for entertaining children, and an opportunity for reflection on fond memories which are passed from one generation to the next. This is not boring text (what McCauly and Lawson call the "tedium effect"[2]), rather it is a vibrant, culturally appropriate communication style that ensures understanding, retention, and ongoing communication, what Daniel Sperber and Deirdre Wilson considered the essence of "relevance theory."[3] The ancient Hebrews and their kind down through the centuries wonderfully preserved their stories as traditions, rituals, and meaningful acts that not only enhanced relevant presentation of stories, but made them memorable and meaningful for audiences across the ages, and around the world today.

In this book Steffen and Bjoraker set out to recapture the wonder of orality and its impact on our thinking. They not only show us how to tell a good story and model what they call "oral hermeneutics" in part 1, they provide a rationale for applying orality to our contemporary globalizing/digitizing existence. Through the well-argued part 2, they provide for orality what has long been the case for literary/textual approaches. They develop an argument to structure our thinking through the implications of using our aural factors rather than our tactile responses. And in part 3 they "represent" (as Martin Noth called it)[4] the past to make it new again in order to reinforce the lesson in part 1. In short, the book models the authors' intent to help nonoral processors rediscover the art of storying on the one hand, and hearing God's word on the other.

---

1. McCauley and Lawson, *Bringing Ritual to Mind*, 38.
2. McCauley and Lawson, *Bringing Ritual to Mind*, 51.
3. See Sperber and Wilson, *Relevance*.
4. See Noth, "'Re-Presentation' of the Old Testament Proclamation."

From his years with the Ifugao in the Philippines, Steffen illustrates his discovery of oral processing, and how that rewired his brain. Bjoraker shows how his interaction with Jewish people around the world enabled him to recognize how orality and textuality combine to help him appreciate a long Talmudic tradition that values story and it's telling in any form necessary for effective communication. Similarly, I cannot communicate without presenting what I have learned from the Samo of Papua New Guinea. That is now a fifty-year story of language and culture learning, translating portions of the Bible, annual visits after we went to Fuller, and now increasing time and ongoing relationships that include renewed efforts to ensure they have God's word in forms they can apply to their lives. Despite many well-schooled Samo engaged as pastors, medical orderlies, and all manner of occupations and activities, they remain, at their core, oral storytellers. For the Samo (as most peoples of this island nation) orality is their primary mode of learning and experiencing life.

In the last several years, my wife and I and the Wycliffe team involved have encouraged the Samo to use their own narrative stories and songs. When they realized that they are part of the metanarrative of the entire canon, they put themselves into God's big picture. Rather than singing songs to petition ancestral spirits to intervene on their behalf, they began to sing translated portions of the Bible that answered the questions of life. As life happened, they found stories and experiences in the lives of biblical charterers that mirrored their own. Similarly, they allowed the biblical message to transform their rituals and ceremonies to reflect their understanding of incarnation, God's word with them. They relied on the Holy Spirit to counter the spiritual powers arrayed against them. All this looked very pagan and unbiblical for the Western-trained national missionaries who brought a linear, logical mindset that mimicked their well-meaning teachers and benefactors from Australia, New Zealand, and the Americas. Gradually literary biblical texts took precedent over stories, and traditional approaches were put aside as Christianity became a Sunday morning ritual rather than an approach to life.

Many questions ensued and the beginnings of revitalization had the Samo asking who they were as a people standing before God's throne with all those "dressed in white" (Rev 7:9 MSG). How could these Samo believers, who carried the texts in their hearts, recapture their first love of Jesus born from translated Scripture they had put to song? Well, they began to sing again—not the pedantic church songs, but rather their traditional song style applied to singing Bible verses that connected God to life.

At the same time, Samo pastors attended a Bible storying workshop (led by a Bible translator), and began to adapt storying approaches around the hearth as well as in church. Rather than reading a biblical passage, translating it, and telling people what it said, pastors began to tell stories using their own narrative style. As they experimented, worship increasingly consisted of telling a story about real people in real places doing real things. Then the congregation would break into gender- and age-specific groups for a time of thinking through the story—discussing the content and its implications for them, much as Bjoraker presents in part 1. The pastor then reconvened excited people and listened carefully as they shared insights he could incorporate into a final sermonette, communicating the relevance of the Bible story to Samo life as expressed by the congregation. The stories made sense because they reflected Samo experience as they dealt with spiritual forces all around them. The Bible affirms this reality, and they increasingly have the tools to apply their logic to worshiping God, who by his grace honors them in the reality of their circumstances. Church attendance is increasing, and oral hermeneutics made it happen.

I present the Samo as a case study of the points the authors of this book make as they present the logic of their argument; orality is not only relevant in today's world, but was the hallmark of biblical approaches to understanding human interaction with God, and God's manifestations in and through those who honored him. Orality came before textuality and was never buried deep in biblical text. They go on to present how Hebrew hermeneutics structured Jewish thought and worship through ritual and song that encased truth, and how strength of character, as God's in-built image, is reflected in each human being. By introducing biblical characters through time and space, they demonstrate the value of establishing identity through genealogies, names, and patterns of behavior, all to help those who hear the stories see the face of God in the human context. They note how questions relate to truth shaped by cultural experience in contrast to questions born of literature and vicarious experience (though the latter provides an awareness of the larger world of ideas). Relevant questions emerge from life and reflect back on God's intervention in the human context as people seek to know God.

None of this is designed to eliminate literacy, books, and all things textual. Rather Steffen and Bjoraker seek to demonstrate how the logic subsumed in literary style emanates from orality that clearly had priority in terms of development, and increasingly impacts our contemporary, digital world. The logic which sociologist Margaret Archer calls "reflexivity" enables human beings to capture their identity, internalize what is meaningful, and apply the results to dealing with social structures on the one hand and personal identity, i.e., "agency," on the other.[5] Centuries of neglecting orality have removed an innate human propensity for deriving logic from story rather than literary text; a focus on relationship and reflection rather than independence and isolated congruity. The nature of our increasingly globalized and digitized existence drives us back to who we are: human beings created in the image of God. The master plan is encapsulated in the first and second commandments, "Love the Lord your God" and "Love your neighbor as yourself" (Matt 22:37–39 NIV). Relationship with God establishes personal identity while relationship with others connects one with sociality. Connecting people to their heritage as revealed in God's eternal story enables each person to experience God in the context of their own reality.

The message of this book is as old as the biblical record and as relevant and contemporary as the latest news report on a smartphone. It is a story of human beings in intimate relationship with God through Jesus Christ in the power of the Holy Spirit. It is the story of each individual intimately connected with the God of the universe. May you rediscover God's story as you place yourself in the flow of God's eternal plan, and experience anew your own identity as a child of God intimately listening to and talking with your Lord. Enjoy discovering your preliterate being.

R. Daniel Shaw

Sr. Professor of Anthropology and Translation,
Fuller School of Intercultural Studies

---

5. Archer, *Structure, Agency and the Internal Conversation*, 153.

Preface

> "The real voyage of discovery consists not in seeing new landscapes, but in having new eyes."
>
> —MARCEL PROUST

THIS BOOK BUILDS THE case for *the return of oral hermeneutics* to better understand, interpret, and teach the Bible ("the book") in the twenty-first century at home and abroad, using oral means. Building this case will take us on a journey back to antiquity when oral hermeneutics had a dominant role among faithful Jewish and then Christian teachers of the Faith—before the canon of Scripture was formed, during its formation, and after its completion—all with the hope you will see how instructive it can be for Bible storytellers/teachers today.

Why Was this Book Written?

Textual hermeneutics, a grammatical approach to hermeneutics, always had a place among the Jewish custodians of Scripture, but it was the specialized task of few, the literate scribes and scholars. The majority of the people learned God's word through oral hermeneutics, i.e., interpreting the interactions within and between characters, the recitation of laws and the poetry, and the retelling of the stories in the annual feast cycle of Israel. Cultural change and developments over the centuries brought about a shift from oral dominance to textual dominance in the learning and teaching of Scripture. One of the pivotal changes in early modernity came through the emergence of the "Gutenberg Galaxy"[1] in the fifteenth century. The invention of the Gutenberg press helped privilege *textual hermeneutics* over *oral hermeneutics,* especially in modern Western culture. *Is it time to recover some of the lost treasures of oral hermeneutics to better understand the Divine Author who came and spoke to us in person—the Word who became flesh?* Because the majority of the world today are oral learners and orality-oriented, we believe the time is ripe to retrieve the practices of oral hermeneutics and thus better connect with the majority of the populace today.

Why Another Book on Hermeneutics?

Books on hermeneutics abound, including multiple editions of bestsellers. They range from the philosophical to the practical, offering various views.[2] Big names in this crowded city from the past and present are readily available: Martin Heidegger, Hans-Georg Gadamer, Gordon Fee, Howard Hendricks, Walter Kaiser, Roy Zuck, Millard Erickson, D. A. Carson, J. Scott Duvall, Elliott Johnson, Scot McKnight, Grant Osborne, N. T. Wright, David Bauer, Robert Traina, and Kevin Vanhoozer, just to name a few. *So why another book on hermeneutics to add to the massive, ever-expanding collection? What could all those sophisticated scholar-writers have minimized or missed? What can two missionary/professors who were called to very different audiences (tribal people and Jewish people) add to the conversation?*

On the practice side, I (Tom) do bring some experience to the conversation, particularly on the oral realities of interpretation. This included fifteen years of missionary involvement in the Philippines, where my family lived for almost eight of those years among the animistic Antipolo-Amduntug Ifugao who reside in central Luzon. My wife Darla, our three girls, and I lived in a rented Ifugao house where we saw a church planting movement emerge, conducted a literacy program for the few who still could not read,[3] organized medical services, and assisted in checking some of the New Testament translated by our colleagues, Dick and Lou Hohulin of Wycliffe Bible Translators.

---

1. Marshall McLuhan coined the term "Gutenberg Galaxy" in a book by that title in 1962 for the communication era and universe of discourse that emerged when, through the printing press, printed materials became widely disseminated, an increasing number of people became literate, and a reading public was constituted. Prior to this, "there was no reading public, only public reading" (Walton and Sandy, *Lost World of Scripture,* 23).

2. See Porter and Stovell, *Biblical Hermeneutics.*

3. Many of these were the elderly or those who babysat younger siblings while their siblings attended school and their parents worked the fields.

Part of that experience included observing a tribal people move swiftly from a predominantly oral society to a functionally literate one. During that time period the Ifugao retaught me the importance of story, something my mother had instilled in her three children years prior, but I had sadly long forgotten, strongly influenced by my formal education. I eventually distanced myself, but not totally, from propositions to Bible stories when evangelizing or teaching Scripture to the Ifugao.[4] At least these propositions now had a concrete home from which they had emerged.

Another related experience involved what was formerly known as Chronological Bible Teaching (presently Firm Foundations). As a former member of New Tribes Mission (now Ethnos360) I was privileged to be in on the foundation of this seven-phase, story-based model that moved seamlessly from evangelism to discipleship as it marched across the landscape of Scripture from creation to consummation.[5]

Initiated by Australian Trevor McIlwain, this model covered the *entire* Bible in a relatively short period of time. It assumed the Bible was one book, one story; the Old Testament provided the necessary foundation for grasping the gospel and other teachings found in the New Testament, and Jesus Christ unified the two testaments. McIlwain's contribution soon went global, culminating in the modern-day Orality Movement.[6]

As the modern-day Orality Movement spread across the globe, including parts of the West,[7] Bible storying models proliferated. Some were lengthy, e.g., McIlwain's evangelism Phase 1 (of seven) alone consisted of sixty-eight Bible stories. Others were compressed to only a few stories. Still others, e.g., Creation to Christ (C2C), could cover Genesis through the ascension in a manner of minutes.[8]

On the professional side, as I came across the various oral-teaching models, I examined how they introduced the story and analyzed the questions that followed. I wanted to discern if and how their introduction, along with the review, application, and accountability questions, were influenced by textual hermeneutic. *How was the story introduced? What was the focus? Ideas? Content? Characters? Clashes? Choices? Inconsistencies? Contributions?*

---

4. See Steffen, "Pedagogical Conversions"; Steffen, "Discoveries Made."

5. We agree with Bates when he says, "Evangelism programs are only accurate and compelling when they are not merely an invitation to forgiveness but an invitation to full-orbed discipleship" (Bates, *Salvation by Allegiance Alone,* 210).

6. See chapters 2 and 3 in Steffen, *Worldview-based Storying* for a brief history of the movement.

7. See Snowden, *Orality in America.*

8. J. O. Terry, a major contributor for the Southern Baptist in the Orality Movement, calls this "fast tracking."

Changes? Consequences? Circumstances? Words? Phrases? Grammar? The individual? The community? How did the questions relate to the various value-moral systems, such as: innocence and guilt, honor and shame, power and fear, purity and pollution?

I soon discovered the typical hermeneutic model used tended to elicit shallow content, abstract ideas, and be driven by the legal value-moral system of innocence and guilt generally preferred in the West. Jayson Georges and Mark Baker define innocence-guilt as "commonly encountered in Western, Anglo contexts." It is "individualistic. It relies on conscience, justice and laws to regulate social behavior."[9] I wondered if our culture had blinded us to other relational value-moral systems cherished by our respective audiences *and* Scripture.

I (Bill) came out of an experience quite different from that of my co-author. Since my college days in the mid 1970s I have had a life calling to the Jewish people. My wife Diana and I have served as missionaries to the Jewish people for over 35 years—eight years in Tel Aviv, Israel, in pastoral and teaching ministries, where we became fluent in modern Hebrew. We have served in outreach to Jewish people in southern California for the last twenty-five years, where over 750,000 Jewish people reside.

The Jewish people, known as "the people of the book," are also people of books. If ever there was a highly literate people, it is the Jewish people. Historically, the high education level and literary skills of Jewish people paved the way for their many successes. I thought, "If I want to be successful communicating theological ideas to Jewish people, I must learn to effectively debate ideas with learned Jewish people."

On the professional side, after achieving my goal of attaining a PhD, I believed I was intellectually prepared for outreach and ministry to Jewish people. I was quite practiced in delivering expositional Bible studies with outlines in a largely lecture form. I could do analytical exegesis. I was well-read in systematic theology.

---

9. Georges and Baker, *Ministering in Honor-Shame Cultures*, 18. This strongly Western, but not exclusively so, value-moral system has strongly influenced Western theology, evangelism, and discipleship. For example, John Piper, like many other Westerners, defines the gospel from a legal perspective, "The good news is that God himself has decreed a way to satisfy the demands of justice" (Piper, *Desiring God,* 59). This is of course true, but it is not the only aspect of the atonement. The *Christus Victor* view of the atonement is not so much a rational systematic theory as it is a drama, a dramatic passion story of God triumphing over Satan and the powers and liberating humanity from the bondage of sin and death. See 1 John 3:8b; Col 2:14–15. God's honor was properly restored and Satan publicly put to shame. See Steffen, "Minimizing Crosscultural Evangelism Noise." See also the blog posted January 17, 2018 on HonorShame.com titled, "4 Problems with Guilt-Based Morality."

But over the years, I became quite weary of using apologetics and argumentation. Jewish people, and especially those schooled in Rabbinic thought, can argue and debate you to a standstill over who is the Messiah and other theological issues. Head-to-head messianic versus rabbinic apologetics was usually futile in terms of winning Jewish people to faith in Jesus the Messiah.

Then, in 2008, I met Larry Dinkins, another missionary with a PhD. He began to tell me his story of how his high-level Bible college and seminary training was not working in Thailand. So he sought a Thai to write a book on systematic theology but could not find one. That is because Thai are largely oral-preference learners, preferring theology drawn from experience.

Through a narrative course at Biola University's Cook School of Intercultural Studies, Dinkins experienced a paradigm shift and with new eyes began using this recent oral way of communicating scriptural truths with the Thai and other Asians using Simply the Story (STS) methodology.[10] It revolutionized his teaching and ministry.

This impressed me, but I assumed storytelling was generally an approach used with nonliterate and uneducated people, so my first response was to think it irrelevant to Jewish ministry. Sure, storytelling is suitable for nonliterate oral learners, but I am trying to communicate with modern-day Jewish people.

But it did not take me long to think twice—stories would be Jewish-friendly, if one used the stories of the Hebrew Bible (the Old Testament). Because Christianity was birthed out of Israel in the first century, the spiritual and intellectual roots of all followers of Jesus are with the Jewish people. Israel and Judaism are the matrix for the Christian faith. Curiously, however, the majority of Jewish people today are secularized, and not well-read in the Bible. Except for the Orthodox minority, they treat the Bible as national tradition and folklore, but not as the word of God.

Here is a peculiar fact—that a very literate people have a high percentage of biblical illiteracy. And they are illiterate in their own great contribution to the world, the eternal book of books—the Hebrew Bible! *Could part of the reason be in the ineffective way modern Judaism communicates its religious knowledge?* There are multiple reasons, but it appears for many modern Jewish people Judaism's messaging has simply not been interesting, engaging, or compelling. *Could a return to an oral hermeneutic be one remedy to this biblical illiteracy among the Jewish people?*

---

10. See a video demonstration of a storytelling event from Ex 17:1–7 at a Jewish Bible Study by Bill Bjoraker: https://www.youtube.com/watch?v=ZhHWeOKM1Wo.

Yet the Jewish people carry at least a vestigial collective memory, an awareness, that the stories of the Hebrew Bible are *their* stories. So I figured these stories of the Jewish people, the stories of Israel, would be nonthreatening and resonate with them. I believed it was worth a try. So I began to use oral storytelling in a weekly Jewish seeker's Bible study that lasted about three years in the Los Angeles area. We had between twelve and thirty who attended each week, and up to one-third of them were Jewish. My Jewish friends loved it! It is the best approach I have ever discovered for engaging Jewish seekers with the word of God.

One Jewish man embraced Yeshua (Jesus) as his Messiah through our group at that time. Several Jewish seekers attended and participated in the story discussions even before they embraced Jesus as Messiah; they participated in the stories and bonded with the group.

A Jewish man is his early eighties, who lived most of his life in New York City, and who came to faith in the Messiah about three years prior, attended our seekers study. He told me, "I grew up in Hebrew school and synagogue and had to learn the stories of the Torah and Hebrew Bible, but I never really knew the stories the way I have learned them now; they have come to life!"

I, like Dinkins, began to have new eyes in the way I saw effective Jewish ministry. I did not see as effective a highly technical approach to exegesis of written texts, giving erudite analyses of Hebrew words and texts to argue my case, titillating the left-brain propensities but not reaching the heart.

Most people today are looking for relational truth or heart truth more than cognitive academic truth. Stories speak to the heart, and discussing them creates relationships. I saw the power of oral storytelling to reengage Jewish people with their own ancestral stories, nearly all of which point to their Messiah. I was becoming convinced we needed a *new* approach to communicating the Bible to Jewish people. Without much further reflection, I realized they just needed to return to an *older* Jewish tradition of interpretation. To engage them in the Bible, we needed to return to oral hermeneutics.

Has our fascination for a fixed printed text that brings precision and exactitude blinded us to other hermeneutic possibilities? Is there something beyond cerebral-cognitive documents, outlines, words, standard and stock phrases, series of editions of printed versions of texts, grammar, semantics, and ideas?

Denver Seminary distinguished professor of Old Testament Daniel Carroll R. ferrets out the obscure: "Seminary courses and books on hermeneutics are not always helpful in acknowledging the influence of one's socioeconomic, ethnic, and racial context on interpretation."[11] *Have we allowed our times (modernism, the Enlightenment, postmodernism) to control and limit how we approach Scripture? Does orality free us from many of these constraints so we can interpret the word more fully as it was intended, particularly the narrative portions? Does orality offer a fuller understanding of not only the cognitive but also the affective/cultural/psychological/motivational context the author had in mind? Is it time for an additional, or retrieved, hermeneutic? Is it time for an additional type of theology and theologizing?* The central question of this book is: *Why is it important to know and practice oral hermeneutics in order to ascertain and communicate biblical meaning?*

The authors wish to state up front that in no way does this book attempt to discount, disavow, demean, or dismiss the many admirable contributions made by textual theoreticians and/or practitioners over the years. These *have* a place and time (Eccl 3). Rather, our desire is to expand and advance the conversation in the hope it will enable many more at home and abroad to experience and internalize the fear of God that results in godly wisdom and in honoring the Anointed One. Our desire for this book is *not to end the discussion—as if we have the arguments all sewed up—but to advance an ongoing conversation* about features and factors that have remained in the hermeneutic shadows for far too long.

Who Should Read this Book?

Whether locally or globally, whether in the majority world or the minority world, whether with oral learners or those who can read but prefer to learn orally, if you give your testimony, evangelize, disciple those in the faith, preach, conduct home, church, or campus Bible studies, plant churches, translate the Bible, go on short-term mission trips, work with refugees and immigrants, the sexually abused, or those enslaved, if you teach the Bible in accredited or nonaccredited institutions, conduct nonformal Bible seminars, or wish to make your institution's Bible courses available to the majority world, then this book is for you. We write this book for pastors, small group leaders, short-termers, missionaries, Bible teachers, Bible professors, Bible curricula writers, evangelists, disciplers, social justice advocates, and those who develop church or business leaders in the majority and minority worlds.

How audiences respond to a hermeneutic used in ministry will determine to a great extent how robust, how fast a Christian movement will birth and grow. *Does the present hermeneutic used come across as foreign to your audience? Too technical? Is it reproducible by the majority?*

11. Keener and Carroll R., *Global Voices*, 2.

All Christian workers who minister, from children to adults, from professionals to practitioners, will find this book helpful in removing some of the foreignness and technicalness found in some textual hermeneutics. Many books on hermeneutics seem daunting and intimidating to ordinary followers of Jesus. Oral hermeneutics help make the Bible more lifelike, natural, inviting, memorable, user-friendly, and reproducible. Possibly most importantly, *it empowers people beyond those in the pastorate to witness, teach, and equip others with confidence!*

How the Authors View Scripture

This book proposes some profound and radically different ways of approaching Scripture that harken back to the centuries before the Enlightenment and the modern Western way of approaching knowledge and authorizing it. We are concerned that these approaches might in some ways give the impression that we are embracing an approach that rejects the universal authority of Scripture and a supreme respect for all that it contains. That is in no way our objective.

The authors understand that what is advocated in the following pages will be seen by some as questionable, if not "another liberal intrusion."[12] We at one time would have been among that contingency. To help calm the fears of our readers we include our assumptions about Scripture by affirming this summary of the 1978 Chicago Statement on Biblical Inerrancy.

A Short Statement

1. God, who is Himself Truth and speaks truth only, has inspired Holy Scripture in order thereby to reveal Himself to lost mankind through Jesus Christ as Creator and Lord, Redeemer and Judge. Holy Scripture is God's witness to Himself.

2. Holy Scripture, being God's own Word, written by men prepared and superintended by His Spirit, is of infallible divine authority in all matters upon which it touches: it is to be believed, as God's instruction, in all that it affirms; obeyed, as God's command, in all that it requires; embraced, as God's pledge, in all that it promises.

---

12. Weathers, "Leland Ryken's Literary Approach," 115. When Ryken explicated the literary art and design in Scripture that had always been there and talked of the Bible as literature, he was criticized as caving to liberalism.

3. The Holy Spirit, Scripture's divine Author, both authenticates it to us by His inward witness and opens our minds to understand its meaning.

4. Being wholly and verbally God-given, Scripture is without error or fault in all its teaching, no less in what it states about God's acts in creation, about the events of world history, and about its own literary origins under God, than in its witness to God's saving grace in individual lives.

5. The authority of Scripture is inescapably impaired if this total divine inerrancy is in any way limited or disregarded or made relative to a view of truth contrary to the Bible's own; and such lapses bring serious loss to both the individual and the Church.[13]

Credit to Contributors

No book is the work of a single (or in this case two) author. We therefore would also like to acknowledge those who have been instrumental in the development of this book. We thank them for their time, insights, and encouragement. These include: Regina Manley, J. O. Terry, Michael Castro, Michael Matthews, and Ray Neu. Special thanks go to Jennifer Jagerson, whose fingerprints can be found throughout the book. We would also like to thank the many Ifugao and Jewish people who taught us so much about the very book we went to teach them. And we would like to especially thank our virtuous wives, Darla Steffen and Diana Bjoraker, for their persistent patience with us.

Breaking Down the Book

This book breaks down as follows. Part 1 demonstrates what we will later define. We begin by setting the stage for making the case for the return of oral hermeneutics. Chapter 1 provides a concrete example of the use of oral hermeneutics in an oral inductive Bible study of the story of "Elisha and the Widow's Oil." This chapter foregrounds, embodies, and demonstrates in action what is to follow in the book. Chapter 2 summarizes key reflections from the Bible story we will later develop and expand.

The two oral inductive story presentations in chapters 1 and 9 serve as bookends of practice enclosing the theory. Sandwiching the theory between

---

13. International Council on Biblical Inerrancy, "Chicago Statement on Biblical Inerrancy."

the two slices of bread of the practice of oral storying gives a place of honor to oral story as the dominant genre of Scripture, and the primary expression of oral hermeneutics. To use another metaphor, we are inviting you to join us as we dip into the flow of the master story of the whole Bible, connecting at that point in the stream where Elisha stories are dominant in 2 Kings. Experience the current with us as we wade in at the beginning and end of the book. In between, we will step out onto the shore, as it were, and reflect on what's going on, and what's going down in the flow. This will help us all wade back in with new vigor as participants in the master story and ride the river to its glorious destiny (Rev 22:1).

Part 2 lays out our *propositional proposals* on oral hermeneutics based on the clues partially provided from the story of "Elisha and the Widow's Oil." It reviews how the canon evolved from voice to text, and how the spoken and written interfaced, and how this is significant for oral hermeneutics today. Over time, scientific logic, theorizing, atomized textual analysis, linear thought, propositions as the main product of biblical interpretation,[14] and systematic theology dominated, and this situation extends to today.

This reality raises a number of questions: *Is strong print-based systemization too one-sided for a complex world where the majority are oral or oral-preference learners?*[15] *Was the Bible designed for only scientific inquiry? Was grammatical breakdown of a text always necessary to secure its meaning? Should systematic theology harken back to its biblical theology roots which captures a deep and comprehensive understanding of the whole unfolding story, thereby providing a rich, Scripture-wide understanding of God and*

---

14. The "dean" of evangelical theologians in the last century, Carl Henry, claims, "As an achievement of the Holy Spirit's inspiration, Scripture presents us with the remarkable phenomenon of a canon concerned primarily with the propositional disclosure of God . . . . By its emphasis that divine revelation is propositional, Christian theology in no way denies that the Bible conveys its message in many literary forms such as letters, poetry and parable, prophecy and history. What it stresses, rather, is that the truth conveyed by God through these various forms has conceptual adequacy, and that in all cases the literary teaching is part of a divinely inspired message that conveys the truth of divine revelation . . . and of course the expression of truth in other forms that the customary prose does not preclude expressing that truth in declarative proposition" (Henry, *God, Revelation, and Authority*, 3:96, 463). Note the emphasis on the conceptual.

15. Grant Lovejoy estimates "5.7 billion people in the world are oral communicators because either they are illiterate, or their reading comprehension is inadequate" (Lovejoy, "Extent of Orality," 5). This percentage would no doubt go higher if limited to the Global South.

In regard to literacy in the US, which has remained static in the last decade, "1. 32 million can not read . . . 14% of the population. 2. 21% of US adults read below the 5th grade level. 3. 19% of high school graduates can not read. 4. 85% of juveniles who interact with the juvenile court system are considered functionally illiterate" (Gaille, "15 US Literacy Rate and Illiteracy Statistics," para. 2.

humans? How does shortcutting, by going from the Bible directly to systematic theology and straight for the categorical and abstract, undermine the deeper, more whole and human meaning of the text?

The question addressed in chapter 3 is: *How does orality influence text and teaching?* To answer this question the authors consider how orality and text interfaced before, during, and postconstruction of the canon, something often overlooked in relation to hermeneutics. In the search for a new way to theologize, we mull over orality, the role of scribes, individual and collective memory, and how manuscripts were delivered and discussed.

Chapter 4 offers a possible course correction to textual hermeneutics without jettisoning it. This chapter calls for a new (actually an old) hermeneutic that specifically addresses the literary portions of Scripture, making Scripture more accessible and meaningful to a large and growing audience of oral-preference learners worldwide. It lays out the need for, and definition of, oral hermeneutics.

Interestingly, what the authors discussed and called for in the former chapter—oral hermeneutics—existed centuries before. Chapter 5 reviews Hebrew hermeneutics that highlight the distinctives between textual hermeneutics and oral hermeneutics, taking some cues from the first custodians of Scripture—the rabbis, scholars, and teachers of the Jewish people. As a wise man once said, "There is nothing new under the sun" (Eccl 1:9 NIV).

In our frailty, humans are continually vulnerable to the biases and emphases of our own age, and each generation has an opportunity to make adjustments and additions even as they build on their strong shoulders. Perhaps we have an opportunity now to recognize the over-emphases embraced by biblical scholars under the influence of the Enlightenment and correct them by incorporating some of the powerful modes of a more oral hermeneutic, resulting in a more robust understanding of Scripture. This chapter focuses the spotlight on the need for another, different type of hermeneutic, theologizing, and theology.

Chapter 6 proposes a different type of theologizing and theology that goes beyond, but does not discard, systematic theology, biblical theology, or narrative theology. We call it *theologizing* as the verbal form fits the dynamic and in-practice process that happens in oral hermeneutics. We call it *theology* as the noun form fits the results—Bible characters who demonstrate and display various aspects of theology—*character theology*. This chapter addresses how oral hermeneutics relies on character theologizing (process) that results in character theology (product) so that we can build an initial and ongoing relationship with the Chief Character.

All hermeneutics find their base steadied on sets of questions. Chapter 7 delves into the questions currently being used in many prominent Bible study models today, such as, Discovery Bible Study (DBS), T4T (Training for Trainers), OT4T (Orality Training for Trainers), S-T4T (Storying Training for Trainers), DMM (Disciple-Making Movements), STS (Simply the Story), Any3, and Simple Church.

Often, the questions used today for drawing out the truth of a Bible story or story set often find their foundational base burrowed deeply in the textual hermeneutic tradition. As well, they evoke and promote strongly Western legal values-morals, such as innocence and guilt (right and wrong, black and white, truth and justice), and neglect the very present values-morals of honor and shame. Building on leading lights such as Meir Sternberg, Leland Ryken, Grant Osborne, Kevin Vanhoozer, and a host of others—who recognized the questions used for the Epistles are inappropriate for the narrative and poetic sections of Scripture—we will question some of the questions currently used in Bible study.

The authors will also offer suitable substitutes from an oral perspective that focus strongly on the concrete characters found in the biblical text. The questions will also highlight other social values and morals consistent within the biblical texts, and the host culture(s), such as the relational language of honor and shame, the control language of power and fear and the hygienic language of purity and pollution. While all of these social values-morals are found in any culture, most likely two will be dominant. Whether one or more, the storyteller can expect it or them to influence the interpretation of Scripture.

Chapter 8 concludes part 2 by reviewing and reflecting on the challenges and contributions of oral hermeneutics highlighted in chapters 4–7.

Part 3 offers a second opportunity to demonstrate what we discussed in the previous chapters, this time to dedicated readers who have clearer vision and better hearing in relation to our intent. We dip back into the narrative flow of 2 Kings where the sounds of previous chapters reviewed here provide Bible communicators echoes of distinctives and overlap between oral hermeneutics and character theology.

Chapter 9 conveys the story of "Elisha and General Naaman" found in 2 Kings 5. As in the former parts, we conclude part 3 by again offering our reflections (chapter 10). We then tender concluding reflections, summarizing echoes of threads and ideas heard throughout the journey of the entire book, as we built the case for the return of oral hermeneutics at home and abroad.

Abbreviations

BAM	Business as Mission
BBC	British Broadcasting Company
C2C	Creation 2 Christ
CT	Character Theology
CBS	Chronological Bible Storying
CBT	Chronological Bible Teaching
CBR	*Currents in Biblical Research*
CJB	Complete Jewish Bible
DBS	Discovery Bible Study
DMM	Disciple-Making Movements
EFL	English as a Foreign Language
ESV	English Standard Version
IMB	International Mission Board
ION	International Orality Network
LOP	*Lausanne Occasional Paper*
JAAR	*Journal of American Academic Research*
JAM	*Journal of Asian Mission*
JBTM	*Journal for Baptist Theology and Ministry*
JETS	*Journal of the Evangelical Theological Society*
JBL	*Journal of Biblical Literature*
MNT	Mace New Testament
NKJV	New King James Version
NIV	New International Version
NT	New Testament

NTM	New Tribes Mission (now Ethnos360)
OBS	Oral Bible School
OH	Oral Hermeneutics
OT	Old Testament
OT4T	Orality Training for Trainers
SBL	Society of Biblical Literature
S-T4T	Storying Training for Trainers
STS	Simply the Story
T4T	Training for Trainers
TESOL	Teaching English to Speakers of Other Languages
TH	Textual Hermeneutics
TLV	Tree of Life Version
TMSJ	*The Master's Seminary Journal*
USSR	Union of Soviet Socialist Republics
WNET	Call letters for a radio station, a subsidiary of thirteen.org

Setting the Stage

"The single biggest problem in communication
is the illusion that it has taken place."

—George Bernard Shaw

"Creativity is always a leap of faith. You're faced with
a blank page, blank easel or an empty stage."

—Julia Cameron

This introduction sets the stage for making the case for the return of oral hermeneutics. Here, in their own words, are some reasons we take this journey:

> I suspect I'm not the first biblical studies instructor in an African theological college to notice the vast gap between what we discuss in class and what our students experience when they return to their home churches. After we spend hours talking about how to understand and use the Bible, honing skills in grammatical-historical exegesis, seeking to produce a careful, reasoned understanding of the meaning a biblical author intended to communicate to his original audience, my students too often find that their churches have little interest in this sort of biblical interpretation. The students' academic contributions sometimes receive a cool welcome when what their congregations long for is a fresh word from the Lord through the Bible, speaking directly to their situation today. In fact, our

students sometimes find that they are labeled as 'unspiritual' because their reading of the Bible lacks spontaneity and immediacy. After observing this for some time, I began to ask myself, 'Is it them? Or is it us?'[1]

I diligently taught my students the 'proper' methods of Bible interpretation and they just as diligently wrote down and memorized everything I said. I taught them the finer points of Bible interpretation, from initial exegesis to sermon preparation. Several of my students did surprisingly well in class. Most struggled. And then, on the weekends, I would accompany them to their rural church field education assignments and listen to them preach in their churches. Here was my chance to observe them putting into practice what they had so painstakingly learned in my classroom. Or so I thought. In stark contrast to the exegetically correct and logically constructed three-point sermons they had prepared in class, what I heard were sermons full of allegories and folksy illustrations, with a storyline that seemed to run circles around a loosely constructed main point. They were exegeting the Bible in ways that would earn them a failing grade in the classroom. I was one disconcerted hermeneutics professor! . . . . Are we really training Asians for Asia?[2]

I grew up in an oral culture but in school we were discouraged from using oral methods to communicate; rather, we are rewarded with good grades for writing fine research papers and other print assessment methods. Unfortunately, when I go back to my home in Korea, they do not understand me anymore. I forget how to communicate using the oral methods that the local people appreciate! I feel like a duck out of water.[3]

I [pastor Dinanath of India] was saved from a Hindu family in 1995 . . . I had a desire to learn more about the word of God and I shared this with the missionary. The missionary sent me to Bible College . . . I finished two years of theological study and came back to my village in 1998. I started sharing the good news in the way I learnt in Bible College. To my surprise my people were not able to understand my message . . . I continued

---

1. Black, "Key Hermeneutical Questions," 3.
2. Caldwell, "Towards the New Discipline of Ethnohermeneutics," 26, 29.
3. Moon, "Encouraging Ducks to Swim," 3.

to preach the gospel, but there were little results. I was discouraged and confused and did not know what to do.[4]

Why Read this Book?

Warning: If you read and digest this book you may experience a paradigm shift in relation to hermeneutics, as we have. We ask you to read our entire book and give it a fair hearing. You may discover what we are discovering from our personal stories, practices, and the literature surveyed.

One reason to read this book is because the world has changed. Today's audiences at home and abroad have a growing penchant for orality—stories, visuals, symbols, rituals, the experiential, the digital—and for recognizing honor and shame (a moral value dynamic that has been downplayed in modern Western culture).

A second reason to read this book is the Bible world has not changed. In antiquity, there was strong preference for orality—stories, visuals, symbols, rituals, the experiential—and valuing honor and shame.

The first two reasons hint at a third: The Bible world and our present postmodern world (modernity being approximately AD 1600–1980) which includes the launching of the digital age, both having strong ties to orality (a preferred way to hear, process, communicate, remember). Both value orality more than did the modern period. We have come full circle. Just add the digital world to the oral world and stir.

The authors believe that biblical eras have much to teach us about how to conduct hermeneutics for today's audiences around the globe. We call it oral hermeneutics. If correct, these discoveries have tremendous implications for today's exegetes/Bible communicators. *Does our weak understanding of orality influence our depth of understanding Scripture and her Author?* We believe it does, and therefore have not written a manual on orality or Bible storying—lots of those exist. Rather, we make the case theoretically and practically to the academic world for a return of oral hermeneutics.

For those who wish to drill deeper, the authors have included extensive footnotes and quotes. Others may wish to continue turning pages. Some will resonate with the theoretical chapters while others the practical ones. Either way, the aggregate reasons provided along the journey make a strong case for the return of oral hermeneutics.

---

4. Lausanne Occasional Paper, *Making Disciples of Oral Learners*, 2.

Boring Bible?

Nothing stays the same for long. Static writing eventually challenged the organic naturalness of orality. As print culture began to predominate in modernity, new ways of thinking were not only possible but now required.[5] And these changes had to be learned not through informal socialization as was orality, but through nonformal and formal study. These changes influenced Bible interpretation as it now became possible to analyze print rather than people. Not without consequences, characters gave way to grammar in Bible interpretation.

Interestingly, once we learned to read or were taught theology, much of that concreteness associated with orality[6] vanished like smoke into thin air. For example, too many sermons we have heard were laced with abstractions, Hebrew and Greek words that the audience did not understand, and "Christianese" (insider jargon), boring us to death! And we are not alone; this has been the experience of many.

I (Tom) have heard many Bible students in various schools claim theology is so boring. While the reasons for this are surely varied, it does raise some questions: *Was it lazy students in the classrooms (or pews) with short attention spans who grew up on sound bites and were unwilling to do the hard work of deep study and research?* Possibly. *But what about we Bible teachers?* While I am not aware of any Bible teacher intentionally trying to make the Bible boring, it happens. I have been a victim, and so have many others, and sadly, I have produced victims!

Research conducted by the American Bible Society in 2018 discovered 54 percent of adults are disengaged from, or indifferent to, the Bible, even as 66 percent of all Americans expressed some interest in learning more about what the Bible has to say![7] *Have we Bible teachers unintentionally made the Bible a stumbling block for certain audiences? Might the growing biblical illiteracy in the West be at least the partial responsibility of we who teach? What is our responsibility in making the Bible relevant and awe-inspiring?*[8]

---

5. See Ong's *Orality and Literacy*.

6. Orality (oral-aural-visual-digital-social) denotes pedagogical preferences designed to process, remember, and communicate verbally and pictorially through social connections, imagining, and identifying with characters in stories rather than through literate instructional forms.

7. American Bible Society, "State of the Bible 2018," 6, 12.

8. Who is having real success in getting people into the Bible and the Bible into people in this age of biblical illiteracy? We note the outstanding impact of "The Bible Project" based in Portland, Oregon.

The Bible Project has produced animated videos on every book of the Bible, available on YouTube. CT reports that just the video on the book of Job has been watched

SETTING THE STAGE

With over half of the Bible delivered in the narrative genre, *what does this signal about interpretation and communication approaches other than our dominant modern ones? With a populace that is posttext, postfacts, and which continues blindly down the road to soulless secularization,*[9] *what does this suggest about how to make the Bible relevant? Have our "text-bound minds"*[10] *blinded us to other possibilities?*

Here are some questions that begin to probe the issues that motivated this book:

> *Why has church attendance continued to drop?*[11] *Why the move of many evangelicals to Orthodoxy and Catholicism?*
>
> *Why are African-Americans with a rich Christian heritage converting to the Black Hebrew Israelites (who believe they are descendants of the ancient Israelites) or drawn to the Nation of Islam?*
>
> *Why do many highly educated African-American millennials, First Nations people, and those from India perceive Christianity as a white man's religion?*

---

more than 3 million times. The Bible Project has more than 1 million subscribers on YouTube, and over 90 million total views on their videos. How have they generated such interest? The key is bringing the Bible to life through portraying its stories visually. Leaders of the project, Tim Mackie and Jon Collins, are of the millennial generation, met at the SkateChurch, and are solidly evangelical Bible scholars. They state their vision of the Bible as "a unified story that leads to Jesus" (Pastor, "How the Bible Project is Using Video," para. 3). They understand the impact of visualized stories. Their videos are keenly in tune with genre, themes, plot, characters, and poetic devices of the biblical literature, and are produced with technical excellence. And a group-learning or discussion-learning aspect is present—Mackie and Collins always narrate and teach together in good rapport in each video.

9. The men's fashion world magazine *GQ* just rated the Bible as the 12th most overrated book of all time. "The Holy Bible is rated very highly by all the people who supposedly live by it but who in actuality have not read it. Those who have read it know there are some good parts, but overall it is certainly not the finest thing that man has ever produced. It is repetitive, self-contradictory, sententious, foolish, and even at times ill-intentioned" (Editors of GQ, "21 Books You Don't Have to Read," 17). He goes on to suggest Agota Kristof's *The Notebook* as a replacement. Contrast that with Jewish talk show host Dennis Prager's bestseller ranked between the top 10 and top 40 of *all* books sold (not just religious) on Amazon today, *The Rational Bible: Exodus*. We wonder if the *GQ* authors have read the Bible. And we wonder if anyone ever brought the Bible to life for them?

10. Ong, *Orality and Literacy*, 153.

11. See Slavsky, "Gallup Poll." See also Pew Research Center, "Why America's 'Nones' Don't Identify with a Religion." The main reason given is that they question much of religious teaching. Could some reality-based Bible stories with similar human thinking make a difference in their perception?

Why do many baby boomers take issue with the numerous contradictions found in Scripture, concluding it is a flawed document unworthy of attention?

Why do so many Western millennials (born in or after 1981) and those who comprise Generation Z (born in or after 1996) perceive Scripture as irrelevant for today?

In a postfactual world, why do we continue to rely predominantly on statements of fact to grasp and communicate God's message?

Could some of the answers possibly lie in the need for an additional hermeneutic?

An additional type of theologizing driven by a different type of questions?

An additional type of theology?

What are the roles of characters and relationships in their world?

How do such audiences prefer to ascertain meaning?

Relationships for humans find their exemplar in the Trinity where relationship has always existed. Trinity Evangelical Divinity School professor of systematic theology Kevin Vanhoozer astutely observes, "The point of Trinitarian theology . . . is that it is the essence of God to be in relationship to other persons."[12] Because of the Trinitarian relationship, we, his creation (Gen 1:26), are born relationalists who naturally connect vertically and horizontally.

We need others in our lives; we think, act, and identify socially. We are social selves in search of relational exchanges; we are interconnected. The need for relationships, reflecting the Trinity, adds natural and necessary value to our lives.

How can the Bible, which focuses on relationships between humans, animals, and spiritual characters (e.g., God, Satan, angels, demons, donkeys, Cain, Job, Rahab, Naaman, Esther, Daniel, David, Solomon, Mary, Onesimus) in concrete contexts (e.g., palaces, temples, deserts, wildernesses, fields, roads, rivers, seas, beds, battlefields), in specific societies (nomadic tribals, pastorals, city-states, kingdoms), ever be boring? There are guts and gore, glee, giants, gems, galaxies, garments, gazelles, grapes, gaffes, greed, guards, goats, grain, gates, generosity, gentiles, guests, greetings, groups, gifts, gods, God, government, genitals, guilt, grief, growth. Put on your crash helmets! Nothing boring here!

---

12. Vanhoozer, *First Theology*, 80.

The Bible is a story primarily featuring relational events about the Supreme Authority encountering humans and humans encountering him. Vanhoozer advances, "God does not play the world drama all on his own; he makes room for man to join in the action. The theme of theology is God and humanity as covenant partners-agents in dramatic relationship . . . at the heart of the biblical action is the relationship, and the conflict, between two freedoms: human and divine."[13] But the divine-human relationship that began in a garden of glamour with daily walks soon ruptured. The first privileged occupants made bad choices. The antagonist won the first round and the garden of glamour became a desert of drabness and restriction to former occupants. Even sin is rooted in relationships (Rom 2:23; 14:23).

Insightful author Philip Yancey adds another perspective to ruptured relationships between the Creator and his created: "More than any other word pictures, God chooses 'children' and 'lovers' to describe our relationship with him as being intimate and personal."[14] The Bible is a story about ruptured and restored relationships[15] (not just ideas and categories) where humans, the spirit world, and the material world interface.

Human and spiritual relationships require conversations, deep conversations often held over long periods of time in multiple settings. Such conversations create opportunity for learning and restoration. Relationships develop through personal and public conversations on both human and spiritual levels in concrete contexts. Conversations serve as the seat of exchanges and changes. Conversations serve the same role in oral hermeneutics.

The Bible is the story about historical, collective[16] relationships played out in time and place through conversations,[17] actions, and interactions.

13. Vanhoozer, *Drama of Doctrine*, 49.

14. Yancey, *Bible Jesus Read*, 33.

15. Tim Keller suggests that "If this world was made by a triune God, relationships of love are what life is really all about" (Keller, *Jesus the King*, 9).

16. Richard Bauckham captures the collective concept this way: "individuals understood themselves and were understood as related to a group as 'dyadic' or, better, 'polyadic' and 'socially embedded' persons" (Bauckham, *Jesus and the Eyewitnesses*, 173). In contrast, we in the West tend to think individualistically.

17. Robert Alter writes, "Everything in the world of biblical narrative ultimately gravitates toward dialog—perhaps . . . because to the ancient Hebrew writers speech seemed the essential human faculty" (Alter, *Art of Biblical Narrative*, 182). Brenda Colijn quotes Martens to contrast contracts with covenants: "Elmer Martens argues that a contract is 'thing-oriented,' is established in order to gain benefits, and depends on performance, while a covenant is 'person-oriented,' is established out of a desire for relationship, and depends on loyalty." And of course, the Bible is about covenants. She then defines reconciliation as "the restoration of relationship between two parties that have been estranged" (Colijn, *Images of Salvation*, 45, 177).

More specifically, it is about a life-changing relationship,[18] a rescued relationship through the efforts of the Chief Character of Scripture—Jesus Christ. Centered on relationships, oral hermeneutics serves as a tool to interpret such relationships.

The Bible is about us becoming corporate members of the community of Christ in a material world that anxiously awaits eschatological redemption (Rom 8:19–21). It goes far beyond gaining an initial spiritual relationship with the liberating King to continually refreshing that relationship that someday culminates in eternal rewards (1 Tim 4:7–8). In a perfected material world it is a reciprocal relationship between unequals (patronage) lived out reciprocally in loyal obedience in time and place. It is about giving him individually and collectively the worship he so deserves. It is the glorious and unrivaled story of creation, the fall, the long, rich saga of Israel, redemption, and renewal of all God's creation that spans the canvas of Scripture from Genesis through Revelation.

The Bible challenges us to become God-conscious in ever-more-deepening ways. When characters experience personal transformation and correction of false beliefs, his agenda—the *missio Dei*—is advanced in ways that address both material and spiritual needs locally and globally. When we image-bearers flourish spiritually, he receives honor! Spiritual restoration restores previously rejected respect for ourselves, others, the material world, and the Creator. Rescued relationships lead to an allegiance change; this results in reciprocity that calls for daily loyalty that evidences itself holistically to the Eternal One (Col 1:19–20). This joyful relational restoration is the ultimate goal of oral hermeneutics.

The voices heard in those many conversations (from congenial to corrosive) documented and demonstrated in Scripture help all to hear his voice—and they are far from boring! This is where oral hermeneutics enters the stage.

Our Modern Penchant for Propositional Philosophy

Why is it, then, as soon as we read, interpret, or teach the Bible, we tend to privilege a theology based on abstract propositional philosophy? I (Tom) vividly remember a certain Bible course I took at a Christian college. I was

---

18. Colijn contends that "Being in Christ is not transactional but relational" (Colijn, *Images of Salvation*, 266). Vanhoozer summarizes thusly: "The purpose of Scripture and theology alike is to draw the people of God into . . . communicative action [in responsive relationship with God] for the sake of communion [with God]" (Vanhoozer, *Drama of Doctrine*, 35).

so excited to be able to learn Scripture in-depth from a godly scholar, but that was short lived.

> "The Anglo-American ear is more accustomed to the spare, fact-dense and proof-structured discourse of pragmatism, empiricism, and positivism."[19]

On the first day of class the young, recently graduated professor outlined how theology finds its roots wrapped tightly around propositional philosophy. As I had just come from a philosophy class I wondered, *Why do we Westerners usually assume philosophical and systematic theology is the most profound expression of truth? Why do I have to know propositional philosophy to understand the Bible? Why is abstractness considered superior to concreteness?*[20]

Expanding the conversation to historical-grammatical interpretation, we find it interesting that when Westerners delve into the concrete historical side of hermeneutics, how often in interpretation individualism supplants collectivism, egalitarianism supersedes hierarchy, or legal values-morals (innocence-guilt) replace relational values-morals (honor-shame). This just shows the power of one's culture to superimpose itself over another culture when interpreting it. As for the grammatical, *How close is our grammar to that of Classical Hebrew or Aramaic or Koine Greek? How necessary is it for all to know such grammar to understand Scripture? And does knowing the grammar rules always ensure correct comprehension?*

We find parallels to oral hermeneutics in language learning. Grammar is better caught than taught as students listen to the language spoken and imitate it. Children don't learn objective, explicit rules of grammar, they

---

19. Swearingen, "Oral Hermeneutics During Transition to Literacy," 140.

20. Interestingly, decades ago language learning moved away from a strong emphasis on memorizing vocabulary and grammar analysis to learning phrases in life contexts, where it has an immediate referent. This user-friendly approach made language learning a concrete event rather than an abstract exercise. Brewster and Brewster's *Language Acquisition Made Practical (LAMP)*, published in 1976, provides an early example. Older textual hermeneutics tended to talk *about* a Bible story (summarize and analyze it), rather than actually *tell* the story the way we do it in oral hermeneutics. The newer Second Language Learning (SLA) methods use kinetics (obeying simple commands to do things in the new language being learned), visuals and concrete object lessons to teach the language. In fact, there is a movement in the SLA field promoting utilizing these methods as the most successful way to teach language acquisition called *Total Physical Response (TPR)* and later *Total Proficiency Through Reading and Storytelling (TPRS)*. See the eighth edition of Ray and Seely, *Fluency through TPR Storytelling*.

absorb it implicitly. Older modern language learning methods tended to talk way too much about the language, rather than using the language, and facilitating students to use it. Children learning their mother's tongue, or native language speakers, seldom talk about their language or analyze its grammar. They learn it by using it.[21]

A few years ago, I (Tom) met with the expatriate head of a Bible seminary in Thailand who had heard I was teaching the course "Story in Scripture and Service." His faculty was experiencing the same issues I faced decades earlier with mostly the same results—students were just not getting it. *If highly literate Western methods used to analyze grammar to isolate propositions to categorize and systematize hinder the West's ability to access the fuller concepts of Scripture, how much more when transported globally?* Recall the quotes at the start of the chapter. *Is it time for some changes?*

Interestingly, the Ifugao of the Philippines have plenty of propositions, so propositions are not the issue. To illustrate, if the red bird flies in front of you, return to where you came from or something bad will happen to you. This proposition, like others, emerged from and was continually tied to concrete contexts and characters. The red bird proposition is nested in stories about those who continued their journey and then experienced some calamity; no bifurcation between proposition (proverb) and experience. For the Ifugao, abstractness required concreteness, and vice versa.

Have we unintentionally placed unnecessary obstacles to the word of God for today's generations? Is there another type of philosophy that differs in form and may be closer to the way the majority of the world actually thinks and processes information today? If culture was influential in the rise of textual hermeneutics for specific generations, could culture also be influential in the rise, or rather the return, of an older hermeneutic for today's generations? Stay tuned.

---

21. Here are further parallels between language learning and oral hermeneutics: "The fundamental factor in successful language teaching is not printed materials, but sound pedagogy" (McQuinn, "Basic Principles."). These language teachers contend that *hearing* the speech is vital for learning to read it. We contend that hearing the Bible's stories using "oral language" provides the greatest potential to grasp their meaning, for all its worth. Speaking reveals what aspects of the language have truly been acquired and forces the learner to learn the syntax and grammar though the experience of using it. We contend that *oralizing* the Bible reveals how well it is really known by a person. *So we might say there are parallels between really learning a language and really learning the Bible.*

Our Taste for Textual Hermeneutics

Hans-Georg Gadamer wrote, "the task of hermeneutics was originally and chiefly the understanding of texts."[22] What may be overlooked here is that such interpretation was viewed primarily through a Western lens. While Bible interpretation had been going on for centuries orally, it did not begin with linear literary analysis. Werner Kelber, retired professor of New Testament at Rice University, puts his finger on an issue often overlooked in relation to Gadamer's observation, i.e., "the tendency among biblical scholars to think predominantly, or even exclusively, in literary, linear, and visual terms.... If [only] we can wean ourselves from the notion that texts constitute the center of gravity in tradition."[23] South African author J. A. Loubser adds,

> In interpreting ancient messages we need to be aware of the historical distance between our own culture and the culture being studied. This especially applies because modern scholars are constantly tempted to understand ancient messages in terms of their present literary frame of mind. Almost by default, most people living in modern literate cultures are 'media blind.'[24]

Graham Furniss of London University addresses the why behind the diminishing role of universal orality in interpretation: "The oral is a set of communicative conditions apparent in *all* societies and it is the implications of those conditions which have been obscured by the focus on the so-called 'advances' purportedly engendered by 'writing.'"[25] "Textual, typographical bias"[26] has reigned in most of the hermeneutic world since Gutenberg invented the printing press in 1447.

---

22. Gadamer, *Truth and Method*, 353. We can thank Friedrich Schleiermacher for expanding hermeneutics beyond philosophy, grammar, and the text to an art of understanding any context, including communication (which would include the oral). He sought to include the intuitive and the experiential (Gadamer, *Truth and Method* 12–14). For a concise overview of the development of hermeneutics with emphasis given to Schleiermacher, see Grossberg and Christians, "Hermeneutics and the Study of Communication."

23. Kelber, "Jesus and Tradition," 2, 163. See also Botha, "Mute Manuscripts."

24. Loubser, *Oral and Manuscript Culture*, 4. Loubser believes most scholars coming from a literary background have a difficult time grasping the relevancy of an oral media, hence "most ... are 'media blind.'" By "media blind" he means that we overlook the first medium of communication of the content we read in our texts—the oral medium. He concludes the nature of and meaning conveyed by orality differs from that conveyed in a print medium. Could the lack of inclusion of orality in our training be one reason why we often fail to see its significance?

25. Furniss, *Orality*, 141 (emphasis original).

26. Kelber, "Oral-Scribal-Memorial Arts of Communication," 237.

Enter the Enlightenment

The "Gutenberg Galaxy" facilitated the Renaissance, the Reformation, and the European Enlightenment when, paraphrasing Immanuel Kant (1724–1804), humans had the courage to use reason to dare to know.[27] But the scientific method that became so dominant was restricted to the natural world, and rational thinking through propositional logic.[28] It was understood to dispel superstition and the supernatural; a new boundary for science was established—only the empirical visible, natural world is researchable.[29] Farewell to the Dark Ages.[30] Hello, Age of Reason! Enter scientific empiricism to enlighten us. Man has come of age![31]

As the Gutenberg Galaxy was launched, changes were eventually made in hermeneutics to remain relevant to a changing audience. One of the developments that emerged out of that early Western-inspired matrix was an evidence-based, seemingly error-proof hermeneutic used to discover pure, objective, propositional truth. Old Testament scholar Walter Brueggemann aptly summarizes:

> All of us are children of the Enlightenment. That cultural reality of the last 250 years has brought us enormous gifts of human reason, human freedom, and human possibility. None of us

---

27. Kant, "What is the Enlightenment?" See also the chapter titled, "The Long Shadow of the Enlightenment" in Matthews, *Novel Approach* for an excellent discussion on its impact on interpretation.

28. This separation of science from biblical truth broke from the early history of modern science in that many of the first scientists where Christians—Galileo, Bacon, Pascal, and Newton. Sociologist of religion, Rodney Stark, summarizes, "Not only were science and religion compatible, they were inseparable—the rise of science was achieved by deeply religious Christian scholars" (Stark, *Victory of Reason*, 12). Can the Great Divide be brought back together?

29. Frei, *Eclipse of Biblical Narrative*, 63; See Groothuis, *Truth Decay*.

30. Kevin Bradt, a teacher at Jesuit School of Theology in Berkeley, California, makes this observation: "Modern science overreached itself and eventually became as dogmatic and authoritarian in its claims as its predecessor, the Church, had been . . . . By discovering 'objective truth,' science and its handmaid, technology, were supposed to release humans from their fears and superstitions, cure disease, and usher in a utopian age of unmatched progress and achievements" (Bradt, *Story as a Way of Knowing*, 89, 90). Also, "all the wonderful, contradictory narrative particularities of the biblical stories were seen only as intellectual embarrassments" (127). Any implications here for hermeneutics?

31. "Exposition is a mode of thought, a method of learning, and a means of expression . . . a sophisticated ability to think conceptually, deductively, and sequentially; a high valuation of reason and order; an abhorrence of contradiction; a large capacity for detachment and objectivity; and a tolerance for delayed response" (Postman, *Amusing Ourselves to Death*, 63).

would want to undo those gifts, but they are gifts not without cost. The reality of the Enlightenment has also resulted in the concentration of power in monopolistic ways which have been uncriticized. Moreover, it has generated dominating models of knowledge which have been thought to be objective rather than dominating.[32]

Jonathan Pennington of the Southern Baptist Theological Seminary adds, "belief in the Bible's truthful history-telling became a function of verifiability, hence the rise of evidentialist apologetics."[33] The omnicompetence of verifiable reason was applied to the biblical texts, which gave Bible communicators credibility in a fast-changing world, but not without cost.

Like all models of interpretation, the revised hermeneutic, which we are calling textual hermeneutics (with all its variants), came with strengths and weaknesses. Vanhoozer addresses one of its excesses, namely the false notion that "human reason can draw out what is implicit in Scripture through a process of logical analysis and inference."[34] Logical analysis can render much of the meaning implicit in Scripture, but not exhaust it. This resulted in reducing meaning to propositional statements abstracted from events. Metaphors were considered deceptive and useless.[35] And the narrative sections of Scripture were analyzed the same as any other genre.

Is there a way to correct some of the overreaches of Enlightenment-influenced hermeneutics? Is only one type of a hermeneutical model sufficient to glean the full meaning of a narrative text? Old Testament scholar and biblical archaeologist G. Earnest Wright concludes, "as the Bible contains no system of theology, it likewise contains no self-conscious hermeneutical methodology."[36] If Wright is right, this opens the door to other possible hermeneutic models to correct Enlightenment overreaches. This is what we call oral hermeneutics (with all its variants).

Are two hermeneutic models (oral and textual-literary) better than one to illicit a fuller meaning of a narrative text? Do the writers of Scripture and the first-century Jesus-followers provide a model for a more inclusive, stimulating, natural hermeneutic model that has relevance for today's listeners/readers/viewers? Does theology have to emerge exclusively from a cerebral-cognitive, rational, analytic, linear, sequential approach?

---

32. Brueggemann, *Hopeful Imagination*, 5–6.
33. Pennington, *Reading the Gospels Wisely*, 103.
34. Vanhoozer, *Drama of Doctrine*, 267.
35. Vanhoozer, *Drama of Doctrine*, 280.
36. Wright, *God Who Acts*, 64.

Is it time for theology to be more expressive (artistic, aesthetic, emotional,[37] relational, storied, mystical, metaphorical, imaginative, non-linear, big-picture, symbolic)? Which hermeneutic model best matches the majority world?[38] *Posttext and postfacts generations in the minority world?* The authors believe primary oral audiences (those who cannot read) and secondary oral audiences[39] (those who can read but prefer other oral/visual/digital means of communication) would benefit greatly by adding a second wing to their hermeneutic aircraft—oral hermeneutics.

Distinguishing Textual Hermeneutics from Oral Hermeneutics

The authors will now attempt to briefly clarify distinctions between textual hermeneutics and oral hermeneutics. We recognize *variants exist within each hermeneutical approach* because different cultural assumptions drive each; that culture—typically conditioned by a preferred type of logic—influences how each is understood and practiced; that each hermeneutic model comes with strengths and weaknesses; and that taught in its purest forms, textual hermeneutics will inevitably overlap some with oral hermeneutics, and vice versa. Expect fuzzy boundaries.

For example, addressing the narrative genre, some use of the imagination, emotions, and communal interpretation will be featured in textual hermeneutics. How these are addressed, and to what level, however, will differ because of the educational background of the interpreter expressed in: (1) preferred philosophical logic, (2) investigative questions, and (3) preferences for social values-morals, e.g., individualism and collectivism or innocence-guilt and honor-shame.[40]

---

37. A quotable quote from Georgia Cates pertaining to emotions is, "Music is what feelings sound like out loud" (Cates, *Beauty from Pain*, 112). The narratives of Scripture sounded "out loud" can be music to many ears today.). So we think the narratives of Scripture sounded "out loud" are music to many ears today.

38. Ramesh Richard notes that of the 2.2 to 3.4 million pastors presently ministering, "only 5% are trained for pastoral ministry." In relation to church planting, Richard relays these dismal numbers, "The Global Alliance of Church Multiplication raised a most serious concern in October 2013. While they envision the planting of five million churches by 2020, they surmise an astounding fail-rate of up to 70% within the first year" (Richard, "Training Pastors," paras. 6 and 5).We would ask several rhetorical questions: How could oral hermeneutics aid in pastoral development? Does the reductionism (limitations) of a training dominated by textual hermeneutics have any role in relation to the stunning attrition numbers noted?

39. See Ong, *Orality and Literacy*.

40. Georges and Baker estimate that "80 percent of the global population (i.e.,

Some readers may prematurely conclude oral hermeneutics allows for anyone's interpretation. "Your truth is your truth and my truth is my truth. It's all good. Relativism reigns! Pass the hot chocolate while we sing Kumbaya." Not so! Not so on the internal level, where the author intentionally inserts literary clues to establish boundaries for interpretation. Not so on the human level, where conclusions must be evaluated against the universal church tradition locally and globally. More to come.

> "Literary analysis seeks to unpack the manner in which stories tell their tales. The question becomes: How does this story mean? That is, how does this story go about the process of communicating what it has to say? Or, as we might phrase the issue today: How does it construct meaning? Literary study presents a new paradigm for readers, raising the question of *how*. Throughout the long, drafty corridors of the history of biblical interpretation textual analysis has focused primarily on the question 'What do they mean?' with very mixed results. Considering *how* texts (construct) mean(ing) is one of the main points of entry to understanding and appreciating *what* they mean."[41]

The following is a preliminary minimalist attempt to distinguish textual hermeneutics from oral hermeneutics, recognizing that multiple variations of each exist. Amplification will follow in the forthcoming chapters.

Textual hermeneutics tends to focus on fixed documents, preferably the earliest Hebrew and Greek manuscripts, grammatical analysis, lexical tools requiring linear, line-by-line, word-by-word studies, definitions. This is then packaged clearly and crisply in systematic categories after hours of often private study and little immediate feedback.

Frequently, only trained professionals from approved schools are trusted as having sufficient scholarly skills of semantics and syntax to ferret out an objective, single meaning intended by the author that meets scientific standards;[42] it values rigid rightness anchored in specificity and preciseness,

---

Asians, Arabs, Africans and even Latin Americans) runs on the honor-shame operating system" (Georges and Baker, *Ministering in Honor-Shame Cultures*, 19). See Steffen, "Clothesline Theology for the World," 257–60, and Appendix F in Steffen, *Worldview-based Storying*, 245–46, for a chart that views the gospel through the eyes of four value-moral systems: innocence-guilt, honor-shame, power-fear, and purity-pollution.

41. Petersen, *Reading Women's Stories*, 8 (emphasis original).

42. Published in 1954, Bernard Ramm's influence on today's hermeneutics remains visible in some circles, particularly through his *The Christian View of Science and Scripture*. Two quotes, with tacit influence from the Enlightenment, point to the emphasis given to systematics and Aristotelian deduction. Ramm posits, "Training in logic and

often separated from events in which they are embedded, even if variant meanings result.[43] Textual hermeneutics limits interpretation to rigid modes of investigation that are highly informed by Western culture and therefore come with strengths and weaknesses.

Textual hermeneutics invites inquirers into the room and tells them where to sit (often based on level of education); it requires they remain offstage. The objective spectator observes the actors' performance before writing a review, usually for the more formerly educated, before communicating to others with accompanying illustrations to make it meaningful. Internal change (application-to-life, spiritual formation) is a goal which may or may not transpire. Textual hermeneutics prefers to define and explain rather than describe and portray. It often serves as a shortcut to identify the assumed most significant point of the passage.

When textual hermeneutics interprets a story it usually talks *about* the story instead of *telling* the story to hearers, bringing it to life, and digging out the truths through questions as the authors do with the "Elisha and the Widow's Oil" story in chapter 1 and again in chapter 9. A standard critical commentary breaks down the parts of the story, conducts a verse-by-verse commentary, defining and explaining words and phrases. The flow of the story is broken up. Things get lost in the dissection process, especially impact on the hearts of the hearer.

Oral hermeneutics, on the other hand, tends to focus on the communal oral telling, demonstration, discussion, interpretation, repetition, and application of the biblical grand narrative and all the smaller stories that compose her. There is (un)planned collective telling, interpretation, with various applications, all unfolded and unpacked through discussion of the Bible characters. Interaction in the group tends to be extemporaneous, experiential, intuitive, verbal, and visual.

Participants collectively hear the Bible story performed (action that includes intonation, energy level, volume, pace, pitch, pauses, posture, rhythm, rhyme, gestures, facial expressions, eye behavior questions), influenced not only by the text, but also by audience reaction. The audience experientially identifies with certain biblical characters, co-constructs possible meanings and life applications, and creatively adjusts (sometimes too creatively as the

---

science forms excellent background for exegesis" (153). This leads naturally to his second posit, "Systematic teaching of Scripture is the Scriptures' final intention" (155). Charles Hodge claimed, "just as the natural scientist uncovers the facts pertaining to the natural world, so the theologian brings to light the theological facts found within the Bible" (Grenz and Franke, *Beyond Foundationalism*, 34).

43. For example, those who prefer covenants and those who prefer dispensations, or modifications of either.

reader will see in chapter 1) interpretations for specific geographical areas and eras. Insights and understanding are often discovered nonsequentially. Deep engagement in the story requires time to reflect, discuss, sound things out with others, let ideas percolate, and form interpretations. Chapters 1 and 9 demonstrate these dynamics.

In oral hermeneutics, the listeners/viewers focus strongly on characters (human and spiritual, individuals, groups, animals [e.g., cattle, 1 Sam 6:12]), considering the historical context, circumstances, conflicts, conversations, inconsistencies, choices and the consequences of said choices. Oral hermeneutics telegraphs values, morals, and theology through character clarification from a context where relationships reign.

Such character reflection often evolves into vivid, vicarious identifications, i.e., those characters to model or avoid at all costs. Bible characters take up residence in the listeners' minds and hearts, offering alternative roadmaps to life. Shared life situations become possible spontaneous moments for long-term transformation on multiple levels. Characters serve as embodied illustrations to convey textual meaning that is absorbed by the audience, and meaning is discovered and transferred through relationships.

Oral hermeneutics champions collectivism, volunteerism, the big picture, comprehensiveness, fulsomeness, and the progressive repetition of repeated themes. It also employs specific schema that assist memory, often enhanced through rhythm, rhyme, echo (references to previous characters/events), the visual, formulaic sayings and structures, group participation, and accumulated meaning, all immediately experienced. Not all of these elements are always present at any given interpretive event. And, rather than programmed in advance, they tend to occur naturally and spontaneously.

To validate the incomprehensibility (spontaneity and mystery[44]) of the Creator, oral hermeneutics advances shades of ambiguity, the affective and

---

44. See Boyer and Hall, *Mystery of God*, 4–11. Brian Howell defines mystery this way: "Mystery, in its Christian theological form, is not a puzzle to be unraveled or the description for that which falls outside the bounds of reason, but a means of intellectually approaching otherness . . . Mystery is considered the beginning of inquiry into transcendent realities from positioned, partial, and spatio-temporal locations that do not deny the possibility of true knowledge, but appropriately contextualize knowledge in relations of the knower to that which is being known . . . . Mystery is used in scripture to refer to the work of God and humanity's relation to it. It is not exclusively hiddenness (although it is that), nor is it the opposite of knowledge. Mystery is frequently used to refer to God, the agency of God, and, most importantly, the revelation of God" (Howell, "Mystery," 34, 40). Howell goes on to quote Vincent Crapanzano, who looks at it from a sociological perspective: "social life relies on mystery, the creative, the imaginative possibilities that the mysterious opens up . . . It is mystery that charms us, inspires us, and even binds us together as individuals and collectives" (Crapanzano, "Hermes' Dilemma," 272–73).

intuitive, and the subjective. All of this results in possible corralled multiple truths (reality as seen by God).[45] The textual meaning is honored through literary markers in the story, in the grand narrative of Scripture, and through traditional parameters, i.e., the universal community of faith locally and globally. These guardrails make some interpretations more viable than others.[46] Interpretations discerned are most effective with immediate collective participation, which may or may not transpire.

Oral hermeneutics attempts to discover the answers to the questions raised by the biblical narrators through co-participation with them. Oral hermeneutics prefers to describe and portray rather than define and explain. Oral hermeneutics not only invites inquirers into the room, but onto the stage to vicariously co-perform with the other actors. Those who exit the stage are changed people; they are never the same because they just lived someone else's life.

Textual hermeneutics, influenced strongly by the Enlightenment, tends to socialize her exegetes to perceive Scripture as a technical user's manual for machines, an inflexible "code book." Oral hermeneutics, influenced by the oral nature of Scripture and the relational Trinity behind the sacred text, tends to socialize her exegetes to perceive Scripture as a "more flexible case book."[47] Textual hermeneutics represents a rational text while oral hermeneutics represents a relational text. *What residue does each hermeneutic imprint on the minds of recipients?*

Textual hermeneutics relies on propositional-based textual analysis and centuries of the Christian faith to discern objective truth. Oral hermeneutics relies on cues inserted in the text by the author (e.g., chiasm, verbal echoes, parallelism[48]), guided questions, communal reputation, and centuries of the Christian faith to discern subjective truth. *Could both be needed? Is there a sequence?*

---

45. Sternberg, *Poetics of Biblical Narrative*, 50–51.

46. Sternberg summarizes thusly, "Whatever the nature and origin of the parts—materials, units, forms—the whole governs and interrelates them by well-defined rules of poetic communication" (Sternberg, *Poetics of Biblical Narrative*, 2). The value of mystery, creativity, and freedom of inquiry in oral hermeneutics is well expressed by this saying: "Without discovery, you have monotony" (James, *Story*, 29).

47. Pinnock, "Work of the Holy Spirit," 8–9.

48. See Iverson, "Orality and the Gospels," 71–106.

Focus of the Book

Denver Seminary distinguished professor of Old Testament Daniel Carroll R. ferrets out the obscure: "Seminary courses and books on hermeneutics are not always helpful in acknowledging the influence of one's socioeconomic, ethnic, and racial context on interpretation."[49] *Have we allowed our times (modernism, the Enlightenment, postmodernism) to limit how we approach Scripture hermeneutically? Does orality free us from many of these constraints so we can interpret the narrative portions of Scripture as intended? Does orality offer a fuller understanding of what the text means? Is it time for an additional hermeneutic? For an additional type of theologizing and theology? Is oral hermeneutics a gift to textual hermeneutics?* The central question of this book is: *Why is it important to know and practice oral hermeneutics in an effort to ascertain and communicate biblical meaning?*

This book focuses on the big picture that frames the issues and challenges that surround Bible storytelling for evangelism and discipleship at home and abroad. This involves multiple topics—orality, literacy, the Enlightenment, inerrancy, hermeneutics, types of logic and theologies, ministry methodologies, pedagogy, andragogy, honor and shame, and Bible study curricula. The authors in no way attempt to bring conclusive answers to all the questions that compose this multifaceted, multidisciplined hermeneutical approach to Bible storying. We leave that to others to bring needed depth and clarity to each aspect. Rather, this introductory text, through theory and practice, introduces the reader to the key players in orality, raises associated issues in relation to Bible interpretation, and demonstrates possible ways to improve present Bible storying at home and abroad.

The authors seek three outcomes: (1) an equal place at the table for oral hermeneutics, (2) user evaluation of the various oral hermeneutic models in use today around the globe, and (3) the beginning of a conversation between professors, pastors, and practitioners as to the rightful role of orality in hermeneutics. This book will be a success if a spirited, mature, in-depth, and ongoing discussion in the academies, assemblies, and agencies about the philosophical-cultural underpinnings and implications of textual hermeneutics and oral hermeneutics takes place. Only when such a discussion happens will a fuller, deeper interpretation of the narrative texts be possible. Only when this happens will a more complete picture of the face of God be drawn.

---

49. Keener and Carroll R., *Global Voices*, 2.

Now Where?

With the stage now set, the authors begin to layer the concepts introduced above which can have a tremendous long-term impact on those with little to no literacy background, as well as those who are highly literate. We begin with a Bible story—"Elisha and the Widow's Oil." We do this to model the major thrust of the book—Bible interpretation should follow a specific sequence—from people to propositions, from concreteness to abstractness, from the experienced to the explained, from the demonstrated to the defined, from the mystery to the meaning. From this Bible story, we also begin to mine many of the principles and practices associated with oral hermeneutics and character theology.

Enjoy the journey. We trust you will gain new eyes to see new peaks, new possibilities, new perspectives, and new pearls from the past and present hermeneutic worlds.

Part 1
Demonstrations

1

Elisha and the Widow's Oil

WHAT FOLLOWS IS A printed version of an oral event. It is a composite of many similar oral events in which I (Bill) have told this story over the past ten years in several countries in homes, schools, a warehouse, parks, and in churches. The group described in this event is a somewhat multicultural group of Americans in Los Angeles at a Jewish seeker's Bible study. Around one-fourth to one-third of the participants were Jewish. This group comprised a mix of educated people, ranging from high school to postgraduate level.[1] The names are pseudonyms.

As a printed version, this lacks essential dimensions of oral hermeneutics that the authors advocate in this book. We therefore can only do our best to simulate the event, and to stimulate the reader's imagination to grasp what the oral performance was like.

Though the three elements of the "storytelling triangle" are constant—the storyteller, the story, the audience[2]—each oral storytelling event has its own chemistry due to the varying contexts and unrepeatable configurations. Some of the variable factors comprising each storytelling event include a different story, audience, time of day, place, energy level of the storyteller and group, distractions, and time constraints. And last but not least, the varying activity of the Holy Spirit who quickens the spoken word differently to different hearers' hearts. Multiple unique takes on the story therefore result.

As you read, imagine the storyteller standing and orally telling the story, and how his/her body language (eye behavior, facial expressions,

---

1. In the evangelical missions world, storytelling and orality methods are often thought of as primarily for use among oral learners, nonliterate or semiliterate people in the Majority World, developing countries, or the Global South. Thus, the use of orality means among literate people in Los Angeles serves to show that these methods are for literate people as well. Storytelling and orality means are effective with all education levels, ages, and ethnicities.

2. Lipman, *Improving Your Storytelling*, 17–18.

voice tone, and emotion)³ might be appropriate to the story's plotline and character dialogue. Effective storytellers vocalize and embody the story as if s/he just saw it happen.

Note the pauses in the speech. As a printed page has both black ink and white space, so oral language has both sound and silence. Pauses are not dead time. They are pregnant; they deliver meaning. In the following text, "pause" refers to an intentional suspension controlled by the storyteller.

"Silence" refers to time lapse between the end of some speech by the storyteller or listener and before anyone speaks again. The number of seconds that constitute each pause is descriptive of what happened in the natural give-and-take of the discussion. They are in no way prescriptive, or a model to be imitated. Each storytelling event is unique and unrepeatable.

As you read this, may the Holy Spirit attend to your reading and aid in the transfer of the imagery from the written language to your imagination and your emotional response. We suggest you read the story itself out loud with the tone of voice and emotion you feel is appropriate.⁴

Oral Introduction to the Story

STORYTELLER (*Standing up from having been seated, with a closed Bible*): Hello. It's good to be with you! I am going to tell you a Bible story. But first, would you like to hear a little about the backstory—who was involved, some of the issues they faced, and where and when it happened?

This story happened about nine hundred years before the birth of Jesus, back when kings reigned in ancient Israel. It was the time just after the great prophet Elijah had ministered in the land. Many generations before, Samuel the prophet had founded a school of prophets. These were men trained to listen to God and then give God's messages to his people.

---

3. Paul Ekman and others at the University of California, San Francisco, identified seven universal emotions: sadness, anger, surprise, fear, disgust, contempt, and happiness (Ekman, *Emotions Revealed*, 58). Life Model Works holds to there being six major unpleasant emotions and then "joy," the biblical promise of the ideal emotion resulting from right and healthy relationships (Neh 8:10; John 15:11, 16:24, 17:13; 1 John 1:4). Instead of "surprise" and "contempt," they identify "shame" and "hopeless despair" (Wilder, *Joy Starts Here*, 44).

4. The text of this story is 2 Kings 4:1–7. Drawing from the New King James Version (NKJV) and the New Living Translation (NLT), I told it in my own conversational language, making it as natural a telling as possible. This version is in my own words, but content-accurate to the biblical text. It is told as if I were a reporter who just saw these things happen and had interviewed a few of the principal characters in the story. Now I have come with excitement to tell it to you face to face.

Later, Elijah the prophet had renewed and developed a school of the prophets, called the "sons of the prophets." They were not their biological sons. This is a Hebrew idiom for "the school of prophets." Elisha was Elijah's successor as leader of the sons of the prophets, inheriting Elijah's mantle of authority and spirit. As a prophet, Elisha performed many miracles and so was the respected man of God of the time in Israel. But even so, he apparently made himself available to ordinary people, and visited their homes.

This was a time of famine and hard times in Israel. Times like these were especially hard for widows. There was no social safety net or programs like we have today in America for widows. Though there is a statute in the Torah stating that debts could be repaid through servitude or working them off, creditors were not to take advantage of the poor or mistreat them. So here is where our story begins.

I will not give you now the scriptural reference for the story. I want you to listen with eye contact, and not to be distracted by rustling through pages to find the printed version in your Bible. I will give you the reference at the end of our session.

Let's pray first—Father in heaven, thank you that you have transmitted your word to us faithfully over the millennia, through prophets and the written Scripture. We ask you to illumine and give us insight, by your Holy Spirit, through this inspired story today. In Jesus' name, Amen.

Telling the Story

Storyteller opens his Bible, begins to read the story, but then lays the Bible down on a nearby table, not the floor or a chair.[5] He gives eye contact to the audience and continues telling the story . . . It is obvious he is not reading the story but telling it by heart.

STORYTELLER: One day a widow of one of the sons of the prophets came to Elisha and cried out,

> "My husband who served you is dead, and you know how he feared the Lord. But now a creditor has come, threatening to take my two sons as slaves!"
>
> "What can I do for you?" Elisha asked. "Tell me, what do you have in the house?"

---

5. To handle holy books with great respect is a value in many non-Western cultures, especially in Jewish and Muslim contexts. So we are careful not to lay the Bible on the floor or a chair, surfaces where people walk or sit.

"I have nothing at all! . . . except . . . well . . . this flask of olive oil," she replied.

And Elisha said, "Go out to your friends and neighbors and borrow as many empty jars as you can. Then go into your house with your sons and shut the door behind you. Pour olive oil from your flask into the jars, setting each one aside when it is filled."

So she did as she was told. Her sons kept bringing jars to her, and she filled one after another. Soon every jar was full to the brim!

"Bring me another jar," she said to one of her sons.

"There aren't any more!" he answered.

And then the olive oil stopped flowing.

When she went and told the man of God what had happened, he said to her, "Now sell the olive oil and pay your debts, and you and your sons can live on what is left over."

The Storyteller picks up the Bible from the table, closes it, and says, "This is the end of the story."

Re-telling the Story

STORYTELLER: Okay, now I want you to turn to your neighbor, and in pairs tell and hear the story again. The person with the longest hair tells the story, okay?! (*Audience laughs and chuckles*) . . . Just tell it to the best of your recall; you won't tell it perfectly . . . it's okay! Start with, "One day a widow of one of the sons of the prophets came to Elisha . . . and go from there." Okay, go ahead (storyteller gives them three to four minutes).[6]

Okay . . . Great! Now you have engaged the story by hearing it told by me, and hearing it again from so and so, and telling it to your partner.

Lead through the Story

To recall the storyline well enough to discuss it, people need to hear it at least twice. They have engaged the story in pairs, but incompletely and/or inaccurately, after the first telling. The storyteller-facilitator leads the group through the story for the third time, accurately for the second time (when they tell it

---

6. An alternative way of doing the retelling phase is to ask for one volunteer to stand and retell the story. But if no volunteer is forthcoming, we pair up.

in pairs, they usually achieve about 50 to 90 percent accuracy). The storyteller asks the group to help him or her tell the story again. S/He begins telling and waits for the group to respond in unison to continue telling it. Often the storyteller begins a sentence and the group finishes it. The storyteller leads but hands off the telling to the group as much as they are able. So the telling proceeds in this responsive interactive way until the end of the story. The storyteller ensures accuracy by naturally chiming into the telling, correcting any errors or omissions as the telling of it proceeds.

STORYTELLER: Okay, now let's go through it for a third time. We will tell it together. I will begin and you continue with me and fill in, okay? . . . So one day a widow of one of the sons of the prophets came to . . .

GROUP IN UNISON: . . . Elisha, and said . . .

STORYTELLER AND GROUP IN UNISON: My husband who served you is dead, and you know how he feared the Lord. But now a creditor has come, threatening to take my two sons as slaves!

STORYTELLER: And Elisha said, "I'm sorry lady, but I can't help you . . ."

A FEW IN THE GROUP: No, no . . . he said, "What can I do for you . . . what do you have in your house?"

The storyteller throws in this obvious error both to keep the participants alert and to draw attention to an aspect of Elisha's character that is highlighted by the error.

STORYTELLER: Right, then the widow replied . . .

GROUP IN UNISON: I have nothing . . . except . . . this jar of oil.

STORYTELLER: Then Elisha said . . .

STORYTELLER AND GROUP IN UNISON: Go out to your neighbors and borrow jars . . . from your neighbors . . . not a few . . . many . . .

This telling together led by the storyteller continues until the story is finished.

STORYTELLER: Okay, great! Now we have been through the story three times. I told it. You formed pairs and retold it. And now we just told it again together. Do you think we know it now enough to talk about it?

GROUP IN UNISON: Yes . . .

STORYTELLER: Okay, let's talk about the main characters some more and unpack what truths their words and actions teach us about ourselves and God. What observations might we make?

Observations: Digging for Truth-Treasures

STORYTELLER: First of all, might someone briefly explain the situation in this story? . . . Just in a few words or a sentence or two? What is the widow's dilemma in this story? . . . What is the point of tension she and her family faces? (*Storyteller pauses for several seconds*) . . .

Another way to get at this basic problem is to ask, "What makes the characters seem real? What makes you feel connected emotionally to the people in this story?" (*Storyteller pauses for several seconds*) . . .

DORIS: Well, she's desperate! This woman is about to lose her sons!

JOHN: The helplessness . . . she has not got much left . . . she needs and loves her sons . . . she is terrified that they will be taken from her.

STORYTELLER: Yes, it may be easier for you who are mothers to imagine this—you are threatened with the loss of your two children. Doesn't this kind of draw you into the story? Do you feel your interest rising as to how this is going to be resolved for the widow?

SEVERAL IN UNISON: Yes . . . Yeah . . . Yes, it does . . .

STORYTELLER: Great! Well, let's go through the story, slowly, part by part, kind of like scenes in a movie, and learn what we can about the characters in the story from what they say and do, the choices they make, and the choices they could have made. And let's observe what we can learn about God too, because every Bible story is ultimately about God. Where do we see the hand of God in the story?

So, let's begin at the beginning and retell the story until we come to a good place to stop and talk about the characters . . .

> One day a widow of one of the sons of the prophets came to Elisha and cried out, "My husband who served you is dead, and you know how he feared the Lord. But now a creditor has come, threatening to take my two sons as slaves!"

Is this a good place to stop and see what we find in this first part?

SEVERAL IN UNISON: Yes . . . Yeah . . . Yup . . .

STORYTELLER: Okay, let's start with the first character that appears, the widow. What might we learn about her from this first part of the story, from what she does and says?

MAX: She is a godly woman, a woman of faith, because she goes to the prophet in her need.

STORYTELLER: Hmm . . . interesting . . . How do you see that?

MAX: Because she goes to the man of God in her need and not some other dark or desperate place.

STORYTELLER: Hmm . . . Yes, we see she goes to the man of God. What other choices did she have at this point of crisis? Could she have done something else? Think of her as a real human being in this situation. (*Five second pause*) . . . What might you have done . . . or thought about doing in this situation? (*Seconds of silence*) . . .

DORIS: She could have taken the boys in the night and ran away.

STORYTELLER: Yes, she could have . . . I wonder about her willingness to take such risks in doing this. . . . Maybe if she had friends who could take her in? . . . Any other options she had? (*Seconds of silence*) . . .

DIANA: She could have tried to steal money to pay the creditor.

STORYTELLER: Yes, she could have done that . . .

JAVIER: She could have tried to find another husband . . .

STORYTELLER: She could have . . . I wonder what her prospects may have been . . . and how long the creditor was willing to wait. It could be months before she found a new husband, no?

JAVIER: Depends on how attractive she was, I guess (*Some general laughter*) . . . But seriously, probably not . . . so probably not a great solution.

STORYTELLER: (chuckles) Hmm . . . any other choices she may have had? (*Seconds of silence*) . . .

JAVIER: . . . If you consider all other options she had . . . she could have just given up the boys and not fight it.

STORYTELLER: She could have, but do you think, as a mother, she would do that?

JAVIER: . . . Well, she could have . . . she was desperate.

LINDA: She could have gone begging for money by day, to get enough to pay the debt.

STORYTELLER: She could have . . . right? (*Pause five to six seconds*) . . . So we see she did have other choices. . . . I am thinking of another choice she could possibly have made (*Turning away from Javier and looking toward those on the other side of the group*) . . . What do some of the rest of you think? (*Seconds of silence*) . . .

JESSE: . . . Ah . . . she could have sold her body . . .

STORYTELLER: Hmm . . . Hmm . . . has this ever happened in the past?

JESSE: Of course! It happens all the time.

STORYTELLER: Okay, so we see the woman did have other options . . . but we know what she did choose to do—she came to the man of God. What does that say about her?

DORIS: Well, she may have felt Elisha kind of owed it to her. Her husband was one of his disciples in the school of the prophets, so he and his family were under Elisha's leadership responsibility.

MAX: She believed that God would meet her need through the spiritual leader over her.

STORYTELLER: Good! Alright, let's shift to another character in just this first scene of the story. Who else do we see?

DIANA: Well, her husband plays a role, doesn't he? Even though dead, he left her with debts.

STORYTELLER: Interesting. . . . What might that mean for this woman?

DIANA: Well, all was not well in the family if they were in debt when he died.

STORYTELLER: Does the story give us any clues about the husband's debt?

MEL: It doesn't seem to. These were hard economic times for everyone then, right?

VALERIE: What about the creditor? He does not say anything in the story, but didn't you say in the intro that creditors were not to be harsh and take advantage of the poor?

STORYTELLER: Yes.

VALERIE: So this creditor seems to be a cruel person.

STORYTELLER: Did the creditor have other choices?

VALERIE: Sure. He could have been merciful and just let it slide for a while . . . until times got better.

STORYTELLER: So his choice does tell us something about his character. Hmm, I'm wondering if Elisha's response in this story has any word of correction to these creditors?

VALERIE: Yes, God is merciful to widows and orphans.

STORYTELLER: Okay. In this first part, do we see the hand of God at all? (*Silence for several seconds*) . . . Okay, well, should we move on to the next part of the story?

SEVERAL IN UNISON: Yes . . . Yeah . . . I think so . . .

STORYTELLER: We recall the story then says:

> "What can I do for you?" Elisha asked. "Tell me, what do you have in the house? I have nothing at all! . . . except . . . well . . . this flask of olive oil," she replied. And Elisha said, "Go out to your friends and neighbors and borrow as many empty jars as you can. Then go into your house with your sons and shut the door behind you. Pour the olive oil from your flask into the jars, setting each one aside when it is filled."

STORYTELLER: What might we learn about Elisha from what he says here?

JOHN: Interesting that he asks her two questions.

STORYTELLER: Yes, Elisha had choices at this point. He asks her two questions. What other choices did he have?

JOHN: Well, he could have just given her some money.

STORYTELLER: He could have. . . . Anything else he could have done?

VALERIE: He was a miracle worker, right? He could have just performed a miracle and poof! There would be food in the house!

STORYTELLER: He likely could have. . . . I'm wondering if there is anything else he could have done . . .?

JOHN: Perhaps he could have gone to the creditor and asked him to hold off and be merciful.

STORYTELLER: Sure.

JESSE: Like you said, he could have just said, "Sorry, lady, I can't help you."

STORYTELLER: Ha, I suppose he could have.

JESSE: And talking about her selling her body, he could have said, "Well, I can arrange something for you, honey," . . . and then accepted sexual favors.

LISA: Sure, you hear about clergy doing that all the time today . . . think of all the sex scandals, the pedophile priests.

STORYTELLER: Since we are looking at all possibilities, yes, he could have. This repulses us, and we would never think a prophet of God would do that. But looking at all the possible choices a character had and then coming back and looking at the choice he did make, gives us insight into his character.

So we see what Elisha does do . . . he asks her two questions. Do you think he just wanted that information? Could there be something more here? (*Silence for 10 to 12 seconds*) . . . I'm wondering . . . and observing the effect of these questions on the woman . . . She says, "I have nothing!" What do you think would have been her tone of voice when she said this?

DORIS: Kind of frantic . . . distressed . . .

STORYTELLER: Yes, a distressed, "Nothing!" . . . But then she catches herself . . . and says . . . "except . . . well . . . this little flask oil." . . . It was an afterthought to the first response of "Nothing!" Can we see the effect of those questions on her? What's going through her mind and thoughts?

DIANA: Ah . . . I see how it forced her to think . . . to realize she did not just have "nothing" . . . she did have something . . . even if it was just a little jar of oil. Elisha's question forced her to see this . . . and then he goes on and has her use that little bit she had . . .

STORYTELLER: Wow . . . Yes!

JOHN: Yeah . . . I see it! I see the wisdom in Elisha's questions! He has her do something . . . not just be a passive receiver of charity. So he sends her out to borrow jars and go inside and follow his instructions . . . so she is an active part of the solution. . . . She is not merely a helpless problem . . .

DIANA: Yes! Wow! Great insight John! So by being part of the solution, using the little she had, she maintains her dignity and her sense of self-worth.

DORIS: Amazing! I see the wisdom of God in this! God wanted more for her than just to give her money and food and save her kids from slavery. He wanted to teach her some things about initiative and faith.

JOHN: Yes, and it is an honor-shame thing. We all hunger for honor and fear being shamed. I think the love and wisdom of God is coming through Elisha in helping her maintain honor as a woman who could act to save her children, and not have to face the shame of helpless dependency. She could save face before herself, her family, and neighbors. The Lord helped her.

LISA: Wow . . . you know I think of so many people today who are just looking for handouts from the government and welfare . . . people today are pretty shameless. They seem to not care anymore about being honorable.

JOHN: Well, that might be true here in the West for many, but in the Middle East or Asia, honor and shame play a huge role in their whole worldview.

STORYTELLER: Yes, great insights! . . . There will be more good applications for today from this. Let's continue to dig for observations about the characters in the story. . . . I'm wondering if we see more wisdom from God in Elisha's strategy here . . . ? Do any of the rest of you see something? (*Silence for several seconds*) . . . I'm wondering . . . what may have been the impact of all this on her neighbors?

MEL: I'm sure they wondered what was going on. It sure alerted them to the fact that something was going on . . . if they spoke to each other . . . they would have been quite curious and would want to follow this whole thing.

STORYTELLER: Hmm. . . . Yes, let's come back to what might have been a longer-term result for the neighbors. . . . Interesting that Elisha tells her to go into the house and "shut the door behind you." . . . What's the wisdom or purpose in this detail? Why might it matter?

LINDA: Well, if they left it open . . . all the lookie-loo neighbors would be peering in . . . perhaps, when they saw the oil flowing into their jar . . . would want it back . . . "Hey that's my jar!" (General laughter all around) . . .

DORIS: Ha-ha! But, yeah, it sure would have changed the experience for the woman and her sons, right? But shutting the door behind them, I'm thinking . . . it's like God was shutting them in with himself . . . like in a private prayer closet. They could have a more intimate experience with him . . . undisturbed.

JOHN: Yes, I see that. The two boys would have a deeper, more impactful experience from God by the miracle.

STORYTELLER: Speaking of the two sons . . . what effect was this having on them? Are they going to have stories to tell their grandchildren one day?

MAX: Absolutely! Our mother and we were desperate . . . we thought we'd be taken away as slaves . . . but God provided! He performed a miracle for us through his great prophet Elisha . . . They would be able to tell their kids that God cares about them and will provide.

SEVERAL CHIME IN: Yeah . . . that's great! . . . Absolutely! God provides!

LINDA: And the neighbors too . . . when they found out what happened . . . they would have received a witness of the power and care of God.

MAX: So the neighbors would have stories to tell too!

JOHN: Again the wisdom of Elisha . . . by having her involve the community in the solution . . . the community received a witness to God's power too. Had Elisha just performed a miracle in the house, only the woman and the sons would have received the witness. Elisha maximized the influence of the miracle.

STORYTELLER: Very interesting . . . Well, because of time, should we go on to the next scene in the story? Let's do that. The story says,

> "So she did as she was told. Her sons kept bringing jars to her, and she filled one after another. Soon every jar was full to the brim! "Bring me another jar," she said to one of her sons. "There aren't any more!" he told her. And then the olive oil stopped flowing.

STORYTELLER: Now the woman, when she was given these instructions, had choices before her, right? We see she obeys and does what Elisha says . . . but what other choices did she have? (*Silence of seven to eight seconds*) . . .

JOHN: She could have balked or argued with Elisha or begged for another kind of help which did not require her to have to go out and knock on doors and ask for jars . . . "Elisha, I don't want to go out and ask the neighbors."

JAVIER: But, wait, this miracle of the oil not stopping surely is speaking of the Holy Spirit. Oil is a symbol of the Holy Spirit. He is supernatural, his power is unlimited and never runs out. The Holy Spirit was ministering to this woman and her kids.

STORYTELLER: Hmm, what from the story tells us that?

JAVIER: Well, it's like anointing oil. It's abundant and outpoured to meet needs . . . God pours out the Holy Spirit, right?

STORYTELLER: Right. Are we sure though, from the information in the story that God intended this to be a picture of the Holy Spirit in *this* story? (*Silence of five to six seconds*) . . . Is there anything that might indicate that this is not a picture of the Holy Spirit?

LINDA: Well, the oil stopped flowing, and ran out. Does the Holy Spirit run out? And she sold the oil. What? . . . do we sell the Holy Spirit?

JAVIER: Well, on the selling part, I guess you have a point, Linda.

STORYTELLER: Does the oil have to symbolize the Holy Spirit in order for this story to bring us its truths?

JOHN: I don't think so. It was a miracle anyway. Miraculous provision. That's the point.

STORYTELLER: Hmm. I'm still interested in the choices the widow could have made but did not. She could have refused to do what Elisha said. If she did not do what he said, do you think the miracle would have happened anyway?

DORIS: I don't think so . . . we have to obey God in faith for him to bless, right?

STORYTELLER: Yes, well, we saw that she is a woman of faith because she chose to go to Elisha in the first place. So this is consistent with her character. Interesting. . . . So they are in the house . . . her sons are bringing her one jar after another and filling them from the oil in the little flask that never runs dry . . . a miraculous provision. But eventually she filled them all, but expects to continue filling more, so says to one of the sons, "Bring me another jar!" We see there were no more, so the oil stopped flowing. Who provided this abundant, miraculous supply of oil?

MAX: God.

STORYTELLER: So might we learn something about God from the fact that the flow stopped?

LINDA: There is a limit. It's not like she just won the billion-dollar lottery! (General laughter all around) . . .

STORYTELLER: Ha-Ha! . . . Good insight, Linda! I'm wondering, what might we learn about God's character or God's ways from this?

MAX: God is not a mechanical, take-your-chances lottery. Or an unlimited ATM machine.

DIANA: Right, Max. . . . And also that, though God provides, he does not just give indiscriminate amounts. She got enough to pay her debts and meet her needs, but not so much that she could splurge and binge-buy . . . if such were possible.

STORYTELLER: Great insight, Diana . . . so from God's choices we see that God is . . . ?

DIANA: He cares and provides, but with wisdom as to how his gifts affect the well-being of his people.

MAX: Yeah, God is not a sugar daddy, but a wise Father.

STORYTELLER: Wonderful truths. Well, let's move on to the last scene in the story. Recall in the story,

> "When she went and told the man of God what had happened, he said to her, 'Now sell the olive oil and pay your debts, and you and your sons can live on what is left over.'"

What questions might we ask about this last part of the story?

DIANA: What might we learn about the woman from what she did here?

MAX: Nice that the widow went and told Elisha what happened. She could have chosen not to go tell him . . . and just carried on with her life, right?

JOHN: Yes, but what she does confirms she is a woman who submitted to authority, God's authority.

STORYTELLER: What other characters appear in this part? . . . Anyone else?

LISA: Elisha, obviously . . .

STORYTELLER: And what questions might we ask about him?

LISA: What we learn about him is from what he says or does.

STORYTELLER: Great! Let's do that . . .

VALERIE: Well, Elisha told her quite clearly about what to do with the oil. He was authoritative.

LISA: He released her to go and pay the debt. It must have given her satisfaction to be able to pay the debt.

DORIS: And there is the creditor. He got his money, not slaves.

STORYTELLER: Right . . . I wonder what the impact on him might have been?

VALERIE: He may also have been impacted by this as to God's care and provision—especially if, when the woman paid the debt, she told him that the prophet Elisha, the man of God, provided miraculously for them. He would have attributed this to God. He must have been reminded that God cares for widows and orphans.

STORYTELLER: Great. . . . So, wow, how many people are impacted by this supernatural provision?

VALERIE: The creditor, the woman, her two sons . . .

DORIS: The neighbors . . .

JOHN: Then what about the friends of the neighbors, the friends of the creditor, who heard about it from them . . . ?

STORYTELLER: Any others?

MAX: Those two boys' children and grandchildren . . . and what about all the people who have, ever since, read this story in the Bible?

STORYTELLER: Isn't the wisdom of God working through his prophet amazing? The way Elisha met the need seemed to involve the maximum number of people who were impacted by the miracle, and thus saw something of the character of God.

Focus on Applications

Storyteller calculates that the group only has another five to ten minutes remaining for the storytelling session until they must close, so he transitions the focus to helping the group identify applications of the story to their lives today. So the questioning shifts focus from analyzing the characters in the story to how they speak into our life situations today. The key word he uses for this transition is "Today . . ."

STORYTELLER: Today . . . are there women in the situation this widow was in, in this story?

LINDA: Are you kidding? Single mothers, raising their kids alone? . . . Who feel desperate about how they are going to pay their bills? . . . Absolutely! Tons of them!

STORYTELLER: Okay, sure there are. What might that look like today?

JOHN: I can share . . . I was recently in India for a short-term mission trip. Just in the three weeks I was there, I read of three instances in the English newspaper of women, without husbands, who had children and were in such despair that they committed suicide. Two of them by drinking acid or pouring it on themselves. Just horrible! There is really no provisions or social safety net for these women in India.

STORYTELLER: Oh, that is terrible! Drawing from this story, how could it have been different for these women? Should there be more government social safety-net programs today?

JOHN: If they had a man of God to turn to for help . . . Godly pastors, like Elisha.

LINDA: But this kind of thing does not just happen in India. America too! Fifty percent of marriages end in divorce today . . . even among Christians . . . and yeah, there are some social programs . . . but still there are many single moms who feel desperate and lonely and who struggle hard to make ends meet.

STORYTELLER: Can you share about someone you know who was or is in a situation like this?

LINDA: Yes, I worked with a woman when I lived in the Bronx in New York about ten years ago. She was my friend. We worked together at a deli there. Sandy had two kids, under ten. Her husband had left her. After the recession of 2008, she was laid off. She barely made enough at the deli to support herself and the kids. After the unemployment ran out, she still could not find a job. They got evicted from the apartment and had to move. All they could find was this cheap run-down place. She had no car. She was really depressed and felt so abandoned. I remember going over there and crying with her a few times. I know she was dating men who had money, just to get money . . . a kind of soft prostitution.

All that was before I made a commitment to Jesus Christ as Messiah and Lord, and I was not part of a church community. I felt so helpless also. Sandy was actually down at the park, begging for money for a while. Finally, Sandy, contacted a cousin who lived in a small town in Maine, and he offered her a place to stay in a small RV behind his house. . . . She was able pack her things and take a bus up there with the kids. I think she got a job as a waitress in the small café there. I lost touch with her . . . because I moved here to Los Angeles.

STORYTELLER: Thanks for sharing, Linda. I think we can all feel the hopeless despair Sandy felt . . . like the widow in our story. I hope she is in a better place now. From what we learned from the widow's story, what do you think can guide or inform us as to how to better help people like Sandy?

LINDA: I really see now that had Sandy and I both been part of a church in the Bronx, where real supportive relationships could have developed, there would have been help for us through the faith community.

MEL: But, you know, it's not just single mothers who are in that condition today. There are now thousands of homeless people, living in the streets in tents and under bridges here in Los Angeles. And the number is growing.

SEVERAL IN UNISON: Yes . . . Indeed . . . True . . . I know it . . . It's really sad . . .

VALERIE: People come and ask for financial help from our church and they often get money given to them, because we have a benevolence fund and take a benevolence offering each month. But these are just handouts. In this story, Elisha does not just give the woman money . . . he involves her in the answer—in meeting her needs. And he involved her neighbors.

STORYTELLER: So who, then, are the counterparts today of Elisha the prophet?

VALERIE: The local pastor or rabbi . . . and the church, or congregation.

LISA: Yes, not to look for the government to help, and become dependent on the government . . . or buy lottery tickets and sit and wait around to win the lottery.

STORYTELLER: So what might be the counsel of this story to local pastors today when faced with needs like this woman had? What do some of the rest of you think? (*Storyteller turns and looks at Jesse, who has not responded for a while.*)

JESSE: So, there is a better way than just giving out benevolence money . . . handouts or charity. I was just at a missions meeting at our church where we talked about how huge mistakes have been made in giving foreign aid and humanitarian giving. Wealthy Western people, and international agencies like the United Nations and the International Monetary Fund, and World Bank, have given money or other material things and it actually hurt the poor people more than helped them. They call it "toxic charity." Just continuing to give money creates dependency, not ingenuity and initiative.

LISA: How was that?

JESSE: One example is when a bunch of American groups were sending loads and loads of clothes to Kenya . . . many people happily got free clothes. But what it did was undercut the local developing cotton and garment-making business. So those local Kenyans, who had jobs and were generating more jobs in a local economy, found themselves out of their jobs, and their industry destroyed because people could just get free clothes from the American shipments. It would have been better to support local enterprises with expertise or other help—not just dump bags of clothes or money on them.

LISA: Ah, I can see that. It's like all these Kenyan widows with their little jars of oil were made to feel they had nothing, and they were just helpless victims who needed handouts. They did not have to do anything, like in the story, to go out to the neighborhood and borrow jars and pour oil. Isn't it so cool that this Bible story has wisdom that the United Nations and the International

Monetary Fund and the World Bank didn't have when it comes to the best way to help the poor? Amazing! Elisha just did not give the widow money.

JESSE: Exactly! Like Elisha, we should ask the needy person questions that make them think about what they still have. She realized that her little jar of oil was something, and Elisha encouraged her to use what she had. Nobody has nothing unless they are dead! If you are a healthy person who has eyes, ears, hands, muscles, strength, that's not nothing! You can do a lot with that. Ask the person, "Do you have friends?" If you have friends, you have something. Think about what you can do with the something you have!

STORYTELLER: Great insight, Jesse! I like that! Let's look a little deeper at this. It has been shown in recent mission studies how just giving money or goods in kind continually just produces dependency and later a kind of entitlement, like the wealthy West owes them. We need to help the people learn to participate in their own solutions, to take initiative, to apply themselves to be entrepreneurs and be creative in this. This is how we facilitate human flourishing and social transformation. Its economic help, but it always should be more than that. It is holistic; it is helping the whole person grow toward health, responsibility, integrity. And what do we think this widow had that was the deepest, most fundamental, most transformative for her? (*Seconds of silence*) . . .

LISA: Her self-respect, her honor.

STORYTELLER: Ah . . . so today, a homeless person comes to the church or synagogue, wants to talk to the pastor or rabbi and ask for money. How should the deacon or leader respond? . . . And they represent us all as the body of Christ. So what is it like for us, as a body of believers, as a people, how it is like us to respond? If we respond out of our group identity, what does that look like? (Silence *for 6 to 8 seconds*) . . .

LISA: Well, we respond in compassion, that is how our Lord responded. That's who we are.

JESSE: Yes, I agree, but with a compassion that is wise . . . that chooses the highest good in the long run for the person . . . like Elisha does with the widow. Truthful loving. That's who we are as the body of Messiah. Ask the person questions to help them see what they do have. Respect them. Don't treat them as a pitiful victim. Affirm their value. Tell them about Jesus' love for them; that he is there for them; try to pray with them. Pastors can then help them share the need with the congregation, involve the congregation with the person in need, so relationships are formed.

JAVIER: I can share . . . from our church years ago. There was a woman who had been through a nasty divorce. Her children had grown and left her. She received some alimony money, which she deserved and also felt she deserved it. She felt she had no skills. She has been a waitress in a restaurant, but felt she had no energy for that anymore. So she asked for aid and handouts. She had a lot of self-pity, really. She felt like she had a been a victim of injustice and was full of resentment and self-pity. But our church really did what Jesse was saying. The pastor asked the woman if she would be willing to do some volunteer work for members of the church. He told her that if she did this, God would meet her needs. After some persuasion, she reluctantly agreed.

So the pastor and the elders talked to some members who had odd jobs around the home . . . not hard dirty jobs, like cleaning . . . but like walking dogs or tending to plants, or babysitting, or running shopping errands, etc. Several members did. The pastor told the woman who they were and gave her their phone numbers, so she could arrange when to come and do what. The people were very gracious to her. She did some work . . . she joined in many mealtimes with people . . . really formed relationships. I can remember after a few months of this, her face, her countenance changed. She began to look joyful and not so sad. I believe it was because she was feeling confident again, that she was not a failure, she could do something. She had value. Her sense of self-worth returned.

Eventually, one of the families, a businessman in the congregation, saw she was very good at details and organizing things. He needed such an assistant at his office to organize his schedules and appointments. So he hired her! She now has a good full-time job.

STORYTELLER: Wow, thanks so much, Javier! That is a contemporary application of one of the truths of this story. When needy people use the little they have it increases. They can maintain or regain their dignity and self-worth and honor. And when the community gets involved . . . needs like this can be met, relationships are formed, networking happens.

Well, we are about out of time, so let's try to wrap up and see what we have learned from the story. What do we believe we learned about God and God's ways from this story?

JOHN: That God provides!

JAVIER: Yeah, and the amazing wisdom of God, through Elisha . . . that he did not just give the woman a handout, but that through his questions and instructions, the woman was able to see that she didn't have just nothing. . . . She wasn't destitute. She had a little bit of oil, but she had neighbors who were generous, she had a prophet of God working on her behalf. She still had her two sons who were with her. And when she acted and used what she had her greater needs were met.

STORYTELLER: Isn't that brilliant? And you just shared, Javier, how this happens today . . . from the similar story of the woman in your church. I like how this expresses our group identity as God's people. She looked to us to help her, not the government. Let's state again, what we learned about how God helped the widow. . . . Was it just giving her a means of paying her debts?

SEVERAL AT ONCE: No . . . no, it was more than that.

LINDA: I think this brilliantly shows that the best counseling, therapy, and help we can give to not just single mothers, but anyone who thinks they are helpless, who have a victim mentality, who feel like failures or losers in life . . . is to help them to see that they don't have to be a victim . . . they are not helpless—if they have hands and feet . . . if they can see and hear . . . if they have friends and neighbors . . . they are not helpless. And if the Christian or messianic community helps them use what they have (a little jar of oil) they will see what they have multiply and expand. . . . Sure, the supernatural provision of God was also there as needed, but that came when the widow acted in faith with what little she had, and in obedience to the man of God.

JAVIER: There are parables of Jesus about this. . . . Use the one talent you have . . . be faithful in little. And as the widow acted, used what she had . . . Elisha helped her maintain her dignity, and not succumb to the shame of failure and helplessness and victimhood.

MEL: Yeah, people today are such snowflakes. . . . Many millennials are so pampered . . . and we are such a litigious society, suing people for emotional damage. . . . People need to use what they have and stop whining and connect with God and his people. That's where they can find mercy, the compassion of God, expressed through his people.

JAVIER: Hey, don't bash the millennials! The baby boomers were radical individualists and lone rangers. Millennials are hungry for community and transformation. Both are in this story. I think this story might really find resonance with millennials. Let's tell it more and more and apply it to today.

MEL: Okay, you're right, Javier.

STORYTELLER: Hmm, so every generation has its flaws in this regard. The woman knew she was getting miraculous help from outside herself—from God . . . I'm wondering what else she learned . . .

DIANA: She would realize and learn through Elisha's teaching that she and her neighbors were not to be passive. We pray for people, pray for healing and divine help. But also call upon the person to rise and act in faith. Giving people money and handouts with no limit, or with no responsibility to do something, just fosters dependency, passivity, and stunts people's character and spiritual growth.

LISA: And it is so important how Elisha had the widow involve the community. He didn't just meet her need alone. The neighbors got to witness the miracle and were taught a lesson that we need to be community, interdependent, not isolated loners. We need to build community, and problem-solving together is a great way to do it.

STORYTELLER: Does anyone have a proverb or a symbol that encapsulates this story?

LINDA: I think it was Anne Frank who said, "No one has ever become poor by giving."

JAVIER: I know it was Jesus who said, "Whoever has will be given more, and they will have an abundance. Whoever does not have, even what they have will be taken from them."[7]

DIANA: I think of the proverb about how "If you give a man a fish, you feed him for a day. If you teach him how to fish, you feed him for a lifetime." This is not exactly the same, because Elisha did not teach her how to fish, like some life skill. He taught her how to trust God. But there is still the element of her learning how to participate in the solution to her problem, rather than being a mere passive recipient of aid.

JESSE: Ah! . . . It just came to me, "No man is an island." I don't know who originally said it, but I know Simon and Garfunkel's song has it, "I am a rock, I am an island," expressing this splendid isolation that the modern individualist thinks he is. This story shows us that no, we need each other, we need the neighbors, we need the man of God, we need each other.

---

7. Matthew 13:12, NIV.

STORYTELLER: Great! Yes, God provides but this story teaches that he does so with the cooperation of his people. Okay, we need to close now because of time. But think this week about how this story can be applied in your life, or in the lives of people you observe around you. The story is from 2 Kings 4:1–7.

Who might you tell this story to this week? The more you tell this story, the more you will own it. Tell it to your spouse, or a family member or a co-worker or friend, best if it is to a group of two or more. Just ask them if they have ten to fifteen minutes and that you want to practice the story you have learned. Tell them the story; ask them to retell it, or you retell it together with them. Then ask a few questions about the characters, and how it speaks to us today, just like we did together for the last thirty minutes. But you can cut it to fifteen minutes; in that case just move more quickly to the application questions, the "Today" questions. Tell us what happened next week.

So, I'd like you to come back next week and report what happened when you told it. We'll listen to your stories on how this story might speak to people in their situations. The more you give a story away, the more you keep it! . . . It will be ready in your heart to pull out and use.

Then we will tell and discuss a story that follows in 2 Kings: the story of Elisha and General Naaman.

Chapter 9 provides the account of the following meeting of this Los Angeles study group to hear and discuss the sequel to this story in the narrative flow of 2 Kings 3–5. We now offer some reflections on this story.

2

Reflections on the Elisha Story

"No man is an island entire of itself; every man is a piece of the continent, a part of the main."

—John Donne

"We don't learn by doing, we learn by reflecting on what we've done."

—Zenworkz Marketing

The authors now reflect on why we did what we did in telling the "Elisha and the Widow's Oil" story in the preceding chapter, and note some implications for oral hermeneutics. Hermeneutics is derived from the Greek ἑρμηνεύω which means "to explain, interpret or to translate to someone."[1] This act of explaining and interpreting or translating the meaning of a sacred text has a long tradition of being done in writing. We contend that, in relation to the narrative sections, it is most successfully done orally, because a live human being explaining to another live human being provides the full range of human communication capabilities (seeing, hearing, emotions, and other body language factors) for the task. This, of course, is a factor in a sermon preached and/or in a monologue (at least potentially). Oral hermeneutics, however, provides relational listening and responding in the immediate give-and-take of discussion, including questions of clarification raised in the process of interpreting, thus ensuring satisfactory explanation and understanding.

God himself explained himself most fully through the incarnation, through coming to humanity in person and speaking with us in person. The

1. Arndt and Gingrich, *Greek-English Lexicon*, 309–10.

incarnation of the Son of God is, of course, unique and unrepeatable. But it does provide a model for our hermeneutics. We seek to enflesh the word in and through our own persons, thereby best communicating its meaning. We might say that oral hermeneutics is the word becoming fresh.[2]

The apostle Paul was convinced that human beings embodying his message were more effective than the message written with ink on paper, as he wrote to the Corinthians:

> Are we beginning to commend ourselves again? Or do we need, as some do, letters of recommendation to you, or from you? You yourselves are our letter of recommendation, written on our hearts, to be known and read by all. And you show that you are a letter from Christ delivered by us, written not with ink but with the Spirit of the living God, not on tablets of stone but on tablets of human hearts. (2 Cor 3:1–3 ESV)

Writing was an important tool, useful to Paul, but his statement here shows he prized oral, face-to-face communication above writing.

We begin our reflections on the oral hermeneutics treatment of this story with an understanding that the most essential factor facilitating deep learning, identity, character formation, emotional maturation, and spiritual formation is full brain engagement.

Full Brain Engagement is Key

We live in a time when our scientific knowledge of the human brain has significantly advanced. As googling the subject will show, there is a vast literature on the subject of neuroscience today, too much to cite here. But I (Bill) summarize some of it for our purposes.[3]

It is clear that the right side and the left side of the brain have different functions. Brain science specialists are quick to point out that this can be understood too simplistically, as if there are two separate compartments in the brain that do not interface, and as if only one side is working at any given time. We do not hold to this erroneous view. The whole brain is active all the time, but either the right side or left side may be dominant (the key word)

---

2. "The Word Became Fresh" is a tagline used by the *Orality Journal*, a publication of the International Orality Network (ION). The journal is published online semiannually (see www.orality.net).

3. I am indebted to E. James Wilder and his associates at Life Model Works for this groundbreaking work in the integration of brain science, biblical theology, and spiritual formation. See https://lifemodelworks.org/. Wilder is affectionately known in the organization as the "chief neurotheologian."

at any given time, depending on the activity. Nor do we hold that a person functions primarily from one side or the other. The brain is sophisticated and integrates different kinds of perceptions, activities, and processes.[4]

The right side is the "master fast-track processor" in that its nerve activity is continually perceiving signals, images and information from outside world events, conditions, and human relationships. This is often thought of as the human sensorium (the perceptual equipment of the human person), because all the human senses are active in sensing, almost like antennae. The data enters the brain near the bottom and is carried to the top to the prefrontal cortex in the right side of the brain about six times per second. As such, it operates on an automatic and superconscious level (beyond our awareness). "Each sweep assembles a 'picture' of who we are and where we are at the moment."[5]

Warner and Wilder call the prefrontal cortex (PFC) the "executive control center"[6] because here is where the important things happen that keep us acting as normal functioning human beings, our proper sensibilities intact. Here is a partial list of PFC functions:

- Maintaining identity (what I do and my people do under these conditions)
- Personal preferences (what values reflect who I am and will guide my behavior)
- Emotions
- Creativity
- Awareness of the body and its states
- Intuition (the popularly termed "gut feeling")
- Imagination
- Moral and social behavior (maintaining healthy relationships, EQ [emotional intelligence], assessing what is fair and compassionate, empathy, social tact, and persuasion)

---

4. For primary sources from neuroscientists, see Siegel, *Pocket Guide to Interpersonal Neurobiology*, especially pages 15-1 to 15-10, 41-6 to 41-7 (there are no sequential pages in the book, rather it is arranged as sections with page numbers under each section; so above are pages 1 to 10 of section 15, and pages 6 to 7 of section 41). Siegel is a clinical professor of psychiatry at the UCLA School of Medicine. See https://www.drdansiegel.com/.

5. Warner and Wilder, *Rare Leadership*, 36. For the scientific and academic case, see Siegel, *Developing Mind*, 177–85.

6. Warner and Wilder, *Rare Leadership*, 36.

- Moral judgement (evaluation, including assessing and reassessing people's behavior and character)
- Trust
- Curiosity
- Feeling Appreciation[7]

It is in the right brain where emotions are regulated. The PFC, on the right side, controls our pathway to emotional maturity. When the PFC or the fast track processing of the right brain is traumatized, it becomes jammed, and we become dysfunctional to some degree. One's emotional maturity becomes arrested until the pain or trauma is processed, resolved, and healed.

The left side of the brain is where intellectual conceptualization, mathematical and logical analysis, reasoning and rationalizing, computing, verbalizing, problem-solving, management skills, using writing skills and more, take place. This is the "slow track" of which we are conscious and aware. It is where we intentionally think. A master chess player has exercised his left brain extensively to compute, test, and review all the possible moves in a game. When he is playing chess, he is left-brain dominant. Though his right brain is still constantly working, it is not dominant.

In contrast to the chess player, a spouse relating well in intimate communication with his or her partner will be right-brain dominant as the cingulate cortex, with its relational circuits,[8] is on and carefully tracking the partner's thoughts, energy, and moods. This produces a state of harmony and mutual understanding. Only when their understanding is not clear does the focus shift to look at some detail demanding more left-hemispheric attention.

It is important to know that it is the right brain fast track that informs the left brain slow track. It is our sensibilities in the right brain that instruct the left brain what to do, what to analyze, what to think about. Moral psychologist Jonathan Haidt uses the metaphor of the elephant and rider to refer to the right brain and left brain, respectively: "The mind is divided, like a rider on an elephant, and the rider's job is to serve the elephant."[9]

To persuade and influence people, we must speak to their "elephants." We cannot change people's minds by utterly refuting their arguments; by

---

7. For some of this list, see Warner and Wilder, *Rare Leadership*, 37.

8. For the relational circuits of the brain, see Siegel, *Developing Mind*, 184–201, 277; Siegel, *Pocket Guide to Interpersonal Neurobiology*, 19-1 to 19-8; Lehman, *Outsmarting Yourself*, 123–64.

9. Haidt, *Righteous Mind*, 1.

direct left-brain confrontations. This elicits shame and the "rider" will fight hard to protect the elephant by any reasoning it can devise. Reason becomes instrumental, a hired gun. This is reflected by common modern proverbs like "a man convinced against his will is of the same opinion still," as well as "you might win an argument but lose a soul," and "people don't care how much you know until they know how much you care." And another common saying shows the power of bias and prejudice (these are elephant functions) is, "I have made up my mind. Don't bother me with the facts." Stories speak to the elephant.[10]

Psychiatrist, clinical director, and fellow of All Souls College, Oxford, Ian McGilchrist entitled his extensive written work on brain science, "The Master and His Emissary." He conveys the same notion—the "master" is the right brain, his "emissary" is the left brain.[11]

So what are the implications and relevance of brain science for oral hermeneutics? Storytelling as a ministry of the word that can transform character, must engage the full brain, and it always does when done right (using good questions to engage the whole brain in group discussion). Life Model Works uses what they call "4+ stories." The "4" alludes to the four levels of the right brain, and the "+" refers to the left brain. Wilder memorably puts these levels in alliteration to aid our memory (a very oral hermeneutical practice). They follow below with a description of how story involves each level:

1. Attachment (thalamus): This deepest part of the brain is the attachment center. As humans, our deepest need and craving is for relationships. This part of the brain is designed to seek, build, and thrive on joyful relationships. If the storyteller and storyhearers are personally and emotionally present and engaged, relational attachments are formed and nurtured.

2. Assessment (amygdala): How the story impacts one emotionally is reflected in bodily experiences and expressed in body language. This level accesses the "library of memories" (stored in the hippocampus) where everything of personal value may be recalled. Unprocessed

---

10. Haidt, *Righteous Mind*, 57.

11. McGilchrist's 2009 book, *The Master and His Emissary: The Divided Brain and the Making of the Modern World* is highly relevant to the subject of our book, and to why we need a return to oral hermeneutics. He contends that modern Western culture has been left-brain-dominant in cultural expression since the Enlightenment and the Industrial Revolution and has resulted in a neglected and stunted human dimension to our society. We might say that in modernity, the tail (left brain) wagged the dog. This includes how we have handled the Bible. Oral hermeneutics is one corrective to this situation.

memories are recalled in their "activated state," still carrying the accompanying emotions.[12] Most people know of this level by its "flight-fight" response. Parts of the story can touch a participant, triggering flight-or-fight emotions, causing self-reflection, greater self-awareness, and perhaps uncovering unresolved pain or trauma. Such "triggered memories" evoked by the story could result in healing prayer and counsel in the group or could be processed later.

3. Attunement (cingulate cortex): This is where we read people, synchronize with their feelings, and track eye contact. Here is where the range of emotions evoked by a story are registered, felt, expressed, and have their effect. This is where the voice gets its tone and energy. "It's the hub of all things nonverbal in the brain."[13] This happens both as participants read the character and emotions of the Bible characters, and once they attune to (or synchronize with) each other in the discussion. Good attunement enhances learning.

4. Action (prefrontal cortex): This is our identity center, what Warner and Wilder call the "executive control center."[14] This expresses what it is like for me and my people *to do* under these conditions. This is where group identity in high-group (collectivist, communal) cultures, where honor and shame are strong values, will be prominently expressed (the "We" whereas in individualistic cultures the "I" will be more prominent). This will become evident in the kinds of applications the participants make in the last part of the storytelling process.

5. Account (left brain): This is the fifth (4+), and refers to just the words and narrated cognitive content level of the story, what you would get if you read, or hear the story read, from a printed page in a monologue with no emotion and in monotone. When the story is read or presented this way, it is very difficult to remember because imagination and emotions are minimally evoked. By contrast, when visualizing and feeling the story, indwelling and internalizing it, it is easily recalled.[15]

So one can readily see that a story has the most impact on identity and character formation, and potential worldview change when it engages the whole brain. And story, of all the genres in Scripture, has great capability of doing that. The Level 5 Account (left brain, intellectual cognition)

---

12. Personal email correspondence with Jim Wilder, August 8, 2019.
13. Personal email correspondence with Jim Wilder, August 8, 2019.
14. Warner and Wilder, *Rare Leadership*, 36.
15. Personal email correspondence with Jim Wilder, August 8, 2019.

is important, but if it is only that then the meaning and transformational potential of the story are greatly reduced.

At the end of each subtitled section below, we will note which of the 4+ levels are engaged and how the telling of "Elisha and the Widow's Oil" in chapter 1 engaged them.

Oral Language Used in the Story

In chapter 1, the authors offered a written-language version through which we attempted to convey what is best experienced in oral language. Written language and oral language have only one element in common—words. But oral language has many additional elements, often called "body language," such as gestures, eye behavior, facial expressions, posture, tone of voice, pauses in the flow of speech, and more.[16] Researchers argue that the majority of communication in face-to-face interaction is nonverbal body language. This is part of oral language. Ideally, teaching the Bible should maximize communication potential. Oral language provides maximal communication and impact and thus greater hermeneutical potential.

Below is the story just told in the previous chapter with notes describing the body language used in the telling. The number of seconds of the pauses report what happened in the natural give-and-take of the discussion. They are in no way prescriptive, or a model to be exactly imitated; they are descriptive of what happened in this particular storytelling event:

> (The storyteller opens a Bible, begins to read the story, but then lays the Bible down on a nearby table).
>
> "One day a widow of one of the sons of the prophets came to Elisha and cried out, (Uses a desperate, high-pitched, shrill

---

16. "Oral language" includes "body language," but comprises more elements than body language. Oral language involves orientation in space and proxemics (meaning of and the use of the relative distance between speaker and audience), the meaning added by the context or place in which the communication event happens, imitation or impersonation of characters portrayed, the meaning that may be conveyed by the gender of the communicator, what culture he or she comes from, and age and social status of the communicator. There are certain kinds of humor that cannot be fully portrayed in writing (would you rather read a joke or hear it told?). There is a multidimensionality in messaging (verbal message, nonverbal body language, and context) as these several factors all congruently convey the same message, thus heightening its impact. Or these elements may be incongruently conveying conflicting messages, thus delivering complexity or dissonance. Oral language also provides transitions in the communication event which are not possible in written language—sound, rhythm, tempo, or movement used to portray scene changes. See Lipman, *Improving Your Storytelling*, 21–39.

voice) ... "My husband who served you is dead, and you know how he feared the Lord. But now a creditor has come, threatening to take my two sons as slaves!" (*A six-to-seven- second pause in speech*)...

(Storyteller shifts to a different position, facing the woman, uses a lower-pitched, male voice) "What can I do for you?" Elisha asked. "Tell me, what do you have in the house?"

(Shifting back into the space for the woman, facing Elisha, uses same voice for the woman, but pauses and lowers the pitch as she catches herself and qualifies her "nothing at all!")

"I have nothing at all! ... except ... well ... this flask of olive oil," she replied.

And Elisha said, "Go out to your friends and neighbors and borrow as many empty jars as you can. Then go into your house with your sons and shut the door behind you. Pour olive oil from your flask into the jars, setting each one aside when it is filled." (Uses same calm low voice for Elisha.)

So she did as she was told. Her sons kept bringing jars to her, and she filled one after another. Soon every jar was full to the brim! (*A five-second pause in speech*) ...

"Bring me another jar," she said to one of her sons.

"There aren't any more!" he told her. And then the olive oil stopped flowing.

(Storyteller makes motion with his hand, as if shaking the oil flask upside down, trying to get the last drop of oil from the flask ... then slowly stops shaking it) (*A four-to-five-second pause in speech*) ...

When she went and told the man of God what had happened, he said to her, "Now sell the olive oil and pay your debts, and you and your sons can live on what is left over." (The storyteller picks up the Bible from the chair, closes it, and says, "This is the end of the story.")

When the story is personally relevant and meaningful to the storyteller, and he or she is fully, emotionally present, is relational, holds good eye contact (depending on culture), is responsive to the feelings, body language, and cues of the group, then attachments are forming—Level 1

Attachment. The group is assessing the character of the characters in the story as they listen—Level 2 Assessment. Some feel flight-fight feelings vicariously for the widow. It was evoking memories with their accompanying emotions, at least for Linda, who later told the story of her friend Sandy, and the hopeless despair she felt. We see through the oral language used (in this case the nonverbal communication) that Level 3 Attunement is occurring. The storyteller's gestures and tone of voice communicate, making the story personal and real.

Vocalization, Inflections, and Pauses in Oral Communication

Being part of oral language, pauses in the speech should not be thought of as dead time. Pauses are a key element in *oral language* and influence meaning. Pauses allow listeners to absorb the story and picture what is happening. Pauses allow the storyteller to think ahead and articulate well, with appropriate body language, and to stay in tune with the listeners. A pause can create anticipation for what is coming next in the story. Silence can elicit emotions, like anxiety, laughter, or excitement. Not using pauses may leave some listeners behind because they are not able to form images from the story fast enough and engage emotionally before the teller advances the story.

The use of various kinds of vocalization is another key element in oral language. A skilled storyteller will use inflections of tone, speed, intensity, volume, stretching and shortening words to communicate appropriate emotions, values, and meaning that are inherent in the story. Think of the different meanings communicated by a shrill, high-pitched voice, or a low-pitched, calm voice. Think of what a whisper, or a rhythmical, lyrical, or melodious tone communicates. If the character's dialogue in a story is demanding, announcing, declaring, questioning, challenging, or merely stating a fact, the intonation and modulation will be different. Good storytellers walk in the sandals of the characters they are incarnating, and their voice brings them to life.

We note however, this should not be something contrived or programmed as a technique. It should flow naturally as the storyteller emotionally internalizes the story and feels it authentically as s/he tells it. This comes through experience and practice.

Here again, we see Level 3 Attunement occurring, as voice intonation, modulation, inflections, and pauses help people attune to each other's mental and emotional states. These vocalizations help embody the characters as real human beings. Perhaps anger toward the creditors is evoked as the group hears the distress of hopeless despair of the widow, as well as the fear the widow felt for the fate of her sons. And we can attune to the joy the widow felt after the miraculous provision from God. The joy came from her renewed attachments to the Lord, gratitude to Elisha, and joy that her attachments to her sons would not be broken. We rejoice with her.

A Method of Oral Presentation and Group Learning

I (Bill) used largely the Simply the Story (STS) method of preparing a story for oral presentation (which closely parallels figure 7.3).[17] Important factors in this method include the storyteller helping the listeners learn the story sufficiently to grasp its plotline and picture it in their mind's eye and thus be able to discuss it. The group hears the story three times and actively verbally engages in telling it twice. This repetition and engagement, so necessary for oral-preference learners, helps hearers retain the story. The participants are thus able to put to memory most of the story so that a thorough discussion to ascertain meaning can follow.

Rather than one person downloading information lecture-style, group learning takes place as participants interact with each other and with the story. The story, through the storyteller and the participants, teaches each one in the group at some level. The storyteller facilitates learning through asking penetrating questions. By concentrated listening that responds to the hearts and minds of the people in the group, the storyteller is able to encourage, recognize, and utilize teachable moments. This enhances memory and life application.

Much facilitating of learning comes from what causes the storyteller to pause, or return, and the energy and emotion s/he has in response to a point, a truth, or an application of a truth, especially when these are catalyzed by personal connection with someone in the group. There is life-on-life teaching in the living moment, thus learning can be transformational, not merely informational. Often the discussion will result in prayer ministry to persons in the group who have been touched by the spoken word. Discipleship or mentoring relationships may be formed and followed up on after the group discussion.

The reader will note the authors stressed the need to keep moving along in the story, and the need to complete the story on time, usually

---

17. See Miller, *Simply the Story Handbook*. This handbook provides an excellent method of inductive oral Bible study. The method works with literate and nonliterate people in that it is totally oral in style.

important in Western culture. This will not be culturally correct in other cultures, where time constraints may not be an issue. One thinks of the saying attributed to guerilla warriors fighting superior forces, "You have the clocks, but we have time." If time is not an issue, the group can go deep and long into a Bible story, including times of prayer and personal ministry which the story may evoke.

When the group engaging the story are adults, they bring with them the experiences, wisdom, and knowledge they have acquired to date. So when the story touches some aspect of their life experience, this knowledge becomes available to others in the group.[18] While the inspired story is the teacher, the Holy Spirit may use the experiences of group members to teach others who might learn from their experience. Note in the story event described how Javier insisted that the oil in the story was a symbol of the Holy Spirit, but when Linda said to him, "What? . . . do we sell the Holy Spirit?" Then Javier gained an insight that changed his mind. The meaning of the story became clearer through the corrective comments of one of the group!

To summarize: The Bible story employed by the Holy Spirit is the teacher; the storyteller-facilitator who leads the group is the midwife. Through character-centric questions, s/he listens and responds and skillfully balances the group discussion of the story; s/he fosters discovery learning experientially through insights into the characters in the story, and each other (or vicariously from the experiences and interpretations and applications to life of others).

This approach aligns well with the way Jesus of Nazareth taught his disciples. His preferred teaching method was through stories, he nearly always taught a cohort (e.g., the twelve or the three), and facilitated group interpretation and application by asking in-the-moment questions.

Here we see Level 1 Attachment happening as group discussion, sharing of emotions and life on life learning surely forms attachments. We see Level 3 Attunement as the participants are synchronizing their feelings about the characters and with each other.

---

18. Adult learning (andragogy) studies show that adults learn differently than children (pedagogy). See for example Knowles, *Modern Practice of Adult Education*. Adults are motivated to learn what they need to know for their life situations. They bring their life experience to bear on what they learn. They have a life-centered, task-oriented approach to learning, rather than content-centered. They like to learn from the experiences of others who are facing what they are facing and who have acquired the insights or know-how that they need for their lives. This story is about hard life experience and economic realities faced by adult care providers. Adults in the discussion group would have a learning readiness to hear the truths in the story, as well as from others in the group, as we saw in the experiences shared by Linda and Javier in the discussion in chapter 1.

Questions Drive Learning

Both Socrates and Jesus of Nazareth, in their wisdom, used questions extensively in their teaching. When a person asks a question, her/his brain is in a state of receptivity to receive and retain an answer. They ask because it is relevant to them to know. When an answer is relevant to them, it will stick and likely be used. When answering a question, a person must think somewhat critically, and draw upon her/his store of knowledge. The answerer knows her/his answer will be public before the group and so could be contested. All of this reinforces the learning process.

In reading the *oral storytelling event* in chapter 1, notice the authors did not use a set of stock or formulaic questions. The *questions are character-centric;* they typically followed the flow of the story, asking questions of or about *each character* unless a question was interjected by someone in the group. The storyteller-facilitator will listen to responses and often ask questions to further draw out a character issue earlier alluded to, or just now being discovered through the discussion. We ask what we might learn about characters from what they said and did and the choices they made, including the choices they might have made. Such questions yield insights into their, our, and God's character. God is always considered a character (even if not explicitly) in every Bible story. The Bible stories are inspired Scripture, so the specific characters, the consequences of their choices, and the trajectories of their lives have divine truth to teach.

Good questions about the story engage the brain, mind, heart, and will to act (or head, heart, hands). They help create Attachment, Assessment, and Attunement, and help one prepare for Action, therefore, engagement of all four levels of the right brain.

When the storyteller shifted to application questions, we saw the Level 4 Action come into play. When Linda confessed how she wished she and her desperate friend Sandy had been part of a good congregation with supportive relationships, she acknowledged she was learning from the story discussion to be less of an individualist and move toward valuing community. When the storyteller asked, "So what is it like for us, as a body of believers, as a people, how it is like us to respond? If we respond out of our group identity, what does that look like?" He was calling for action, and there had already been application from anecdotes from both Linda and Javier.

Thus, in the language of Life Model Works, we can say that "Elisha and the Widow's Oil" story is a 4+ story.

Who is in Control?

A story told in its entirety like this in a group setting engages the listeners and brings it to life through discussion. The experience of the characters in the story touches the experience of the "characters" discussing it. Parts of the story touch different parts of the listeners' lives. When it touches a life-need—for insight, correction, comfort, guidance, healing—needs can be met, and life-change can happen. But the storyteller-facilitator is not in control of this. The Holy Spirit is, through the story demonstrating meaning to hearts and lives, as he wills and as listeners are receptive.

In textual hermeneutics, by contrast, the exegete uses lexical tools to deliver what s/he understands is the exact and accurate (usually one) authorial intended meaning. Her/his tools give a sense of control over the text and its meaning as s/he delivers it to the listeners. Perhaps due to the prevalence of our late-modern technologies, we are especially conditioned to want to be in control.

Ambiguity and Multiple Truths

Listener engagement of the imagination with the story, acting upon it by talking about it (thinking out loud), actually brings meaning that may not have occurred by merely hearing it in a lecture or sermon. A listener's experiential and emotional identification with a character in a story will have a deeper impact on that person's heart and behavior than will merely gaining cognitive insights.

This means an element of ambiguity will be present.[19] Every Bible storytelling leaves gaps and omits information that was available at the original event. Think of the story of Noah and the great flood. The events took place over many years, but all we get is less than four chapters (Gen 6–9). It is left to us to imagine what else happened and read between the lines. As a story is discussed, it is not always clear and certain to us what meaning or application a person may be getting from the story. There may be possible multiple truths (John 14:26; 16:12–13 may be applicable) and dimensions in different parts of the story. By multiple truths we mean the author (and the Divine Author) has purposely not necessarily limited the text to a single truth. This can be beneficial in different ways to a wide array of hearers, stimulating deeper thinking and imagination.

There may be more than one truth drawn from parts of the story by different people. In the above story, for example, *why did Elisha tell*

---

19. Walton and Sandy, *Lost World of Scripture*, 196, 204, 210, 214, 279, 308.

the widow to "shut the door behind you" after she had borrowed the jars from the neighbors? Was it merely practical (so that the neighbors would not disturb, or that she would not be vulnerable to robbers)? Was it for a spiritual formation reason for the woman and her sons so that they would experience an intimate time in the presence of God with the miracle he would be performing—similar to when Jesus taught in the Sermon on the Mount, to "go into your room and shut your door and pray to your Father who is in secret and your Father who sees in secret will reward you" (Matt 6:6 ESV)? It is not an either/or proposition. Both interpretations may be true. One saw God's wisdom, another saw his provision. One listener may find truths where another does not. This is part of the genius of story.

A Different Style of Teaching

As a storyteller-facilitator, one is still a teacher, but the teaching style shifts. We shift from the lecture mode, which can often devolve to a mere download of cognitive information, to a facilitator of discovery-learning mode.[20] If you are used to teaching by the lecture method, learning this style will be a challenge. We are constantly tempted to start lecturing or preaching, rather than asking questions that evoke discovery learning. We shift from being, as noted in a famous article, "The Sage on the Stage" to being "The Guide at the Side."[21] Think of these styles of teaching:

- *The Learned Professor* who looks for the right answers from his/her students.
- *The Knowledge Policeman* who looks to correct the wrong answers of his/her students.
- *The Fellow-Climber* who leads in seeking to find answers with his students.

In the Fellow-Climber model the teacher may well know (and perhaps should) more than her/his students, but has the wisdom and skill of making the students feel encouraged to think, to venture out in the climb of learning together with their teacher, and to discover wisdom and knowledge

---

20. A classic image of the cognitive download lecture method is the mother bird who predigests food which she then regurgitates and drops into the open mouths of the baby birds in the nest. Such a lecturing approach is sometimes necessary to impart information to students which they could not otherwise acquire, but active discovery-learning facilitated by the teacher is the more effective way to learn and produces the best retention and use by the student.

21. King, "From Sage on the Stage," 30–35.

embedded in the characters storied in the event(s).[22] The Fellow-Climber teacher helps the rest of the group truly hear, visualize and feel, and make life applications from the story as they climb the mountain together.

Why Ask for a Summary Symbol or Proverb?

One of the challenges of oral hermeneutics is that in some settings the participants do not have the text visually to refer to, so it is particularly important to create memory markers along the way. Symbols (jar of manna, an oil flask, a shepherd's staff, twelve stones) and proverbs serve as metaphorical memory markers for the storytellers and listeners. These succinct memory markers capture the essence of the story, making it easy to recall the storyline that fleshes out the story. This is especially true for cultures who highly value visual images and proverbs. If the story group is not forthcoming with a proverb or symbol, the storyteller could offer suggestions.

To summarize, whether through body language, use of pauses in oralizing, painting pictures in the mind's eye, group learning (that includes correcting each other), character-centric questions, personally directed questions, symbols and proverbs, emotions, ambiguity, and possible multiple truths, Bible communicators who facilitate discovery learning of the truths in a story (instead of lecturing) utilize oral hermeneutical methods to evoke meaning and enable wise and relevant application to life. These experiential learning components, among others, comprise oral hermeneutic.

Part 2 begins to provide the theoretical and theological reasons for the oral hermeneutic components demonstrated in the story modeled, as well as others.

---

22. I owe this delineation of three types of teaching styles to Dorothy Miller. Miller used this illustration in her practical training and coaching in *Simply the Story Handbook* workshops.

Part 2

Propositions

3

Orality's Influence on Text and Teaching

"How can people invoke His name when they do not believe? How can they believe in Him when they have not heard? How can they hear if there is no one proclaiming Him?"

—Romans 10:14 VOICE

"Fully literate persons can only with great difficulty imagine what a primary oral culture is like . . . Try to imagine a culture where no one has ever 'looked up' anything."

—Walter Ong

I (Tom) had really never even thought about it.[1] Christianity had always been a book religion for our family and church family. We were people of the book. Home Bible studies, personal (in contrast to communal) devotions, Sunday school, church services all centered on the printed text. Touting, quoting, and hearing the collective swish of turning pages was the expected norm for Sunday mornings, not to mention we thought it pleased God.

I learned my version of textual hermeneutics (TH) informally through Bible teachers and formally through Christian scholars and deeply researched textbooks. I had never known anything but TH, that is, until I started to

---

1. I (Tom) introduced the topic of textuality trumping orality in relation to canon construction in a paper presented at the Evangelical Missiological Society Northwest, in Spokane, Washington, on April 1, 2017. This paper was expanded into, Steffen, "Saving the Locals from Our Theologies, Part 1," and Steffen, "Saving the Locals from Our Theologies, Part 2."

teach Scripture to the Ifugao. The looks on their faces immediately informed me my message (I spoke their language with a high degree of fluency) was not being understood, even as they tried valiantly to follow my twisted topical teaching that bunny-hopped from one passage to another across Old and New Testament terrains. I knew I was in trouble but had no solution: *Why could they not get it? Was it them? Me? What was I missing?*

Have you ever noticed how frequently Scripture refers to variations of speaking, telling, hearing, listening, proclaiming, preaching? The author of Genesis tells us, "then there was the voice of God" and the results were "beautiful and good" (Gen 1:2, 4 VOICE). In the New Testament, Jesus spoke and lives were radically changed forever. From beginning to end, orality plays a significant role in Scripture. I certainly had read these words on numerous occasions, but my literate background blinded me to their oral significance and implications. One of those implications was the ability to interpret and communicate Scripture in a more comprehensive way.

Years later I was able to conduct some in-depth research that demanded new eyes. I realized that at least twenty to forty years passed from Jesus' crucifixion to when the first Synoptic Gospel (Mark) was written.[2] That time period could shed light on the implications of how orality and textuality interfaced. So I began reading, one book being Werner Kelber's *The Oral and the Written Gospel: The Hermeneutics of Speaking and Writing in the Synoptic Tradition, Mark, Paul, and Q*. Drawing from the classicists, linguists, and cultural anthropologists, this book became a watershed in New Testament studies.

I immediately recognized the close connections between orality and text in first-century Christianity and the Ifugao as they transitioned from a predominantly oral society to a more literate one. I later read *Jesus the Voice and the Text: Beyond the Oral and the Written Gospel*, that celebrated and challenged twenty-five years of Kelber's ground-breaking volume in New Testament studies, primarily because of the pertinent questions he raised.[3]

Following are some of the things I discovered on this journey that have specific implications for another hermeneutic. My experience working with oral and oral-preference Ifugao was about to meet the predominant

---

2. "It was not until approximately twenty years after Jesus' public ministry that the first written accounts of his words and deeds were inscribed in the Gospels" (Walton and Sandy, *Lost World of Scripture*, 108). "For about thirty to forty years the memory of what Jesus had said and done would have been in *oral* form" (Dunn, *Jesus According to the New Testament*, 27 [emphasis original]). See also Berger, *Oral Interpretation of the Bible*, 6; Loubser, *Oral and Manuscript Culture*, 7.

3. For example, "What was the tradition like out of which the gospels have grown, and in what manner are the latter related to tradition?" "Can one not expect the little stories to fall in line with the larger story so as to produce an oral gospel?" "Does the gospel reflect estrangement from oral life and alienation from its linguistic heritage" (Kelber, *Oral and Written Gospel*, xx, 77, 95)?

first-century oral/aural Christianity, i.e., how orality influenced the text and how the text was taught. A major insight I was about to discover on this journey was that *without an understanding of orality, one's understanding of Scripture would be minimized*. Warning! The discoveries that follow may shake you to the core as they did us. Seatbelts suggested.

To answer the question, "*How did orality influence the biblical Text and teaching?*," the authors begin with a succinct overview of the central components that comprise orality. We do this to help grasp what the ancients experienced during their transition from a strongly oral text[4] to a written Text (we focus primarily on the New Testament). We then consider the role of scribes in manuscript-making (scribality), followed by memory—how all this was kept as pristine as possible and stored in strongly oral-based cultures where few if any libraries existed (see figure 3.1). A look at the vast volume of oral type literature in the totality of Scripture follows, concluding with the delivery and dialogue that surrounded completed manuscripts. This section briefly touches on the teaching-learning patterns during antiquity and oral societies today. While we isolate these categories for discussion purposes, we consider them all tightly integrated.

Orality

As to the primacy of oral speech in human communication, anthropologists and cultural historians have clarified that oral speech is the fundamental and essential nature of human language. Linguist Ferdinand de Saussure (1857–1913) developed the study of phonemics, showing the way language is nested in sound, made up not of letters but of functional sound units or phonemes.[5] Orality specialist Walter Ong asserts, "sounded words are not things, but events."[6] Oral expression can and mostly has existed without writ-

---

4. "A text is a tissue of words. The term comes from the Latin *texere*, meaning literally to weave, join together, plait or braid; and therefore, to construct, fabricate, build or compose (Greetham, 1999: 26). That is what this book is about: the universal human work of weaving or fabricating with words. People put words together to make a mark, to leave a trace. They do this orally as well as in writing. Though many people think of 'text' as referring exclusively to written words, writing is not what confers textuality. Rather, what does is the quality of being joined together and given a recognizable existence as a form" (Barber, *Anthropology of texts, Persons and Publics*, 1).

5. Ong, *Orality and Literacy*, 5.

6. Ong, "Before textuality," 265. He adds, "words modify the holistic situation and in one way or another they explain or interpret it, make something known in it that was not know (sic) before . . . . The oral word is . . . an event, an action. The oral word is a call from someone to someone, an interpersonal transaction. No interactive persons, no words . . . the oral word is essentially explanation or interpretation or hermeneutics, a clarification by one person of something that to his or her interlocutor or interlocutors is otherwise not evident" (Ong, "Before textuality," 266–67).

ing. Conversely, writing has never existed without orality. "Orality, far from being primitive and savage, is pervasive and cohesive."[7]

In everyday life, we unconsciously focus on the oral. Our personal worldview received significant development long before we ever learned to read. "Don't touch that!" "Did you hear what happened to Joe?" What does that mean?" "Why did Jane do that?" "Did you notice how he did that?" Oralists, which we all were until we learned to read, discern meaning primarily by listening to and observing what others say and do, and then attempt to replicate or avoid it.

We grew up in an oral world that defined, determined, and distinguished how we leaned into life.[8] That oral-based identity[9]—"an internalized and evolving life story or personal myth"[10]—however, would be challenged along our journey to adulthood.

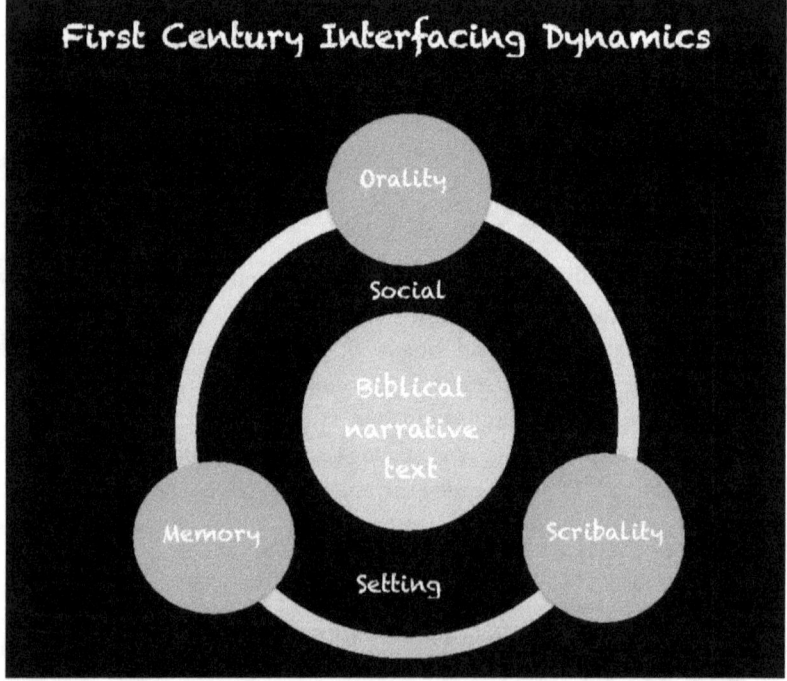

Figure 3.1. First-Century Interfacing Dynamics within the Biblical Text

---

7. Knighton, "Orality in the Service of Karamojong Autonomy," 149.

8. Eric Havelock notes, "the natural human being is not a writer or a reader but a speaker and a listener" (Havelock, "Oral-Literate Equation," 20).

9. Steffen, "Foundational Roles of Symbol and Narrative"; Bruner, *Acts of Meaning*, 34–38; Wright, *New Testament and the People of God*, 42–43, 123–26.

10. McAdams, "What Do We Know?," 382.

Our formal educational system added literacy to orality and changed the way we learn and communicate. Learning the technology of reading and writing changed the way we take in information, think, communicate, and remember it. Ong captures this worldview change this way, "writing restructures consciousness."[11]

After some 500 years of reading (since Gutenberg made it accessible to a significant percentage of people), here is one way it has changed us: "Readers, in a sense, are no longer asked to see; they are simply asked to interpret the code."[12] Abstract ideas, fragmentation, and learning in private, among others, received strong attention, often placing orality's concreteness, comprehensiveness, and communal learning on the backburner. *Did the addition of literacy eventually blind us to the continued role of orality? What can Israel and first-century oral/aural audiences teach us today about interpretation and communication?* To answer these questions some basic understanding of orality is necessary.

While many have written about orality, Ong's landmark *Orality and Literacy* has received possibly the most attention. First published in 1982, the release of a 30th Anniversary Edition in 2012 argues for its staying power. For Ong, speaking differs greatly from writing.[13] And he believes this has major implications for Bible communications: "Orality-literacy theorems challenged biblical study perhaps more than any other field of learning, for, over the centuries, biblical study has generated what is doubtlessly the most massive body of textual commentary in the world."[14]

Building on but expanding beyond his mentor, Marshall McLuhan, famous for the phrase "the medium is the message," Ong helped distinguish orality from literacy and identified implications literacy added to orality in relation to communication. The authors will make one major distinction from Ong and other earlier writers who perceived literacy as totally separate from orality. We view orality and literacy as a continuum rather than a great divide. Very few people in the world are totally oral, and no literate is oralless.

The time has arrived for us in our day to take orality's concreteness, comprehensiveness, and communal learning off the backburner and place it on the frontburner to identify central components and concerns. Many of these components will be more fully developed in later chapters. These components apply specifically to primary orality and collectivist societies, though some components will apply more broadly to more individualistic societies.

11. Ong, *Orality and Literacy*, 77.
12. Stevens, *Rise of the Image*, 64.
13. See Ong, *Orality and Literacy*, 37–56.
14. Ong, *Orality and Literacy*, 169.

Spoken Words have Power

In orality, spoken words carry power—they can create from nothing or bless or curse.[15] *Remember Simon the sorcerer's immediate response to Peter's comment,* "May your silver rot right along with you, Simon!" "*Please*—you must pray to the Lord for me. I don't want these terrible things to be true of me" (Acts 8:20, 24 VOICE).[16] Simon knew immediately that Peter had just cursed him; he intuitively knew the ramifications of the power of spoken words.

Concentrates on the Concrete

Orality focuses on the concrete rather than the abstract, the tangible over the intangible. The symbol of the cross requires the story of Jesus' crucifixion. A miracle requires an event—Moses and the Israelites crossing the Red Sea, and a retelling of that event.

Concentrates on Conflict, Changes, and Clashes

Conflict, changes, and clashes serve as flashpoints for orality, as evidenced in both of the Elisha stories (chapters 1 and 9). Tied to the plot, these flashpoints signal the significant in a story.

Calls for Communal Face-to-Face Dialogue

Orality spotlights the need for people to communally interact in concrete events. Communal face-to-face interaction supersedes individualism and privateness. Community serves as the basis for culture transmission and transformation.

A Preference for Whole to Parts

Orality focuses on the unified whole, the global, the big picture; "the oral mind totalizes."[17] The parts are not excluded but rather seen as nested in

---

15. "His voice explodes in great power *over the earth*. His voice is both regal and grand" (Gen 29:4 VOICE).

16. Italics in a Bible passage is considered "emphasis original" unless otherwise stated.

17. Ong, *Orality and Literacy*, 171.

the whole from which they originate (more inductive). In contrast, much of modern methodology starts with the dissected parts and deducts.

Nonlinear Processing Preferred

While many from the West prefer to process things linearly or chronologically based on cause-and-effect, oralists find more satisfaction in other ways of processing, such as successive independent episodes, associations, echoes, or circular thinking.

Learning through Apprenticeship

Orality emphasizes learning by observing and imitating someone (usually) known, rather than from instructions gleaned from a written text by an unknown author. Personal mentoring is a key activity. And where the apprenticeship takes place is also part of the immediate, practical learning process. Apprenticeship focuses on living issues in life settings in the moment.

Aggregate Learning

Orality relies on learning over time, i.e., adding what was learned from one event to the next to the next. This is cumulative learning and is more convincing. It tends to result in greater retention than relying on the critical analysis of isolated events.

Experientially Based

Orality is based on what people experience. From such subjective experiences, theories emerge. Both experience and theory (or propositions) are present and utilized, but there is a sequence, from experience to theory. Oralists, therefore, place a high priority on action and active learning.

Communal Relationships are Central

Orality focuses strongly on relationships between people and does all it can to maintain harmony within the community.[18] Communal relationships,

---

18. Referencing the many significant changes experienced by the community of Israel, Bradt says this: "For this is what story does: it creates relationships of shared

therefore, surpass the desires of the individual. In collectivist cultures, anyone who attempts to challenge communal tradition can expect social humiliation, which may require a mediator to arbitrate the case.

These negotiated relationships are usually hierarchical—patrons and clients. Patrons are expected to meet the needs of their clients. In return, clients compensate by honoring their patrons publicly.

Participation Required

Again, in most collectivist cultures, orality calls for all to participate in communal events. Not to participate is to bring shame on oneself, one's family, the community, and even one's nation, that could result in feared social isolation. Literacy, on the other hand, affords the opportunity to distance oneself from the text being read and from others while reading it.

Focuses on Stories, Symbol, and Rituals

Orality relies on repeated stories, symbols, and rituals to remember and reinforce what society considers significant. "Symbols seek to summarize and synthesize complex issues through images that project meaning through silent speech."[19] Rituals recall, reenact, reexamine, reactivate, renew cultural values, behavior, and relationships.[20] The triadic repetition of stories, symbols, and rituals fosters deep engagement, thereby enhancing long-term communal memory.

Imagination and Emotion Required

Orality requires engagement of the imagination and emotions; it expects these God-given capacities to assist in communication, interpretation, and application.

---

experiences, of communality, of compassion and empathy . . . And in the storying of human experience, an alternative world is evoked, an alternative world with alternative values, alternative ways of knowing and relating" (Bradt, *Story as a Way of Knowing*, 149).

19. Steffen, *Worldview-based Storying*, 136.
20. Steffen, *Worldview-based Storying*, 180.

Concentrates on Conversations and Actions

What characters say and do or don't say or do (involving themselves and/or others) in a story are signposts of meaning significance.

Meaning is Discovered through Demonstration

Orality begins the "aesthetic experience"[21] of discovering meaning by focusing on the actions, interactions, and conversations of the portrayed characters. Meaning, therefore, is demonstrated and absorbed through speech that is "performance-oriented,"[22] rather than defined and expounded.

Descriptions Preferred Over Definitions

The Song of Moses (Deut 32:1–43) serves as a great example in that it is full of imagery and metaphors describing God and his ways but has no stated conceptual theological propositions.

Focuses on the Relational Value-Moral System of Honor and Shame

Honor and shame, reflecting relationships, will typically be evidenced in collective communities. In contrast, Western individualist societies tend to focus more on guilt and innocence.

Artistic Rhetoric Appreciated

Oral communities have deep respect and appreciation for oratory. Like sharp-witted wordsmiths who continue to better their script, so speakers continue to hone their speaking skills, but with different tools. Part of their rhetoric toolbox may include rhythm and rhyme, poetry, song, visuals, gestures, voice fluctuation, and so forth. We might think of Homer and his great works—*The Odyssey* and *The Iliad*—which were originally oral compositions that were sung. Every traditional society has had its bards.

---

21. Prior, *On Reading Well*, 21.
22. Ong, *Orality and Literacy*, 173.

Bounded Ambiguity Assumed

Orality assumes ambiguity within boundaries. Meaning, whether comments, symbols, or rituals, relies heavily on the visual and is therefore tolerable of some wiggle room in interpretation (which is always culturally negotiated). It is *not*, however, open to *any* interpretation.

Collective Memory Required to Maintain Oral Tradition

The collectivist community sees herself as the holder and preserver of oral tradition. Anyone who challenges oral tradition will be subject to dreaded social isolation.

Repetition Required for Collective Memory

Because remembering over time is always an issue in oral societies where books and libraries are absent or rare, multiple ways are required to keep people from forgetting the significant. Orality therefore relies on repetition to keep memories alive and meaning boundaried. On the communal level this is accomplished through public repetition of songs, dances, dramas, drums, reading, poetry, proverbs, and art (see Deut 6 and the Passover).

It should be noted that just as there are variations of oral hermeneutics and textual hermeneutics, so there are variations of orality. While there are universal features connected to orality, these are expressed locally and generationally. Orality is expressed through oralities.[23]

Summarizing, orality refers to a preferred way to hear, process, communicate, and remember. It is a multisensory mode of communication that weds the ear (sound) and eye (symbols, rituals, body language).

Oral learners are those who prefer to learn through oral means, think holistically and more circularly (in contrast to linearly), remember visually, and prefer to communicate concretely and affectively. A Native American captured orality this way, "Ours is an oral tradition. It can be heard in the way we think and speak. An oral tradition schools the memory and makes the spoken word a poem. Stories are a treasure of oral tradition, passed on in eloquence."[24] And it will be passed on with local seasoning.

Author and professor of theology Kenneth Bailey (1930–2016) will now illustrate some implications from Middle Eastern orality.

---

23. See Bush, "Synthesizing the Orality Debate."
24. Bowman, "Finding My Real Father," 57.

Middle Eastern Tellings

Bailey resided in the mountain villages of Lebanon for some thirty years. From this extensive experience, he concluded there were three ways Middle Easterners told proverbs, riddles, poetry, parables, stories, or biographies: (1) informal uncontrolled—such as rumors, urban legends or tragic events easily embellished, (2) formal controlled—where teachers ensure message integrity often through word-for-word drilling and memorization or dictated writing, and (3) informal controlled—where certain genres allow for some deviation within the control of the community.[25]

Bailey concluded from his studies that informal control characterized Middle Eastern village life,[26] and thereby provided a methodological framework for interpreting the Synoptic Gospels. *Why do we have four gospels?* His experience and writings opened a window James Dunn has yet to close, even if it took him twenty years to open. "What excited me when I learned about this characteristic feature of oral transmission was that it spoke immediately to the character of the Synoptic tradition."[27]

In *The Oral Gospel Tradition* Dunn defends informal control[28] when he declares, "In oral performance there is no original version, only a storyline retold in diverse and divergent versions, only a teaching of the same in substance, but diverse in detail."[29] As Jesus' teachings were heard, they were retold over several decades with some flexibility, yet some fixedness, not atypical of any oral-based society.

---

25. Bailey, "Informal Controlled Oral Tradition," 34.

26. Bailey may go too far in claiming that contemporary storytelling in the Middle East is the same as that from the first century. For sure there would be similarities, but also differences. In *Honor and Shame and the Unity of the Mediterranean*, the edited volume by E. E. Gilmor found similarities, in addition to some differences across the Mediterranean in relation to honor and shame during the first century. This is probably also true of how stories were told and guarded.

27. Dunn, *Oral Gospel Tradition*, 306.

28. In *Jesus and the Eyewitnesses*, Richard Bauckham, who prefers *formal control*, critiques Bailey's and Dunn's model: "It is the weakness of Bailey's and Dunn's models that they focus on the early transmission of Jesus traditions in Palestinian Jewish villages, ignoring the Jerusalem church . . . after the resurrection it was the Jerusalem church, under the leadership of the twelve and later of James the Lord's brother, that became the mother church of the whole Christian movement" (Bauckham, *Jesus and the Eyewitnesses*, 298). While both *formal control* and *informal control* existed, orality still dominated during the time of the Jerusalem church. Eyewitness accounts were still vulnerable to fluidity even as there was fixed understanding of the storyline (a retelling of actions witnessed).

29. Dunn, *Oral Gospel Tradition*, 244.

Referencing orality, Kelber correctly notes, "*tradition is almost always composition in transmission.*"[30] In an oral culture, one would expect to find "plurality, uniformity, and variability."[31] Dunn concurs, "Ambiguity and fuzziness around the edges are an integral and essential part of Christianity's canonical tradition and heritage."[32] He further claims, a "stable core and substance with variation"[33] remains. Vanhoozer calls this "creative fidelity" and "ruled spontaneity."[34]

Out of these repetitious fixed-fluid expressions, an authoritative oral tradition developed that was collective-individual[35] in nature. Stories, songs,[36] scrolls, symbols, sayings, chants, rituals, genealogies, and the like, expressed and maintained oral tradition.

What is often overlooked today is the oral process that preceded and influenced the written text. History reminds us, however, that orality served as the bedrock for biblical oral texts for centuries. For the most part, *spoken Scripture was lived long before it became written word.*

The Window between the Spoken and Written Word

The generational handing down of spoken Scripture was a significant part of the sovereign, divine process. Those earlier oral presentations did not become inspired, they *were* inspired. This must be the case because the biblical author who wrote it down was drawing from an oral and community tradition. The authors could claim that inspiration was only at work when he wrote, but the evidence suggests otherwise.

---

30. Kelber, *Oral and Written Gospel*, 30 (emphasis original).

31. Kelber, *Oral and Written Gospel*, 5.

32. Dunn, *Oral Gospel Tradition*, 359.

33. Dunn, *Oral Gospel Tradition*, 359. See Sternberg, *Poetics of Biblical Narrative*, 50–51.

34. Vanhoozer, *Drama of Doctrine*, 129.

35. We prefer to see the interconnection between communal and individual rather than an either/or. The first term, in this case "collective," signals the dominant side. It's a both/and, while the first word identifies the dominant side.

36. Aminta Arrington, professor of intercultural studies at John Brown, discovered in her research among the Lisu of Yunnan Province, China, a ministry begun by J. O. Fraser in 1914, that two books influenced their Christianity for over a century. Book one, the written word, and book two, the hymnbook. The hymnbook served as a bridge, a theological mediator, between the written word and their oral world. While the missionaries stressed personal Bible study, the Lisu learned and maintained most of their theology for generations through hymns. And they continue to do so today. See Arrington, *Songs of the Lisu Hills*. See also Deut 31:19.

Oral texts were rarely told word for word (Bailey's "formal controlled"), rather they were told with some creative fixedness (Bailey's "informal controlled"). In those multiple retellings, some changes naturally occurred because of memory loss, the current context and audience, and the cultural filters of the teller and those of the audience. They illustrate the boundaried fluidity of orality.

Anyone who has given the same sermon multiple times on the same day (using notes) knows there were differences in each presentation, even with basically the same type of audience.[37] Pure oral duplications then and now are difficult unless rote memorization is involved. Even then, an exact duplicate is never guaranteed. Ask any professional storyteller. What may be overlooked, however, is the oral process that preceded and influenced written texts. In the case of the New Testament, that process lasted decades while its influence remained for centuries.

Were Jesus' words, spoken mostly in Aramaic in rural Galilee, consistently told by eyewitnesses word for word for twenty to forty years, even as they transitioned from rural areas to urban centers where Greek predominated? Did Jesus speak Hebrew? Surely he knew and used it at least in the synagogue liturgy and in Scripture reading (Luke 4:16–19). *Did Jesus speak Latin to the centurion whose servant he healed (Luke 7:1–10)? Were his spoken or translated words by others retold with consistency and exactness over decades, geographical areas, and four different languages and cultures? Were Jesus' words inspired? Which, the Hebrew or the Aramaic?* The gospels, written in Greek, are already a translation from the original. A more important question is: *Was the meaning consistent over time?*

> "When Jesus . . . narrated a story at one place, and then proceeded to retell it, with modifications, at a different place, he was not in this second instance rendering a variant of the so-called original. He was rather in both instances presenting an authentic version of the story."[38]

In the thousands of hours Jesus would have taught in his three years of public ministry, *how many times did he orally teach on the same topic? Did*

---

37. Vanhoozer concludes, "*every* speech and *every* act after the closing of the canon are a kind of improvisation. A false picture of improvisation must not hold us captive" (Vanhoozer, "One Rule to Rule Them All?," 113 [emphasis original]).

38. Ong, quoted in Kelber, "In the Beginning were the Words," 73.

eyewitnesses at one setting hear variances from eyewitnesses at other settings due to different group chemistry and context? It is hard to imagine in an oral culture that Jesus' teachings were exactly the same word-for-word reiteration in every place every time.[39] Nor would oral audiences expect that of him or any orator! Jesus was not a robot, or an audio tape recorder. *Which version did eyewitnesses consider original?*

In one sense, every story rehearsal was an original. Good storytellers often intentionally repeated the rehearsal *without* becoming verbatim repetitive. Rhetoric demanded some level of oratorial creativity. Every telling of a story was different because the chemistry of the setting, the audience, the emotional ambiance, and the communicator's response to these were never exactly the same from one telling to the next. Possibly the first to capture this concept was Harvard University professor Albert Lord (1912–1991) when he wrote, "each performance is 'an' original, if not 'the' original."[40] British anthropologist Jack Goody concurs, "Repetition is rarely if ever verbatim."[41]

There has been a debate in modern biblical and Gospel studies of (using the Latin phrases) the *"ipsissima verba"* (the very words) and the *"ipsissima vox"* (the very voice) of Jesus. *Do we have in our written gospels the very words or the very voice of Jesus?* Based on our foregoing discussion, immediately above, the authors are convinced the *ipsissima vox* position most reflects reality. To summarize the argument: Jesus spoke mostly Aramaic and Hebrew so our Greek gospels are already a translation, Jesus spent hundreds of hours teaching, yet his words in the gospels can be read in less than an hour, and we have variations in wording in the parallel passages of the gospels. The gospel writers do *not* agree word for word, but they *do* agree thought for thought.[42]

---

39. Based on her extensive research or oral unwritten literature in Africa, Ruth Finnegan puts forth this challenge: "The variability typical of oral literary forms has tended to be overlooked by many writers. This is largely because of certain theoretical assumptions held in the past about the verbatim handing down of oral tradition supposedly typical of nonliterate societies. The model of written literature has also been misleading in this context, with its concept of exact transmission through manuscripts or printing press . . . There is not necessarily any concept of an 'authentic version,' and when a particular literary piece is being transmitted to an audience the concepts of extemporization or elaboration are often more likely to be to the fore than that of memorization" (Finnegan, *Oral Literature in Africa*, 12).

40. Lord, *Singer of Tales*, 101.

41. Goody, *Domestication of the Savage Mind*, 118.

42. See Bock in Wilkins and Moreland, *Jesus Under Fire*, 73–99, and Osborne, "Historical Criticism and the Evangelical," 193–210. For an opposing view, see Green, "Evangelicals and *Ipsissima Vox*," 49–68. We wonder if our theological sophistication has blinded us to the simple yet significant supporting role orality has in the discussion.

Voice preceded text and therefore came with some fixed fluidity which would *not* have been a major issue for the strongly oral audiences of antiquity (or today); it only becomes an issue for those superimposing modern scientific models of exactitude onto a very human oral context. That does not mean that meaning was lost as we shall shortly see. With this backdrop of orality, we now investigate scribality.

Scribality (Handwritten Manuscripts)

Over the years the spoken word became handwritten manuscripts through the tedious efforts of scribes (mostly the "literate elite"[43]). With the addition of a written text, significant changes followed. Some of those resultant changes included the location of reality. Summarizing Ong, cognitive developmental psychologist David Olson observes, "writing lifts speech out of its context and turns it into an object of thought and interpretation."[44] Writing moved the more fluid, concrete spoken event into fixed, abstract words. This change removed some of the experiential impact found in spoken text.

Stock, referencing the eleventh and twelfth centuries, adds depth to our understanding of the transition from the spoken to the written, "Man began to think of facts not as recorded by texts but as embodied in texts,

---

Why must "bring to your remembrance" (John 14:26 NASB) mean precise words? To those with literate backgrounds they might, while oralists would understand it as *meaning* (words could vary, meaning stays the same). Could not conveying meaning also be historical? Authoritative? Does orality offer a better solution for the data we have?

Anne MacKay provides some history on the matter: "The Judeo-Christian Bible reveals its oral traditional roots; medieval European manuscripts are penned by performing scribes; geometric vases from archaic Greece mirror Homer's oral style . . . . Indeed, if these final decades of the millennium have taught us anything, it must be that oral tradition never was the other we accused it of being; it never was the primitive, preliminary technology of communication we thought it to be. Rather, if the whole truth is told, oral tradition stands out as the single most dominant communicative technology of our species as both a historical fact and, in many areas still, a contemporary reality" (MacKay, *Signs of Orality*, 1–2).

43. Kwok Pui-lan reminds us that, with the exception of Koran (or Qur'an), other major Asian religions went through a similar process: "Comparable to the Bible, many Asian scriptures went through a period of oral transmission, some for a long period of time, before they assumed written form. The Confucian *Analects,* a compilation of the saying of Confucius and his disciples, were recorded long after the death of the master. The Daoist classic *Dao de jing* consists of sayings that embodied the spirit of a living tradition. Shortly after the Buddha's death, his disciples met to recite his teachings in order to establish an authoritative body of doctrine for the future. But the actual writing down of the Dharma was not achieved until hundreds of years later" (Pui-lan, "Hearing and Talking," 78).

44. Olson, *World of Paper,* 38.

a transition of major importance in the rise of information retrieval and classification."[45] Professor of Hebrew Bible and Northwest Semitic languages William Schniedewind adds, "Writing locates authority in a text and its reader instead of in a tradition and its community."[46] Writing replaced the spoken as the source of reality and authority. Individuals could now break up embodied text into fragments, categorize them, and retrieve as needed, thereby giving more of a sense of control over knowledge. The text, rather than the community, became the go-to place for wisdom.

Psychotherapist Kevin Bradt believes another change occurred, namely, that it "emphasizes exactness over interaction."[47] Writing moved reality and authority away from the fluid to the fixed. Dialogue, with all its shades of gray, gave way to preciseness. *But how much?*

We easily forget those early handwritten texts had no indentations, no word divisions, no chapter breakouts (developed in 1220 by Stephen Langton for commentaries), no verse numbers (developed in 1555 by Robert Estienne for a concordance). Author at the Institute for Bible Reading Glenn Paauw perceptively posits:

> We created a Bible exoskeleton . . . Columns, numbers, headings, footnotes, cross-references, callouts, colored letters, etc., etc., etc. Our overindulged addiction to addition has given us everything we could ask for except the text itself in a clean, natural expression . . . Such a Bible becomes something other than a mere carrier of the ideas found within . . . . Our Bible practices change when the form of our Bible changes.[48]

Such elaborate Bible exoskeletons and apparatuses can influence a hermeneutic, and is imposed upon the reader by the theology of the creators of the exoskeletons. To counter such fragmentation, the six volumes of the *ESV Reader's Bible* and *The Books of the Bible* offer readers a clean read, free of the artificial additives of chapters and verses. More steps, however, would be necessary to replicate antiquity—having it read out loud (proclaimed[49]),

---

45. Stock, *Implications of Literacy*, 62. In relation to "facts," Ong claims, "The term 'fact' in our ordinary sense of that which is actually the case, appears very late in English (in the *Oxford English Dictionary* the first record of its use dates only from 1581). Human utterance is concerned basically with more than announcing or disputing 'facts'" (Ong, "Before textuality," 266).

46. Schniedewind, *How the Bible Became a Book*, 114.

47. Bradt, *Story as a Way of Knowing*, 22.

48. Paauw, *Saving the Bible from Ourselves*, 33, 207.

49. Winger writes, "there is no distinct vocabulary in Old Testament Hebrew for the activity of reading. There is no verb which directly and uniquely means 'to read.' In both Hebrew and Aramaic the most common verb used is קָרָא (to proclaim or to call aloud)

ORALITY'S INFLUENCE ON TEXT AND TEACHING

explained, and discussed in community (Exod 24:3–4, 7; Deut 31:11–13; Josh 8:34–35; Neh 8:8–9; Col 4:16; 1 Thess 5:27; 2 Thess 2:15; 1 Tim 4:1; Rev 1:3).

New Testament texts, including many of the Epistles,[50] were mostly collaborative efforts. Their collective efforts (certainly not uncommon within collective societies) of the New Testament derived from eyewitnesses,[51] collections of sayings, and in some cases the previous works of earlier authors and scribes. Luke, for example, explains how his two-volume book Luke-Acts (25 percent of the New Testament) came into being through his research to discover the main ideas (not the precise words, because these varied) being made in various oral and textual versions.[52]

> For those who love God, several other people have already written accounts of what God has been bringing to completion among us, using the reports of the original eyewitnesses, those who were there from the start to witness the fulfillment of prophecy. Like those other servants who have recorded the messages, I present to you my carefully researched, orderly account of these new teachings. (Acts 1:1–3 VOICE)

The apostle John, a strong representative of visual orality, adds:

> This testimony is true. In fact it is an eyewitness account; and he has reported what he saw so that you also may believe. (John 19:35 VOICE)

> We want to tell you about the One who was from the beginning. We have seen Him with our own eyes, heard Him with

---

. . . Reading is aloud and interpersonal. There simply is no way of naming private, silent reading in Hebrew" (Winger, "Spoken Word," 144).

50. At least seven of Paul's Epistles included multiple authors (Sosthenes [1 Cor 1:1]; Timothy [2 Cor 1:1]; brothers and sisters [Gal 1:1–2]; Timothy [Phil 1:1; Col 1:1]; Silas & Timothy [1 Thess 1:1; 2 Thess 1:1]).

51. "These eyewitnesses did not merely set a process of oral transmission that soon went its own way without reference to them. They remained throughout their lifetimes the sources and . . . the authoritative guarantors of the stories they continued to tell" (Bauckham, *Jesus and the Eyewitnesses*, 93).

52. An Old Testament example using past authoritative *spoken words* is found in Jeremiah 36:2: "Write down on a scroll all that I have told you *over the years* about Israel, Judah, and the *surrounding* nations" (VOICE). An example of using existing authoritative *written documents* is found in 2 Kings 12:19: "Is not the rest of Jehoash's story—his actions *and lasting legacy*—documented in the book of the chronicles of Judah's kings" (VOICE)? Note the Old Testament's absence of the "Great Divide" between oral text and written text. Note also that each was considered authoritative primarily because of the God-chosen messenger, not because of preciseness of content. The same holds true for the New Testament.

> our own ears, and touched Him with our own hands. This One is *the manifestation of* the life-giving Voice ... What we saw and heard we pass on to you so that you, too, will be connected with us intimately *and become family.* (John 1:1, 3 VOICE)

Note how John attempted to keep the experiential and relational (both oral based) in the written text. Peppered with aspects of orality, the collective efforts of canon construction offered sound research and could therefore be *trusted as authoritative!*

In the book of Revelation, e.g., seven times (repetition) John ends each brief letter to the Asian churches with the equivalent of, "Let the person who is able to hear, listen to *and follow* what the Spirit proclaims to all the churches" (Rev 2:7 VOICE; see 2:11, 17, 29; 3:6, 13, 22). Literate scribes, influenced by the needs of the oral recipients of their tedious task, provided a trustworthy translation that reflected oral preferences, in this case through repetition.

Scribal writings did include unintentional errors, different spellings, additions, deletions, rearrangement of word order, often influenced by their specific social setting. In the process, "*the flexibility of the oral transmission period carried over into the written forms of the tradition.*"[53] Dunn describes it this way:

> Scribes were not merely copying a fixed tradition, but were doing (in a more modest way) what the story tellers of oral tradition were doing before them—retelling the story in the text, with the sort of modifications, elaborations and improvements which the oral performance had much more readily facilitated. In other words, the scribal task was not simply issuing copies of the text, but as providing something more like versions and editions of the text.[54]

Much like modern Bible translations, scribes continued to make minor changes in the text.[55] Even so, meaning remained relatively constant, as evidenced in the Dead Sea Scrolls.

---

53. Dunn, *Oral Gospel Tradition*, 309 (emphasis original).

54. Dunn, *Oral Gospel Tradition*, 345.

55. Can one assume that a Bible translator (or committee) today comes to the project with no cultural, theological or religious tradition biases that influence the translation? Why do some theological groups gravitate to certain translations while denouncing others? Does a Bible translation exist that has no such biases? Does one's preference for certain translations project certain biases? We must never forget that the text and translations will always differ. The former is authoritative, the latter are not, even if some come closer to the text than others. Since we all are biased, so will be our hermeneutic, our theology, and Bible translations.

Manuscripts, however, did not change everything in the conduit of oral culture, nor did it for Augustine,[56] Luther,[57] or the Ifugao.[58] Oral communication tended to carry the day even in the midst of growing literacy, literature, and reliable scribal transmissions. "Textuality was a tool of orality."[59]

While those who assess the changes made by scribes while copying texts from today's text-based background may find some discomfort or even outright disagreement,[60] this would *not* have been the case for first-century oral societies. As Wheaton professors Walton and Sandy sagely state:

> Written texts were shaped by their oral origins. They began as oral texts and were derived from oral texts. Scribes preserved the marks of orality in inscribed forms, which meant the differences between the two were almost negligible . . . slight differences in details were not considered errors within the oral culture of the Bible. They were simply discontinuities resulting from the transmission of oral texts, or from the freedom of authors in choosing what or how to write about certain events, or from scribes' alterations as they copied texts.[61]

---

56. Winger, "Spoken Word," 134–35.

57. Luther considered the oral superior to the written: "The gospel should not really be something written, but a spoken word, which brought forth the Scriptures, as Christ and the apostles have done. This is why Christ himself did not write anything but only spoke. He called his teaching not Scripture but gospel, meaning good news or a proclamation that is spread not by pen, but by word of mouth . . . . So it is not at all in keeping with the New Testament to write books on Christian doctrine. Rather in all places there should be fine, goodly, learned, spiritual, diligent preachers without books, who extract the living word from the old Scripture and unceasingly inculcate it in the people, just as the apostles did" (Luther, quoted in Lotz, "Proclamation of the word," 346–47).

58. Ong called this "oral residue," which he defined as "habits of thought and expression tracing back to preliterate situations or practice, or deriving from the dominance of the oral as a medium in a given culture or indicating a reluctance or inability to dissociate the written medium from the spoken" (Ong, *Rhetoric, Romance, and Technology*, 25).

59. Walton and Sandy, *Lost World of Scripture*, 85. Referencing the Gospels, Darrell Bock concludes in *Jesus According to Scripture* that differences do not evidence "contradiction and inauthenticity," rather they add depth to the account (Bock, 17–18).

60. Werner Kelber attempts to expose the strength of one's pedagogical socialization when he states, "One should not underrate the role of print and the seductive perfection of the printed page in making us believe that the perfectly constructed print format is the carrier of a perfectly unified content" (Kelber, "Oral-Scribal-Memorial Arts of Communication," 249).

61. Walton and Sandy, *Lost World of Scripture*, 176–77, 307.

> **Media Changes Change Hermeneutics**
> "The Bible in Oral Culture"
> "Manuscript Culture"
> "Culture of Silent Print/Documents"
> "Bible in Electronic Media"[62]

For example, in relation to what to include in the Gospels, *was it an error that Mark and John, unlike Matthew and Luke, focused on Jesus' adulthood rather than his childhood, as did the latter? Why did Matthew and Luke include extensive, albeit different genealogies (one starts with Adam while the other with Abraham)? Did someone forget the contributions of eyewitnesses in their research?* Orality influenced the written text.

Rather than resort to convoluted scientific logic to justify variances (e.g., the Synoptic problem), the answer may simply be found in how orality influenced text development. Walton and Sandy go on to say, "Our thesis is that we will not interpret the New Testament correctly if we fail to grasp the oral dimensions involved in its creation and transmission."[63] *What insights can the foundational role of orality in manuscript making, interpretation, and communication provide?*

> "For those who love God, several other people have already written accounts of what God has been bringing to completion among us, using the reports of the original eyewitnesses, those who were there from the start to witness the fulfillment of prophecy like those other servants who have recorded the messages, I present to you my carefully researched orderly account of these new teachings. I want you to know that you can fully rely on the things you have been taught about Jesus, God's Anointed One."
>
> (Luke 1:1–5 VOICE)

It could be added, if one assesses the change from orality to text as an evolutionary advancement, and thereby jettisons orality, s/he will miss much that can be learned about discerning meaning.[64] "Have you heard?" and

---

62. Boomershine, "Biblical Megatrends," 145–47.
63. Walton and Sandy, *Lost World of Scripture*, 86.
64. Long ago, Milman Parry (1902–1935) perceptively challenged the ethnocentric

"Have you not read?" interfaced during first-century Christianity. Just as the oral, literacy, and digital worlds interface today (see appendix A), so oral and literacy interfaced in antiquity. God-inspired voice (Deut 18:18–20; 1 Kgs 17:24; 2 Sam 32:2; Ezek 3:27; Acts 28:25; 1 Thess 2:13; 2 Pet 1:20–21) and God-inspired script (2 Tim 3:16–17) co-existed. No "Great Divide"[65] then, nor should there be today. *The written text speaks because it is spoken text!*

As Wheaton's Leland Ryken and Westmont's Tremper Longman conclude, "To read the Bible is to become an implied listener of the spoken voice."[66] Holly Hearon, Professor of New Testament, adds, "Reading is not a silent activity, but a reoralization of written words . . . The written word is perceived as having voice, a voice that is vocalized in the act of reading."[67] Both voice and text encourage dialogue because each was formed through dialogue.[68]

What percentage of literacy features are possible without some orality base? Probably none. Literacy is built on and champions an oral foundation. Interestingly, the Ifugao maintained a healthy respect for both.[69] They

---

evolutionary view that the literary surpassed orality. Parry highlighted the brilliance of Homer's works oralized (orality as their original medium). For a collection of Parry's essays, see Kirk, *Songs of Homer*, and Lord, *Singer of Tails*. Both Lord and Kirk continued Parry's work after his early death. Sam Chan adds, "To insist that we must privilege one form of communication over another is to confuse orthopraxy with orthodoxy, form with content, method with message, and pedagogy with theology. It is also a failure to recognize that we are all influenced by our culture. The traditional expository Bible talk is a product of Western, logical, linear, Enlightenment, and inductive communication methods. So, when we accuse anyone else of 'selling out' to culture and 'trying to make the Bible relevant,' we must also be attuned to our own failure to see that we might be doing the same thing. Are we like the American who cannot hear his own accent, who laughs at the funny way everyone else speaks English" (Chan, *Evangelism in a Skeptical World*, 194)?

65. Ruth Finnegan, emeritus professor at Open University, critiqued the distinction made by some between the "superior" written and the "inferior" spoken, literate societies and oral societies, identifying it as the "great divide." She believed they interfaced on a continuum, constantly crisscrossing and cross-fertilizing each other, not unlike the spoken and written word of God (Finnegan, *Literacy and Orality*, 39–105).

66. Ryken and Longman III, *Complete Literary Guide to the Bible*, 32.

67. Hearon, "Interplay between Written and Spoken Word," 58.

68. While referencing late Medieval times, the implications would be similar to first-century Christians: The written text "was essentially a transcription which, like modern musical notation became an intelligible message only when it was performed orally to others and to oneself" (Saenger, "Silent Reading," 371).

69. Rosalind Thomas provides this noteworthy backdrop of the interface of orality and literacy in ancient Greece, "Yet most Greek literature was meant to be heard or even sung—thus transmitted orally—and there was a strong current of distaste for the written word even among the highly literate: written documents were not considered adequate proof by themselves in legal contexts till the second half of the fourth century

highly welcomed the text and sang its praises but continued the familiar oral. *Is there anything here the Ifugao can teach us?*

> "We think of the Bible as a book, neatly bound, printed, read silently or quoted or studied, a set text... Turning our ancestors into ourselves, we call the Israelites 'people of the book' and reinforce this proverbial image of a community well versed in *the skills of literacy.*"[70]

Just as there were creative variations (flexibility) within parameters (fixed) with the spoken-written Scriptures, so it was in the scribal world; whether accounts were retold or documents transcribed, variations occurred. This was inevitable in the multiple transcriptions and translations that included both the spoken[71] and eventually the written.[72] Nevertheless, the manuscripts remained trustworthy and authoritative, thereby providing a foundation and a tether or touchstone, a helpful corrective to expansive orality.

Manuscripts preserved the spoken word. The spoken word made manuscripts relevant to oral recipients. Each benefited from and required

---

BC. Politics was conducted orally . . . the art of speaking was a major part of Greek education . . . Socrates pursued his philosophical enquires in conversation and debate and wrote nothing down. His pupil Plato attacked the written word as an inadequate means of true education and philosophy . . . The written word was more often used in service of the spoken" (Thomas, *Literacy and Orality in Ancient Greece*, 3, 4).

70. Niditch, *Oral World and Written Word*, 1 (emphasis original).

71. Walton and Sandy conclude, "those of us under the influence of a text-dominant culture may be inclined to respond, 'But Paul did say God-breathed about the written text, and he didn't say that about the oral texts.' That logic fails, however, because the context does not suggest that Paul wanted Timothy to have greater confidence (or less confidence) in one over the other. Further, although only implied here, elsewhere Paul explicitly claimed divine source for his oral texts (e.g., 1 Cor 2:13)." They go on to say, "*It is safe to believe that Scripture is verbally inspired*" (Walton and Sandy, *Lost World of Scripture*, 272, 293; emphasis original).

72. The "books" which resulted in small libraries were first compiled into the "book" one could hold in one hand (mostly by seminary students and Bible teachers) in the thirteenth century when scribes standardized the handwritten Latin Bible. Renaissance scholars, now with printers, made the King James Version (with page numbers, verses, and tables of contents), affordable to many. See Boynton and Reilly, *Practice of the Bible*.

We appreciate David Dockery's summary of inspiration that values the human-divine connection that results in the trustworthy word of God: "The superintending influence the Holy Spirit exerted on the biblical writers, so that the accent and interpretation of God's revelation have been recorded as God intended so that the Bible is actually the word of God" (Dockery, *Christian Scripture*, 240).

the other. One made the other trustworthy while the other made one truthful.

Memory

How does an oral society preserve meaning over generations? How do they store stories when few can read or have access to books or libraries? How did Jesus' followers preserve oral tradition for decades before Mark was written? What and who governed oral speech? Part of what lies behind these questions is memory. "Memory organizes the past in meaningful narrative patterns; it 'acts to organize what might otherwise be a mere assemblage of contingently connected events.'"[73]

The Communal Role

Dunn rightly recognizes that "oral tradition—is *communal memory.*"[74] James Fentress and Chris Wickham remind us of the scope of social memory, "Social memory is not stable as information; it is stable, rather at the level of shared meanings and remembered images."[75] In relation to Scripture, William Graham adds, "a shared text—one that can be chanted in unison and constantly referred to as a proof text common to an entire community—is a powerful binding factor in any group."[76]

> "Then the Lord said to Moses, 'Write this in a book as a memorial and recite it to Joshua.'"
>
> (Exod 17:14 NASB)

Communal songs, chants, readings, symbols, rituals, among others, rehearsed publicly helped preserve communal memory over time. Such activities included the oral attributes of relationships, participation, imagination and emotions, repetition, metaphor, and memory that reflected the social setting.[77]

73. Kirk, *Memory and the Jesus Tradition*, 7.
74. Dunn, *Oral Gospel Tradition*, 75 (emphasis original).
75. Fentress and Wickham, *Social Memory*, 59.
76. Graham, *Beyond the written word*, 160.
77. Holly Hearon accurately reminds us the Mediterranean world was not monolithic when it comes to stories, "The ubiquity of storytelling in the ancient

In relation to Scripture and the community of faith, the Holy Spirit must be included. "The Christian community provides the dynamic context in which the Spirit is actively invited to participate because without the Holy Spirit's participation there is no authentic Christian community."[78] The community of faith's memory, driven by Bailey's *informal control*, becomes the repository of the meaning of the message, safeguarded by the Holy Spirit.

This does not mean reliance on the Holy Spirit guarantees infallible interpretation for anyone, including "Bible scholars."[79] Even so, the supernatural spoken-written word demands supernatural assistance—the Holy Spirit who guards, guides, and gladdens. Such assistance is not only for the giving of the word (from oral to written), but also for discovering its meaning, and for deepening our relationship with others and the Father.

Ensuring generational integrity in some societies goes beyond the living to include the ancestors. For the Israelites, that included the likes of Abraham, Moses, David, and Isaiah, among others. The spoken-written word of the living-dead served as checks and balances for the living to help assure long-term memory purity. Such interaction helped bury meaning deep in the recesses of the communal mind-soul and remain there, thereby ensuring generational integrity.

Actions, dialogue, stories, and listening also perpetuate long-term memory. Osborne astutely observes, "Narrative does not merely inform; it acts."[80] Dialogue is an event because it is more than spoken words. As "speech act" theory[81] has shown, three facets are involved in spoken language: (1) the explicit words spoken (locution), (2) what the speaker meant by those words (illocution), and (3) the acts that result from the words (perlocution). The community monitors more than words spoken, it also monitors the meaning of those words and their resulting actions. Stories make the voices and actions of characters sticky.

As oralized stories become speech-acts, narratives sometimes tangled threads surrounding the strengths and struggles of characters weave themselves from episode to episode within events centered in place(s) and

---

Mediterranean world is signaled by the many kinds of stories that have been preserved in written sources . . . The wide range of stories encompassed in this list points to the difficulty of assigning to 'story' and 'storytelling' a single form, content, context, or purpose" (Hearon, "Storytelling in Oral and Written Media Contexts," 94).

78. Archer, *Pentecostal Hermeneutic for the Twenty-first Century*, 183.

79. Zuck, "Role of the Spirit in Hermeneutics," 125. This is one of fourteen propositions from Zuck.

80. Osborne, "Historical Narrative and Truth in the Bible," 684.

81. See Searle, "Austin on Locutionary and Illocutionary Acts."

time(s).[82] These events eventually cultivate identifiable themes[83] (macro and micro, unifying and opposing[84]). Think Saul and David. For Saul, one theme could be that jealousy has consequences. And the very telling of the events becomes an event in and of itself, aiding long-term community memory.[85] Oralized stories help the community (who is prone to forget)[86] preserve tradition across generations, genders, and geography.

The antidote to communal forgetfulness is acting, repeating, representing, and remembering in multiple ways. But before a community can do such, its citizens must first be able to listen—to themselves, others, and especially their Creator. Whether a whisper, a cry, or a loud voice, the collective ear must be listening.[87] The model for such sequence (and resulting benefits) is demonstrated early in Genesis—when the cosmos listened to the Voice, order replaced chaos. The same holds true for a listening community long term.

The Role of Eyewitnesses

In his challenging book *Jesus and the Eyewitnesses*, Richard Bauckham identifies the pertinent role of the many eyewitnesses to preserve Jesus' sayings: "These eyewitnesses did not merely set a process of oral transmission that soon went its own way without reference to them. They remained throughout their lifetimes the sources and . . . the authoritative guarantors of the stories they continued to tell."[88] The memory of the eyewitnesses was paramount in maintaining the integrity of Jesus' verbal teachings, all made possible by a culture that daily socialized minds for long-term memory.

---

82. Referencing cities or similar human settlements, Orum and Chen say this about our strong connectedness to "*places—that is, specific locations in space that provide an anchor and a meaning to who we are*" (Orum and Chen, *World of Cities*, 1; emphasis original). Place provides individual and communal identity, all tied to history.

83. In the 1960 publication, Albert Lord defines a theme as "groups of ideas regularly used in telling a tale" (Lord, *Singer of Tales*, 68).

84. See Opler, "Themes as Dynamic Forces in Culture," 198–206.

85. Imaged stories are stored in the same part of the brain as lived experience (Caine and Caine, *Making Connections*).

86. In relation to God's community, "remember" is used some 130 times in the Old Testament and thirty-six times in the New Testament in the NIV translation.

87. For an instructive book on a seldom-discussed topic, see McHugh, *Listening Life*.

88. Bauckham, *Jesus and the Eyewitnesses*, 93. See 297–98 for a list of the eyewitnesses.

> "Bind cords around your fingers to remind you of them; meditate on them, and you'll engrave them upon your heart."
>
> (Prov 7:3 VOICE)

That does not necessarily mean word-for-word memorization of all of Jesus' sayings. Rather, it was often an expression of the internalization of the meaning of the message, symbols, and rituals.[89] As Jesus' teachings were retold through creative performances in diverse social settings through different languages, variances naturally occurred, just as evidenced in the Synoptic Gospels (note the differences, similarities, inclusions, absences, and rearrangement of sequences). Nor must we overlook John's claim that much was excluded. In fact, "if these accounts were also written down, the books could not be contained in the entire cosmos" (John 21:25 VOICE). Memory recall is not necessarily static retrieval.

Rather than viewing this as a Synoptic problem that calls for forced harmony, we view it as the authors' expression to communicate to specific, strongly oral audiences through narrative features. Even so, the community knew it was ultimately responsible for meaning integrity, both verbal and textual. Every rehearsal was subject to collective correction in a public gathering. That is because the community's collective honor and face[90] in the villages and cities were at stake.[91]

The Storyteller's-Performer's Role

Just as the community had responsibility for meaning's integrity, so did the individual storytellers-performers. To help accomplish this they telegraphed meaning through "alliteration, appositional equivalence, proverbial and aphoristic diction, contrasts and antitheses; as well as synonymous, antithetical, and tautological parallelism, rhythmic structures, and so forth."[92] All of these oral discourse features,[93] not to mention symbols, stories, and

---

89. See Ong, *Orality and Literacy*, 62–68.

90. Those socialized strongly into the individualist innocence-guilt, value-moral system may have a difficult time appreciating the strength and effectiveness of communal honor and shame.

91. "One is more likely to get the truth straight right in community, for here are present other Christians illuminated by the same Word and Spirit" (Johnston, "Orthodoxy and Heresy," 29).

92. Kelber, "Works of Memory," 233.

93. Following Douglas Campbell and others, Lucy Peppiatt, in *Women and Worship*

rituals,[94] were designed to spotlight truths rehearsed so that they can stick in communal memory.

As with the community, the storyteller's individual honor and face were at stake. Tellings that veered too far from circulating oral tradition resulted in the storyteller being publicly shamed. Communally transmitted oral tradition was the communal cultural treasury. It must therefore be safely secured, and the storytelling tradition-bearer was responsible to make sure oral tradition remained. Individual creativity[95] must always submit to tradition or face feared shameful consequences, namely, social separation.

The Scribal Role

Scribes also participated in aiding memory in ways those of us coming from a literacy-based hermeneutic often fail to recognize. This has to do with how the texts were constructed. Distinguished Professor of Liberal Arts and the Study of Religion Richard Horsley provides a clue when he calls them "oral-derived texts" that "functioned in communal contexts."[96]

Professor of New Testament David Watson becomes more specific: "these written texts are structured as if they were composed to be spoken aloud and heard, rather than read silently."[97] Ryken adds, "To read the New Testament is to become a listener of the spoken word."[98] Concordia Lu-

---

at Corinth, provides a powerful argument for Paul's use of rhetoric to show "a more excellent way"—unity must prevail over schisms. Jews and gentiles, slaves and free, men and women are equal under the new covenant. Her conclusions show Paul not as a theologian continually contradicting himself, or a misogynist, but rather one who uses "diatribal discussion" (83) or "speech-in-character" (72) (Campbell's term) to make his case (Peppiatt, *Women and Worship at Corinth*, 83, 72.). Paul either quoted or summarized the Corinthians' argument from their letter to him *before destroying it:* 1 Cor 11:2–16 (head coverings); 14:20–25 (tongues); 14:33b–36 (speakers). This is difficult to pick up strictly from reading the text; it would not have been for those, however, hearing the text read by the reader-performer delivering Paul's letter because of verbal and nonverbal clues he would give the audience. This rhetorical technique was not uncommon inside or outside Paul's letter.

94. For a chapter on each—symbol, story, and ritual—see Steffen, *Worldview-based Storying*, 116–36, 137–60, 162–81.

95. "Creativity in oral cultures is strongly interactive and performative (Goody, 1977), governed not so much by the question 'what can I do that is totally new?' but 'how can I truly engage my audience in a memorable way' (Watson, "Interpreting across the Abyss," 164)?

96. Horsley, *Whoever Hears You Hears Me*, 60.

97. Watson, *Honor among Christians*, 116.

98. Ryken, *Words of Delight*, 459.

theran Theological Seminary professor Thomas Winger narrows the focus to the Epistles:

> The epistolary authors use language which suggests a conversation is going on between them and the receivers of the letter. Rather than a prosaic, philosophical 'What shall we think/reason/suggest/propose about this? Paul poses the dialectical question: 'What then shall we say?' Such oral engagement continues as the 'writers' use verbs of speaking rather than verbs of writing.[99]

Swedish biblical scholar Birger Gerhardsson provides some historical background: "In antiquity, words were written down in order to be read out loud. Even the written word was formulated for the ear."[100] Loubser goes so far as to call Paul an "oral theologian"[101] because he generously mixed the oral within his written letters. The psalmist provides another example of how, like written text, creation speaks, "Day after day they pour forth speech . . . from here to the ends of the earth, their voices have gone out; the whole world can hear what they say" (Ps 19:2 NIV; Ps 19:4 VOICE). Written words, like creation, pour forth oral speech.

Not only did voice precede text, it also followed text. For centuries after the written text, voice still played a major role in interpretation and communication. Hearon expands:

> Alongside this perception of the text as 'written,' however, is the experience of the written text as, principally, a spoken word that is read aloud, heard, and remembered. This is also how the text is most often employed: it is quoted in discourse and appealed to in debate. Equally strong is both the perception and encounter of the text as a living voice that continues to speak to the present . . . The Hebrew Scriptures, therefore, are representative of the complex relationship between written and spoken word. They are perceived of as both written word and spoken word (as having 'voice'), yet they are most often encountered and employed as spoken word.[102]

The spoken Voice is never detached or distanced from the written Voice.

As an Asian recently told me (Tom), the worst sin she ever committed was making patron Jesus wait outside as he persistently knocked at her heart's door, calling out to her by name. Because the Bible came to us

---

99. Winger, "Orality as the Key," 226.
100. Gerhardsson, "Gospel Tradition," 519.
101. Loubser, "Orality and Literacy in the Pauline Epistles," 67.
102. Hearon, "Interplay between Written and Spoken Word," 65.

formidably through oral means, the text continues to speak forth through print used by the Holy Spirit. *Do you hear someone calling and knocking at your door?* Oral-dominated audiences do not find such things strange.

The Role of Symbolic Images

John's Revelation[103] includes a feast of symbolic images (e.g., numbers, colors, armies, thrones, animals, horns, heads) communicated through a narrative (dream) framework. Many from the West, if given the chance to intervene in canon inclusions, may have encouraged the apostle John to tone it down a little. Too mysterious. Too ambiguous. Too circular. Too uncomfortable.

> "If we want to understand the Bible, we have to consider what its symbols stand for, what story they're telling, and how they're interpreting and summarizing what has gone before as they point to what is and will be."[104]

Luther and Zwingli would have been among that group, preferring the book of Revelation *not* become part of the New Testament. Even the prolific commentary writer John Calvin (living in the first rushes of the Gutenberg Galaxy) passed on Revelation, confessing "I can't make heads or tails out of what most of it means."[105]

The oralist ancients took a very different perspective in that these narrative-based images (symbols)—recall John's preference for visual orality—would not have seemed so foreign as they did to sixteenth-century theologians, or to many today. Symbols made the experiential normal, inviting, comprehensible, and memorable.

Symbolic images[106] communicate and aid individual and communal memory. Kelber captures this concept when he concludes, "This interior visualization, the forming of images from what is heard, is deeply rooted in

---

103. "When John sees a vision, he sees it in terms of scenes and pictures from the Old Testament places and occasions when God had already revealed Himself and His truth to His people" (Barclay, *Revelation of John*, 1:56).

104. Hamilton, *What is Biblical Theology?*, 65.

105. Third Millennium Ministries, *Book of Revelation*, 22.

106. Clifford Geertz defines symbol as "vehicles for a conception . . . abstractions from experience fixed in perceptible forms, concrete embodiments of ideas, attitudes, judgments, longings, or beliefs" (Geertz, *Interpretations of Cultures*, 91).

orality and conceptualized by rhetoric . . . memory is the treasurehouse of rhetoric, which is filled with the furniture of *imagines* and *loci*."[107] Revelation speaks forthrightly to John's oral audience, and is mightily memorable, primarily because of its symbolic visual imagery.

From Mouth to Ear/Eye

Scripture was written strongly for the ear/eye. Collective cultural memory relied on the meaning of oral clues, symbols, stories, and rituals to preserve not only the past, but also the community's present identity.[108] Manuscripts were scripted to be read out loud and discussed communally. All this relied heavily on the relational social values-morals of honor and shame to maintain integrity. In antiquity and centuries beyond, validity rested primarily in what one heard and saw in the mind's eye, *not* in printed texts.

Christianity began mouth to ear/eye; it relied heavily on eyewitness accounts of what Jesus declared and did. The early Jesus-followers found revelation and spiritual meaning foremost in a Person, not just the written text. The human side of Jesus, the incarnation, overwhelmed the meticulously handwritten scribal manuscripts. Orality reigned.

> "At its core, commemoration is a hermeneutical activity . . . it is the 'effort to fix the meaning and purpose' of the past . . . . 'Memory flowed [in Jerusalem] . . . through two channels: ritual and recital.' Both along with and independent of rituals and material artefacts groups make use of the verbal arts, oral or written, for commemorative ends. Commemorative ritual draws the community together on a regular basis which in turn supplies the context for utterance of group memory."[109]

Many of these oralists therefore tended to envision the text from a liturgical perspective. When they heard Scripture read, they envisioned a parade of events and sacred images calling for community participation. They saw memorable word pictures in the mind's eye that unwittingly pulled

---

107. Kelber, "Modalities of Communication," 204–5 (emphasis original).

108. What is true for the Western working class is also true of first-century Christianity, another minority group, "Perhaps the most powerful element we have met is the memory of the community in opposition to the outside world, for this is one of the most effective recourses any social group has to reinforce its own social identity in opposition to that of others, and it is a memory everyone can participate in, through personal memories and family traditions" (Fentress and Wickham, *Social Memory*, 114).

109. Kirk, *Memory and the Jesus Tradition*, 19, 21.

them into the event. What they heard, they visualized; what they visualized, they acted upon, thereby glorifying the Most Majestic One.[110]

What was true in antiquity remains true for many oralists today. A Thai missionary married to an American made this challenging confession, surprising many, when they returned to the United States and began attending an Eastern Orthodox parish:

> I was born and raised in Thailand. When I became a Christian in many ways I felt that I had to give up being Thai. But now worshiping God in a liturgical way, for the first time in my life, I feel that I am fully Christian and fully Thai. When I worship God in the liturgy, my body understands what I am doing. It is not like I am getting confused and think I am worshiping Buddha or some idol, I know I am worshiping the true God, it is just that *as a Thai person I understand the language of liturgy, this is my language, and I am finally able to speak it in worship.*[111]

Most Westerners have a difficult time appreciating the muscle of memory of those coming from strongly oral-based societies compared to those of text-based societies. I (Tom) have observed bus conductors in the Philippines watch people board from multiple stops for hours, and when approaching the final destination, go through the bus charging riders according to when they boarded. The oralists' ability to remember things short- and long-term is sharpened daily, making recollection as normal to them as locating a verse on BibleGateway.com is to us.

For oralists, the preservation of memory is based on multiple entities. These include the roles of community, eyewitnesses, storytellers, scribes, symbols, and rituals, all of which are protected by individual and communal honor and humiliation.

Volume of Oral Literature in Scripture

A significant component of orality is narrative or story. This begs the following questions: *What percentage of Scripture is written in story? How significant is the narrative text compared to the other genres the Holy Spirit chose to include?*

---

110. See Okholm, *Learning Theology through the Church's Worship.*
111. Wu, "Desiring the Kingdom in Missions," 26 (emphasis added).

Trying to discern what percentage of the Bible is narrative or story is a difficult task. Definitions differ.[112] Genres interface,[113] e.g., poetry and narrative in Psalms,[114] as well as Isaiah and other prophetic books. Laws are embedded in narratives in the Pentateuch. Songs tell stories, e.g., the Song of Moses (Exod 15:1–21; Deut 31:19). Even some sections of the Epistles focus on characters that require background narrative (Rom 4; 9–11; 1 Cor 5; Phlm) and everyday conversations (1 Cor 7:1; Col 1:4). Revelation is a dream (which we count as story[115]). Distinguished Professor of Theology at Western Seminary Millard Erickson concludes:

> Indeed if one does a comparative analysis of the content of the Bible, the New Testament books that seem to deal most explicitly with narrative constitute only 56 to 62 percent of the content, depending upon whether one treats Revelation as narrative. In the Old Testament, the narrative books (Genesis–Job) constitute 57 percent of the material. It can, of course, be argued that the prophetic books contain considerable narrative, which they surely do, or even that they represent interpretation of the narrative and that the narrative is an interpreted narrative.[116]

---

112. "Narrative is present in myth, legend, fable, tale, novella, epic, history, tragedy, drama, comedy, mime, painting . . ., stained glass windows, cinema, comics, news item, conversation. Moreover, under this almost infinite diversity of forms, narrative is present in every age, in every place, in every society; it begins with the very history of mankind and there nowhere is nor has been a people without narrative . . . it is simply there, like life itself" (Sontag, *Barthes Reader*, 251–52).

113. "The casting of speeches into poetic form is a general feature of Hebrew narration, even in the historical books which are usually described as being written entirely in prose" (Anderson, *Job*, 45).

114. "The 'narrative' mode is evident throughout the Psalter, especially in a number of psalms in which Israel's praise takes the form of recounting Yahweh's 'deeds of salvation') e.g., Ps. 66:5–7; 71:15–16; 75:1; 77:11–15; 98:1–3; 107:31–32; 145:4–6) . . . . One gets the impression from reading and contemplating these psalms that they have a strong didactic interest: history is recounted in order to teach people the meaning of their history" (Anderson, *Out of the Depths*, 53–54).

115. In regard to eyewitness testimony before text, Brian Stock points out that "historical and epic narrative was not sharply drawn; and, within histories, personal accounts, dreams, visions, prophecies, and poetic insights were all taken to be reliable witness to events" (Stock, *Implications of Literacy*, 74). The apostle John makes this claim: "This testimony is true. In fact, it is an eyewitness account; and he has reported what he saw so that you also may believe" (John 19:35 VOICE). Peter adds, "we were relying on what our eyes had seen of His glorious majesty, not on cleverly told fables" (2 Pet 1:16 VOICE).

116. Erickson, *Evangelical Left*, 58. McGrath writes, "Narrative is the main literary type found in Scripture" (McGrath, "Biography of God," 23).

While the percentages are certainly guesses, they can, however, be informed guesses.

Presently, I (Tom) put the percentages as follows: story: 55 to 65 percent; poetry: 25 to 35 percent; and propositions: 10 percent.[117] See Figure 3.2. Scholar, author, and poet Eugene Peterson persuasively posits, "The Holy Spirit's literary genre of choice is story."[118] *How should such percentages influence our choice of hermeneutic?*

Another significant component of orality is poetry,[119] which would include the wisdom literature, such as the Psalms, Proverbs, Ecclesiastes, and poetry interspersed throughout Scripture from Genesis to Revelation. Often, in both the Jewish and the Christian traditions, the Psalms were sung; sometimes, like Proverbs (dehydrated wisdom stories), they were told. If story and poetry were combined, possibly around 65 to 75 percent of Scripture could be classified under orality.

Delivery and Dialogue

From Old to New Testament the faithful gathered publicly to hear God's word read and explained.[120] Veritas College Malawi director Davidson Chifungo concludes, "We need congregations as spaces and locations where wise readings of Scripture are exemplified in faithful and wise actions and practices. Congregations are distinct communities of interpretation . . . the Bible is the Church's book."[121]

---

117. Steffen, "Pedagogical Conversions," 150. While there are multiple genres in Scripture, I reduced them to three for convenience.

118. Peterson, *Leap Over a Wall*, 3.

119. "Poetry makes up about one-third of the whole Bible and would alone constitute a book the size of the whole New Testament" (Longman III, "Literary Approaches to Biblical Interpretation," 168).

120. See Deut 31:11–13; Josh 8:34–35; 1 Sam 31:11–13; Neh 8:7–9; 1 Kgs 22:11; 2 Kgs 5:5–7; Neh 8:8–9; 2 Cor 1:13; Col 4:16; 1 Thess 5:27; 2 Thess 2:15; Acts 8:30; Rom 10:17; 1 Tim 4:13; 2 Tim 2:2; 1 John 1:1, 3; Rev 1:3; 2:7.

121. Chifungo, "Oral Hermeneutics," 153, 157.

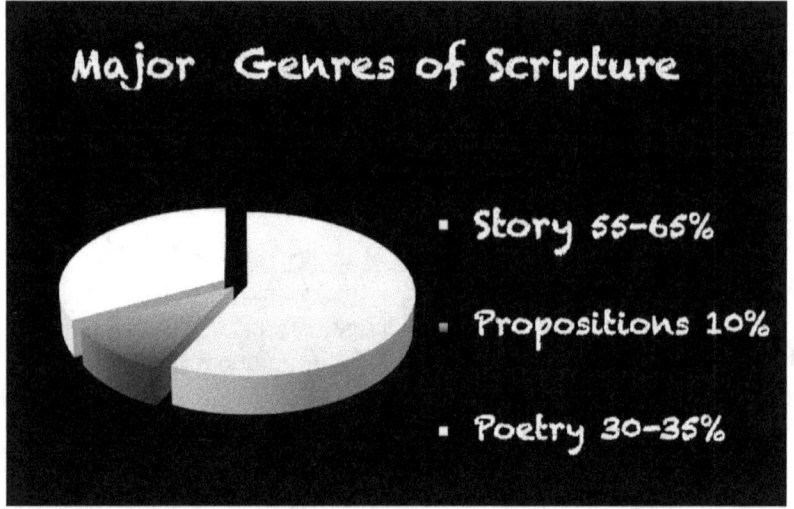

Figure 3.2. Dominant Genres of Scripture Percentages

A community document requires readers and interpreters. Nehemiah notes Ezra read out loud from the "Book of the Law of God" and the Levites "clearly explained the meaning" (Neh 8:8 NLT). We do well to recall Jesus' conversation with the scribes of his day: "You search the Scriptures because you think that in them you have eternal life; and it is they that bear witness about me, yet you refuse to come to me that you may have life" (John 5:39 ESV). The purpose of the writings was to facilitate communal encounters, relationships, and memory. As someone once quipped, "The purpose of the book of the Lord is to know the Lord of the book."

The concept "You sit still while I instill" would have been foreign to most in the early church. Group participation was expected, thereby demonstrating the need of individual input for the benefit of the faith community as a whole. Not to participate—whether through silence or failure to attend—would indicate disapproval in these strongly shame-based societies.

Coming from a literate background, we may conclude that once a manuscript existed, audiences were immediately fixated on it. The written sacred text, however, even with its strong oral bent, did *not* immediately replace voice, whether the Gospels or Paul's letters.[122] That would take

---

122. "*Jesus' oral texts became the oral texts of the eyewitnesses, and those oral texts became the basis of the written Gospels, yet the written texts did not replace the oral texts*" (Walton and Sandy, *Lost World of Scripture*, 139; emphasis original). Theylater add, "While written texts of Paul's gospel began to be circulated, they did not take the place of, or supersede, his oral texts. Luke preserves records of Paul's ongoing preaching even though he had already written letters to churches (e.g., Acts 18–23)" (162).

centuries. *Why?* Besides being the custom of the day, there is something unique about hearing the sound of a human voice. Voice often carries an intuitive invitation to join in, harmonize, reciprocate, debate, and challenge, including with those who comprise the spirit world. Audible words heard are *experienced* because they *vocalize* events. In relation to first-century written texts, they were mainly "conceived as realizable only in the vocal act of reading aloud."[123]

The written word was most often conceived as the spoken word, even after it was handwritten. Voicing, hearing, and responding to the oralized-written-word continuum completes its intended purpose. Because the ancients assumed sound to be superior to script, they therefore believed reading should not be conducted silently or in solitude. Reading required voice; reading required the script be read out loud in community.

There is also something unique about public gatherings, particularly among oralists. When combined with voiced script, an intrinsically memorable, social moment occurs. Comparative oral tradition scholar and founder of the *Oral Tradition* journal John Miles Foley adds definition:

> When you voice a text, wherever and whenever you do, you cause it to live and to mean by being present; when you perform within a community, you bind the community together in a shared experience that far supersedes the authority of any artifact. That is the inimitable power of voice—to give presence, literally to 'em-body.'[124]

Walton and Sandy go so far as to say Paul's letters "were surrogates for oral communication."[125] Note Romans 6:1, where Paul asks an oral-based group question, "What shall we say then?" Notice the apostle did not ask an individual-oriented, propositional question like "What do you think?" "There was a prevailing preference for the 'living voice.'"[126] Most considered voice superior to script, including the sacred script.

---

123. Graham, *Beyond the written word*, 32.

124. Foley, "Riddle of Q," 139.

125. Walton and Sandy, *Lost World of Scripture*, 163. John Harvey captures it this way, "Orality continues its influence long after the introduction of the alphabet and writing" (Harvey, "Orality and its Implications," 101).

126. Botha, *Orality and Literacy in Early Christianity*, xii. William Graham concludes, "Silent, private reading appears to have become dominant only with the advent of widespread literacy in much of Western Europe, which was largely a nineteenth-century phenomenon" (Graham, *Beyond the Written Word*, 41).

Delivery through an Authorized Spokesperson

The first-century practice was that a trusted spokesperson would be used to deliver and read written messages from apostles or important spiritual leaders. So when Paul instructed that his Epistles be read aloud, there would be a designated person of honor and integrity who would deliver and read the message, not just any old messenger. The trusted spokesperson ("emissary-performer"[127]) chosen to convey, read, and interpret[128] the text to a faith community would require a certain level of authenticity to be heard. This is because, "The authenticity of the oral text . . . was held to be guaranteed by the authenticity of the performer."[129] Interaction on the development of text with the author (who also required authenticity) of known status would provide the required authenticity for the spokesperson.

> "The 'voice of John' is the voice of the Christian prophet . . . the voice that is heard within the assembly room is not a text, but is at one and the same time the voice of the lector and the voice of John . . . his voice is also the voice of the Spirit that speaks in the charismatic worship of the Asian congregations, which is the voice of Jesus, which is the voice of God."[130]

Bauta Motty, lecturer at Jos ECWA Theological Seminary, Nigeria, posits, "for oral people the person who says something is often more important than what is said."[131] Winger writes, "The use of authorized messengers

---

127. Winger, "Orality as the Key," 303.

128. This seems to challenge many of the church planting movement's (CPMs) models and strategies today that give little emphasis to the role of outside teachers in ongoing discipleship. This, they believe, leads to outside control and less dependence on the Holy Spirit. See Smith and Kai, *T4T*, 77–78; Schattner, *Wheel Model*, 107–12. Valid warnings about outside control, but does that mean no Holy Spirit-gifted foreign teachers can teach a new group of local believers in their own language because of potential problems? David Sills provides some background: "The need for speed that drives many mission efforts today causes them to streamline the missionaries to something humanly manageable and something results in jettisoning the half of the Great Commission that would require missionaries to stay and pour their lives into the hearts of their people to teach them all Christ has commanded them" (Sills, "Competing and Conflict Mission," 43).

129. Draper, "Vice Catalogues as Oral-Mnemonic Cues," 113.

130. Boring, "Voice of Jesus," 350.

131. Motty, "Spreading the Word," 9. It is not uncommon in certain parts of Africa to have a speaker first present his/her testimony *before* teaching so the audience

was part of a system of keeping the word *alive*."[132] The *force* of a story is tied directly to the *source* who delivers the story.

Paul partially unfolds the oral-communal-liturgical process in 1 Timothy 4:13 VOICE: "Until I get there, make sure to devote yourself to the public reading of Scripture, to exhortation, and to teaching." Until Paul arrives, his trustworthy spokesperson "would either read the texts aloud or memorize and recite them. The delivery was oral and the reception aural."[133] This would be often followed by communion, tying them to the historical, global community of faith and its Head, concluding with prayer (Acts 2:42).

After the public reading of the delivered manuscript, listeners would have opportunity to dialogue with the spokesperson by asking questions, making comments to gain clarification, or offer a challenge, among other things.[134] See Appendix B for more details. Those who rejected the reading and explanation of the message (and consequently the messenger representing the author and the Divine Author) were to be shamed by isolating them from the group (2 Thess 3:14). Accepting the voice of the messenger was to accept the Voice. Conversely, rejecting the voice of the messenger was to reject the Voice.

The Teaching-Learning Process

First-century Christians experienced the teaching-learning process much differently than most from the West today. Here are a few pedagogical variations from first-century, oral-dominant Christ-followers that can prove instructive when interpreting Scripture today.

Dialogue Reigned

Identifying patterns superseded identifying isolated, fragmented content. Horsley correctly concludes, "Cultural memories do not consist of mere fragments, discrete dates, and names and proverbs, but rather of patterns

---

can discern the speaker's legitimacy. This corresponds well to the classical Aristotelian modes of persuasion in effective rhetoric: *logos* (the words, logic, reason), *pathos* (the emotion, passion, sympathy), and *ethos* (the character or reputation of the speaker; his/her credibility, authority, reliability). *Logos* and *pathos* without good *ethos* was much less persuasive or effective in moving people to action.

132. Winger, "Orality as the Key," 282 (emphasis original).

133. Winger, "Orality as the Key," 177.

134. Gerhardsson, "Gospel Tradition," 524. Mark writes, "Let the one who reads and hears understand" (13:14 VOICE).

that inform group identity."[135] Thatcher tells us why, "Oral words are tied to the concrete human situations from which they draw their shape, meaning, and energy and do not aspire to transcend those situations or point to abstract concepts."[136] This is because, "oral words are *events* that draw their meaning from human interactions, written words are *things* that exist independently of the people who use them."[137]

Concrete human situations such as those found in story, e.g., our featured story of "Elisha and the Widow's Oil" (2 Kgs 4:1–7), or expressed in poetry (Exod 15; Ps 59; Prov 31) or symbols (Mal 3:1–3; Rev), were the primary mode of comprehending meaning. Spoken words from conversation about people, symbols, or events carry power because they add color, depth, and character, and they can bless or curse, as Simon the sorcerer discovered (Acts 8:20, 24; Rev 11:12).

Critical Thinking or Character Thinking?

"Critical thinking" for oralists differs greatly from how most Westerners understand it.[138] In fact, it requires an entirely different term. Rational, objective analysis, evaluation, conceptualization, and synthesis are not the oralists' typical starting or end points. Rather, concrete social situations, case studies, events, or incidents driven by the voices and actions of characters requires a different form of thinking. The equivalent of critical thinking for oralists may be considered "character thinking."

Character thinking is driven by questions with a different focus from those of critical thinking. For example, the question is not, *what does it mean?* Rather, *what do the characters communicate through their words, choices, deeds? And what kind of character is this who is communicating?* Critical thinking tends to focus on reading ideas; character thinking focuses on reading characters. Oralists are more practiced in the use of the attunement level of the right brain (the cingulate cortex). This is where we read people, their nonverbal communication signals, and where we

---

135. Horsley, "Oral Performance and Mark," 59. Thomas Farrell would add, "Generally speaking, in live oral communication the hearer will not need many 'logical' connections, again because the concrete situation supplies a full context that makes articulating, and thus abstraction, at many points superfluous" (Farrell, quoted in Ong, "Literacy and Orality in Our Times," 131.

136. Thatcher, "Beyond Texts and Traditions," 7.

137. Thatcher, "Beyond Texts and Traditions," 7 (emphasis original).

138. In *Preface to Plato*, Eric Havelock argues Greek alphabetic literacy was influential in the development of critical thinking (Havelock, *Preface to Plato*).

synchronize our emotions with another (see chapter 2 on the four levels of right brain function).

The first focuses on abstract ideas, while the latter concentrates on concrete actions and the discernment of their personal significance. Both require intelligence but have a different subject of focus. Interestingly, oralists tend to do character thinking intuitively while many educated Westerners are so practiced in left-brain skills that they need to train their attunement skills for character thinking.

As for listening audiences (in contrast to reading audiences), Kelber claims "knowledge is gathered and multiplied more than critically developed."[139] What is learned from one story heard is added to what is learned from another story heard. The repetition of words, phrases, themes, the actions and deeds of people, communal events, and like features of storytelling, aid in the concrete, aggregative[140] way of gaining knowledge we call character thinking.

Delivery and dialogue of the text required respected personnel who used oral-based teaching methodologies. Minimally, this included dialogue (questions and answers), repetition, and character thinking driven by narrative logic. Identifying first-century oral distinctives and their influence on text and teaching can provide Bible communicators helpful insights into how to interpret and communicate Scripture today to various audiences—oralists, post-Christian, and posttext, postfactual, late-modern people.

What Joanna Dewey determined about the Gospel of Mark could easily be said of the entire New Testament, at least until print media triumphed centuries later. She concluded that, "The gospel remains fundamentally on the oral side of the oral/written divide. It is best understood using oral hermeneutics."[141] Making the ancient narrative texts conform to present-day literary expectations is as mistaken as making orality conform to textuality. Both require the other because both influence each other. Both find themselves on a continuum. Yet there is a sequence. Just as orality

---

139. Kelber, *Oral and Written Gospel*, 80.

140. Joanna Dewey notes other oral features in written text that aid memory: "It [Mark] consists of short episodes connected paratactically [i.e., by no more or little more than 'and,' thus placing events side by side rather than subordinating one to another]. The narrative is additive and aggregative [short narratives accumulate rather than creating a climactic linear plot]. Teaching is not gathered into discourses according to topic but rather embedded in short narratives, which is the way oral cultures remember teaching. Indeed, I would suggest that it is the lack of a more literate chronological and topical order that Papias had in mind when he said Mark's story was 'not in order.' . . . It followed oral ordering procedures, not proper rhetorical form" (Dewey, "Survival of Mark's Gospel," 499).

141. Dewey, "Gospel of Mark as Oral Hermeneutic," 86.

influenced text and teaching in the past, so it should influence interpretation and communication of biblical truth in the present.

For first-century oralists, the incarnation of Jesus trumped (not denied) manuscripts that transcribed his life, authenticity trumped words, speech trumped writing, rhetoric[142] trumped reading, reverence trumped rules, memory trumped manuscripts, and meaning trumped words. This requires something beyond textual hermeneutics. *What then is needed to complement textual hermeneutics?* We believe the answer is oral hermeneutics.

---

142. "Rhetorical culture is basically oral culture shrouded in writing" (Ong, *Rhetoric, Romance, and Technology*, 261).

4

Oral Hermeneutics

"There's truths you have to grow into."

—H. G. WELLS

"We treat words primarily as records in need of interpretation, neglecting all too often a rather different hermeneutic, deeply rooted in biblical language that proclaims words as an act inviting participation. A sophisticated oral hermeneutic opens the way to deeper understanding not merely of orality but of texts themselves."

—WALTER ONG

A MILLENNIAL STUDENT RECENTLY told a group I (Tom) was with that in all but one of his Bible classes he was "taught *what* to believe, not *how* to believe." For whatever reason, right or wrong, he viewed most of his Bible classes as *indoctrination to conform* rather than *discovery to transform*. He felt he was offered tasty delicacies before feeling hunger. Clarity came before confusion; answers before questions; meaning before mystery.[1] If the stu-

---

1. If we approach the word of God as modern technicians who seemingly think they can exhaustively command and control these sacred texts via our exegetical tools, we are surely missing significant dimensions of God's revelation. Annie Dillard captures the magnitude of mystery when she concludes, "We wake, if ever we wake at all, to mystery" (Dillard, *Pilgrim at Tinker Creek,* 4). Shuan Gallagher adds, "A mystery is something that involves the person in such a way that the person cannot step outside of it in order to see it in an objective manner. She is caught within the situation with no possibility of escape, and no possibility of clear-cut solutions. Indeed, *ambiguity is the*

dent's perception was reality, how antithetical to the way the Bible presents itself, the way Jesus taught, and to life itself.

We *can* do better. We *must* do better for that audience, and other oral-preference audiences around the globe. If millennials, Gen Z, and others find themselves on the oral/digital[2] peripheries of oral/written/digital media, *could oral hermeneutics provide a more engaging, attractive onramp to the Bible?*

> "But it is not the 'facts' themselves that one tries to redeem through narrative tellings. Rather, it is an articulation of the significance and meaning of one's experiences. It is within the frame of a story that facts gain their importance."[3]

Those socialized in a "literary-molded mind-set,"[4] which includes most in the West, may be reluctant to return to an ambiguous, semispontaneous, multi-sensory, emotive oral media; too much of a "slippery slope" leading to subjectivism. Walton and Sandy perceive a different outcome: "We will not interpret the New Testament correctly." *Why?* Because we will "fail to grasp the oral dimensions involved in its creation and transmission."[5]

Dunn drills deeper: "We naturally, habitually, and instinctively work within a *literary paradigm*. We are, therefore, in no fit state to appreciate how a *non*literary culture, an *oral* culture, functions."[6] The contributions of first-century oral media, which has overlap for today's oralists, offers much to consider. If accurate interpretation of the meaning of the text is

---

rule within a mystery" (Gallagher, *Hermeneutics and Education*, 152; emphasis added).

2. Notice how relationships dominate in technology: "The biggest impact these technologies have had, and will have, is on relationships between people and between organizations. *The so-called 'information revolution' itself is actually and more accurately, a 'relationship revolution.'* Anyone trying to get a handle on the dazzling technologies of today and the impact they'll have tomorrow would be well advised to reorient their worldview around relationships" (Michael Schrage, in Hapgood, "Simulations Help Make Better Businesses," para. 2). Social media reveals the hunger for relationship out there. But an important question to ask is: How much does social media actually hinder authentic relationships, as everyone puts forth their best persona in selfies and on Facebook? Oral hermeneutics interacts with real people, face to face, offering more authenticity.

3. Bochner, "Narrative Virtues," 153.
4. Dunn, *Oral Gospel Tradition*, 57.
5. Walton and Sandy, *Lost World of Scripture*, 86.
6. Dunn, *Oral Gospel Tradition*, 44 (emphasis original).

the goal, rather than wooden word equivalency,[7] capturing substance and significance rather than precise definitions, then oral media should be game on! If so, this makes the God behind the words the focus, rather than the mere words themselves. As someone sagely suggested, "We are too suspicious of subjectivity." The question that requires an answer is: How well do we understand the differences between orality and literary cultures?

In the previous chapter, the authors considered how orality influenced the text and teaching by considering the basic components of orality, narrative as the dominant genre in Scripture, the role of scribes in textual construction, and how manuscripts were delivered, discussed, and remembered. To continue to answer the central question of this book—*Why is it important to know and practice oral hermeneutics in order to ascertain and communicate biblical meaning?*—this chapter drills deeper into the dialogue and discussion components in relation to interpretation—oral hermeneutics (see figure 4.1).

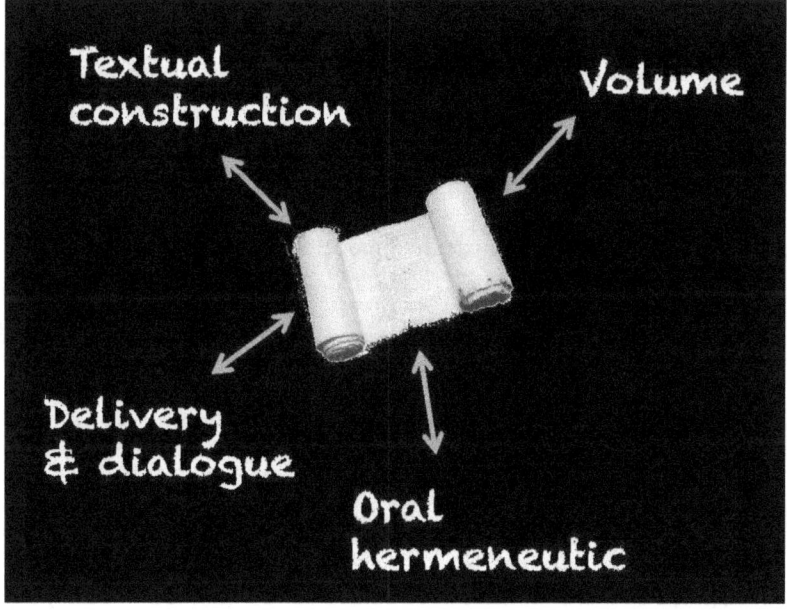

Figure 4.1. The Robust Role of Oral Hermeneutics

---

7. For a fascinating overview of the various viewpoints of theologians such as Luther, Calvin, Charles Hodge ("free from all error"), Frances Turretin (the Bible is errorless), A. A. Hodge, and B. B. Warfield (a proved error would discredit all of the Bible), see Fitzgerald, *Evangelicals*, 77–79.

In this chapter the authors map out the parameters of oral hermeneutics (OH), consider the robust role of narrative/story in relation to OH, the experiential aspects of OH, several different forms of preferred logic, contributions OH offers, and the need to recalibrate our present hermeneutic assumptions. We begin by mapping out the parameters of OH.

Mapping Out Oral Hermeneutics Parameters

Abstract concepts such as anger, abuse, stinginess, generosity, laziness or leadership, faith, and salvation come alive as they are lived out positively or negatively through Bible characters. Such demonstrations beg for deeper discussion as to the (in)validity of their actions, values, morals, and theology. Since "Scripture is composed of 'ordinary' language and ordinary 'literature,'"[8] such investigation becomes possible. This is where OH enters the interpretative process. Focusing on the narrative sections of Scripture, OH attempts to experientially interpret the congenial to corrosive conversations and conflicts characters face on a daily basis. To discern meaning, OH, in contrast to textual hermeneutics (TH), which centers on grammatical-historical analysis, centers on character analysis in the context of story.

The authors recognize there are multiple models of OH presently in use today at home and abroad and in rural and urban settings.[9] Some are more robust than others. We therefore encourage all those using variations of OH in any context to evaluate their model for strengths and weaknesses. For those using variations of TH, *how could OH enhance your model?*

The Robust Role of Narrative/Story in Oral Hermeneutics

Unlike TH, which focuses on atomized *disconnections* dissected from words and grammars that result in principles and theological concepts placed in systemized categories,[10] OH explores the *connections* between ac-

---

8. Vanhoozer, "Semantics of Biblical Literature," 85.

9. Steffen, *Worldview-based Storying*.

10. French philosopher René Descartes may provide some clues as to the origin of such a rationale for fragmentation: "The second [precept] was to divide all the difficulties under examination into as many parts as possible, and as many as were required to solve them in the best way" (Descartes, *Discourse on the Method*, 17). The Cartesian tradition casts a long shadow down through modernity. Descartes's famous dictum, *"I think therefore I am,"* and the philosophical stream that followed him, contributed much to modern Western autonomous rationalism and to the radical individualism of our time. A formulation more in line with our human nature and to oral hermeneutics would be *"I yearn, therefore we are."* (We owe this formulation to Michael Sullivant,

tors as well as their verbal and visual actions, all of which call for "the moral reform of the multitude."[11] The conversations, clashes, and changes made by the characters in the story (plot) upset equilibrium[12] (the death of the widow's husband and her connection to Elisha through him) thereby providing an investigative starting point to discern how disruptive episodes of life will mysteriously be returned to normal. Unraveling dialogue is where OH begins, and not without reason.

Yale professor Hans Frei argues persuasively in his pioneering *The Eclipse of the Biblical Narrative* that narrative and human relationships go hand in glove, unlike anything found in any other media. "Realistic narratives" (ones that could actually happen)[13] are where humans and meaning intersect.

Frei courageously challenged the compromise that hermeneutic constructors had made to the Enlightenment's perception of interpreting Scripture. He contested: (1) limiting interpretation to abstract propositions and logic that distanced connection to human life and the depth of all its complexities, (2) the rejection of the Eternal One's ability to interact with and have a personal relationship with humans in all areas of life, and (3) the demotion of literary (poetic) precepts to a secondary form of authoritative information. Frei sought to restore a literary-driven hermeneutic that the Enlightenment had debunked and dismissed.

To ensure the strength of human interaction in interpretation, Frei called for the return of story to drive the interpretation of Scripture (something common up to the seventeenth century) to replace the so-called "neutral," scientific-based hermeneutics. Frei asserted, "the meaning emerges from the story form, rather than being illustrated by it."[14]

CEO of LifeModelWorks, from his presentation at a seminar in Laguna Niguel, CA, June 2019.)

11. Murrin, *Veil of Allegory*, 39.

12. "Plot" could be defined as conflict, chaos, or confusion—that can be brief, extended, multiple, internal, or external—created within and/or between characters through a sequence of author-directed events and episodes that seek resolution. Sternberg states, "No ignorance, no conflict, no conflict, no plot" (Sternberg, *Poetics of Biblical Narrative*, 173). Plot answers three basic questions: What happened? What will happen next? How will it all turn out (Mays, *Norton Introduction to Literature*, 85)? Ong contends, misguidedly, that plot has no place in orality: "An oral culture has no experience of a length, epic-size, or novel-size climactic linear plot, nor can it imagine such organization of lengthy material" (Ong, "Oral Remembering and Narrative Structures," 15). For Ong, plot was associated with writing, not episodes told orally. That seems odd. Do the spoken-written words of the Word demand a hybrid type of analysis?

13. We go beyond Frei and his Yale associates who are influenced by postmodernism. We believe biblical narratives are realistic because they are historical.

14. Frei, *Eclipse of Biblical Narrative*, 280.

Frei considered story, rather than science, the natural hermeneutic. This emphasis moved hermeneutics beyond abstract propositions and logic to concrete characters driven by narrative logic. It highlighted the Eternal One's intimate interactions with humans, experiencing their greatest joys and worst nightmares. And it restored story as an equal, authoritative hermeneutic.

Modern-day hermeneutics (TH in all its variations) influenced by the Enlightenment comes with compromises. Old and New Testament authors and Jesus would have found such an interpretative approach difficult and distant. What Frei advocates are the principles and practices promoted by OH (in all its variations), which would have been familiar to the biblical authors and Jesus.[15] And they add what the Enlightenment missed—life itself in the context of story interacting with the Divine Author!

Ryken and Longman would concur with Frei, but add this caveat, "literary texts are irreducible to propositional statements and single meanings. The whole story or the whole poem is the meaning. A propositional statement of a theme can never be a substitute or even the appointed goal of experiencing a literary text."[16] The propositional statement "Cain murdered Abel" tells us little that is embedded in the story. In the story we discover they are brothers and that their parents are Adam and Eve, their occupations, how each perceived God, God's perspective of their offerings, the motive for the killing, how the murder happened, and so forth. As some one quipped, "Story is not the icing on the cake. Story *is* the cake!" Story serves more than being a statement—*story is metaphor for life's meaning!*

In *The Rule of Metaphor* and *Time and Narrative,* published in sequence, French philosopher Paul Ricoeur argues metaphor and narrative take discourse *to a higher level* than prosaic words or sentences.[17] In relation to metaphor he based its superiority on the difficulty of capturing its denseness in words. In relation to narrative he based its superiority on the powerful interplay of plot and imagination that leads to action.[18]

To illustrate, my (Tom) granddaughter does not perceive our barn as just being big, red, or a place for her favorite Gypsy Vanner horse, but rather as a "sanctuary in an unsettled world, a sheltered place where life's true priorities are clear."[19] When there is internal or external conflict (plot)

---

15. Sadly, Frei missed, for the most part, the historical aspect of Scripture. While his contributions to hermeneutics are fundamental, foundational, and formative, they must be seen from this erroneous perspective.

16. Ryken and Longman III, *Complete Literary Guide to the Bible,* 17.

17. Ricoeur, *Time and Narrative,* 1:ix.

18. Ricoeur, *Time and Narrative,* 3:ix.

19. Lauren Davis Baker, "New Freedom Barn." https://www.facebook.com/

there is no better place to seek shelter than the sanctuary barn. Metaphors and conflict, as Ricoeur points out, go beyond words, serving as conduits to deeper meaning.

While Ricoeur recognized the full interpretation of discourse required objective analysis, he also recognized interpreters must advance beyond scientific methodology. That is because "there is always a *surplus of meaning* to be found in discourse that goes beyond what such objective techniques explain."[20] Narrative analysis offers what objective linguistic hermeneutic techniques often fail to offer—a "*surplus of meaning.*"[21]

OH mines the vast and deep recesses of the whole story, revealing insights often missed by textual types of analysis. Searching the "full arc" of cause-and-effect (plot destined to some conclusion as it advances through events linearly, circularly or by chiasm [ABCB'A']) in a story makes new discoveries possible.[22] This does not mean OH is superior to other hermeneutical models, just different, distinct, and unique to the narrative genre.

Oral Hermeneutics Relies Heavily on the Grand Narrative of Scripture

OH engages the metanarrative or grand narrative of Scripture as well as individual Bible stories. The Bible, all sixty-six books, divided into multiple acts, is a unified book with plays within plays,[23] driven by a plot as it mysteriously, magnetically, and majestically advances to the Author-chosen conclusion. All the main characters, events, and scenes have interpretive significance as they have some relationship to the primary Protagonist[24] who unifies the grand narrative in the midst of a losing chaotic cause perpetrated by the primary

---

NewFreedomFarmVA/posts/2075075162815121.

20. See Ricoeur, *Paul Ricoeur Interpretation Theory*, 57 (emphasis added). Pellauer, "Paul Ricoeur."

21. Vanhoozer, *Drama of Doctrine*, 88 (emphasis added).

22. Steffen, "Clothesline Theology for the World," 238, 254, 265, 267. See Wu, "Chiasm, Oral Peoples."

23. Vanhoozer, *Drama of Doctrine*, 52. Karl Barth perceived Scripture as "one vast, loosely structured nonfictional novel" (Willimon, *Conversations with Barth on Preaching*, 34).

24. "Apart from the Old Testament we will always have an impoverished view of God. God is not a philosophical construct but a Person who acts in history: the one who created Adam, who gave a promise to Noah, who called Abraham and introduced himself by name to Moses, who deigned to live in a wilderness tent in order to live close to his people" (Yancey, *Bible Jesus Read*, 27).

Antagonist, Satan. Each individual story, along with its featured characters, adds more distinct clarity to the fingerprint of God.

> "Some suggest, 'We must examine each thread carefully, and once we have exhaustively considered each separate panel of the tapestry, only then can we attempt to reconstruct the whole.' Others say, 'Let us look at the earliest part of the tapestry sewn, and we will be able to see how it has developed from there.' Still others urge, 'Let us consider what is central to the tapestry and read its more contingent or secondary elements in that light.' To all these voices one is tempted to answer, 'But why not step back once more and try again to look at the *whole*, which is much more than the sum of its parts, even the dominant and colorful ones.'"[25]

Of the cast of nearly 3,000 characters who help demonstrate and embody the Chief Character, it is neither possible nor necessary to know them all. *So how then should the interpreter proceed to gain a better grasp of the embodied threads of truth of Scripture?*

Paauw prefers to search for two factors: "Contrary to what most people think, a chapter-and-verse Bible is not essential for referring to a particular passage. It would be healthier and show a great knowledge of the Bible itself if we were to adopt the practice of referencing by *context and content*."[26]

Rather than context and content, Trinity Evangelical Divinity School's Emeritus Professor of New Testament, D. A. Carson, chooses to comb the text for turning points that break up the grand narrative:

> That stance is most likely to be deeply Christian which attempts to integrate all the major biblically determined turning points in the history of redemption: creation, fall, the call of Abraham, the exodus and the giving of the law, the rise of the monarchy and the rise of the prophets, the exile, the incarnation, the ministry, death, and resurrection of Christ, the onset of the kingdom of God, the coming of the Spirit and the consequent ongoing eschatological tension between the 'already' and the 'not yet,' the return of Christ, and the prospect of a new heaven and a new earth.[27]

---

25. Witherington, *Paul's Narrative Thought World*, 1–2.
26. Paauw, *Saving the Bible from Ourselves*, 41 (emphasis added).
27. Carson, *Christ and Culture Revisited*, 81.

Cross-cultural church multiplier Paul Koehler proposes the most concrete scenario. Rather than context and content or turning points, Koehler identifies fifteen central characters:

> Consider the fact that one can think through most of the stories of the Old Testament by following the lives of no more than a dozen individuals and their families or associates: Adam, Noah, Abraham-Isaac, Jacob, Joseph, Moses, Joshua, Samuel-Saul, David, Solomon, Elijah-Elisha, and Daniel. These 12 characters cover most of the historical eras of the Old Testament. The Gospels chronicle the life of only one Man (with many supporting characters), and Acts can be told by simply following the experiences of Peter and Paul. If someone were to learn the stories that pertain to these fifteen people, they would have a mastery of a large portion of the Bible.[28]

If characters can demonstrate the meaning of a single section of Scripture of a book, could they not also do the same for all sixty-six books of the Bible?[29] *For a collection of books (e.g., Pentateuch)? Could the big picture of Scripture, the grand narrative, emerge through the cumulative, varied voices, actions, interactions, and interfacing of characters?*[30] *What role does the Chief Character—Jesus Christ—who spans both testaments, have?*

Biblical scholars Gordon Fee and Douglas Stuart observantly note the embedded nature of stories, and consequently the characters within them, as the biblical authors layer Scripture into three levels:

> Every individual OT narrative (bottom level) is at least a part of the greater narrative of Israel's history in the world (the middle level), which in turn is a part of the ultimate narrative of God's creation and his redemption of it (the top level). This ultimate narrative goes beyond the OT through the NT. You will not fully do justice to any individual narrative without recognizing its part within the other two.[31]

---

28. Koehler, *Telling God's Stories with Power*, 104.

29. An interesting experiment would be to take a narrative book of the Bible and let the author-selected controlling characters define the theme of the book.

30. Jennifer Jagerson offers an interesting possibility for discovering the grand narrative of Scripture when she asks, "Is it possible to teach a paradigmatic story from each book of the Bible that makes clear to the oral learner what the big picture of the book is about? Might these paradigmatic stories be used to knit together the larger picture of God's overarching historical work to help insure a strong understanding of the metanarrative" (Jagerson, "Hermeneutics and the Methods of Oral Bible Storytelling," 260)?

31. Fee and Stuart, *How to Read the Bible*, 80.

The twelve characters Koehler identified above could easily be placed within Fee and Stuart's three levels.[32] From their voices and actionized beliefs, individual narratives begin to emerge. If these narratives were collated, a grand narrative of Scripture begins to emerge. As the arc of biblical history passes through time, OH asks: *Who are the quintessential controlling characters*[33] *that advance the plotline of the grand narrative of Scripture?*[34]

Why is knowing the grand narrative of the Scripture important? One reason is because significant populations of the world, from which we literates have much to learn, have less of a fondness for fragmentation found so profusely in the West.[35] Rather, as social psychologist Richard Nisbett puts it, "Asians view the world through a wide-angle lens, whereas Westerners have tunnel vision."[36] Oral-based audiences tend to see things more holistically, more harmoniously, more globally, in a more unified manner.

---

32. The number three is highly recognized in many parts of the West—from nursery rhymes (three blind mice, three little pigs) to three-point sermons. The number four carries negative connotations in parts of Asia where it means death. The different global perceptions of numbers should alert the wise cross-cultural Bible teacher to investigate how locals perceive numbers (in this case related to levels) *before* making indiscriminate divisions. More significantly, numbers have significance in the Bible—the number three permeates the story of Jesus (three in the inner circle of the disciples, three denials of Peter, three crucified together, resurrection after three days and nights [as for Jonah in the fish], three times Jesus asked Peter, "Do you love me?," and more—all point to the Trinity which permeates Jesus' life. This symbolism gives fine mnemonic value to Fee and Stuart's three levels. The number four symbolizes the "four winds," "four corners" of the earth. The number seven is wholeness, completion, perfection. The number twelve is for governance or authority, as the twelve tribes of Israel and the twelve apostles. Koehler's twelve OT characters can be nicely remembered by this meaning of twelve. The wise Bible teacher will make good use of biblical numerology to redeem or displace negative or dark symbolism of numbers in a given culture.

33. See Appendix D for how Jennifer Jagerson astutely identified the quintessential characters, stories, and texts of the Old Testament.

34. Abraham serves as a controlling character not only in specific stories in Genesis, but also in the entire redemptive story of Scripture, as Paul narrated in Romans 4. See Sailhamer, *Pentateuch as Narrative*.

35. Peter Senge elaborates, "From a very early age, we are taught to break apart problems, to fragment the world. This apparently makes complex tasks and subjects more manageable, but we pay a hidden enormous price. We can no longer see the consequences of our actions; we lose our intrinsic sense of connection to a larger whole. When we then try to 'see the big picture,' we try to reassemble the fragments . . . the task is futile . . . Thus, after a while we give up trying to see the whole altogether" (Senge, *The Fifth Discipline*, 3).

36. Nisbett, *Geography of Thought*, 89.

> "... the Old Testament supplies the New Testament with its normative theological and historical markers, while the New Testament witness to the risen Messiah supplies the subject matter for a Christian hermeneutic by which the Old Testament becomes Christian scripture."[37]

We appreciate noted theologian N. T. Wright's insight into how the whole shapes the parts: "When the early church told stories about Jesus these stories were not . . . mere random selections of anecdotes. They were not without a sense of an overall story into which they might fit, or of a narrative shape to which such smaller stories could conform."[38] New Testament scholar Richard Hays believes the same holds true for Paul: "The framework of Paul's thought is constituted neither by a system of doctrines nor by his personal religious experience but by a 'sacred story; a narrative structure.'"[39] Scripture could be portrayed through concentric circles that share the same axis—Jesus Christ. These circles highlight central characters and contexts that synthesize into a grand narrative that influences the interpretation of all its individual parts.

One of the most important reasons for being able to articulate the grand narrative of Scripture is it becomes the foundation, the *heart hermeneutic (in contrast to a head hermeneutic) for interpreting each individual part of Scripture*. Whenever a single verse, story, or section of Scripture is heard, read, or viewed, we intuitively interpret it through the framework of our understanding of the grand narrative of Scripture. This is significant because *no story or passage can be interpreted accurately or fully if taken out of context of the grand narrative of Scripture*. OH can help move us beyond the fragmented, incomplete interpretations so common today in the West.

The individual stories all tie together because all Scripture is embedded in other Scripture. Therefore, Scripture is best interpreted through Scripture—the immediate text, the section, the book/letter, other books/letters by the same author, and writings of other authors. Canadian literary critic and theorist Northrop Frye aptly summarizes: "The primary understanding of any work of literature has to be based on an assumption of its unity . . . Further, every effort should be directed toward understanding the whole of what we

---

37. Wall, "Significance of a Canonical Perspective," 536–37.
38. Wright, *New Testament and the People of God*, 78.
39. Hays, *Faith of Jesus Christ*, 6.

read."⁴⁰ Therefore, "we have to study not only the spiders, or the Bible characters; it is equally important to study the web, or the meta-narrative . . . because God has chosen to weave his grand story with the smaller stories of particular people."⁴¹ OH takes seriously the interfacing of the biblical parts and the role of the whole in the interpretation of those parts.⁴²

Nor dare we overlook the nesting of all theology in Genesis 1–3 that provides clues to the rest of the Bible as it unveils beginnings and projects the finale of the grand narrative. The beginning of Scripture telegraphs theological clues as to what will follow in the remainder of the book, e.g., relationships, rest, rule, rot, redemption, and restoration (make a new story). Knowing the grand narrative of Scripture allows one to think, speak, and act with a coherent message because the spoken-written word is perceived as a unified manifesto from beginning to end.

Story, Symbol, and Ritual (De/Re)construct Worldview

Another powerful and praiseworthy contribution story makes is its ability to (de/re)construct one's identity or worldview. Many have written on the topic, e.g., philosopher Alasdair MacIntyre, who concludes, "I can only answer the question, 'What am I to do?' if I can answer the prior question, 'Of what story do I find myself a part?'"⁴³

Psychologist and education theorist Jerome Bruner believes, "It is only in the narrative mode that one can construct an identity and find a place in one's culture."⁴⁴ Professor of Counseling Psychology Donald Polkinghorne paints the picture of narrative as "the primary form by which human experience is made meaning."⁴⁵ N. T. Wright writes, "worldviews provide the stories through which human beings view reality. Narrative is the most characteristic expression of worldview, going deeper than the isolated observation or fragmented remark."⁴⁶ Wright continues, "The stories which characterize the worldview itself are thus located, on the map of human

---

40. Frye, "Literary Criticism," 75.

41. Steffen, *Facilitator Era*, 148.

42. "*Narrative criticism views the text as a whole.* Narrative critics are interested in narratives as complete tapestries in which the parts fit together to form an organic whole" (Resseguie, *Narrative Criticism of the New Testament*, 38–39 [emphasis original]).

43. MacIntyre, *After Virtue*, 216.

44. Bruner, *Culture of Education*, 42.

45. Polkinghorne, *Narrative Knowing and the Human Sciences*, 1.

46. Wright, *New Testament and the People of God*, 123.

knowing, at a more fundamental level than explicitly formulated beliefs, including theological beliefs."[47] Ricoeur offers a more nuanced reflection:

> To state the identity of an individual or a community is to answer the question, 'Who did this?' 'Who is the agent, the author?' ... The answer has to be narrative. To answer the question 'Who?' ... is to tell the story of life ... the story of life continues to be refigured by all the truthful or fictive stories a subject tells about himself or herself ... an examined life is, in large part, one purged, one clarified by the cathartic effects of the narratives, be they historical or fictional, conveyed by our culture ... Individual and community are constituted in their identity by taking up narratives that become for them their actual history ... Subjects recognize themselves in the stories they tell about themselves ... Is there ... any experience that is not already the fruit of narrative activity?[48]

OH emotionally and rationally recognizes the robust power stories have to construct, deconstruct, and reconstruct worldviews;[49] it does so through the voices, actions, and interactions of characters, symbols, and rituals as they dramatize life from sufferings to successes. Stories concretely demonstrate our emotions, our reason, and our rationalizations. *But is there more involved in worldview (de/re)construction than just story?*

In *Worldview-based Storying: The Integration of Symbol, Story, and Ritual in the Orality Movement,* I (Tom) expanded the framework to discern worldview through story by adding symbol and ritual. The triad could be expressed this way: "Reality [worldview] and relationships are symboled, storied, and reviewed through ritual."[50]

> "Symbols are created and communicated ultimately as stories meant to give order to human experience and to induce others to dwell in them in order to establish ways of living in common, in intellectual and spiritual communities in which there is confirmation for the story that constitutes one's life."[51]

---

47. Wright, *New Testament and the People of God*, 38.
48. Ricoeur, *Time and Narrative*, 3:246–48.
49. Steffen, "Foundational Roles of Symbol and Narrative," 477–94.
50. Steffen, *Worldview-based Storying*, 181.
51. Fisher, *Human Communication as Narration*, 63.

As a prime example of the triad, consider the annual feasts of Israel, still observed by Jewish people today. At Passover, the *ritual* cleansing of the home of leaven occurs again. During the meal the *story* of the exodus from Egypt is told again, and the *symbolic* foods—the bitter herbs, the lamb and the unleavened bread—are consumed again. This annual *ritual* of history reinforces collective Jewish identity and worldview.

Since worldview is at least constructed by this triad, it can be deconstructed and reconstructed by the same. Transformation (in contrast to fictional faith transactions) leading to a rival worldview will require the illumination of new stories, new symbols, and new rituals through the power of the Holy Spirit. Former stories of substance that dishonored God must be restoried; former false symbols of significance that dishonored God must be resymboled; former false rituals of relevance that dishonored God must be reritualed. As transformation happens, a new identity and worldview emerges. In the case of the Jewish story, existing symbols and rituals should be infused with new messianic meaning. OH recognizes that other components of orality—symbols and rituals—bring life changes as well.

Oral Hermeneutics Relies Heavily on the Experiential

Discerning meaning through the experiences of characters is as true for the grand narrative formed by the cumulative stories as it is of individual stories. The whole and parts are never really divorced. Stories (individual or cumulative) unpretentiously pull us into a "world of discourse"[52] where we discover what demands dialogue and internal and external expression. We react, reset, extend encouragement, disparage, give direction, offer hope, lose hope, and then dismiss it.

As humans, we mature and change through emotional relationships. Professional storyteller Loren Niemi notes: "If the narrative plot is how we get from the beginning to the end of a story, the emotional arc is how we want the audience to feel as we make the journey."[53] Relational interaction with the characters, therefore, even though vicariously through a story, leads to experiential learning, offering the possibility of transformation.

For Ricoeur, imagination, along with cognition and emotions,[54] stand behind one's ability to interpret the experiences of the characters,

---

52. Crites, "Narrative Quality of Experience," 19.
53. Niemi, *Book of Plots*, 39.
54. Ricoeur, *Time and Narrative*, 1:50. See also Hays, *Conversion of the Imagination*.

metaphors, symbols,[55] and rituals within a story.[56] Ryken and Longman add, "The Old Testament does more than inform readers' intellect with facts about God and history. It also arouses emotions, appeals to the will, and stimulates the imagination."[57] Imagination allows for alternative views and actions dramatized by various characters, offering legitimate life alternatives. The past offers new possibilities for the present, thereby generating new expectations for the future.

Even so, imagination "is not born from nothing. It is bound in one way or another to tradition's paradigms [worldview]. But the range of interpretation is vast. It is deployed between the two poles of servile application and calculated deviation."[58] Risk therefore results for those brave enough to move beyond tradition, especially for early adapters to live like (or unlike) the characters depicted in the story (look for what Naaman risked and pioneered in chapter 9). There is something about imagination and story that provides the listener/reader/viewer confidence to move beyond her/his present prison.

> "Jesus changed lives because he was able to change the way people *imagined* their lives. He dared them to imagine the stranger as neighbor, the child as teacher, the enemy as mirror, the deity as loving father. He helped them imagine lepers, women, and Roman centurions as exemplars of faith. He asked them to imagine that the most important person at the table was the waiter, and that the end of the line was the place to be. At the moment I cannot think of a single story he told that was not intended to change the way his listeners imagined the world."[59]

Theologians Stanley Hauerwas and David Burrell offer possibilities as to what these incentives may be: "Any story which we adopt, or allow to adopt us, will have to display: (1) power to release us from destructive alternatives; (2) ways of seeing through current distortions; (3) room to keep us from having to resort to violence; (4) a sense for the tragic: how

55. Ricoeur refers to symbol as "rule-governed behavior" (Ricoeur, *Time and Narrative*, 3:58).
56. Ricoeur, *Essays of Biblical Interpretation*, 144–66.
57. Ryken and Longman III, *Complete Literary Guide to the Bible*, 97.
58. Ricoeur, *Time and Narrative*, 3:69.
59. Taylor, quoted in Cooke, "Insight that Changed the Way," para. 1 (emphasis original).

meaning transcends power."⁶⁰ Challenging social memory is never easy, but narrators supply clues through characters' words and works on how this can be accomplished, not to mention convictions advanced by the Holy Spirit (John 16:13).

Experiential-based OH recognizes the robust role stories, symbols,[61] and rituals have in discerning a surplus of meaning. The interaction of characters—their inconsistencies, courage (or lack thereof), charisma, contributions, choices and changes made, and the consequences of such, ignite the imagination and emotions of listeners/readers/viewers as they seek models to imitate. They observe echoes of their own lives in the lives of those in the story, and therefore are challenged to make choices to better align their lives with kingdom truths. OH is experientially based.

Some characters serve as cautionary tales; others serve as role models and heroes to emulate despite inevitable backlash. Wise listeners/readers/viewers recognize choices made have short- and long-term consequences. Used properly, OH is common-sense, visually based, socially driven, experientially oriented hermeneutics, relying heavily on the relational role of characters to telegraph and clarify meaning as the plotline progresses. OH is character-centric theologizing driven by a specific form of logic to highlight the Chief Character. *But what is that logic?*

Types of Logic

Subjectivity and objectivity find their roots in forms of logic. Yes, there is more than one form of logic—there is more than the scientific propositional or formal logic that dominates the Western world. Bruner makes this helpful distinction. The scientific side is "preoccupied with the epistemological question of how to know truth" while the narrative side prefers to focus on the "broader questions of how we come to endow meaning to experience, which is the preoccupation of the poet and the storyteller."[62]

According to this line of thinking, logic could simply be defined as an underlying mental system of principles that determines how one hears and processes information toward conclusion. Most times we are not cognizant of the logic that drives our decisions. For example, members of Western cultures tend to "habitually, and instinctively work within a literary

---

60. Hauerwas and Burrell, "From System to Story," 185.

61. For example, Vanhoozer identifies Jeremiah's use of the symbols of a yoke and Hosea's marriage as a form of drama (Vanhoozer, *Drama of Doctrine*, 51). Repetition results in remembrance.

62. Bruner, *Actual Minds, Possible Worlds*, 12.

paradigm."[63] Most of us, therefore, tend to take literary logic for granted, *and* project it on those of different cultures.

Utilizing different forms of logic is never easy. That is true even if another form of logic could provide different views into the same room, thereby providing a more comprehensive understanding of the room's contents and history. Logic, a part of worldview, is a sacred cow.

Could a different form of logic give a much more comprehensive picture of the liberating King? If so, what is that form of logic?

Narrative Logic

Formally educated Westerners are probably most familiar with the kind of logic first developed by Aristotle—syllogistic logic. Syllogistic logic presents a proposition (major premise), followed by another proposition (minor premise), and then one infers a logical conclusion. For example,

> All dogs have four legs.
>
> Rover is a dog.
>
> Rover has four legs

Syllogistic or propositional logic, unlike narrative logic, is something that has to be learned formally. It does not come naturally through informal means, as does narrative logic. And it requires regular usage to be remembered.

I (Tom) approached the Ifugao with propositional logic, or what Jerome Bruner calls "logico-scientific."[64] I did so to help assure an objective interpretation of Scripture would result. The Ifugao were totally unimpressed, not to mention perplexed. Most were not wired or trained to think in formal logic. That left me with several options: (1) teach them to use propositional logic, or (2) learn their form of logic. The prospects of the first choice did not look achievable nor wise as I was on their turf, so I chose the latter.

As I explored their consternation, I discovered the Ifugao preferred a form of logic that discerned a more subjective meaning—narrative logic.[65] Here is how the distinguished, ground-breaking narrative theorist Walter Fisher defines narrative logic:

---

63. Dunn, *Oral Gospel Tradition*, 44.
64. Bruner, *Actual Minds, Possible Worlds*, 12.
65. See Steffen, *Worldview-based Storying*, 146–49.

> Narrative rationality is its logic. The essential components of this logic are the following. Human communication is tested against the principles of probability (coherence) and fidelity (truthfulness and reliability). Probability, whether a story 'hangs together,' is assessed in three ways: by its argumentative or structural coherence; by its material coherence, that is, by comparing and contrasting stories told in other discourses (a story may be internally consistent, but important facts may be omitted, counterarguments ignored, and relevant issues overlooked); and by characterological coherence.[66]

Narrative logic relies on coherence (the audience senses an acceptable building of the argument in that the story hangs together through their internal narrative dynamics), truthfulness, and reliability (the story rings true with other stories in their universe). The recognizable flow of the argument and the instantaneous connection to the characters would lead the listener/reader/viewer of a story to exclaim, "Aha! Been there, done that. That happened to me too! I know her/him. I can identify with that person!"

Susan Shaw sagely surmises, "The truths of stories are made, not by logical persuasion, but by experiential engagement. *Stories do not convince by argument; they surprise by identification.*"[67] Narrative logic relies on coherence, truthfulness/reliability, interconnectedness, and identification to discover meaning. Narrative logic is the logic of association.

While TH relies on factual evidence to reach a proven verdict, OH relies on experiential evidence to demonstrate a verdict. OH discovers truth, not through a coherent logical argument, but through "characterological coherence,"[68] i.e., the character's life experiences that mirror ours or those of others, offering paths to follow or avoid. Even so, both types of logic rely on reason. But as Pascal perceptively pronounced, "The heart has its reasons

---

66. Fisher, *Human Communication as Narration*, 47 (emphasis original). Fisher goes on to say that, "Before the advent of philosophy in ancient Greece, all modes of human communication were regarded as *mythos/logos, form/content, and feeling/reason.* No instance of human communication was privileged over another as having a special capacity to convey knowledge, truth, or reality" (192). Sachs adds to the timeframe, "The oral tradition that dominated human experience for all but the last few hundred years is returning with a vengeance" (Sachs, *Winning the Story Wars*, 20). Sadly, most of us fly one-winged aircraft when it comes to the use of logic. Interestingly, while the Greeks developed a rigorous and helpful form of philosophical logic, their entire culture was based on their mythic narratives by Homer, which were understood according to narrative logic and informed their understanding of beauty and life, all the while setting the stage for their pursuit of philosophical truth.

67. Shaw, *Storytelling in Religious Education*, 61 (emphasis added).

68. Shaw, *Storytelling in Religious Education*, 47. See also Olson, "From Utterance to Text."

that reason knows not of."[69] Narrative logic, which is the engine that drives OH, finds legitimacy in experiential meaning.

Contributions of Oral Hermeneutics

Like textual hermeneutic models, OH makes a number of contributions in discerning textual meaning. Here are a few. These contributions not only help define OH, they also represent how the authors envision a healthy hermeneutic designed specifically to interpret narratives, and have attempted to illustrate it through two Bible stories. The authors, like all of us, are on a steep learning curve. Again, as you read through them, ponder how they compare to the hermeneutic model you are presently using.

Oral Hermeneutics Encourages Laity Participation

Oral hermeneutics offers multiple powerful contributions for specific and general audiences. For example, Chifugo concludes:

> When we speak of the interpretation of old texts, we tend to regard this as a remote exercise whereby only those who have the privilege of knowing the ancient language and church history are the only ones who can interpret biblical texts. But, to regard interpretation as an imaginative and communal process could revolutionize that view and will enable oral lay people to begin to consider Bible interpretation.[70]

Unleashing the nonprofessional, oral, or oral-preference audiences to use *their* preferred hermeneutic—the imaginative within a communal process—has the potential to unleash Scripture to the majority of God's faithful and future followers. Through communal connectivity (relationships) OH discovers meaning that helps cement communal memory.

Oral Hermeneutics Utilizes the Imagination

Another contribution OH makes is the unleashing of one's imagination. Recall all the imagination unleased in the "Elisha and the Widow's Oil" story. While some may immediately bristle at the thought of using one's imagination to perceive God, Jonathan Edwards was not ready to throw the proverbial

---

69. Pascal, "Manifest Propensity," para. 1.
70. Chifugo, "Oral Hermeneutics," 139.

baby out with the bathwater even as he recognized that reason raised questions about some of its weaknesses. Edwards expresses it this way:

> As God has given us such a faculty as the imagination, and so made us that we cannot think of things spiritual and invisible without some exercise of this faculty; so it appears to me that such is our state and nature that this faculty is really subservient and helpful to the other faculties of the mind, when a proper use is made of it.[71]

For Edwards, imagination was an essential component to spiritual growth.

> "Literature speaks the language of the imagination and the study of literature is supposed to train and improve the imagination."[72]

Imagination, with its etymology rooted in image, is necessary because it takes us beyond our other God-given faculties, such as disembodied linear reason. When we hear and contemplate the stories of Scripture, we must use our imaginations to envision the characters and events surrounding them. Many of the Hebrew prophets would agree as they not only *heard* God's word, they *saw* it (Gen 15:1; 20:3–4; Isa 13:1; Ezek 1:1–3; Zech 5:2).

The Gospel of Mark's abrupt end provides another example. Dunn offers this reason why hearers were left "in some suspense." Such an ending "presumably helped bring a listening audience to their own experience of the risen Jesus."[73] Such suspense fires up the imagination.

> "popular, devotional interpretation does contribute an insight that many of us academicians, for all our methodological precision have missed. That is, we need to hear Scripture with faith, embracing it in our personal lives . . . Hermeneutical distance has advantages at one level of interpretation but place the interpreter at a severe disadvantage when it comes to living the text's message."[74]

---

71. Edwards, "Distinguishing Marks of a Work," para. 10.
72. Northrop Frye, https://www.azquotes.com/quote/1101737.
73. Dunn, *Jesus According to the New Testament*, 51.
74. Keener, *Spirit Hermeneutics*, 24.

C. S. Lewis insists that "reason is the natural organ of truth," yet does not stop there. He continues, "but imagination is the organ of meaning. Imagination . . . is not the cause of truth, but its condition."[75] In other words, Bible communicators do not grasp the meaning of a word or concept *until* they have a clear image to which it connects.[76] For Lewis, this is what the imagination is all about—not just the ability to dream up fanciful fables, but the ability to identify meaning, and to know when we have discovered something truly meaningful.

Have you ever heard statements or principles repeated for years that never had any personal meaning, until a concrete, living example ignited your imagination, illuminating the principle and presenting you with that "Aha" moment? I (Tom) could never figure out Simon the sorcerer's fearful response to Peter until I observed demonic activity among the Ifugao. Simon's response then made total sense.

Meanings we discover in "aha" moments are easily retained. Propositional, abstract knowledge, therefore, must be connected to some image for there to be meaning and sustained memory. Stories are full of images that ignite the imagination, leaving behind a trail of long-remembered meaning. Meaning grows from the roots of imagination thereby aiding long-term memory.[77]

Oral Hermeneutics Utilizes the Emotions

OH not only unleashes the imagination, it also unbridles the emotions. Listeners/readers/viewers feel with the characters who are being portrayed, whether about their conversations, charisma, courage, clothes, contexts, circumstances, conduct, inconsistencies, contributions, comedic abilities, convictions, conflicts, or choices. They vividly, vicariously experience laughter, sadness, shame, dirtiness, depression, dejection, anger, betrayal, acceptance, pain, fear, frustration, comfort, confusion, contagiousness, and hope. They even try to warn other characters about impending danger. They laugh at their good jokes and boo their bad ones; they interrupt, cheer, jeer; they wince at repugnant actions or comments, e.g., when Gordon Gekko (played by Michael Douglas) infamously said in the 1987 movie *Wall Street*, "Greed

---

75. Hooper, *C. S. Lewis*, 570.

76. Chinese drama is instructive: "The text of a play is but one component entering into the finished performance. In the Western dramatic tradition, the text is central; in China it plays a more modest role. It is impossible to do justice to the Chinese drama by studying texts apart from the actual performance" (Idema and Haft, *Guide to Chinese Literature*, 193).

77. Ryken, *Words of Delight*, 53.

is good. Greed is right. Greed works." That comment in the movie was latent with emotion and stirred emotions, so much so that it is still repeated today.

> "The ancient rabbis exhorted Jews studying the Torah to 'turn it over, turn it over, because everything is inside of it.' First you 'open' the Story, then you 'turn it over, turn it over.' There is a Story—turn, turn, turn. It is the turn of the Story that turns lives back to God. This bad habit of Jesus will lead us to never underestimate the power of story to cultivate the imagination and change the heart. We don't just read the stories of the Bible; we live in them, and they live in us."[78]

Imagination writes truth on our hearts. Emotions trigger values. OH is designed to activate faculties with which we have been endowed by our Creator—our imaginations and emotions. In *Desiring the Kingdom*, Calvin College's professor of philosophy, James K. A. Smith, maintains we have misidentified the human race, and therefore, by extension, our ministry models and strategies. Influenced by Greek tradition, we tend to identify humans as thinkers or thinking things. Our models and strategies of discipleship therefore tend to concentrate on the abstract, the cognitive. Smith offers an alternative identification: "we are, first and foremost: loving, desiring, affective, liturgical animals who, for the most part, don't inhabit the world as thinkers or cognitive machines."[79] He continues by stating that humans are "more affective, embodied creatures who make our world more by feeling our way around."[80] Smith's insights are applicable not just for evangelism and discipleship models and other ministry strategies, but also for the review and application questions for discussion of stories (ch. 7). OH engages the affective aspects of the actors without leaving reason in the shadows.

OH recognizes humans do not live by facts alone; it recognizes emotionality has the ability to write truth on our hearts. That is because stories of the Bible "'tell of mankind's experience at its most moving and most memorable in words that go beyond the mere chronicle: words that strike the heart and light up the vision.'"[81] Such subjectivity, however, could

---

78. Sweet, *Bad Habits of Jesus*, 76.
79. Smith, *Desiring the Kingdom*, 34.
80. Smith, *Desiring the Kingdom*, 47.
81. Paul Roche, quoted in Ryken and Longman III, *Complete Literary Guide to the Bible*, 16.

be dangerous. Dutch biblical scholar J. P. Fokkelman offers this response: "Good readers control their subjectivity: they do not deny it and know they need not be ashamed of it; on the contrary, they are able to employ it in a disciplined way."[82] OH is designed to activate in a disciplined way what we have inherited from our Creator—imagination and emotions.

Oral Hermeneutics Allows for Multiple Boundaried Truths

OH, built on orality, recognizes that a single meaning of a narrative text is often inadequate. In certain cases, therefore, it offers the audience truths on multiple levels, thereby meeting the needs of a diverse audience that addresses gender, generations, and geographical areas, all within the oral parameters of said story. In the narrative genre, "one main point" is too often insufficient.[83] The "big idea" just may be "big ideas." Or, it may not even be an idea; it may be a person!

> "The life of narrative inheres in the potency of the literal, and also, paradoxically, it is the literal that creates the potential of narrative to mean many things."[84]

What are the truths conveyed in the story of the prodigal son? Will it be the same from son number one's perspective? Son number two's? The father's? The community's?[85] *How did the widow of the deceased prophet interpret what happened? Her sons? Her neighbors? Elisha? And what about the meaning to the multiple and diverse audiences who have read or heard the story told over the centuries? In each story, who were the big characters? How do these characters define the big idea(s)? Did the reader note the sequence?*

Duke's Professor of History of Christianity, Stephen Shoemaker, takes a very different perspective from that of the scientific model driven by

---

82. Fokkelman, *Reading Biblical Narrative*, 25.

83. "It is impossible to summarize the meaning of a parable, when viewed as a metaphor, in either one or several points. Instead all one can do is describe the impact which it creates" (Blomberg, *Interpreting the Parables*, 35. See also 69, 76, 92, 137, 165).

84. Alter, *World of Biblical Literature*, 106.

85. Researching African songs as a means to discover oral theology, Emeka Ekeka notes how different audiences within a single audience are addressed: "A song may challenge the men, then the women, the young people, the preachers, a different target in each verse, with the same theme" (Ekeka, "Oral Expression of African Christianity," 155).

propositional logic, one that may actually reveal the Divine Author more fully: "Recognizing multiple meanings in a story is more reverencing to the holiness of God than straining after one meaning."[86] Scientific structure argues there is one legitimate answer. God is comprehensible. Thus, he can be predicted, characterized, compartmentalized, and controlled; there is certainty, providing the investigator a sense of power and control.

Additionally, conversations and interactions claim possible multiple truths. Much about God is incomprehensible. He is deep, mysterious, magnetic, and difficult to compartmentalize. *Is a single truth, as in the prodigal son or the widow stories noted above, an insult to the Author's awesomeness? Does the exegete's or storyteller's uncertainty and curiosity cause hermeneutic humility?* Orality argues meaning is multiintentional, multilayered, and multidirectional.

People respond to different things in a text due to a host of reasons—needs, hopes, fears, age, health, education, status, and role, as well as experiences such as war, tsunamis, wealth, poverty, and exploitation. Possible multiple interpretations (within the literary and traditional parameters noted above) demonstrate God's ability to meet all human needs at any place, at any time, among any gender and generation. *Can any speaker or writer assume his or her words will be limited to only one interpretation?*

OH recognizes possible multiple interpretations (multivocal) within author-provided parameters (which preserves the historical and present meaning).[87] Presuming that those from a propositional logic perspective have learned the oralist's narrative logic, or at least put themselves in their logic sandals for the moment, multiple truths seem not only plausible but probable and profitable.[88] Multiple truths, however, does not mean any

---

86. Shoemaker, *Godstories*, xxiii.

87. Seeking a betwixt and between, Sze-kar Wan compares the weaknesses of historical criticism and ideological criticism: "While historical critics replace the text with an imputed original meaning behind it, ideological readers might also be guilty of bypassing the text to reconstruct a symbolic universe based on their own perspectives. As a result, the text vanishes from view, the dialogue between reader and text weakens to a monologue by the interpreter, and the rupture between interpreter and text becomes unbridgeable. While both camps tend to regard understanding as a conception out there that must be captured and formulated, Hans-Georg Gadamer, following Martin Heidegger's phenomenology of being, regards understanding as an event that unites the interpreter to the text, because both participate in a tradition that is centered in and defined by language. In the final analysis, true understanding is a creative encounter between the interpreter and the text, with the result that neither is left by the wayside" (Wan, "Betwixt and Between," 140).

88. Maybe the reason theologians often cannot reach a unanimous decision on the meaning of a particular passage is that that passage requires multiple meanings. It is not an either/or binary, but a both/and possibility.

truth. The discoveries must correlate with the inspired written documents and the church's accounts over the centuries.

Bailey believes that each parable contains a "theological cluster."[89] By this he means "a group of interlocking themes."[90] As the themes in tension infuse each other (Bailey identified four in the parable of the sower[91]), a single general response (not a single meaning) based on action is expected: "Hear the word of the Kingdom and bear fruit."[92] For example, a hearer of the parable may perceive one theme while another hearer focuses on a different one, all directed by the Holy Spirit. While the themes may vary, they find themselves embedded in a single general response tied to the parable. As St. Augustine claimed centuries ago, "All truth is God's truth."

Truth may be much more elastic than modernity proposed, but less elastic than postmodernism presumes. We purport that because of the limitations of humanity, our ability to grasp truth requires a more elastic and humbled approach than modernity takes into account. Even so, truth *is* discernible. Interpreters can trust the text to unveil truth.

Referencing Bible narratives, Ryken and Longman contend that readers have a great likelihood of locating truth when reading Scripture. *Why?* Because "the Bible seems to have a built-in safeguard against misinterpretation that goes beyond what we find in literature generally. Israeli literary critic and biblical scholar Meir Sternberg calls it 'foolproof composition.' By this he means that while the Bible is hard to interpret correctly or definitely, it is nearly impossible to misread totally."[93]

Sternberg states, "follow the biblical narrator ever so uncritically, and by no great exertion you will be making tolerable sense of the world you are in, the action that unfolds, the protagonists on stage, and the point of it all."[94] There is a common saying, "The main things are the plain things and the plain things are the main things." The main things in the story will be plain in any good translation, whether heard, read, or viewed.

---

89. Bailey, *Poet & Peasant*, 41.

90. Bailey, *Poet & Peasant*, 28.

91. The theological cluster of four themes in tension with each other includes: (1) the kingdom, like a seed, grows slowly, (2) unprepared ground still gets planted because of God's grace, (3) the kingdom requires fruit bearing, and (4) a harvest is guaranteed no matter what happens (Bailey, *Poet & Peasant*, 28–29).

92. Bailey, *Poet & Peasant*, 28.

93. Ryken and Longman III, *Complete Literary Guide to the Bible*, 31.

94. Sternberg, *Poetics of Biblical Narrative*, 51.

Oral Hermeneutics Aids Long-Term Memory

The narrative nature of OH aids in reinforcing communal memory, partially because it does not require abstracting conceptual deductions into isolated chunks of knowledge categorized for memorization. Rather, it prefers to keep events tied to concrete concepts. If and when abstract concepts are needed, they can be drawn from the narrative by the listener/reader, often emerging from discussion, or pointed out by a teacher, as Jesus did with his disciples after he told them parables and they asked him what they meant (Matt 13:36–43). Further, it uses repetition in the text (furthered through discussion) to drive home and retain the truths.

Summing Up

OH is an experiential interpretation method to understand more fully the narrative genre in Scripture. It accomplishes this by focusing on the conversations, actions, and interactions of characters found in a biblical text. This ancient-modern art based in orality ponders passages of Scripture characterologically, considers the era, event(s), setting and surroundings, plot, attire, gestures, posture, direct and inward speech, symbols, rituals, conduct, conflicts, choices, and consequences of choices as characters embody and demonstrate (rather than define and explain) meaning. To discover the story's meaning it conducts character analysis (in contrast to textual analysis) through primarily character-centric questions (in contrast to content-centric) that follow the plotline. Multiple OH versions are presently in use globally.

While Christianity is based solidly on reason, it is not based solely on reason; we get there intuitively through God-given imagination and emotions, thereby making OH the preferred starting point for grasping the meaning of a story and the divine story. Emotional choices tend to precede rational choices, even as both are intertwined. The attachment center of the brain is where all relationships are formed and consist. This is how the brain works in relationships with others—we perceive and experience another person first in the fast track of the right brain from which character assessments and attunements are made. Only after these perceptions (which we have called "character thinking" in chapter 3) do we, when needed, analyze and compute facts logically, in the slower left-brain functions. It is the same as we relate to the characters in Scripture, or at least this can and should be the case. Oral hermeneutics helps facilitate such relationships. We attune to the character of biblical characters, and even become attached to them.

See chapter 2 for the reflections on how this worked in the "Elisha and the Widow's Oil" storytelling.

If God's word came to humanity first as oral text, and orality influenced how texts were written, discussed, interpreted, and remembered, and narrative and poetry (significant parts of orality) dominate the pages of Scripture, *would it seem unusual for narrative logic to be the philosophical underpinning of OH?* OH uses narrative logic to investigate the voices, actions, and interactions of Bible characters in search of authoritative, memorable, applicable truth. Stories that depict the struggles of characters gain our attention, raise questions, provide warning and hope, and create ongoing meaningful conversations. Oralists find narrative logic to be a very natural way to discover demonstrated biblical values, morals, and theology. With the help of the Holy Spirit, teachers, and others, creative-correct theology[95] can emerge (see figure 4.2).

A good story (or poem) does not end with a period. Rather, it ends by raising a host of unanswered questions that demand answers in the minds of listeners/readers/viewers. Think for example: *What was the response and ongoing life trajectory of the older son in the prodigal son story?* We are not told. It is up to you to use character thinking to imagine what may have been. These questions create curiosity, mystery, suspense, fascination, surprise, and often challenge the official sociocultural map. Good stories (like good poetry) end by beginning a creative, constructive, ongoing conversation in search of godly wisdom. The Eternal One's talking book is designed to do the same—it creates continued conversations to address all those nagging unanswered questions about life that clamor for answers. OH aids in the continued conversation through its strong focus on characters, imagination, emotion, and audience discussion.

OH not only investigates individuals in a single story, it is also interested in how all the individual stories and their controlling characters form a grand narrative. OH relies on the grand narrative of Scripture to safeguard the meaning of the individual parts and fight the fragmented understanding of Scripture so prevalent in the West today.

If Bible stories require a response, which we assume they do,[96] Scripture can make truth understandable to the listener/reader/viewer through the text itself, through teachers (Acts 8:30), other Jesus-followers, nonfollowers,

---

95. We are indebted to Arden Autry for the hyphenation of the terms "creative" and "correct." Interpretation includes some subjectivity as well as objectivity. "The language of the Bible does seem to have a dynamic quality not always exhausted by the author's original intention... The 'correct' reading serves the 'creative'; and the 'creative' measures itself by the 'correct'" (Autry, "Dimensions of Hermeneutics in Pentecostal Focus," 37, 49).

96. Ryken and Longman III, *Complete Literary Guide to the Bible*, 34.

and of course the Holy Spirit. Biblical historical times and settings will meet contemporary times and contexts revealing transgenerational and multigenerational biblical truths. OH embodies relational discourse across generations and social-cultural differences as it communally searches for divine truth, whether resulting in a single truth or multiple truths.

The ultimate goal of OH is God-honoring behavior and veneration. Bible character(s) who ring true become virtual close friends, helping facilitate this outcome. That is because, typically, *friends, not facts, change minds*.[97] The words and actions of these vicarious, trustworthy friends, unbridle the listeners'/readers'/viewers' imaginations and emotions,[98] thereby allowing transformative identification to occur and godly wisdom (Prov 9:10) to reshape lives.

The contribution OH has made to the world cannot be estimated and therefore should never be underestimated.

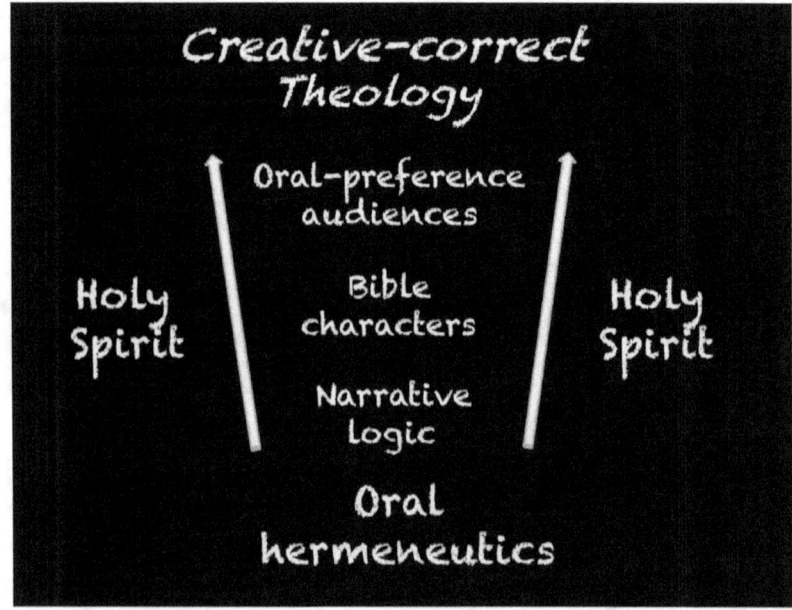

Figure 4.2. From Oral Hermeneutics to Creative-Correct Theology

---

97. Clear, "Why Facts Don't Change Our Minds."

98. "By questioning our feelings, we open ourselves up to question our stories. We challenge the comfortable conclusion that our story is right and true" (Patterson, *Critical Conversations*, 114).

Recalibrating Hermeneutic Assumptions

If Bible communicators are not to lose the richness that Scripture offers from the narrative sections, especially to oral and oral-preference audiences, another hermeneutic beyond TH will be required to complement it. This hermeneutic will be different and distinct, yet equally sophisticated. This is what we call oral hermeneutics (OH), with all its variations. For this addition to happen, some recalibration of basic hermeneutical assumptions is required. These recalibrations will include at least changing the following false assumptions where held:

> Orality had little to do with textual construction and teaching.
>
> Orality has little to do with interpreting Scripture.
>
> The ear and eye should be separated.
>
> Scripture is best read and understood when done personally and privately.
>
> The rational and cognitive supersede imagination and emotions.
>
> Propositions dominate Scripture without requiring a story base.
>
> All oral texts are "originals."
>
> Textual hermeneutic theories, emerging in the Enlightenment era, are sufficient and superior because they result in objective truth separated from the contaminants of subjectivism.
>
> Biblical authors have a single meaning in mind for the individual parts and the whole of their writing(s).
>
> The distinctive fragments of the text (grammar, phrases, individual words) and word studies are of *topmost* importance for discerning textual meaning.
>
> Topical studies supersede studies of complete books or letters or narratives.
>
> Belief in theology supersedes participation in theology.[99]

---

99. Commenting on Liberian revival evangelist and "prophet" William Wade Harris (1860–1929), Kwame Bediako notes he "appropriated the truth of the Bible not as patterns of 'belief in' the truth, but more in line with the African pattern of 'participation in' the truth" (Bediako, "Biblical Exegesis in Africa," 16). Harris is a celebrated and dynamic figure in the expansion of Christianity in Liberia, Ivory Coast, and Ghana in the early twentieth century. Mission historian Andrew Walls states that he "owed little in any direct way to church mission, and nothing from any commission to one. . . . Harris was convinced of his prophetic call, and he meditated deeply on Scripture, which,

Behind every assumption lie rival questions leading to better answers. *What are the foundational questions that surround a hermeneutic that wishes to resurrect oral forms of media?* Here are a few questions distilled from the above discussion:

> *Why should oral-preference people interact with a finished biblical text?*
>
> *Why should text-preference people interact with the oral basis of the biblical text?*
>
> *How does the spoken word differ from the written word in relation to inspiration?*
>
> *What components are required in an oral hermeneutic?*
>
> *How well does our preferred hermeneutic tie abstractness to concrete events (history)?*
>
> *Which hermeneutic portrays practice and participation best?*
>
> *What role should imagination and emotion have in interpretation?*
>
> *Because the Bible is earthy, historical, sensory, mysterious, how can we align our hermeneutics accordingly?*
>
> *How do we keep hermeneutics communally focused locally? globally?*
>
> *How does oral hermeneutics promote a holistic human experience?*[100]
>
> *How does oral hermeneutics help ensure textual meaning?*

---

as Shank shows, he read in a way quite different from that of the missionaries but one quite intelligible from within his own frame of reference. He called people to repentance; he persuaded thousands to abandon traditional African religious practices; he pointed them to the God of the Scriptures, which as yet they could not read." Walls, *Missionary Movement in Christian History*, 87–88. Harris's story is surely a testimony to the effectiveness of oral hermeneutics a century ago among non-Westerners.

100. Part of holism will include the discovery of themes or patterns within the story because "the story-pattern provides a map for construing the narrative as a whole, the themes forecast further developments both immediate and long-range" (Foley, *Oral Tradition in Literature*, 217). That is because, "the whole story is the meaning" (Ryken, *Words of Delight*, 19). The themes that comprise a story build a sense of the whole. For example, in the "Elisha and Widow's Oil" and "Elisha and General Naaman" stories in chapters 1 and 9, several themes converge—use what you have, and God will multiply it.

Why does it matter if the individual stories are not presented chronologically?

How does hearing or viewing the Bible depicted visually differ from reading the Bible?

How did orality influence textual construction?

How did orality influence how the text was taught in antiquity?

The above foundational rival questions find their basis in the multiple components that comprise orality, and by extension, OH. A partial list of these components would include:

1. **Delivery**

    Face-to-face dialogue where the ear and eye dominate

    Authority of the human author and spokesperson(s); the value of the word made fresh via human vehicles.

    Repetition of key words, names, phrases, expressions, characters, incidents,[101] topics, and themes

    Descriptions over definitions

    Sensory dialogue

    Concrete events/history preferred over conceptual ideas

    Indirectness over directness

    Rhythm and rhyme

    Pitch and pace

2. **Message**

    Contrasts/comparisons of paired characters (foils), names, taglines, and lineage

    Conflict-driven conversations, changes, and clashes between characters

    Observed (un)justifiable actions/practices in specific time(s) and setting(s)

---

101. Sternberg argues that "twice told stories" (e.g., Jacob and Esau [Gen 25:29–34 and Gen 27]) reinforce the author's point: "A series of two enables the narrative to strengthen, diversify, or balance the grounds for reversal and to draw out its execution" (Sternberg, "Time and Space in Biblical (Hi)story Telling," 127).

The relational value-moral system of honor-shame (privileges "we" over "I") tends to dominate in oral-based societies and the biblical text

3. **Meaning**

    Flexible meaning within textual parameters

    Imaginative resourcefulness

    Emotional connection

    Actions performed have societal implications

4. **Collectivism (vs. Individualism)**

    Communal interaction and accountability

    Collective consensus of meaning

    Collective participation in truth application

    Collective memory to maintain a communal faith tradition

5. **The Grand Narrative**

    Multiple episodic presentations comprise the big picture

    Individual stories sense, point to, and anticipate a grand narrative

    Individual stories echo back to former stories, thereby reviewing and advancing a grand narrative that guards all truth.

The authors will unpack many of these categories and components in the subsequent two chapters.

Fokkelman focuses our attention on something sad, "The most widely read book in the world is not necessarily the best-read book."[102] The authors would add, nor the best heard or best viewed. The above assumptions and oral components can help challenge and change that critique in that they call for a new (or is it really new?), sophisticated, legitimate, yet natural hermeneutic—an OH.

Is OH just another new fad or is it actually a return to ancient aspects of Hebrew hermeneutics that incorporate most, if not all, of the above components?

---

102. Fokkelman, *Reading Biblical Narrative*, Preface.

5

Hebrew Hermeneutics

"God made man because He loves stories."

—Elie Wiesel

We have titled this book *The Return of Oral Hermeneutics* with the intention to communicate that oral hermeneutics is not some new postmodern *fad-du-jour*. Rather, it is a very ancient approach to preaching, teaching, and interpreting Scripture that the ancient custodians of Scripture themselves—the Jewish rabbis and scholars—used. Yeshua (Hebrew for Jesus) said, "Every Torah scholar discipled for the kingdom of heaven is like the master of a household who brings out of his treasure both new things and old" (Matt 13:52 TLV). These old treasures of oral hermeneutics can be renewed with great effect in our day. By retrieving some ancient lost Hebraic treasure, we can benefit from what Bible teachers in the past found effective and see how their insights are especially relevant in our digital, postmodern, globalized, and "secondary orality" moment of history.

The authors want to now offer a perspective that comes from Hebraic thought and the Jewish interpretive tradition to illustrate the differences between *textual hermeneutics* (TH) and *oral hermeneutics* (OH).[1] The emphasis here will be on OH.

This chapter unfolds in this manner: the authors will show that Israel was a hearing-dominant society and that true hearing and heart-transformation correspond. The authors note how repetition, story, symbol, and ritual are integral to the annual feasts of Israel, effecting greater memory and transmission over generations. We then observe that the Hebrew language and Hebraic thought is concrete, relational, and experiential, rather than

1. Parts of this chapter are adapted from my (Bill) article titled "The Place of Story in Messianic Jewish Ministry," 3–37.

abstract, conceptual, and theoretical. It follows that Hebraic epistemology claims that *story* is a true, and in fact the ultimate, way of knowing. From there we look at the oral modality of the teaching and learning approach of the Jewish rabbis and Yeshua the Messiah. We then examine the power of story in biblical and Jewish tradition. Finally, we discuss the Jewish interpretive tradition and practice—Hebrew hermeneutics.

"Hear O Israel!"

Though shifting to a digital-screen-dominant culture, modern Western society is still a literacy- and text-dominant society; Israel was a hearing-dominant society. Though written or printed texts became very important later in Jewish history, the Hebraic tradition involves the hearing ear more than the distancing eye. Biblically, we see God always speaking personally to his people, not writing to them. The *Shema* reads: "Hear O Israel!" not "Read O Israel!" That Israel was a hearing-dominant society is in harmony with the way humans are made and how they most authentically communicate. In a major part of the Shema passage, God instructs the people this way:

> And these words that I command you today shall be on your heart. You shall teach them diligently to your children and shall talk of them when you sit in your house, and when you walk by the way, and when you lie down, and when you rise. You shall bind them as a sign on your hand, and they shall be as frontlets between your eyes. You shall write them on the doorposts of your house and on your gates. (Deut 6:4–9 ESV)

> "The *Shema* reads: 'Hear O Israel!' not 'Read O Israel!' That Israel was a hearing-dominant society is in harmony with the way humans are made and how they most authentically communicate."

Note the emphasis on repetition, and the oral telling of these truths in all situations of life, including the use of mnemonic devices (memory aids) that were visual and physical. These methods all aided the effort of inculcating them to heart. There are very few times in Scripture where God or Yeshua wrote anything: the Ten Commandments, the handwriting on the wall in Daniel, and Yeshua's writing in the sand in front of the woman caught in adultery. Yet the phrase "Thus *says* the Lord" is repeated over 400 times.

Presently, each year at Passover, the Jewish people are commanded to tell their children the story of the nation's founding—of God's awesome deliverance from Egypt. "You shall *tell* your son on that day" (Exod 13:8 NASB). Hence the Passover story and its oral retelling through the *Haggadah* (the telling) are an essential Jewish practice. The annual retelling of the story reinforces the Jewish people's identity as a nation and people. Passover includes ritual and symbolic foods. Virtually all the feasts of Israel provide an opportunity to retell one of the stories of God's gracious acts on behalf of his people, and they include ritual and symbol. Each of the Jewish feasts features the triad of story, symbol, and ritual.

Psalm 78 is a retelling of the story of Israel. This is a model liturgy for Israel and is what is practiced in most Jewish feasts—telling and retelling the story and stories of Israel from generation to generation. Many of the Psalms give a story sweep through Israel's story (e.g., Ps 76, 78, 105, 106:6–12, 136). And there is Psalms 78, this exhortation to keep on telling the story generation to generation:

> Psalm 78: A *maskil* of Asaf
>
> Listen, my people, to my teaching;
>
> turn your ears to the words from my mouth.
>
> I will speak to you in parables [Hebrew: "mashal," a wisdom saying, poem, or story]
>
> and explain mysteries from days of old.
>
> The things which we have heard and known,
>
> and which our fathers told us
>
> we will not hide from their descendants;
>
> we will tell the generation to come. (1–4 CJB)

Doctrinal formulation and systematization of theology as propositional dogmatics (as we prefer in the West) were alien to the Hebrews/Israelites of the biblical period. They favored the concrete and shunned the abstract. The theologians of Israel were primarily narrative theologians.

The God of Israel modeled for us how to embed something in the memory of a group or peoplehood. When God instructed Moses in matters pertaining to the ongoing tutelage of Israel, he tells Moses the reason for the great "Song of Moses" that will follow in Deuteronomy 32. This song proclaimed God's ways, his honor, his judgment, and his salvation. God wanted Israel to take this to heart, to hear it, to internalize it. So, he says, "Now write down this song and teach it to the Israelites and have them sing it ['by heart' MSG], so that it may be a witness for me against them" (Deut 31:19 NIV).

They were to learn the song by heart. So, the song of Moses is in memorable poetry and was to be formally articulated in ways to facilitate memorization by the community. It was to be sung, oralized. But we note also that it was to be written down.[2] The textual version of the poem was necessary for maintaining its permanence from generation to generation, to check its accuracy. Here we see the dynamic dialectic between the written word and the oralized word—the oralized word can be ephemeral, so must be preserved in writing. The written word is enduring but must be oralized.[3]

"Let Me Write the Songs of a Nation"

"Let me write the songs of a nation and I care not who writes their laws."

"Let me make the ballads of a nation, and I care not who makes its laws."

In discussing the song of Moses above, we can gainfully move to discuss the nature of song itself as it relates to communication theory and hermeneutics. The above two variations on this saying are attributed to Andrew Fletcher (1653–1716), a Scottish writer, politician, and patriot.[4] As a politician he was a keen observer of what it takes to start a movement of social change, even a revolution, in a society. Songs are surely more effective than laws to change the hearts and minds of the masses. Songs and stories embed in the heart; laws embed in the intellect, if they embed at all.

---

2. There are three forms of the word of God: (1) Yeshua the Messiah is the *Living Word, the Logos,* who became flesh (John 1:14). (2) The inspired canonical *written word*, which is the authoritative standard for the testing of truth in teaching for faith and life. (3) The oralized word, "Hear O Israel!" existed before the written word and completes its purpose. The purpose of the book of the Lord is to know the Lord of the book. Yeshua delivered his teaching orally and it was transmitted orally (he said his words are "spirit and life"); he did not write a book.

3. The Pauline Epistles were circulated and read orally aloud in the churches. When the apostle John sent the letters to the seven churches of Asia Minor, here were the instructions, "Favored is the one who reads the words of this prophecy out loud, and favored are those who listen to it being read, and keep what is written in it, for the time is near" (Rev 1:3 CEB). Reading the Scriptures is not exactly equal to listening to God. To do the former is not *necessarily* to do the latter. Atheists can read Scripture. Hearing the word out loud is more arresting than reading it; the reader of a text controls the time, the place, and the pace of reading. One who listens is summoned to hear and respond.

4. Sometimes attributed to Plato, but likely mistakenly so. Fletcher has the strongest claim. https://en.wikiquote.org/wiki/Andrew_Fletcher. https://historeo.com/web/?tag=andrew-fletcher.

The God of Israel wanted to inculcate the song of Moses into the hearts of the people so that having internalized it—"by heart"—their old cultural ways would change and they would live out his new ethical ways, thus becoming an examplary society, a "light to the nations." For a culture change phenomenon from our times, consider how powerfully the music of the 1960s (the debut of rock and roll to the masses) both expressed and shaped the culture then and until now (the moral character of the shaping is not the point). It is often underestimated just how powerfully that music shaped late-modern culture.[5]

King Saul, Israel's first monarch, found this out as the increasingly storied David was celebrated in the streets, the women singing and dancing to, "Saul has slain his thousands, and David his ten thousands" (1 Sam 18:7 NKJV). The story became a ballad that permeated and mobilized the whole culture, and songs emerged from the hearts of the people. King Saul correctly observed after this, that "Now what more can he [David] have but the kingdom" (1 Sam 18:8b NKJV)? Saul's law had been overtaken by the songs of the people. David had captured their hearts.

The Psalms are Israel's songbook. These songs have arguably shaped the nation of Israel and the people of God more than the laws of the Torah. They have been profitably put to music ever since the days of King David by Jews and later by Christians. John Calvin said he was accustomed to call the Psalms "'An Anatomy of All Parts of the Soul' for there is not an emotion of which anyone can be conscious of that is not here represented as in a mirror."[6] This feature of the Psalms is a major reason for their endurance and widespread popularity in every Jewish and Christian tradition. They help us express our souls vertically to God.

What if musicians could put the stories of Scripture into the contemporary and beloved and popular forms of music as inspired ballads,[7] and into more

---

5. Award-winning British documentary film maker Leslie Woodhead produced a documentary entitled "How the Beatles Rocked the Kremlin" aired by the British Broadcasting Company (BBC). http://www.thirteen.org/beatles/video/video-watch-how-the-beatles-rocked-the-kremlin/. In 2009, WNET, a radio station, produced the documentary, showing how the Beatles' music was a strong factor contributing to the collapse of the USSR. The film argues persuasively that their music—banned in the USSR and bootlegged by Russian teenagers—inspired dreams of hope and freedom of expression for a whole generation, which eventually helped lead to the collapse of communism. Little did the dour totalitarian rulers of the USSR know that their iron laws would be brought down at least in part by songs. A good story is powerful in itself. Put it to music and verse and it heightens the power to cast vision, to inspire, and to motivate social groups. If you want to know what people hold as valuable, investigate their songs. See King, *Music in the Life of the African Church*.

6. Calvin, *John Calvin's Bible Commentaries on the Psalms 1–35*, 19.

7. See King, *Global Arts and Christian Witness*.

dramatic visual and film media to express these stories (which reach all parts of the soul) in society today and in each generation? Concerned with long-term memory, OH also relies heavily on the auditory and visual worlds.

The Hebrew Language is Concrete, Relational, and Experiential

The language of the Old Testament is Hebrew. The Hebrew language has at least three characteristics relevant to orality, as it is: (1) concrete, (2) relational, and (3) reflects experiential knowledge.

Hebrew is Concrete

From the very beginning, in the account of creation, God pronounced the created physical world "very good" (Gen 1:31 NIV). This has echoed down through Jewish history in the Jewish affirmation of life, *"L'Chaim!"* Marvin Wilson quotes George Adam Smith as saying:

> Hebrew may be called primarily a language of the senses. The words originally expressed concrete or material things and movements or actions which struck the senses or started the emotions. Only secondarily and *in metaphor* could they be used to denote abstract or metaphysical ideas.[8]

Examples of graphic, vivid use of concrete language to communicate abstract concepts include the following: to look is to "lift up the eyes" (Gen 22:4 ESV); to be angry is to "burn in one's nostrils" (Exod 4:14 in the Hebrew); to have no compassion is "hard-heartedness" (1 Sam 6:6 NIV); to be stubborn is to "stiffen your neck" (2 Chr 30:8 NAS); to be determined is "to really set your mind" (Jer 42:15 NAS).

There are also the anthropomorphisms of the living God of the Hebrews. He is not a distant, ethereal deity, but a concrete person: "Behold, the LORD's hand is not shortened, that it cannot save, or his ear dull, that it cannot hear" (Isa 59:1 ESV). Also, "the eyes of the LORD are in every place" (Prov 15:3 NKJV). These concrete images are common in Hebrew.[9] Stories tell real events and actions relayed by the sensory experience of the storyteller. Often metaphors and similes from the vernacular are the most expressive terms at hand.

---

8. Wilson, *Our Father Abraham*, 137.
9. Wilson, *Our Father Abraham*, 137.

Hebrew is Relational in Terms and Perceptions

Why is orality (the oral-aural process) so singularly valuable? It is due to the interpersonal-relational dimension that is the basis of orality. *Would you rather read a joke or have it told to you?* We think you will say, "Have it told." Right? The joke is told with paralinguistic features, such as tone, inflections, sounds, eye and eyebrow behavior, and gestures that bring it to life. And it's relational—you have someone with whom to share the laugh.

German Jewish philosopher Martin Buber (1878–1965), in his classic work, *I and Thou*, explains that "I-Thou" encounters with persons are fundamentally different than "I-It" relationships with things.[10] Persons know other persons by encounter (character assessment, attunement, and attachment). A major theme of Buber's book (and which is certainly biblical) is that human life finds its greatest meaning in relationships with other persons.

Storytelling is inherently relational. A story is told *by* someone *to* someone. The hearers of the story vicariously encounter the characters in the story, identify with them because of interconnectedness, and have emotional and moral responses to them (positively or negatively), sometimes in life-changing ways. The relationship between teller and hearer is direct, instantaneous, powerful, and personal.

Hebrew Reflects Experiential Knowledge

When thinking about God, Israelites do not ask, *"What is divinity?"* (the philosophical essence of divine being). Rather they ask, *"Who is Yahweh?"* The Hebrew word *yada* refers to an experiential knowing, more than to mere cerebral cognition. Genesis 4:1 says, "Now Adam knew (*yada*) Eve his wife, and she conceived and bore Cain" (NKJV). That is indeed personal, experiential knowledge. "And this is eternal life, that they may know You, the only true God, and *Yeshua* the Messiah, the One You sent" (John 17:3 TLV). Stories relay real-life experiences, encounters, first-hand experiences, and often the accounts of eyewitnesses. The more direct the experience, the more impact it has.

Like the Hebrew language, OH focuses its attention on concrete, experiential relationships to ascertain clarity of meaning; it analyzes their descriptions, conversations, and actions. These three characteristics—concreteness, relational, experiential—of the Hebrew language are commensurate with the Hebraic epistemology.

---

10. See Buber, *I and Thou*.

Hebraic Epistemology: Story as a Way of Knowing

In contrast to the European Enlightenment epistemology of *disengaged reason*,[11] *Hebraic epistemology is receptive of divine revelation and is a narrative epistemology* that embraces story as a way of knowing. A story—in its whole telling and hearing—imparts a quality of psychological and intuitive knowledge, a thicker description of reality, than can lists or abstracted statements derived from it. As Gordon Shaw states, "We dream, not in bullet points, but in narratives."[12]

Professor of Old Testament Walter Brueggemann (b. 1933), widely considered one of the most influential Old Testament scholars of the last few decades, recognized the importance of narrative as a way of knowing. He is known for his advocacy and practice of rhetorical criticism which studies how the elements of oral speech—in oral performances, films, and discourse in general—work to affect and influence people through imagery, symbols, body language, and other rhetorical elements.

This, of course, has everything to do with orality, storytelling, and OH. Brueggemann's emphasis on the importance of knowing through oral methods brought into question the core categories of modernity and the Enlightenment and how the Enlightenment epistemology had become a "tyranny of positivism," generating "models of knowledge"[13] that are thought to be

---

11. In order to compare and contrast the dominant modern Western epistemology (the study of how we know what we know, or the ways of knowing) with the Hebraic epistemology, I (Bill) will first describe the Enlightenment epistemology. A major epistemological shift from medieval knowledge and learning to modern science (empiricism and rationalism) as the major way of knowing occurred during the European Enlightenment of the eighteenth century. It was a shift from reliance on authority as moral sources (Scripture, religious tradition, established venerated philosophers), to empirical observation (and application of the new rational scientific method of inquiry to interpret the data of experience) as the primary source of knowledge. The results of the new science then became the new dominant public source of authority in the West for several centuries, weakened only somewhat with the postmodern shift. The moral sources, in this case epistemological, become disengaged reason [Definition: The concept of reason or rationality disengaged from external, objective and transcendent verities and/or moral absolutes that had served as guideposts (touchstones, anchors, tethers) for the practice of rationality and the ascertaining knowledge] and the deliverances of such reason via the highly acclaimed modern scientific method. Disengaged reason became supreme in Enlightenment thought such that all knowledge and any alleged authority had to pass the bar of this now-presumed omnicompetent reason. Starting from itself, this rationality was assumed to be able to ascertain certain, universally true, and objective knowledge. Reason was presumed to be unconditioned and to operate from a totally neutral vantage point.

12. Shaw, quoted in Seymour, *Creating Stories that Connect*, 24.

13. Bradt, *Story as a Way of Knowing*, 121.

objective and neutral but are actually dominating. For example, educated Westerners are inclined to lend credibility more to statistics in a textbook than we are to an oral presentation. Brueggemann has championed that aspect of the postmodern critique and postmodern epistemological shift that allows for a loosening from the oppression and reductionism of the scientific method of modern rationalism (or positivism).

Brueggemann scholar and psychotherapist Kevin Bradt has researched and written on story as a way of knowing. Much of his research focused on Brueggemann's work on Israel's storying. Bradt observes when Enlightenment thought became dominant:

> Debates raged about the historical facticity behind the biblical texts while the study of Israel's rhetorical practices, her long traditions of alternative speech, orality, and storying went into eclipse. Now all the wonderful, messy, contradictory narrative particularities of the biblical stories were seen only as intellectual embarrassments.[14]

Brueggemann discovered how a narrative epistemology could sustain a community's sense of hope and history in the face of systemic repression and violence. Through Israel's tradition of storying, a defiant, shared imagination powerful enough to activate an alternative future reality had been born.[15]

Bradt is referring to Israel's sojourn as slaves in Egypt and how Israel's story (transmitted from their patriarchs) was an alternative story to the dominant mythic story propounded by the Pharaohs to legitimize and absolutize by their imperial state power. Israel's story defied Pharaoh's story. That mythopoetic ideology was the official sociology of knowledge that dominated the civilization of that era. For people in Egypt there was no alternative story to that of the Pharaohs.

But Israel had another story! And it empowered their dissent. They defied an empire and changed the world. Out of their story, the story of the Exodus was able to occur, the story of the birth of the nation that would impact human civilization more than any other story in history. It was the story—or more accurately, the true and living God of Israel's story—that not only liberated and transformed Israel, but defeated imperial Egypt, the most powerful nation on earth. Bradt continues, "The story of Israel and the land could not be reduced to a thesis. Only the narrative tension

---

14. Bradt, *Story as a Way of Knowing*, 127.
15. Bradt, *Story as a Way of Knowing*, 129.

of the stories could hold together the complexity of the revelation of God's relationship with Israel."[16]

For Brueggemann, the stories of the Bible reveal a relationship between Israel and her God that is so complex, inexhaustible, and fraught with all kinds of confusion, dark mystery, and shocking tensions that to try to reconcile what must ultimately remain irreconcilable can only be an exercise in futility and madness. It is only narrative modes of knowing and relationship that can embrace and tolerate such ambiguity, wonder, paradox, pain, grief, and surprise; it is only an alternative imagination called into existence through storying that can help us understand Israel's situation as a model of our own in this postmodern age.[17]

Brueggemann calls story "Israel's primal mode of knowing."[18] Story is the foundation from which come all other knowledge claims; "story can be told as a base line."[19]

> "For people in Egypt there was no alternative story to that of the Pharaohs. But Israel had another story! It empowered their dissent. They defied an empire and changed the world. Out of their story, the story of the Exodus was able to occur, the story of the birth of the nation that would impact human civilization more than any other story in history. It was *the story*—or more accurately, *the true and living God of Israel's story*—that not only liberated and transformed Israel, but defeated imperial Egypt, the most powerful nation on earth."

The Hebrew slaves lived out of an alternative worldview, an alternative consciousness that enabled them to defy a totalitarian state power through faith in the God of their story. Their story has since empowered other oppressed people throughout history, e.g., the African-American slaves in the antebellum South of the United States. Many of us know the negro spirituals which sang of that overcoming faith, e.g., "Heaven Boun' Soldier." We might think of "We Shall Overcome," a protest song that became a key anthem of the African-American Civil Rights Movement (1955–1968).

What Israel knows is if the story is not believed, nothing added to it will make any difference—not more commandments, rituals, or laws. Israel knows that pain, like story, can never be abstract or universal, so she trusts

---

16. Bradt, *Story as a Way of Knowing*, 131.
17. Bradt, *Story as a Way of Knowing*, 131–32.
18. Bradt, *Story as a Way of Knowing*, 15.
19. Bradt, *Story as a Way of Knowing*, 15.

the expressions of both. Israel knows long after all the dissertations have been read, defended, and forgotten, her stories will remain. It is her mission.[20] "Story in Israel is the bottom line. It is told and left, and not hedged about by other evidences . . . Israel understands them not as instruments of something else, but as castings of reality."[21]

In this vein, Rabbi Michael Goldberg states, "there is no issue of theological substance detachable from the stories' substance. That is, these recountings of the Exodus and the Christ story are not fables, such that once their point or moral has been gleaned, the actual narratives can then be discarded."[22] We cannot cash in the stories for some abstracted universal timeless truth that leaves the story behind. There is not some pure kernel of truth that we should extract and leave the story-husk in the refuse.

Like Hebrew epistemology, OH recognizes that meaning is mined from the story. It values a story's wholeness, knowing it is through such that we learn to know not only our own stories, but his story as well. OH treasures the possibilities of a new, sustainable identity through knowledge gained from the stories of others.

Hebraic Logic

In our discussion of narrative logic in the previous chapter, we touched on the various types of logic. Anthropologist Paul Hiebert describes five types: algorithmic, analogical, topological, relational, and evaluative. We in the modern West have majored in the first two, originating from the Greek and Enlightenment heritage. So dominant have they been that many moderns think these linear, binary, and syllogistic forms are the *only* kind of logic that exist. The Hebrews/Israelites, however, majored in the fourth and fifth types.

Relational Logic

In much of the world, people define reality in relational terms. So, a man is the husband of Mary, father of Peter and Lois, grandfather of Mark and Helen. As the oldest male, he is the head of his clan, and a village elder. Traditional societies around the world use this concrete, functional, relational logic, whereas modern Westerners use a more abstract logic. So, in the modern West the man might more likely be described by his age, gender,

---

20. Bradt, *Story as a Way of Knowing*, 157.
21. Bradt, *Story as a Way of Knowing*, 162.
22. Goldberg, *Jews and Christians*, 15.

ethnicity, height, weight, and profession, rather than by his functional relationships, such as described above.

Evaluative Logic (or Wisdom)

This form of reasoning may draw on any logic above but makes a considered assessment of a matter based on the knowledge at hand, on past experience, or other factors that might be involved, in order to evaluate a situation or matter at hand. The Hebrew Scriptures are full of the wisdom found in proverbs (short sentences drawn from long experiences), stories, parables, fables, riddles, jokes, and creative literature, all of which arise from evaluative logic.[23]

These descriptions converge well with and are actually featured in "narrative logic" as defined in chapter 4 by Fisher.[24] Narrative rationality observed in the flow of the story about real life as it rings true in characters as they relate to each other, and in what Fisher terms "characterological coherence"[25] (the characters are authentic, convincing, believable). So, TH generally uses a more formal logic and intellectual tools needed to analyze texts. Like Hebraic logic, OH uses narrative logic as the stories of the characters featured in Scripture are brought to life in oral tellings and in group discussion.

The Rabbis and Oral Learning and Teaching

The existence of the Rabbinic tradition of oral Torah (*Torah sh b' al peh*) with its expansions and explanations of the written Torah, though it was later put into writing, is testimony to Jewish awareness of the need for texts to be oralized and for the word of God to reach into and speak to the ongoing human social situations that arise in the complexities of life in the succeeding time periods. The oral origins of Rabbinic literature and its study are quite clear:

> Even when put into writing, it remained a record of oral discussions going on among multiple personalities . . . . In a *rabbinic* work, each contribution quoted comes originally from an oral context . . . and even if there are intermediate written sources,

---

23. Hiebert, *Transforming Worldviews*, 39–44.
24. Fisher, *Human Communication as Narration*, 47.
25. Fisher, *Human Communication as Narration*, 47.

none of these sources has lost its oral atmosphere or its character as a record of oral discussions.[26]

Yeshua's Oral Forms of Teaching

We might classify academic systematic theologians as "conceptual theologians" in that they use more abstract and philosophical concepts and logic in their theologizing. This is not to say that conceptual theologizing and writing is wrong or without value. But in the modern West, we have often majored in the conceptual in theological education, to the neglect of the more Hebraic concrete and narrative approach. Yeshua, by contrast, was not a conceptual theologian.

> Jesus was a *metaphorical* theologian. That is, his primary method of creating meaning was through metaphor, simile, parable, and dramatic action rather than through logic and reasoning. He created meaning like a dramatist and a poet rather than like a philosopher.[27]

For example, we are told that at a specific point in his ministry, when it was clear that the religious leaders were out to reject him, he shifted to parables so that only those with "ears to hear" would understand his message. "He did not say a thing to them without using a parable; when he was alone with his own *talmidim* he explained everything to them" (Mark 4:34 CJB).

Was Yeshua then but a simple teller of folktales for fisherman and farmers? Hardly. *Could Yeshua have given the most erudite, learned, scholarly lecture of any of his contemporaries? Or ours?* Of course! When he was twelve years old he amazed the learned rabbis in the Temple with the profundity of his knowledge and wisdom (Luke 3:46). He was the most profound of theologians. But his primary teaching method was through stories, word pictures, and metaphors.

A metaphor communicates in ways that a rational argument cannot. A word or concept takes on meaning when we have a clear image with which to connect it. Recent studies in neuroscience confirm this—specific parts of the brain light up when words stimulate images in the brain, and hence meaning occurs. And when the listener or disciple discovers the meaning himself/ herself (the Aha moment), then s/he retains that truth much better, owning it! If facts are spoon-fed by lecture or monologue to a more passive mind or

---

26. Maccoby, *Early Rabbinic Writings*, 8 (emphasis original).
27. Bailey, *Jesus Through Middle Eastern Eyes*, 279 (emphasis original).

a mind that cannot connect a propositional concept to an image (imagine it), they may go in one ear and out the other.

Yeshua's use of stories as his primary teaching method was not merely due to his cultural context; rather, story is a universal means of communicating. Yeshua knew that stories are what stick in hearts and minds because they address intellect, imagination, and emotions, thereby engaging the whole brain. In short, stories grip the heart (the metonomy used in Scripture to refer to one's whole brain, conscience and sensorium, one's core and whole consciousness), and as the proverb says, "out of the heart are the issues of life" (Prov 4:23 NKJV).

Another major reason Yeshua's method of choice for teaching is story is that a lecture often only speaks to the intellectual cognition; it provides data or information that may or may not affect that person's heart or will. By contrast, a story with its characters with whom the story hearers will identify, either positively or negatively, evokes response—a heart response. Thus, the story stirs and stimulates moral responses that can lead to change and character growth in the listener. Yeshua sought moral decisions and character transformation in his followers.

Regarding orality and Yeshua, the authors find it relevant that "In the beginning was the Word" (John 1:1 NKJV). In the Greek lexicon of the New Testament, the Greek word *logos* is denoted as an "utterance, chiefly oral."[28] In the modern West, we tend to think of it as a written word on a page. "The evidence from the Gospels is unanimous about the word 'word.' When the context was the ministry of Jesus, *logos* (or *rhema*) denoted speech."[29] And speech implies an event.

The oral origins of the four Gospels are evident within the gospels. It was not until at least twenty years after Yeshua's public ministry that the first written accounts were inscribed. Yeshua's teachings were delivered orally and transmitted orally. His delivery system as a teacher was face to face and oral. His teaching methods were predominantly nonformal, mostly among the *am ha aretz* (the people of the land) in the villages and countryside. But, with his chosen twelve, it was also highly intensive, twenty-four hours per day, life on life; an apprenticeship model with much coaching and personal mentoring, and therefore highly oral and without the aid of books or classroom lectures. Yeshua did not write a single book—he did not need to. He stated, "The words I speak to you are spirit and they are life" (John 6:63b NKJV). Apparently, it was sufficient for Yeshua that his oral texts remain oral.

---

28. Arndt and Gingrich, *Greek-English Lexicon*, s.v., "Logos."
29. Walton and Sandy, *Lost World of Scripture*, 127.

Yeshua taught using many questions and stories, with a cohort of twelve adult learners for discussion learning. His method was effective, such that at the end of the three short years of training, Yeshua was able to report to his Father, "For I have given them the words which you have given to me; and they have received them . . ." (John 17:8a NKJV). The young leaders Yeshua trained went on to change the world. A simple application for Bible communicators today is the necessity to recover the lost treasures of storytelling and the oral and relational teaching methods of Yeshua.

Like the three years of Yeshua's oral teaching, most of what was finally put into writing was *first* expressed orally. Even when the oral became print, the speech-sourced writing reflected a strong oral bias, including the New Testament Epistles. This fact makes it natural for us to oralize it today.

Insights from a Rabbi about the Power of Story

Rabbi Jacob ben Wolf Kranz of Dubno, known as the "Dubner Maggid," was a Lithuanian-born preacher who lived from 1740 to 1804. *Maggid* is Hebrew for "storyteller" (from the same Hebrew root as *Aggadah* and *Haggadah*). A contemporary of the Vilna Gaon, the Dubner Maggid was famous for explaining Torah concepts by using a *mashal* or parable. Moses Mendelssohn named Kranz, "the Jewish Aesop."[30] The Dubner Maggid was once asked: "Why do you always tell stories? Why are stories so powerful?" Kranz's legendary reply was to answer by telling a story:

> There was once a poor old woman. She was, well . . . ugly . . . very ugly. She had a bent back and hooked nose. Her chin was covered with warts and pimples. Her eyes bugged out. Her mouth was crooked, and her teeth broken. She dressed in old rags that smelled. No one would listen to what she said or even look at her. If they saw her they would run away . . . slam doors in her face. So, she was very sad because all she wished for was some company, some companionship. But no one would pay attention to her or talk to her. So, she wandered from place to place looking for friends.
>
> She crossed a great desert and came to a city in the middle of the desert. She thought to herself, "Surely I'll find friends in this city. People in the desert know how hard life is and will take pity on me, and I'll find a friend." But, alas, this city was like all the rest. People ran away and slammed doors or closed their shutters. No one would talk to her or listen to her. She became

---

30. Steinbarg, *Jewish Book of Fables*, xii.

very upset. "Why go on? What's the point? Life is too hard. I think I should just give up on life." So she wandered out of the city and sat down on the dusty road just outside the city. She waited, watching life pass her by.

Before long a good-looking young man dressed in beautiful clothes arrived in the city and received a great reception. The people came out to shake his hand. Some even hugged him. They brought him food and drink and lavished him with gifts. The old woman said, "Life is so unfair. When you are young and good looking, everyone loves you, but when you are old, ugly, and sick, they forget you and ignore you. It is so unfair!" After a while the young man gathered up his gifts, said "Good-bye," and headed out of the city. He stopped on the dusty road and sat down opposite the old woman to pack up his gifts.

The old woman could keep her tongue no longer, "What is going on? What's with you? Is it like this everywhere you go? Do you always get treated so well?"

The young man blushed and said, "Well . . . yes . . . I guess . . . Everywhere I go they treat me well."

"Well, why? Why?! You must be someone special! Someone extraordinary," said the old woman.

The young man said, "Oh, no, Ma'am! Actually, I am quite ordinary."

"I don't believe it. You must be an emperor, a king in disguise, or a prince or a general," she said.

"Oh no . . . I am not like that . . . I am very common. You find me everywhere—me and my type," he said.

"Well then, what are you?" asked the old woman. "Who are you that people are so happy to see you when you come along?"

"Well, I am a Story, and I think I am a pretty good Story at that. Because people like a good story they are happy to see me. But, old woman, what are you? Who are you? Why don't people like to see you?" asked the young man.

"Ah, that is the problem. It's what I am. I am Truth, and nobody likes to hear the truth."

(Narrator: This may seem a bit strange to some . . . but when you think about it what the old woman said is really true, isn't it? . . . If someone said to you, "I'm going to tell you what your friends really say behind your back. Do you really want to hear it? If you are destined to die a horrible death, or to die early, do you really want to know the truth about that now? No, some truth is ugly, especially truth about ourselves. We avoid it, we resist it, we don't want to know it. We welcome Story but we reject the Naked Truth.)

The young man said, "I'm sorry about that." He then began to think how he could help the old woman. "I've got an idea, old woman," he said. "Let's team up . . . let's journey together! You and I can travel together and wherever I go, you'll go. Anything I am given, I'll share with you."

"That won't work," she said. "They'll see me. They'll take one look and run away from both of us!"

"No, you don't understand! You'll hide behind me—behind my cloak. Whatever they give me I'll share equally with you. Let's try it."

The woman agreed, and they partnered up and travelled together. Wherever they went, the old woman hid behind the young man's cloak, and anything he was given he happily shared with the old woman.

This worked out so well that their arrangement lasts to this very day. That is why to this very day the truth always hides behind a good story.[31]

Just as Rabbi Jacob ben Wolf Kranz assumed stories were a powerful means of unlocking truth, so OH assumes truth is discernable and can be discovered through stories.

The Nathan Principle

What follows is a biblical example of truth hiding behind a good story. Imagine with me: had Nathan the prophet approached King David, after his sin with Bathsheba, and told him the propositional truth, "You have committed adultery and murder, O King. You have broken four of the Ten Commandments" (Bjoraker paraphrase), *would the king have readily received this truth?* Likely not. He may have rid himself of this troublesome prophet. Off with his head! He did not want to hear the ugly, naked truth. But instead of presenting him with the naked truth, Nathan told him a story:

> There were two men in a certain city, the one rich and the other poor. The rich man had very many flocks and herds, but the poor man had nothing but one little ewe lamb, which he had bought. And he brought it up, and it grew up with him and with his children. It used to eat of his morsel and drink from his cup and lie in his arms, and it was like a daughter to him. Now there came a traveler to the rich man, and he was unwilling to take

---

31. This is Bjoraker's version of the tale originally told by Rabbi Jacob ben Wolf Kranz of Dubno, but that is told in many variants, often under the title "Truth and Parable."

one of his own flock or herd to prepare for the guest who had come to him, but he took the poor man's lamb and prepared it for the man who had come to him. (2 Sam 12:1–14 ESV)

This story brought David into a house and figuratively opened a window for him to see. He vividly saw the injustice done. David bought into the story. He was caught in the powerful rhetorical trap of the story. The king became enraged and said, "As the LORD lives, the man who has done this shall surely die! And he shall restore fourfold for the lamb, because he did this thing and because he had no pity" (2 Sam 12:5, 6 NKJV). David thus judged himself. Nathan said, "You are the man!" (Bjoraker paraphrase) Nathan opened a window that became a mirror to David. Herein is the power of story to bring truth home to the heart and core of a person.

A story is an oblique way of coming at truth and helpful in getting past the defenses of a hearer or audience. Bible storyteller and trainer, the late Dorothy Miller, called this "the Nathan Principle,"[32] and added this verse as explicating its effect, "See, the word of God is alive! It is at work and is sharper than any double-edged sword—it cuts right through to where soul meets spirit and joints meet marrow, and it is quick to judge the inner reflections and attitudes of the heart" (Heb 4:12 CJB).[33]

In thinking of communication of messages as taking a route from source to receptor, direct route communication and processing uses logical argumentation; whereas a peripheral route circumvents argumentation, uses narrative logic, and goes to a deeper place in the heart. This is critically needed in Jewish evangelism because of the high resistance among Jewish people to direct communication of the gospel. This is the Nathan Principle.

Like the Nathan Principle, OH builds its uniqueness and strength on its ability to take us by surprise through the words and deeds of others rather than the directly declared propositional statement. We do not just hear something—as did David, we discover we cannot stop listening to it and acting upon it! It grips us at a deeper level than left-brain cognition.

Seventy Faces of the Torah and the Orchard

Though the rabbis are better known for their laws and statutes, the authors have been focusing in this chapter on the ancient and continuous biblical, Jewish, and rabbinic storytelling tradition—the *Aggadic/Haggadic* (Hebrew

---

32. http://simplythestory.org/oralbiblestories/index.php/practitioner-audio.html. Dorothy Miller was the founder of Simply the Story (STS).

33. See Miller, *Simply the Story Handbook*.

for "telling") tradition—whose focus is on the literary-artistic, the aesthetic, the emotionally and relationally expressive, the holistic, and on metaphor, imagery, and story.[34] The "people of the book" are the people of the story.

In Jewish tradition, the Torah has seventy faces. Hebrew scholar John Parsons explains:

> 'The Torah has 70 faces.' This phrase is sometimes used to indicate different 'levels' of interpretation of the Torah. 'There are seventy faces to the Torah: Turn it around and around, for everything is in it' (Bamidbar Rabbah 13:15). The Torah is a work of literary art, written by the LORD Himself, and therefore shares characteristics with all other works of art.[35]

"Seventy Faces" will be seen as hyperbole for those holding to a grammatical-historical hermeneutic alone. And indeed, hermeneutical controls and tethers must be applied so as not to fall into a free-for-all mode. However, the notion of the seventy faces of the Torah jolts us moderns away from the only-one-true meaning literalist mode when dealing with biblical stories and is a reminder of the depth and riches of the inspired word of God. When interpreting the nonnarrative genre, like the law codes of Leviticus or the logical, more linear Pauline letters (Romans being a favorite), careful historical-grammatical exegesis must be used. However, in contrast, stories require more than just historical-grammatical exegesis; they often have multiple, many-faceted interpretations and applications, depending on the audience hearing the story.[36]

The major Jewish and rabbinical hermeneutical tradition goes by the acronym PaRDeS (*peshat, remez, darash,* and *sod*). Nicely, the Hebrew word

---

34. "*Aggadah* or *Haggadah* (Heb. הַגָּדָה, אַגָּדָה; "telling," "narrative"), one of the two primary components of Rabbinic tradition, the other being *halakhah*, usually translated as 'Jewish Law.' . . . The *Aggadah* comprehends a great variety of forms and content. It includes narrative, legends . . . its forms and modes of expression are as rich and colorful as its content. Parables and allegories, metaphors and terse maxims; lyrics, dirges, and prayers, biting satire and fierce polemic, idyllic tales and tense dramatic dialogues, hyperboles and plays on words, permutations of letters, calculations of their arithmetical values (*gematria*) or their employment as initials of other words (*notarikon*)—all are found in the *Aggadah*" (Jewish Virtual Library, "Encyclopedia Judaica," para. 1).

35. Parsons, "Seventy Faces of Torah," para. 1.

36. For example, the story of Mephibosheth in 2 Samuel 9 demonstrates the same powerful truth about how to treat the vulnerable and the meaning of God's covenant in ways that would have felt very different to King David and his close aids, Ziba, Mephibosheth, the house of Saul who had lost the war, and to the Philistines who were learning that this was a whole different kind of kingdom than they had known. The core truths of the story (loyalty, mercy, and kindness for the vulnerable) can be stated propositionally, but story invites us to deeper contemplation of how that truth applies, what it means in application, and how it is experienced among diverse audiences.

for "orchard" is "pardes" which offers the helpful image of the Bible as a fruitful orchard with truths to be picked from the trees of the supernatural Scriptures like ripe fruit. Here are the definitions:

> *Peshat* (פְּשָׁט)—"plain" ("simple"), literal, direct meaning—the historical-grammatical interpretation. This is the on-the-face-of-it reading; like you would read a newspaper article. It simply says what it means and means what it says, on the surface of it.
>
> *Remez* (רֶמֶז)—"hints" at a deeper (allegoric, symbolic or typological) meaning beyond just the literal sense; type and anti-type. Careful Christian scholars have found many allusions and hints of Yeshua the Messiah in the Hebrew Scriptures.
>
> *Derash* (דְּרַשׁ)—"inquire" ("seek")—the interpretative, applicational teaching (midrashic) meaning (a *darasha* is a homily or sermon).
>
> *Sod* (סוֹד)—"secret" ("mystery") or the mystical, esoteric meaning. Proceed with caution at this level. The Kabbalah (the Jewish mystical tradition) is rife with this approach and takes fanciful flights to mysterious (and sometimes occultic) realms. It needs tethers, controls, and discernment.

Those with an evangelical view of Scripture can learn much from the first three levels but will find difficulty with the fourth level.

Before discussing two of these forms in more detail, the authors refer to an insight and writing theory of one of the greatest literary figures of the twentieth century, which reinforces and aligns with the Jewish PARDES hermeneutic—Ernest Hemingway (1899–1961). Hemingway received the Nobel Prize for Literature in 1954 when he asserted the "iceberg theory."[37] An iceberg is only one-eighth above the water, whereas seven-eighths are invisible below the water. The words on the page are only part of the story. The rest, the underwater part of the iceberg, is always just beneath the surface, giving life and depth to what is written. Hemingway held that only the tip of the iceberg shows in good fiction—your reader will see only what is above the water—but the knowledge you have about your character that never makes it into the story acts as the bulk of the iceberg. However, a

---

37. "I always try to write on the principle of the iceberg. There is seven-eights of it underwater for every part that shows. Anything you know you can eliminate and it only strengthens your iceberg. It is the part that doesn't show. If a writer omits something because he does not know it then there is a hole in the story—Ernest Hemingway" (Plimpton, "Ernest Hemingway," 26).

perceptive reader will detect what you the author know. And that is what gives your story weight and gravitas.

What is not said by the writer—but somehow emanates through, is implied but left for the reader to imagine—was to Hemingway the mark of the good short story. Hence his writing style is terse and compressed. Though its origin is disputed, and it is something of an urban legend, this six-word short story (often used by writing teachers) is attributed to Hemingway: "For Sale, Baby Shoes, Never Worn." Let your imagination read between the lines and tell you this tragic story.

In other words, Hemingway affirmed and employed the use the Jewish hermeneutical principle *Remez* (above) in his writing. And surely the Jewish tradition of interpretation understood that the inspired Scriptures use the iceberg theory. Listen to the dialogue between Abraham and Isaac in the *Akedah* (binding of Isaac) story (Gen 22), such as when Abraham says to the two servants, "You stay here with the donkey, and I and my son will go up the mountain and then we will return to you," and when Isaac asks his father, "Father, we have the wood and the fire but where is the lamb for the sacrifice?," and is answered with, "My son, God will provide for Himself the lamb for a burnt offering" (Gen 22:8 NKJV). Surely, there is much to read between the lines here. And in contrast to the six-word short story above (from which you could imagine many stories), this Bible story has many rich clues and information in the rest of the Bible to help us fill in the gaps or read between the lines accurately.[38]

Could it be that the very sparse nature of the texts of the Old Testament stories are not evidence of poor writing skills on the part of the author, but are rather to provoke imagination and discussion about the seven-eighths of the story below the surface? These characters in a given story are real people in a rich context. *Can we read between the lines and imagine, with the help of directive questions, what it must have really been like?* The rabbis thought so. So do we. So does OH.

Pashtan and *Darshan*

Of the four in the *Pardes* (orchard), I will focus here on the *peshat* and *darash* methods (or levels) of biblical interpretation. In Hebrew, the practitioner of *peshat* (simple, literal) was called a *pashtan*. The practitioner of *darash*

---

38. This is in contrast to a practice observed among very intellectual exegetes who like to say, "Where the text is silent, we must be silent." This sounds very disciplined and responsible. But it certainly limits discussion that brings the story to life, it limits application, and may even limit the Holy Spirit.

(applicational, sermonic exposition) was called a *darshan*. The interpretive product of the *darshan* is a *midrash*. Midrash is from the Hebrew root *drsh*, meaning "to seek, consult, inquire of . . . seek with application, study, follow, practice."[39] And we might add—to read between the lines.

The *pashtan* and *peshat* exegesis, like the modern evangelical historical-grammatical exegete, aims to uncover and elucidate only what he believes to be the authorial intent and original meaning of the passage, what it meant to the first generation of its hearers. This meaning is usually thought to be the one-and-only true, authentic meaning. The tools of the *pashtan* are technical and objective—philology, grammars, and lexicons of the original languages and historical, cultural, and archeological studies. The goal of the *pashtan* approach is to arrive at the accurate and final, best reading of the text.[40] This is what we are calling herein textual hermeneutics (TH).

The tools of the *darshan* tend to be more subjective—s/he applies creative imagination to the text in order to squeeze out more meaning. As s/he deals with the narrative genre, s/he will not be limited by the strict rules of the *pashtan*. S/He knows every Bible story has large holes—things not told in a sparse ten-, twenty-, or even 100-verse story. To use the anthropological term for detailed cultural description, the biblical stories are not "thick description"; they are often thin-on-the-ground. *What are the features, the motives or goals of this or that character? How does one view his fellow characters? What psychological, cultural or other factors in the biography of each character are influencing him or her in the story situation?* As Israeli literary scholar Meir Sternberg, a master of the literary art of the biblical narrative, states:

> From the viewpoint of what is directly given in the language, the literary work consists of bits and fragments to be linked together in the process of reading: it establishes a system of gaps to be filled in. This gap-filling ranges from simple linkages, which the reader performs automatically, to intricate networks that are figured out consciously, laboriously, hesitantly, and with constant modifications in the light of additional information disclosed in the later stages of reading.[41]

It could be said that the *darshan* is practiced in employing the *remez* level of interpretation. The *darshan* aims to bring the real people and events in the story to life for the present generation or audience. He believes it to be the right and obligation of every generation of Scripture exegetes to uncover relevant meaning to the hearers of any generation. He believes the threat of

---

39. Brown, *New Brown-Driver-Briggs Hebrew and English Lexicon*, 205.
40. Zion, "Origins of Human Violence," 22.
41. Sternberg, *Poetics of Biblical Narrative*, 186.

misinterpretation (which the *pashtan* fears) is less dangerous than the threat of irrelevance.[42] He believes Scripture has a dynamism that is translatable to the needs of people of all ages and social situations in life; and he knows this requires oralization in a group setting to create the robust framework that allows for a wider, richer application to the complexities of life.

> "He [*darshan*] believes it to be the right and obligation of every generation of Scripture exegetes to uncover relevant meaning to the hearers of any generation. He believes the threat of misinterpretation (which the *pashtan* fears) is less dangerous than the threat of irrelevance. He believes Scripture has a dynamism that is translatable to the needs of people of all ages and social situations in life; and he knows this requires oralization. The needs of God's people call for the manna of fresh *midrash*, applicable to present needs of hearts and lives."

The needs of God's people call for the manna of fresh *midrash*, applicable to present needs of hearts and lives. A good example of the kind of existential pressures of life that provoke new meanings and answers is when the matriarch Rebecca, Isaac's wife, was bewildered by her unusual pregnancy (the battling fetuses) and sought *Adonai*, "*v' tilech l'drosh et Adonai.*" Her need moved her to inquire, search out, seek the Lord (Gen 25:22). *Adonai* answered her and gave her meaning.[43] This prayerful, oral searching out of the meaning of the narratives of God's word is what we call oral hermeneutics (OH).

Midrash Aggadah, Broadly Considered

For an example of gap-filling, consider the story of Noah and the great flood that comprises eighty-five verses (Gen 6:1—9:17). So, eighty-five verses cover decades of tumultuous life as Noah is commissioned to oversee the humanly overwhelming and daunting task of God's near genocide of the human race, the destruction of the world. For this story, as for all the others,

---

42. We would agree with this, generally, for most believers in their ordinary Bible study. Of course in such extreme cases as interpreting an Old Testament passage about the genocide of the Canaanites as justification for performing a massacre today, or to take the Hebrew form "slavery" (a way of paying off debts) as justifying slavery today (as was done in the American antebellum South), in these matters of great moral magnitude, misinterpretation is more dangerous than irrelevance.

43. Zion, "Origins of Human Violence," 22.

the *darshan* seeks to fill in the gaps through imaginative reconstruction of the storyline between the lines of the text.

One could ask, *what kind of world was Noah living in if all humans were being as bad as possible in their every action and motivation? What did that look like and feel like for Noah and his family on a daily basis? What did it mean to live that way for 100 years? What was it like to build a massive unusable boat on land among horrific people during that time? What did he have to put up with? What fears must he have had for his family? What was it like to get on and be on a boat as every person outside of your family died?*

Another way to describe a *midrash* is as a narrative commentary (as opposed to a critical, analytical commentary, with lexical studies, etc.). Such imaginative reconstruction, together with drawing out applications and relevance to today, is called *midrash* or a *midrash Aggadah*. This kind of expansive exploration of biblical narratives is part and parcel of OH.[44] *Midrash halacha* is a different style, which this book will not address.

Jewish writers and producers Darren Aronofsky and Ari Handel produced an example of a *midrash* on the Noah story that came to the big screen in 2014. Simply called *Noah*, and starring Russell Crowe, the movie is a visual *midrash*. The Noah story is an epic, archetypal story and begs for *midrash*.

In the movie, after Noah has heard from God, his wife asks him, "Noah, what did he say?" Noah responds, "He is going to destroy the world." What kind of man was this, entrusted by the Creator with overseeing such a daunting, overwhelming venture? The human drama of this for Noah and his family, their relatives and neighbors, would have included times of high anxiety, tension, and emotion. These were real flesh-and-blood people, like you and me. That Noah got drunk and naked in his tent after it was all over is surely human realism. After years of high stress, Noah unwound, released his inhibitions; his inner moral restraints had collapsed.

Brad Jersak commented on the "evangelical panic" caused by the movie in his blog after *Noah* was released:

> I don't think anyone should be surprised at the usual course of Evangelical reactions decrying the movie for its 'biblical inaccuracies.' . . . Of course, citing inaccuracies implies that the measure of faithfulness to Scripture is somehow photocopying Genesis 6–9 into the screenplay in a sort of word-for-word

---

44. Other archetypal Genesis stories which have been treated in this expansive exploratory form we may call a literary midrashic genre, broadly considered, are Genesis 3, the Fall of Man in Eden by John Milton in his epic poem *Paradise Lost*; Genesis 4, Cain and Abel by John Steinbeck in his novel *East of Eden*; and Genesis 27–50, the Joseph Story by Thomas Mann in his massive *Joseph and His Brothers*.

depiction. It's this paint-by-numbers mentality that keeps many an Evangelical trapped within the lines of their own assumptions—as if taking the text literally was remotely akin to taking it seriously. Not so![45]

Those who love Scripture and want to see its stories reach the broadest possible audience have cause to applaud this visual *midrash*, the *Noah* movie. The *Christian Post* reported in the days following the release of the movie, "Two of the most popular online destinations for Bible readers reported robust increases in traffic in the first book of the Old Testament following the release of *Noah* last week."[46] YouVersion reported "in the days after *Noah* hit theaters, people opening the Noah story in Genesis 6 increased about 300 percent in the US and 245 percent globally on @YouVersion."[47] BibleGateway reported "visits to the Noah story in Genesis 6–9 . . . saw a 223 percent increase over the previous weekend."[48]

The *Christian Post* reported "in addition to *YouVersion*, an app of the Scriptures which hit 100 million downloads last summer, and the website, BibleGateway, trends also showed a spike in substantial increase in search queries for the Old Testament text" as a result of *Noah*.[49] "Film analysts believe *Noah* attracted a wider audience, and not just the religious, due to Hollywood touches given to the film by Aronofsky."[50] "'It certainly feels like the biggest film of 2014,' Tim Briody, analyst for Box Office Prophets, told *USA Today*."[51]

The movie stimulated the public interest in the story of Noah, making people wonder what the real original story is about, and why it is so compelling. It stirs people to go home and look it up in the Bible. Because this was a mainstream Hollywood film, the number of people and the demographic segment of people reached by this movie was far greater than would have been the case by a Christian movie about Noah. This gives Bible-believers opportunity to tell the more accurate story to those with awakened interest in the home and workplaces of social life. The producer of *Noah*, Aronofsky, is not a follower of Messiah Yeshua. This begs the question—*What if messianic Jews and Christians would produce movies which would be even more accurate*

---

45. Jersak, "Noah," lines 4–9.
46. Lee, "'Noah' Movie Sparks Massive Spike," lines 1–4.
47. Lee, "'Noah' Movie Sparks Massive Spike," lines 5–7.
48. Rau, "'Noah' Generates a Flood of Bible Readers," lines 3–5.
49. Lee, "'Noah' Movie Sparks Massive Spike," lines 8–11.
50. Kumar, "Hollywood's 'Noah' Tops Box Office," lines 15–16.
51. Lee, "'Noah' Movie Sparks Massive Spike," lines 48–50.

to the biblical text than Aronofsky's production (and indeed we should honor the text more than they did), but would have as large a public impact?

Noah was controversial and featured much imaginative reconstruction, some of which piqued some people's sensibilities.[52] In the Jewish style of midrashic discussion, if one does not like someone else's picturing of events to fill the gaps, they can offer their own; in synergistic conversation, milking the story for all it's worth. This, while always avoiding notions that flatly contradict the text of the story, and the kind of fanciful allegorizations spun out from the parables by many church fathers.[53]

---

52. The "watchers" in the film were shocking to some. They were sort of sci-fi creatures, having fallen from heaven into molten lava. When the lava hardened to stone, they were lumbering rocky creatures. The angelic "watchers" are mentioned in canonical Scripture in Daniel 4:13, 17, and 23. They are featured in the apocryphal books of 1 Enoch and Jubilees. The New Testament Epistles of Peter allude to angels who were disobedient in the days of Noah who had fallen (1 Pet 3:19–20; 2 Pet 2:4–5; Jude 6). The Epistles state they are kept "in prison" and "Tartarus," (in 2 Pet 2:4), a term borrowed from Greek mythology, for a place lower than Hades, whereas Aronofsky and Handel's movie has them wandering the earth, helping men, and some return to heaven in light form, escaping their stony condition. Jude 14–15 cites 1 Enoch directly (probably 1 Enoch 1:9), stating that Enoch (the great-grandfather of Noah) himself had uttered these prophecies. If Peter and Jude can allude to them, surely a visual midrashic version of the Noah story can legitimately do so and imaginatively depict what they were like. There is enough mystery here to allow speculation. No one owns or has copyright to the biblical stories; they are surely in the public domain. And if they were thought to have ownership, they belonged to the Jewish people before ever they did to evangelical Christians.

53. The storyteller is responsible to clarify and correct when a *midrash* or interpretation of a story is offered that does clearly contradict the authoritative inspired written text of a Bible story. In the case of *Noah*, the most glaring dissonance with the biblical story was the way the character of Noah was portrayed as having so badly misunderstood the Creator he believed he and his family were also to be destroyed and only the animals were to be saved, this to the extreme point of planning to kill his two granddaughters to help the Creator exterminate every last human being. These notions clearly reach the zone of "Phiction" and the "Deniable" and the tethers apply (see alliterative "Four P's" and "Four D's" below). This confusion in Noah was perhaps because, in the movie, God never speaks audibly or in clear language to Noah. This contradicts the authoritative biblical story stated in Genesis 6:9b, "Noah was a righteous man, blameless in his generation. Noah walked with God," (ESV). And it states God spoke clear and intelligible instructions to Noah, quoting the words of God, which included the promise of a covenant with Noah (Gen 6:13; 7:1; 8:15; 9:1, 8, 12). However, considering the possible choices by the characters in the story, choices they could have made but did not make (such possible, hypothetical ones as portrayed in the movie), illumines the choices they did make (as told in the Bible). Noah *could have* acted as confused as he was in this movie version but did not. God *could have* been as silent as he was in this movie, but he was not. What light does this *midrash* then throw upon the way they did speak and act in the biblical story? This kind of exploratory questioning is the method we used in the two demonstration stories in chapters 1 and 9—looking at possibilities, but then using character thinking to arrive at the best, most accurate interpretations.

If we wish to assess whether or not a midrash is within the pale of faithful interpretation and application of the inspired Scriptures, there are two helpful, alliterative rules-of-thumb that provide hermeneutical tethers to restrain midrashic exploration. A tether is a rope or a leash that restrains, usually an animal. An interpretation, application, or imaginative reconstruction of story may be tested by these "Four P's" and "Four D's:"[54]

Table 5.1 Four P's and Four D's

Provable	OR	Dogma
Probable	OR	Debatable
Possible	OR	Doubtful
Phiction (fiction)	OR	Deniable

When the midrashic exploration reaches the "Phiction" and "Deniable" zone, that is to say that it clearly contradicts the biblical text, then the storyteller must state unambiguously that this is no longer the biblical story; it is outside the pale of the biblical account. One is free to write fiction, but such should no longer be considered an interpretation and application of the word of God.

We will always need careful *pashtans*, the strict exegetes and their technical tools to stay loyal to the historical meaning of texts, especially for the nonnarrative genres. However, messianic Jews and evangelicals today need to recover and ply the approach of the *darshan*—*imaginative reconstruction* of the Bible stories, using insightful character-centric questions to search out and to squeeze out more relevant meaning from the inexhaustible treasures of the word of God. We need to fear less a misinterpretation of the historical-grammatical one-and-only true meaning (if there is such in stories or we are capable of isolating such a singular one) and fear more the relegation of Scripture to irrelevance. The stories are rich and deep, having multiple truths and applications; they should not be reduced to or frozen to one exegete's one-and-only-true-best rendering.

A good storyteller (*darshan*) will be able to guide a group's discussion if it gets out of hand. A storyteller, performing like those in the demonstrations of the Elisha stories in our chapters 1 and 9, and using the tethers the authors suggest above (the "Four P's" and "Four D's"), can trust the story

---

54. The "Four P's" are attributed to Grant Lovejoy. The "Four D's" I (Bill) learned from Dr. Marvin Wilson, professor of Old Testament and Jewish Studies, Gordon College.

itself and the work of the Holy Spirit to attend to his word, applying it to the needs of the hearts and lives of any group who hears it, across cultures and generations, in multiple and various applications. Such formative work is Divine and out of the *pashtan's* or the *darshan's* hands.[55]

The rhetorical and homiletical arts are always central to ministry of the word. The oralizing of the word described through the cluster of word gifts—teaching, exhortation, prophecy—are endowed by the Holy Spirit to equip the church for ministry (Rom 12:6, 7; 1 Cor 12:8, 10; Eph 4:11). Bible storytelling is an expression of the gifts of teaching and exhortation, but in a form often not recognized as real teaching due to our Western orientation to use primarily the lecture method. OH recognizes, relishes, and relies on oralized Bible stories to evangelize future followers and equip current followers of Yeshua.

"Just Give 'Em Chocolate, Bill"

I (Bill) close this chapter with a delightful memory I hold from a dear mentor I was blessed to have in the practice of storytelling—the late Dorothy Miller, founder of Simply the Story. When I first was introduced to storytelling as Bible teaching, I, being a scholar from the Western tradition, had to intellectualize everything, dissect it, and analyze it. Some of my first presentations on the topic were PowerPoint presentations full of theoretical propositions about orality, literacy, communication theory, the digital age, secondary orality, and so forth. Dorothy watched me in this and saw some of my representative writing. I had mentioned to her that some people were a bit bored. Dorothy countered (paraphrased):

> "Well, Bill, were you to give a lecture to a group of people on how chocolate is made . . . you could describe the origin and history of chocolate from the Cacao bean from Central and South America. You could tell about how the native Americans made a beverage out of it, to get the bitter taste out. You

---

55. A missionary to Africa tells of the African bush lady who heard the story of Joseph and Potiphar's wife. She heard the story and then said, "I've never seen a man turn down such an opportunity. I want to know the God behind this man. This God must be very powerful to help Joseph turn down such a temptation." The storyteller reminded her that this story was not evangelistic, but God used it to bring her to faith in Yeshua. The authorial intent of the Genesis story was to show God's power to preserve Joseph through the testing of Joseph's character by resisting temptation, but the nature of story *genre* allows it to be used evangelistically. (Personal communication with Larry Dinkins, as told to him by African indigenous Christian leaders in a Simply the Story summit meeting held at Hemet, California, September 13, 2014.)

could tell how the Europeans adapted it, added ingredients like sugar and invented processes to turn it into pastes, and blocks and bars. You could talk about the many kinds and types of chocolate, its various blends and forms. You could talk about the processes of 'conching,' 'tempering,' 'melanging,' and 'crystalizing' chocolate. You could talk about the chemical processes involved in its crystallization. You could talk about its nutritional value, the antioxidant properties of dark chocolate. You could talk about its sale and marketing and why people everywhere seem to like it so much. All this would be very interesting to a chemist, a culinary artist, or perhaps a scholar like you, Bill. But most ordinary people would be bored with all of this. Just give 'em chocolate, Bill!"

> "You could talk about its nutritional value, the antioxidant properties of dark chocolate. You could talk about its sale and marketing and why people everywhere seem to like it so much. All this wouldn't be very interesting to a chemist, a culinary artist, or perhaps a scholar like you, Bill. But most ordinary people would be bored with all of this. Just give 'em chocolate, Bill!"

Indeed, as a Jewish studies specialist, I should have known the Hebrew Bible is not so much about the origin of or the theory of making and processing chocolate and the chemistry and science about how it is constituted. It is mostly chocolate (the stories themselves). Like chocolate, this is what most people delight in. They want to taste the chocolate! Do not the Hebrew Scriptures say, "O taste and see that the LORD is good" (Ps 34:8 NKJV)? The two example stories we offer you in this book are chocolate. Enjoy! The rest is theory and table setting, which has its place on certain tables. Thank you, Dorothy!

Thus, the *oral hermeneutics* (*OH*) we are arguing for herein is not a new fad, nor is it anti-intellectual, nor is it just storytelling for children's ministry, nor is it just for tribal people. *OH is the retrieval and adaptation to our times and audiences of an ancient and venerable Hebrew hermeneutic.*

You will have noticed the prominence of characters in the above discussion, so it is to character theology we now turn.

6

Character Theology

"And what more shall I say? I do not have time to tell about Gideon, Barak, Samson and Jephthah, about David and Samuel and the prophets."

—Hebrews 11:32 NIV

"Biblical writings do not teach us concepts of God; they show us how people encountered God, learned to know him and walked with him."

—Tite Tiénou

"The lives of the saints are the hermeneutical key to Scripture."

—Stanley Hauerwas

Oral hermeneutics, with strong ties to Hebrew hermeneutics, leads naturally to the role of characters in Bible interpretation. Characters in a single story or those who drive the grand narrative serve as a means to grasp what the authors and Divine Author wish us to assimilate. At the same time it provides a strong solution to meet the pedagogical preferences[1] (how people prefer to learn and be taught) of oral and oral-preference audiences

---

1. "Pedagogy is never innocent. It is a medium that carries its own message" (Bruner, *Culture of Education*, 63).

globally. This approach calls for a different type of theologizing (process) and theology (product) that will complement systematic theology and biblical theology. Using oral hermeneutics as a means to theologize leads inevitably to character theology.

In this chapter, the authors build on the previous chapters that discussed the influence orality had on the text and teaching, dominance of the narrative genre in Scripture, delivery and dialogue of manuscripts that impact memory (ch. 3), Oral Hermeneutics (ch. 4), and Hebrew Hermeneutics (ch. 5). OH calls for a theologizing process that leads naturally to another required type of theology—character theology (see figure 6.1). We begin by identifying some of our basic assumptions, clear a path to define character theology, consider possible contributions character theology makes in discovering truths within a story, and conclude with the need for character theology.

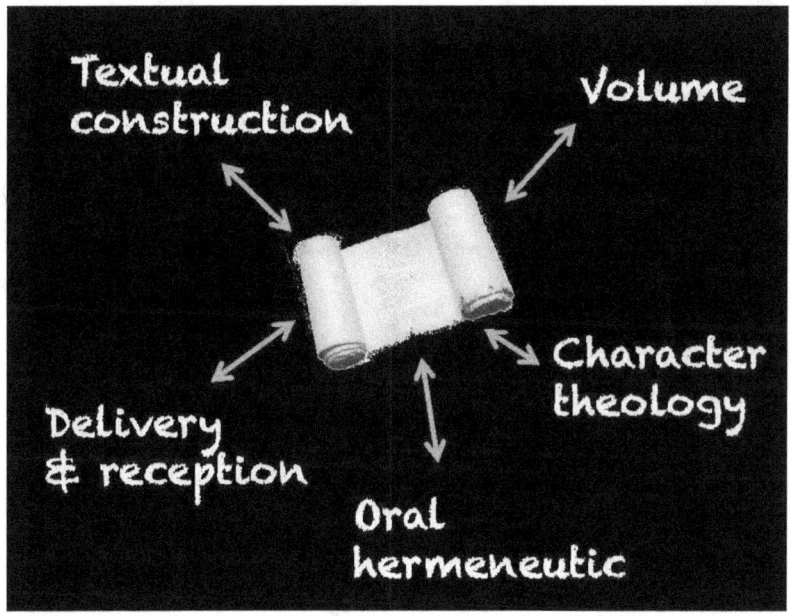

Figure 6.1. Character Theology Extends Existing Theologies

Assumptions

Before delving into character theology (CT), the authors underscore some of our basic assumptions. The authors assume there is no one perfect, superior, complete, or global hermeneutic model or method for interpreting Scripture. All humans are fallible when interpreting the infallible. All models and methods are influenced by individualism and/or collectivism, and social values-morals. All have denominational/theological biases (and specific Bible translations to back them), including the multiple versions of OH presently in use. But there are, however, better hermeneutic models (best practices) for seeking meaning within the narrative genre. And there are better pedagogical models that match more precisely the oral preferences of postmodernists,[2] posttextualists, postfactualists.

The authors also assume the hermeneutic models of faithful Jews and Christians have changed over the generations (see table 6.1). For example, the allegorical, philosophical, empirical-scientific, historical-critical, redemptive-historical, motif-driven, and more. We remember (and cheered) when "literary" was added to "grammatical-historical" in the 1970s. All of these changes, of course, were influenced by the spirit of the times and/or the Spirit.[3] What we propose here is a modest, general, adaptable oral hermeneutical model to interpret narratives and the grand narrative of Scripture through characters so the stories can be understood in a more comprehensive, deeper, natural way.[4]

---

2. Kenny Woodhull's research identified two cultural strands to the "receptivity to narrative parabling:" (1) "the post-modern adolescent's predilection to participate in their stories," and (2) "the digital native's ear as a post-literate secondary oral learners" (Woodhull, "Art of Parabling," 81).

3. To grasp the metanarrative of the early modern Pentecostal movement requires asking a certain set of questions of them as a religious community. These questions influence her hermeneutic filter (which was experiential) to interpret Scripture. They include favorite texts and verses, stories (testimonial experiences), characters, symbols, and rituals. In this case, the book of Acts and the outpouring of the Holy Spirit with the evidence of speaking in tongue, becomes a central choice. The story of Pentecost, the work of the Holy Spirit (as cited in Joel 2:28–29), "last days" fulfillment restoration of the power and purity of the church, and the call and destiny for their God-ordained movement offered a "full gospel" to the whole world. See Archer, "Pentecostal Story."

Why is this important? Because what was true of the Pentecostal process in search of meaning and identity is true of *every* Christian denomination/tradition: a metanarrative, stories that are teleological (beginning, middle, end), specific grounding question sets that seek meaningful answers, a specific hermeneutic, favorite Bible text(s) and verses, stories (including testimonies), characters, symbols, rituals that express and endorse their cohesive theological worldview, all thereby providing meaning and impetus to the communal movement. Think of the Anabaptist tradition with its narrative of persecution by the magisterial Reformation and thus resistance to the state, its pacifism, and its emphasis on believer baptism. The historical canon of Scripture has contemporary relevance and continues to the final curtain call. What is the metanarrative of your denomination/tradition that drives your hermeneutic? How does it match up with historical traditions? Jaroslav Pelikan offers this piece of advice when comparing the contemporary with tradition: "Tradition is the living faith of the dead; traditionalism is the dead faith of the living" (Pelikan, *Christian Tradition*, 9).

4. "What biblical scholars need to hear most from literary critics is that old-fashioned

Defining Character Theology

The authors define *characters* as humans, animals (donkeys, cows, roosters, whales), spiritual beings (angels, demons), individuals (Paul, Rahab) or groups (Pharisees and Sadducees), real (Mary) or fictional (good Samaritan), marginalized (poor blind Bartimaeus) or prominent (Pilate), good (Moses) or evil (Pharaoh) who participate in a story.

Most stories have characters who play a significant, small, or insignificant role. The authors are especially interested in those who advance the story's plotline. We call these controlling characters. The characters of Israel serve as an example. Paauw states: "The Bible has something universal to say, but it will only say it through the very down-to-earth story of one particular tribe of people struggling to make its way in an old Mediterranean world."[5] And Brown adds: "Israel is the grand theater of God's redemptive play."[6]

> "The Torah spoke in human language."
> ~ Rabbinical saying ~

Controlling characters drive and determine a story's direction (plotline) as a series of events manifest the "manysidedness of real life,"[7] offering models to follow, modify, or avoid. These can include protagonists (e.g., Elisha and the widow) and antagonists (e.g., debt collector).

"Theology" breaks down into two parts, *theos* and *ology* or *logos*. *Theos* is Greek for God, while *ology* (words) or *logos* (events) are words as events.[8] We define *theology*[9] simply as humans attempt to understand

---

critical concepts of plot, character, setting, point of view and diction may be more useful than more glamorous and sophisticated theories" (Sider, quoted in Ryken and Longman III, *Complete Literary Guide to the Bible*, 23).

5. Paauw, *Saving the Bible from Ourselves*, 91.
6. Brown, "Spiritual Lessons from the Land of Israel," para. 7.
7. Ryken and Longman III, *Complete Literary Guide to the Bible*, 22.
8. Werner Kelber notes, "Gerhard Kittel has stressed the activist character of *logos* with a seriousness rarely encountered in Pauline scholarship: 'In all this the *logos* is always genuine *legein*, or spoken word in all concreteness. One of the most serious errors of which one could be guilty would be to make this *logos tou theou* a concept or abstraction.' As a rule, the Pauline reference to *logos* or *logos tou theou* is to the living, preached word of the gospel" (Kelber, *Oral and Written Gospel*, 144). For a tidy summary, see also Walton and Sandy, *Lost World of Scripture*, 121–27.
9. Kosuke Koyama points out the life-sustaining abilities of "theology" which he defines as "an exciting report on our having rice with Jesus" (Koyama, "We had Rice with Jesus," 19).

God as revealed through characters and events documented in Scripture. In *Worldview-based Storying*, I (Tom) provided a summative overview of CT:

> By character theology I mean utilizing some of the more than 2900 human characters in the Bible, including groups, such as the Pharisees or Sadducees, along with those associated with the spirit world, such as the Holy Spirit, Satan, angels and demons, to teach abstract doctrines, morals, and ethics. Character theology relies on earthy, concrete characters to frame abstract truths and concepts, thereby providing ideas a home. It does so even as it retains God as the center of the story, and the individual story's place within the broader sweep of Scripture ... For example, rather than teach the abstract doctrine of justification by faith, let the earthy lives of Abraham and David define this abstract doctrine (Romans 4). Dogma without spiritual and human characters defining it is on the fast track to coldness. Bringing Bible characters out of the closet will heat up the conversation.[10]

CT analyzes people and parties in place and time in search of practices that position God at the center of our daily lives. CT uses characters to teach ideas with the goal of glorifying God in more extensive ways.

> "Narrative speaks in the idiom of the earth."[11]

The Bible's "compelling immediacy"[12] makes CT human, natural, and immediate. This is brought about in part through participatory history, i.e., the human experience the listener/reader/viewer encounters in a story. Harry Stout explains, "history stories are neither past nor present but both simultaneously."[13] The past is simultaneously the present, and vice versa, thereby making relational connection possible, often instantaneously, with the character in the story (Level 3 Attunement; see ch. 2).

---

10. Steffen, *Worldview-based Storying*, 211; Steffen, *Facilitator Era*, 149.
11. Fackre, "Narrative Theology," 345.
12. Alter, *World of Biblical Literature*, 210.
13. Stout, "Theological Commitment and American Religious History," 48.

Strategies for Biblical Criticism

David Smith

Source Criticism seeks to understand what written sources the author of a particular text depended on when composing a text.

Form Criticism proceeds on the assumption that most biblical books existed orally before being written down. Form criticism seeks to reconstruct that oral stage and locate it in the *Sitz im Leben* (life setting) in which it originally arose and functioned.

Redaction Criticism seeks to understand how various ancient versions of biblical texts were edited and compiled by a later redactor. This approach seeks to discern how the redactor shaped the final form of the text to make particular theological points.

Genre Criticism identifies the literary genre of a text. This is done by comparing the text with similar ancient texts to discern how the original author and audience would have understood it.

Historical Criticism seeks to reconstruct the world in which a text was first written and read. It shows how investigation of historical background can shed light on the Bible.

Tradition Criticism is concerned with how a text has been understood by various traditions contained in the Bible. For example, how was Moses understood by the communities of Josiah and Ezra?

Canonical Criticism asks what meaning texts have in their final canonical arrangement. It is concerned with how the rest of Scripture elucidates a text and vice versa.

Literary Criticism refers to the application of literary theory to the study of the Bible. It includes, but is not limited to, analysis of rhetoric, plot, character development, themes, imagery, and poetry.

Copyright Westminster Theological Seminary © 2010. Used with permission.

https://students.wts.edu/resources/westminster_center_for_theolog/paper_formatshtml/wc_exegisis2/approaching_the_biblical_studi.html.

Table 6.1: Strategies for Biblical Criticism

The Bible's compelling immediacy is also brought about through the voices, actions, and interactions of God-chosen characters[14] used by the Holy Spirit to comfort or disrupt our lives, challenging us to change beliefs and behaviors that demonstrate godly wisdom that brings increasing honor to the King. He does so, not through evidential apologetics, i.e., proving something systematically and abstractly, but through experiential apologetics, i.e., demonstrating something concretely through performing, enacting, embodying, exhibiting, illustrating, actionizing, echoing, encountering, mirroring, presenting, and describing. As my friend Marco Diaz told me (Tom), "I didn't change because someone told me who Jesus was, I changed because someone showed me who Jesus was." We will now consider how CT discerns textual meaning.

CT Explores the Setting, Social Status, and Time

Characters converse and act out in social settings (tent to palace). Characters also convey meaning through social positions held in society (slave to king), during specific times (war to peace). Bible narrators provide listeners clues through these backdrops as to themes being constructed. To discern meaning, CT recognizes the roles of setting, social status, and time.

CT Concentrates on the Characters in a Story

CT recognizes that meaning is strongly determined by the characters portrayed in a story. CT assumes that most, if not all, author-chosen characters have causes and campaigns.

CT Explores Conversations and Actions

James Resseguie, Distinguished Professor of New Testament, concludes, "Characters reveal themselves in their speech (what they say and how they say it), in their actions (what they do), by their clothing (what they wear), in their gestures and posture (how they present themselves)."[15] Gifted novelist Flannery O'Connor adds, "In good stories, characters are shown through the action and the action is controlled through the characters."[16]

---

14. Note how the created model their Creator in Genesis 1:1–5, 26, 28. God spoke ("*Then there was the voice of God*" 1:2 VOICE), acted (created, separated, named, blessed), interacted ("let Us conceive a *new creation*" 1:26 VOICE); and blessed ("God blessed them and gave them *this directive*" 1:28 VOICE).

15. Resseguie, *Narrative Criticism of the New Testament*, 121.

16. O'Connor, quoted in Shaw, *Storytelling in Religious Education*, 291.

> "As Laurence Perrine says, the way a protagonist responds to a crucial situation in his or her life will 'likely be the surest clue to the story's meaning.' And 'to state and explain the change [in a character] will be the best way to get at the point of the story.'"[17]

Part of exploring the conversations and actions of characters will include a focus on conflict and chaos. CT concentrates on changes,[18] conflicts, and clashes[19] within the conversations and actions. That is because when a life is disrupted or dashed[20] e.g., the death of the widow's husband noted in chapter 1, revealing choices result. From the insights detected, a plotline emerges.

> "The literary analyst though he should certainly be aware of the differences of ancient mind-set and ancient literary procedures, presupposes a deep continuity of human experience that makes the concerns of the ancient text directly accessible to him. These millennia-old expressions of fear, anguish, passion, perplexity, and exultation, speak to us because they issue from human predicaments in some respects quite like our own and are cast in the molds of plot, character, dialogue, scene, imagery, wordplay, and sound play that are recognizable analogues to the modalities of literary texts more easily familiar to us, closer to us in time and space."[21]

17. Resseguie, *Narrative Criticism of the New Testament*, 126.

18. "*Frequently*, the point of a narrative can be found in the changes a character undergoes in a narrative" (Resseguie, *Narrative Criticism of the New Testament*, 12 [emphasis original]).

19. Leland Ryken writes, "The conflict can consist of physical conflict, character conflict, inner psychological conflict, or moral/spiritual conflict. A plot ordinarily consists of the progress of the conflict(s) toward a point of resolution" (Ryken, *Words of Delight*, 62).

20. "Defamiliarization [not familiar with] works best when textual disruptions cause the reader to slow down and take notice, or when norms and values firmly held by an implied audience are developed and then dashed. An unusual context, a difficult saying, an unexpected twist, a puzzling response, a violation of readers' expectations, a shattering of commonplace assumptions—any of these disorients readers, forcing them to attend to something new ... A defamiliarized ending is one that is less automatic, less able to glide smoothly over the text; it is more aware of the bumps in the road and the disruptions in the text. It is a close reading that slows down and attends to the nuances of the text—aware, often for the first time, of the text's strangeness" (Resseguie, *Narrative Criticism of the New Testament*, 38).

21. Alter, *World of Biblical Literature*, 205.

Why does CT focus so strongly on the conversations and actions of Bible characters? Because the Author knows that we generally face the same uncertainties in life as did the characters in Bible times. "Characters, like us, reveal who they are in what they say and do. Their speech and actions are open windows to their biases, concerns, values, and worldview."[22] These Bible characters are then "recreated in the reader's imagination."[23] This character thinking is what James models for us in his Epistle when he said, "Elijah was a man with a nature like ours, and he prayed fervently that it might not rain, and for three years and six months it did not rain on the earth. Then he prayed again, and heaven gave rain, and the earth bore its fruit" (James 5:17 ESV). Their journey becomes our journey. Their choices become our choices.[24] CT recognizes we become the characters we review and rehearse. Osborne summarizes the last two considerations:

> The reader must study carefully the plot and miniplots within narrative books in order to determine the developing themes and characterizations of the author. This is the best indicator of the basic message(s) of a literary work. The interplay of opponents and the interaction between major and minor characters are the clearest guidelines to the meaning of the passage . . . In this way theology may be better served by narrative material rather than didactic. We not only learn the truth but see it enacted in living relationships.[25]

CT Explores the Meaning of Names, Taglines, and Occupations

Other ways God revealed himself concretely in Scripture were through given or changed names/nicknames, genealogies, taglines,[26] and occupations. Examples of names could include: Abram (high father) to Abraham (father of multitude);[27] Saria (my princess) to Sarah (mother of nations);

---

22. Resseguie, *Narrative Criticism of the New Testament*, 20.
23. Resseguie, *Narrative Criticism of the New Testament*, 121.
24. Sternberg, *Poetics of Biblical Narrative*, 48.
25. Osborne, *Hermeneutical Spiral*, 208.
26. Merriam-Webster defines "tagline" as "a reiterated phrase identified with an individual, group, or product." It is similar to the use of a #, or "hashtag," in today's social media.
27. And God blessed Abraham's name, i.e., made it great, so that all the families on earth could be blessed (see Gen 12:3).

Moses (one drawn out of the water); Jacob (heel grabber) to Israel (one who argues/strives with God);[28] and Ananias (the Lord shows grace).

Jewish background specialist Lois Tverberg provides this insight in relation to a name: "The word *shem* often referred to a person's reputation, authority, or identity within a community, rather than to the verbal label that was attached to them."[29] Theology professor Jerome Neyrey adds, "Although individual children have their own names (James, Joses, Judas, and Simon), their worth is symbolized by their family name, that is, the name of their father and his ancestors."[30] And most of these communal expressions within a hierarchical society would carry the relational implications associated with honor and shame.

Nor dare we overlook how God revealed himself through the use of personal names. Old Testament scholar G. Ernest Wright contrasts the names of pagan gods with those of the God of Israel, concluding:

> God is known and addressed primarily in the terms which relate him to society and to history. The language of nature is distinctly secondary. God is Lord, king, judge, shepherd, father, husband, and the like, but these appellatives are not superimposed upon a central image in nature . . . *Consequently, the only image of him possible is the mental image of a person, and the only language by which he may be addressed is drawn from the institutions of human society.*[31]

God's powerful and praiseworthy names reveal his "primary concern for, and relation to, man, society and history."[32] God's many names express and exhibit his many attributes in human ways.

Examples of taglines could include Noah: "a good man, a right-living man, the best man of his generation; and he walked closely with God" (Gen 6:9 VOICE); Sodom: "wicked—utterly defiant toward God" (Gen 13:13 VOICE); Hanani: "honest and faithful, and in the fear of God he surpassed most men" (Neh 7:2 VOICE); Esther, regarding Haman: "he was vile, and an enemy to my people" (Esth 7:6 VOICE); Judas Iscariot: "who would betray Him" (Matt 10:4 VOICE). Examples of nicknames and occupations could include Simon the "Zealot" (Matt 10:4) and Matthew the "tax collector"

---

28. Interestingly, Islam means to submit to God. What a contrast to the God of Israel, with who one can have an interactive authentic personal relationship!

29. Tverberg, *Reading the Bible with Rabbi Jesus*, 258.

30. Neyrey, *Honor and Shame*, 22.

31. Wright, *God Who Acts*, 49 (emphasis added).

32. Wright, *God Who Acts*, 49. A. W. Tozer contends there is no religion that has ever risen above its own perception of God (Tozer, *Attributes of God*, 1:40).

(Matt 10:3). Scripture narrators, however, rarely provided such character descriptives; that is left to the hearer.

CT concentrates on characters as a means to illuminate the Chief Character.[33] Selected Bible characters "appear to be caught in *characteristic* action, at that moment in their lives when they are most themselves, when they reveal themselves most precisely and definitely."[34] Their sheer spontaneity seizes our attention as we observe their virtues, vices, attitudes, attire, actions, decisions, paraphernalia, and the context surrounding them, including the weather (Luke 8:23–25)! Through the actions of actors, positively and negatively, we capture glimpses of the Chief Character.

Alert Bible storytellers pay close attention to the controlling characters who advance the plotline of a story and the grand narrative of Scripture. They intentionally note genealogies, contrasts, changes, conflicts, and clashes between characters, the meaning of names, nicknames, taglines, occupations, and the interaction assigned by the author to various biblical characters. *Why?* Because "a prime prerequisite for reading the stories of the Bible is the ability to empathize with the characters in the story."[35] Resseguie adds, "The enjoyment of the narrative lies in the discovery of complex, developing characters that help define or redefine our own quests."[36] Empathy with various characters can begin a journey towards personal and collective godly wisdom.

Empathy and identification with a character can lead to a full-frontal assault on one's identity if personal honor is affronted. Or, it can lead participants who experienced failure and shame to deeply engage those characters who experienced the same but have progressed beyond humiliation to honor. The characters within the story become the characters outside the story—us. Case studies of lifelike characters divinely chosen to be included in the unfolding sacred story innately force listeners/readers/viewers to take the lives of the ancients seriously, as well as their own, and most importantly, the Chief Character. Empathy begins the journey to personal, societal, and/or national transformation.

Empathy connects people, which can lead to identification, which can lead to discussion, which can lead to godly wisdom, which can lead to imitation, which can lead to transformation. Bible characters become tutors who parade possible pathways to avoid or ones that lead to more God-pleasing

---

33. Ryken and Longman III, *Complete Literary Guide to the Bible*, 36.
34. McFague, *Speaking in Parables*, 122 (emphasis original).
35. Ryken, *Words of Delight*, 53.
36. Resseguie, *Narrative Criticism of the New Testament*, 122–23.

attitudes and activities. CT not only connects people, it connects hearts. CT is relational theology.

CT Relies on Genealogies to Generate Genuineness

Genealogies (chronologies of related characters) provide groups an unforgettable heritage as well as a contemporary identity.[37] Recorded names are remembered names. The identities of those included in a genealogy matter over generations!

Genealogies also help distinguish extended family lines and insiders from outsiders. For example, the Hebrew Bible identifies Yahweh as the "God of Abraham, Isaac, and Jacob" thereby maintaining group purity, "These are the generation of . . ."

Genealogies also determine social status and roles (including some impure women now purified), establish lines of loyalty and obligations, pinpoint historical feats or other notable events, and locate abstract borders and boundaries. They determine eras through genealogy, tie the past to the present, and build the cumulative individual stories (God and Satan, Adam and Eve, Abraham, Moses, Israel, David, prophets, Jesus, the Twelve, Peter, Paul, the community of faith, Satan and Jesus) of controlling characters into an authoritative, ever-expanding, grand narrative driven by the Name above all names.

Some stories are best framed through genealogies (Matt 1:1–17; Luke 3:23–38). Where such need exists, *should the individual story or story set include the controlling characters found in the genealogy? Would such give credibility to the narrator's claims being made?* Bloodlines (ancestral linage) bind not only kinship, they also bind Bible stories and story sets.[38]

---

37. For a helpful article on the use of genealogies in ministry, see. B. "Genealogical Storying in a Nomadic Context."

38. "I've had interruptions, e.g., a woman listening to the story of the Annunciation and Mary's following visit to Elisabeth. When the story said that Mary went to visit her relative Elisabeth, someone asked, 'How were they related?' My initial impression was to disregard this interruption. But the woman really wanted to know. So I paused the story and went back to the earlier story of Jacob's sons, mentioning Levi and Judah. Then briefly tracing the two stories through Aaron and David, and briefly mentioning that the line of priests were descendants of Aaron who was the son of Levi, the son of Jacob. I did the same for David, telling he was from Judah, also Jacob's son. Apparently, this satisfied the woman who said to continue Mary's story. I thought about that later how it was important when a word like 'relative' was used that it immediately triggered a need to know how the relation existed." J. O. Terry, personal communication, December 30, 2017. Kinship, relationships, including genealogies, are foundational to many group-oriented societies. People are always interested in roots and the ties that bind.

Genealogies are not just for people in biblical times or today's tribal people, but also for the many who currently wish to discover their ancestry through genealogical research. As Larry Dossey, MD, declares, "We yearn for unity with one another. The recent explosion of interest in genealogy, the study of one's family origins, can be seen as a hunger for oneness expressed through the attempt to restore historic connections."[39] CT recognizes there are modern-day audiences who, like the ancients, resonate with genealogies.

CT Relies on Poetic Images Rather than Textual Tools

Marshall McLuhan memorably coined the phrase, "the medium is the message."[40] Ryken and Longman claim, "With a literary text, form is meaning. This implies that we cannot grasp the truth of story or poem . . . without first interacting with the story qualities or poetic images."[41] This means, e.g., if Bible communicators wish to understand the story of Abraham offering Isaac or the possibility of one's sons being taken as slaves to pay off a debt, they must first relive the unfolding of the story. Then, and only then, can they fully appreciate the characterization development of Abraham and Isaac, and the widow, her husband and sons, and the Supreme Authority behind and within each story.

> "The enjoyment of a narrative lies in the discovery of complex, developing characters that help define or redefine our own quests."[42]

The authors have offered and discussed many principles and not a little technical scholarship in this book. *So are not special textual tools required to accomplish such narrative analysis?* Not so, claim Ryken and Longman: "For the most part, observant reading will reveal what is in a text."[43] We would add observant listening or viewing for oral audiences. Rather than master Scripture through specific textual tools, listeners/readers/viewers absorb its meaning through identifying and emulating characters in a story. *Is it time for the specialist to retreat briefly (not disappear forever [Acts 8:31, 13:1; Rom 12:7;*

---

39. Dossey, "Our Identity Crisis and a Solution," 395.
40. McLuhan, *Understanding Media*, 7.
41. Ryken and Longman III, *Complete Literary Guide to the Bible*, 17.
42. Resseguie, *Narrative Criticism of the New Testament*, 122–23.
43. Ryken and Longman III, *Complete Literary Guide to the Bible*, 22.

Heb 5:12; Eph 4:11; Jas 3:1]) *so the common oralist can learn to interpret a story in a conventional, natural, everyday manner?* As philosopher Shaun Gallagher correctly concludes, "Interpretation is built into the oral performance."[44] *Is it time to turn the lion loose under the power of the Holy Spirit?*

Through CT, character analysis happens naturally through descriptions, questions, gestures, attire, explanations, and evaluation; all in the format of group discussion. All tend to blend together in character analysis, frequently haphazardly (to some literates). Yet such analysis can result in life shifts accompanied by long-term memory. The two despondent disciples serve as a case in point, "*Amazing!* Weren't our hearts on fire within us while He was talking to us on the road? *Didn't you feel it all coming clear* as He explained the meaning of the Hebrew Scriptures" (Luke 24:32 VOICE)? Characters, including strangers, present new alternatives to the mental prisons that hold us captive.

We all grew up not only hearing and telling stories, but also interpreting them, and being interpreted by them. "Master stories," argues Goldberg, "not only inform us, they form us."[45] CT prepares a path to personal, communal, social, and national transformation through intuitive character analysis. This cast of characters includes those in a range from fatally flawed to fence sitters to the exemplars worthy of emulation. Through their actions and conversations we adopt and demonstrate personal convictions. CT recognizes that poetic images alone have the ability to impart a story's meaning.

CT Seeks to Contrast Characters to Help Define the Craftsman

Another way God revealed himself concretely in Scripture was through contrasting pairs of characters (foils),[46] e.g., Adam and Eve, Cain and Abel, Rahab and the spies, David and Goliath, the widow and the creditor, Paul and Philemon, Philemon and Onesimus. Old Testament sage Walter Kaiser observes:

---

44. Gallagher, *Hermeneutics and Education*, 322.
45. Goldberg, *Jews and Christians*, 13.
46. The *Cambridge Dictionary* defines "foil" as "someone or something that makes another's good or bad qualities all the more noticeable." https://dictionary.cambridge.org/dictionary/english/foil.

In Genesis 1, everything God created becomes a foil to reflect honor back to him. The author of Hebrews uses the foils of angels, prophets, covenants, and so forth, to show Jesus' superiority.

> Since Hebrew narrative does not describe character in much detail, the interpreter must pay special notice to the details that are given in the Bible . . . Characters are often contrasted in Hebrew narrative. Thus, as they are played one off the other, a better idea of each is gained. Rahab stands over against Achan; Samuel against the sons of Eli; Ruth is seen as opposite to Orpha.[47]

CT and character-thinking is alert to detect foils and recognizes that contrasting the differences and similarities between binary characters provides a more nuanced glimpse of the Craftsman.

CT Focuses on Personalities to Discover Propositions and Principles

God revealed his character *seldom* through ideas, *seldom* through propositions, but predominately through his actions and his interaction with the characters in the Bible. God did not provide us a list of his attributes, rather they emerged over time as he revealed himself through his actions and interactions with people. Characters and events preceded attribute disclosure. These gave propositions and principles their home and that is why character studies should proceed content studies. CT operates from the concrete to the abstract. No wonder the Ifugao were unimpressed with my finely tuned, systematic theology-based lesson on the attributes of God.

Mission historian Ruth Tucker highlights what can happen when propositions are prioritized over personalities:

> Every predicament and emotion and enchantment found in the twenty-first century is somewhere lurking on the pages of Scripture. Yet for many publishers and preachers and ordinary people, the Bible is largely a manual of propositions. The colorful personalities pushing their way out of its pages are seen as secondary—if that.[48]

Tucker continues, "any attempt to turn this incredible chronicle into a theological dissertation destroys the very essence of its message. We learn how to live and how to die by putting ourselves into the narrative. Indeed, we recognize these characters by looking in the mirror."[49]

---

47. Sandy and Giese, *Cracking Old Testament Codes*, 74.

48. Tucker, *Biographical Bible*, 2.

49. Tucker, *Biographical Bible*, 2. See also Ryken and Longman III, *Complete Literary Guide to the Bible*, 21.

What happens when one looks into the mirror? The "examiners become the examined."[50] God preferred to reveal himself through concrete characters rather than abstract propositions, thereby making it natural and therefore easier to see our true self in the mirror. As Ryken and Longman note, "Reading the Bible has a strong element of encounter to it. The Bible does not merely invite response—it requires it."[51] As King David was forced to see himself in the story that Nathan the prophet told him about the rich man stealing the poor man's little lamb (2 Sam 12:1–6), so Bible characters call us to a long, hard look in the mirror.

The repetition of Bible characters within or across testaments, books, and letters is not by chance. Robert Tannehill, Professor of New Testament, tells us why this is important—the echo effect. By repeated mention, "The echo adds emphasis helping to specify and ensure communication of central meanings."[52] Repetition reveals the significance of a character (and his/her causes) and/or that characterization can be cumulative. Some necessary questions therefore arise: *Who is mentioned the most in individual books or letters?*[53] *Who from the Old Testament are noted most in the New Testament? Who is mentioned in the summary sections or chapters?*[54] What do these characters exhibit to us?

> "Thus, it is through the face of others that we first come to know the divine Face. . . . It is in the experience of being faced by the Face of God that we gain a new and true face."[55]

If inquirers want to discover the face of God, the Hero behind the story,[56] they can do so by hearing the stories of his interaction with charac-

---

50. McClendon, *Biography as Theology*, 171.

51. Ryken and Longman III, *Complete Literary Guide to the Bible*, 34.

52. Tannehill, "Composition of Acts 3–5," 229.

53. See https://blog.logos.com/2007/05/top_50_people_i_1/. The top tier of fifty includes: Jesus, David, Moses, and Jacob. Tier two: Abraham, Aaron, Solomon, Judah, Isaac, Saul (Son of Kish), Joseph, Paul, Joshua, and Peter.

54. In the Acts 7 summary, Stephen makes eleven mentions: Abraham, Isaiah, Jacob, Joseph, Harnor's sons, Shechem, Moses, Aaron, David, Solomon, Jesus. The author of Hebrews 11 mentions nineteen characters in his summary: Abel, Cain, Enoch, Noah, Abraham, Sarah, Isaac, Jacob, Esau, Joseph, Moses, Rahab, Gideon, Barak, Samson, Jephthah, David, Samuel, Jesus Christ. For a comprehensive summary of summaries, see Hood and Emerson, "Summaries of Israel's Story."

55. Flanders, *About Face*, 197–98.

56. "If we miss God in the story, then we have missed the story" (Duvall and Hays, *Grasping God's Word*, 349. Walter Kaiser rightly concludes, "For the biblical narrative,

ters in community and in isolation. That is because every controlling character in Scripture, positively or negatively, whispers some characteristic of the Chief Character.[57] Bible characters draw the face of the Hero—the Chief Character. CT recognizes a certain sequence—abstract concepts about the Creator and godly principles to imitate him emerge through embodied conversations and actions.

CT Focuses on the Big Character

Narrative authors typically began composing a story with a big character in mind rather than a big idea. In the story "Elisha and the Widow's Oil," the prophet Elisha would be the start point, rather than an abstract idea—the miraculous provision of finances. As strong oralists, Bible authors naturally preceded from big characters.

Most of us have been taught to read Bible narratives for one-liners or the big idea. A succinct statement is sufficient. No need to take the time to get into all that emotional, periphery fluff. Just get to the heart of the matter as fast as possible.

Few on the literacy side of spoken-written Scripture have been taught to engage Bible characters to discover the significant in a story. If the narrative sections of Scripture are to have the transformative power they were authored to have, some changes from the textual hermeneutics tradition must happen. Our hermeneutic must focus first on characters—the real heart of the matter. From the characters who compose a story, a big character will emerge, and from this character a big idea[58] or big ideas will materialize. CT recognizes that the big character(s) initiate the big idea(s).

---

one of the most distinguishing features is 'the pervasive presence of God.' Often God is one of the two 'characters' in the scene. In the early chapters of Genesis, it was God and Adam (chap. 3), God and Cain (chap. 4), God and Noah (chap. 6), and God and one of the three patriarchs in the rest of the book of Genesis. Even when God was not directly mentioned as being one of the participants in the scene, his presence often was implied from the point of view taken by the narrator, writer, or the prophet who spoke on his behalf" (Kaiser, "Narrative," 71). Charles Koller adds, "the Bible was not given to reveal the lives of Abraham, Isaac, and Jacob, but to reveal the hand of God in the lives of Abraham, Isaac, and Jacob; not as a revelation of Mary and Martha and Lazarus, but as a revelation of the Savior of Mary and Martha and Lazarus" (Koller, *Sermons Preached without Notes*, 51).

57. Alter, *Art of Biblical Narrative*, 189.

58. Blomberg offers this warning (which has application beyond parables) to those who wish to pare down all the main points into a concise statement: "The shorter and more concise such a statement becomes, the more it risks missing some of the wealth of the parable's detail." He concludes that the, "interpretation must result in that which would have been intelligible to a first-century Palestinian audience" (Blomberg,

CT Relies on the Whole Text to Discern Meaning

From a literary perspective, most tend to see a "text as a unified whole."[59] For O'Connor, meaning results "from the whole presented experience... which is the story itself."[60] She deduces a story "cannot be reduced to one thematic statement about its meaning" because "the story itself is the meaning."[61] That is because "a story says something which cannot be said any other way ... One tells a story because a statement would be inadequate."[62]

A story talks, offering a surplus of meaning. The complete conversations and actions of chosen characters create textual meaning that offers on-ramps and off-ramps to the multidimensionality of life. CT recognizes that the whole story is necessary to discern its fullest meaning.

CT Focuses on Meaning that Evolves Indirectly

As an anthropologist was writing down a Zuni story, the Zuni storyteller abruptly interrupted the story, asking, "Do you picture it, or do you just write it down?"[63] The Zuni intuitively knew that literary genres indirectly paint their meanings on the hearer's mind through images, but was unsure the print-dominated anthropologist was capable of seeing such.

Ryken and Longman quote O'Connor, who claims the storyteller speaks "*with* the character and action, not *about* the character and action ... Literary texts do not come right out and state their themes. They embody

---

Interpreting the Parables, 163). We differ with Blomberg somewhat in this latter statement, in that we hold to a "surplus of meaning" and "multiple truths" wherein the Holy Spirit may impart meaning to a listener that a first-century audience may not have known. Though not referring to parables, the apostle Peter says of the prophets' messianic writings that they were for our sake, about which even the angels longed to know (see 1 Pet 1:10–12). This, together with how Jesus opened the minds of the two on the road to Emmaus to understand truths that were all along in the Hebrew Bible, but which they did not understand (Luke 24:25–27), show us that there are truths in Scripture that would not have "been intelligible to a first-century Palestinian audience" but may be to later generations.

59. Ryken and Longman III, *Complete Literary Guide to the Bible*, 19.
60. O'Connor, in Shaw, *Storytelling in Religious Education*, 55.
61. O'Connor, in Shaw, *Storytelling in Religious Education*, 55.
62. O'Connor, in Shaw, *Storytelling in Religious Education*, 55.
63. Tedlock, *Finding the Center,* xxxi.

them."[64] They add, "The power of story as a literary form is its uncanny ability to involve us in what is happening."[65]

In relation to theology, values, or morals, Bible characters do not normally define or try to prove them, rather they demonstrate, exemplify, embody, and illuminate them (positively or negatively) through lived life. Their words and actions paint pictures on the mind, creating what storyteller Jay O'Callahan often calls a "theater of the mind."[66] Jon Spelman adds, "Stories ultimately do not really consist of words; they consist of images that the teller translates into words, which the listener hears and then translates back into images."[67] Characters paint pictures on the mind of predicament and promise. There is a transfer of imagery from one mind to another through the symbols of words.

The Zuni storyteller mentioned above continued, "If someone tells a story, you can just imagine it."[68] Characters communicate meaning indirectly through emotive images triggered by the imagination and emotions, all aiding in making the message motivating and memorable. CT recognizes that it is difficult to unsee what one's mind has seen!

CT Recognizes the Possibility of Multiple Truths within a Single Story

Ryken and Longman claim, "literary texts are irreducible to propositional statements and single meanings. A propositional statement of a theme can never be a substitute or even the appointed goal of experiencing a literary text."[69] This is because Bible stories show rather than tell, enact rather than explain, illuminate rather than spell out, demonstrate rather than define, embody rather than conceptualize, encounter rather than detail, and present rather than assert, thereby leaving much to the imagination, emotions, and conversation within the listening and examining group. CT recognizes that Bible stories are not particularly amenable to a single truth.[70]

---

64. Ryken and Longman III, *Complete Literary Guide to the Bible*, 17 (emphasis original).

65. Ryken and Longman III, *Complete Literary Guide to the Bible*, 34.

66. Cordi, "How Storytelling Serves as Actors," para. 7.

67. Spelman, quoted in Mooney and Holt, *Storyteller's Guide*, 33.

68. Tedlock, *Finding the Center*, xxxi.

69. Ryken and Longman III, *Complete Literary Guide to the Bible*, 17.

70. Ryken and Longman III, *Complete Literary Guide to the Bible*, 31.

CT Relies on the Grand Narrative to Guard against False Securities

The authors saved the most significant aspect of CT for last—its focus on the characters who comprise the grand narrative of Scripture to protect all against false securities. Theologians Craig Bartholomew and Michael Goheen warn that having a fragmented understanding of Scripture easily leads to all kinds of culturally specific false securities:

> If we allow the Bible to become fragmented, it is in danger of being absorbed into whatever *other* story is shaping our culture, and it will thus cease to shape our lives as it should. Idolatry has twisted the dominant cultural story of the secular Western world. If as believers we allow this story (rather than the Bible) to become the foundation of our thought and action, then our lives will manifest not the truths of Scripture, but the lies of an idolatrous culture. Hence, the unity of Scripture is no minor matter: a fragmented Bible may actually produce theologically orthodox, morally upright, warmly pious idol worshippers![71]

As discussed in chapter 4, one's understanding of the grand narrative of Scripture, whether cognizant of it or not, becomes one's hermeneutic for interpreting all of Scripture (and life). The issue is, when the grand narrative is neglected or minimized, interpretation is distorted. We cannot interpret any story or passage correctly or fully if it is taken out of the context of the grand narrative of Scripture. The grand narrative of Scripture serves as guide and guard to a more correct, fuller interpretation of all its parts.

Elsewhere, based on God's interaction with the controlling characters of Scripture between the bookends of Scripture (the first two chapters of Genesis and the last two chapters of Revelation),[72] and incorporating four influential value-moral systems, I (Tom) scripted a possible grand narrative of Scripture, now slightly adapted:

> The counterfeit Adversary tried to usurp the Creator's authority and glory but was ultimately defeated. Even so, Adversary managed to influence Creator's highest creation—humans. They became haughty, disloyal, unclean, guilty outcasts. This required the Creator to reestablish his rightful rule and glory over all his creation (human/spiritual/material). To accomplish this,

---

71. Bartholomew and Goheen, *Drama of Scripture*, 12 (emphasis original).

72. T. Desmond Alexander rightly concludes that, "a story's conclusion provides a good guide to the themes and ideas dominant throughout" (Alexander, *From Eden to the New Jerusalem*, 10).

Creator selected Israel to bring forth the mediator Jesus to restore broken relationships through his life, death, resurrection, and ascension. Jesus defeated the spiritual powers and paid the full penalty for sin. Justice through grace prevailed; the Creator's authority and honor were restored, as was human honor. Those from the nations who chose to follow the Spirit and honor Jesus demonstrated their collective loyalty and obedience as worshiping co-laborers; they spread the gospel through word and works, resulting in a global movement. Some experienced suffering. Others experienced rest. All impatiently awaited the Creator's final restoration of this world.[73]

This grand narrative influences all my interpretation of individual passages, paragraphs, and stories found in Scripture.[74] And it continues to morph as I gain new insights. *What is your grand narrative that interprets all the individual parts of Scripture?*

Having a grand narrative of Scripture, such as the above, challenges the widespread belief of fatalism. It demonstrates how the powerful Patron-Father can be trusted because he is personally interested in the everyday life of everyone and every family he has created. He invites each to figuratively walk securely and shamelessly by his side as he did with Adam and Eve prefall,[75] and is in total control of what transpires in the future, the climax being the establishment of his eternal kingdom.

Nothing just happens in life (Matt 10:29–30). Individual response is therefore not only necessary or encouraged, but required. The grand narrative of Scripture—which incorporates the gospel (good news) from beginning to end—displays the evil force and face of fatalism. In its place it offers the Supreme Authority, who sovereignly controls the present and future, just as he has the past. The grand narrative of Scripture encourages and emboldens people to place their confidence in the Sovereign and act boldly for him as they find their place in his story. CT recognizes that the grand narrative of Scripture protects against all untruths.

---

73. For more details related to fragmentation and tools to discern the grand narrative of Scripture, see, Steffen, "Saving the Locals from Our Theologies, Part 1" and "Saving the Locals from Our Theologies, Part 2."

74. The hermeneutic circle finds its totality tied to the integration of the parts and the whole. "The meaning of the whole has to be derived from its individual elements, and an individual element has to be understood by reference to the comprehensive, penetrating whole of which it is a part" (Gallagher, *Hermeneutics and Education*, 207).

75. "He has never let you down, never looked the other way when you were being kicked around. He has never wandered off to do his own thing; he has always been right there listening" (Ps 22:24 The Message).

Summing Up

To avoid reducing the narrative sections of Scripture to less than all their worth, and minimizing life-applications, CT calls for a theologizing process that concentrates on how characters challenge us positively or negatively. Author-selected characters demonstrate attitudes and actions, challenging how we lean into life. Their contributions also help unfurl the Bible's grand narrative that guides and guards all the individual stories.

> "This is Jesus' genius. He tells what seems like a simple story and yet, as you encounter it, you find your own self-righteousness coaxed gently out into the open. You aren't just told about your sin. You are almost provoked to enact the very transgression he is discussing."[76]

Character theology is analysis by the audience, i.e., investigation (intuitively and formally) of the conversations and actions of the character(s) in the story. From concrete actions and interactions, abstract concepts, doctrines, values, ethics, morals, and worldviews emerge, offering the hearer choices to make. At the same time they reveal imaged characteristics of the Chief Character of the Bible. CT brings clarity to our lives through the choices Bible characters made.

Why the Need for Character Theology?

Following are some reasons for the necessity of CT for today's world. Westerners tend to be experts in disrobed propositional theology. Theological propositions ("naked truth"), however, require clothing made out of event-based stories (whether told, sung, symboled, ritualed, sculpted, drawn, acted), and the characters who interact within them. Osborne provides a reason that rings true:

> The unity and lines of causality within the dramatic sequence of the story first draw the reader into the narrative world and then help the reader relive its point and understand its purpose. In this way theology may be better served by narrative material

---

76. Cawley, *Myth of the Non-Christian*, 22.

rather than didactic. We not only learn the truth but see it enacted in living relationships.[77]

Theology is conveyed most strongly and completely when lived out through living relationships.

Bible doctrines ("timeless truths") require earthy, particular historical events expressed through characters. Denarratized and deevented theological ideas require clothing, i.e., a concrete story conveyed through the lives of characters. Following Irenaeus, Swiss theologian Hans Urs Von Balthasar captures this concept when he concludes Jesus Christ is "the Idea made concrete, personal, historical, universal, concretum, et personale."[78]

Osborne concludes that the interaction between characters leads directly to discerning the meaning behind a story:

> The reader must study carefully the plot and miniplots within narrative books in order to determine the developing themes and characterizations of the author. This is the best indicator of the basic message(s) of a literary work. The interplay of opponents and the interaction between major and minor characters are the clearest guidelines to the meaning of the passage... We not only learn the truth but see it enacted in living relationships.[79]

Just as culture is necessary to understand words, so the lives of storied characters acted out in events in place and time are necessary to make theological principles comprehensible, communicable, and memorable.[80] Until an event becomes storied characters where relationships reign, theology remains unclothed ideas having minimal impact.

A decade ago, a Chinese seminary student in the US had a conversation with a fellow Korean student about the difficulty in translating

---

77. Osborne, *Hermeneutical Spiral*, 208.

78. Von Balthasar, *Theology of History*, 89. He argues, "In Jesus Christ, the Logos is no longer the realm of ideas, values and laws which governs and gives meaning to history, but is himself history. In the life of Christ the factual and the normative coincide not only *in fact* but *necessarily*, because the fact is both the manifestation of God and the divine-human pattern of true humanity in God's eyes.... For the business of theology is not to keep one eye on philosophy, but, with its gaze obediently turned toward Jesus Christ, simply and indirectly to describe how it stands in time and in history as the heart and norm of all that is historical" (Balthasar, *Theology of History*, 18, 20).

79. Osborne, *Hermeneutical Spiral*, 208. See also Resseguie, *Narrative Criticism of the New Testament*, 197.

80. Walter Ong argues, "[T]ruth can never be simply propositional.... Every propositional truth is limited in explicitness and thus demands interpretation. Every statement is embedded in history, nonverbal history even more than verbal history.... The truth of the most clear-cut proposition is never within the words alone, but in the words-plus-existential-context" (Ong, "Hermeneutic Forever," 18, 19).

the Chinese term *han* (suffering, patience, pain, environmental, social anguish). The Korean struggled to provide a typical Western textbook definition. Finally he responded, "Look at the lives of Ruth and Naomi. They experienced *han*!" The Chinese student followed up, "Do you mean something like the suffering they experienced in a famine, pain over the death of loved ones, leaving a community . . . ?" The Korean student excitingly responded, "Yes, yes, all those things!"

The Chinese student, now a missiologist teaching in a seminary in Southeast Asia, has not forgotten the Korean student's answer even after the passing of many years! He reflects, "Talk about the power of the story enfleshing and giving clothing to the naked definition. His explanation of what *han* meant was more memorable than a dictionary-defined phrase." It also signaled to the professor an alternative way to teach theological definitions.[81]

Focusing exclusively or even minimally on theological ideas deplatforms, demystifies, denarratizes, deevents, deenfleshes, and decharacherizes the dominant literary genre of Scripture—narrative. Worse yet, it deincarnates the Chief Character—Jesus—making him an idea.[82]

In The Table Podcast, Denver Seminary Distinguished Professor of Old Testament Daniel Carroll-Rodas (who is half-Guatemalan) said this to the moderator, Professor of New Testament Darrell Bock of Dallas Theological Seminary:

> They're [students] used to the visual movie. But they actually just stop and read, so when I teach my Old Testament narrative sections, a lot of it is very self-consciously acting it out, very self-consciously raising my voice or speaking in a whisper, you see? And taking on the different characters. And they begin to get into it. And they'll say to me, 'I've never seen it this way. *It's a shame because they've been taught to read it for principles, not to engage it as literature. . . . Life isn't a one liner.*'[83]

Later in the interview Darrell Bock made this poignant observation, "You did something today that I thought was interesting, that I thought might be worth also getting people to think about how narrative works as we move to talking about ethics, and that is *you told the story of Abraham as*

---

81. John Cheong, personal communication, May 8, 2019.

82. "The Voice took on flesh *and became human* and chose to live alongside us." (John 1:14 VOICE).

83. Bock and Carroll-Rodas, "How Does Narrative Teach Theology and Ethics?" (emphasis added)

an immigrant. And normally in our circles, when we go to Genesis, we go to Genesis for the Abrahamic Covenant."[84]

Until interpreters can acknowledge the significant role of stories and characters in robing (incarnating) theological ideas and definitions, the less fully they will comprehend Scripture and the Author behind it, remember it, or communicate it enthusiastically and impactfully to others. *If the emperor needs clothes, how much more naked biblical truths? What changes must take place if Bible stories are to be understood more fully and communicated more impactfully?*

Vocalized or written theological principles devoid of concrete events and characters will likely experience a boring death in some remote corner of a dusty library or find themselves in a "cold-storage locker for preserving dogmas."[85] They may fill the minds of students with cognitive facts, like the frustrated millennial Bible student noted in chapter 4. Or, using the naked metaphor, clothing that ends up hung in a dark closet waiting to adorn, advertise, protect, comfort, conceal, reveal, warm or cool, date or define its wearer.

> "[I]n speaking to us God chooses to work through people, including the human authors of Scripture. Nicholas Wolterstorff describes Scripture as 'divinely appropriated human discourse' that is, words spoken and/or written by human beings which God inspires and then uses to carry out his own 'speech acts' such as asserting, promising, prohibiting or commanding."[86]

It is time to unleash the listeners/readers/viewers' imagination and emotions in relation to interpretation, remembering these must be tethered to and critiqued by not just the entire individual story, but also the clothed truths laid out by the Holy Spirit in Genesis through Revelation—the grand narrative of Scripture. When such occurs, a more complete and accurate understanding of Scripture will occur, and the Bible will come alive not only for the participant, but also for those who interact with the participant. All this encourages long-term memory and reputable replication with implications for the individual, his/her neighbor, and the environment. Jesus'

---

84. Bock and Carroll-Rodas, "How Does Narrative Teach Theology and Ethics?" (emphasis added)

85. McClendon, *Biography as Theology*, 68.

86. Black, "Key Hermeneutical Questions," 25–26.

infectious character is reflected and embodied not only through the actors of antiquity, but through today's living actors as well.

The bifurcation between naked propositions and clothed ones, doctrine and events, statements and stories, points and people, definitions and demonstrations, explicitness and ambiguity, principles and participants, publication and performance, all limit understanding of the spoken-written word. And this is the same spoken-written word the Holy Spirit uses to bring conviction (John 16:8), empowerment (Acts 1:8), illumination (John 14:26), and transformation (Titus 3:5) to individuals and groups. Theology demands and deserves better in the West and beyond. Healthy theology calls for a bifurcation breakdown; it calls for a both/and following a preferred sequence.

We appreciate how G. Ernest Wright summarizes the integration of the abstract and concrete in relation to theology:

> [Theology] is fundamentally an interpretation of history, a confessional recital of historical events as the acts of God, events which lead backward to the beginning of history and forward to its end. Inferences are constantly made from the acts and are interpreted as integral parts of the acts themselves which furnish the clue to understanding not only contemporary happenings, but those which subsequently occurred. The being and attributes of God are nowhere systematically presented but are inferences from events.[87]

Vanhoozer adds, "Doctrine is . . . a species of scriptural reasoning that makes explicit the implicit story-logic and meaning of the biblical text."[88] Ong furthers the discussion: "Oral cultures know few statistics or facts divorced from human or quasi-human activity . . . orality situates knowledge within a context of struggle."[89]

Is it time to rerobe naked doctrinal truth? The authors would answer in the affirmative and believe the CT process helps make such possible; it serves as a means to make truth not only mysterious, but also magnetic, understandable, applicable, multipliable, and memorable.[90] CT serves as a

---

87. Wright, *God Who Acts*, 57.

88. Note the order from implicit to explicit. Vanhoozer, "One Rule to Rule them All?," 110.

89. Ong, *Orality and Literacy*, 43, 44.

90. Early in the modern-day Orality Movement, in 1984, Dell and Rachel Sue Schultze, in their widely used book *God and Man*, introduced a chart of six characteristic of God to be used with each story taught chronologically. These were: God is righteous; God is all powerful; God knows everything; God is the source of grace; God hates sin; and God keeps his promises. Listeners were alerted to the six characteristics

means to make Bible history relevant today through God-chosen storied characters acting out in events in place and time.

> "Truth can never be simply propositional . . . Every propositional truth is limited in explicitness and thus demands interpretation. Every statement is embedded in history, nonverbal history even more than verbal history."[91]

Concrete events provide shelter and security for abstract constructs (Acts 1:1). For example, the theological abstractions found in the Epistles are nested firmly in earthy historical events (note God's promise to Abraham and justification by faith in Romans 4). The Epistles, which contain and refer to earlier conversations and actions on multiple occasions, are embedded in the Acts stories, which are embedded in the Jesus story, which is embedded in Israel's story, which is embedded in Abraham's story, which is embedded in Adam and Eve's story, all of which are embedded in God's story.[92] "There is no story that is not embedded in other stories."[93]

First-century Christianity did not begin with a set of principles, rather, principles emerged over the years (as evidenced in the Epistles[94]) as young faith-followers of Jesus attempted to readjust their lives in light of the gospel of grace and mercy. Even so, abstractions were seldom if ever left naked.

---

prior to each Bible story so they could identify them as they listened. The continuous repetition of the characteristics soon made them part of collective memory. Note the order—propositions to events. While we would recommend story precede propositions, a strength evidenced in *God and Man* is *both* propositions and events were included. The abstract had a home.

J. O. Terry called it the "oral chart." He found many listeners used the characteristics as a confession in their worship services. In Bangladesh, someone silkscreened the characteristics on banners. Many hung in the churches (personal communication, January 4, 2018).

91. Ong, "Hermeneutic Forever," 18.
92. Steffen, *Reconnecting God's Story to Ministry,* 90–94.
93. Fisher, "Narrative, Reason, and Community," 316.
94. Long ago German systematic theologian Martin Kähler (1835–1912) claimed that mission is "the mother of theology." For Kähler, theology began as "an accompanying manifestation of the Christian mission." Bible authors had no choice in an "emergency situation" but to theologize (Bosch, *Transforming Mission*, 16). Mission historian Andrew Walls concurs: "Theology emerges out of mission" (Walls, "Spirituality and Theological Education," 1).

Rather, they were clothed in community-influenced characters living out their lives through symbols, stories, and rituals.

Referencing the Epistles, Asbury's New Testament Professor Ben Witherington is convinced that

> *all* Paul's ideas, all his arguments, all his practical advice, all his social arrangements are ultimately grounded in a story, a great deal of which is told in the Hebrew scriptures, but some of which is oral tradition reflecting developments that happened after Old Testament times. Paul's thought, including both theology and ethics, is grounded in a grand narrative and in a story that has continued to develop out of that narrative.[95]

All principles centered around doctrines, values, and morals in Scripture tie back to some biblical story(ies) and the character(s) within them,[96] weaving together a grand narrative construct.

Another reason for the necessity of CT is that its approach more closely matches the pedagogical preferences of many of today's audiences. While modernity sought the "progress of doctrine," postmodernity prefers an "unfolding story."[97] Darrell Bock posits, "For boomers, it's getting the content of your faith right; for millennials, getting the ethics of your faith right is more important . . . Ministries that are going to address both the content level and the ethical outreach level in a relevant way are going to be powerful ministries."[98] *How well does your hermeneutic model match the pedagogical preference of your audience?*

---

95. Witherington, *Paul's Narrative Thought World*, 2 (emphasis original). See also Longenecker, *Narrative Dynamics in Paul*, and Hays, *Echoes of Scripture*.

96. One example of this is Paul's reference to Abraham and David (Rom 4) to help define justification by faith; it is not based on good works. Based on the concrete lives of two highly respected Jewish ancestors—Abraham, a man of deep faith (Gen 15:6), and David, a man after God's own heart (1 Sam 13:14)—Paul defines one of his major abstract doctrines, justification by faith. Witherington expands: "One of the keys to a proper Pauline reading of large portions of Galatians, Romans, and also some of the Corinthian letters is a proper reading of the story of Abraham and his descendants and of the relationship of Abraham's story to the story of Moses, and a proper understanding that both stories are being read in the light of Christ" (Witherington, *Paul's Narrative Thought World*, 38).

97. Baxter, *Master Theme of the Bible*, 20. Note also the changes in Bible titles from the word of God to the story of God, e.g., *The Voice: Step into the Story of Scripture*.

98. Bock, quoted in Pardo-Kaplan, "Bible Study's New School," 40.

> "Images call for interpretation and to leave biblical imagery uninterpreted is a great waste. The images of the Bible exist to tell us something about the godly life, something they will not do if they are allowed to remain as physical phenomena only."[99]

Whether in liturgy or service, the sensory (images and imagination) will connect with millennials and Gen Z through the use of oral-digital means. As noted earlier, these generations will want to participate not only in the discussion, debate, and dialogue, but also in emotive-driven practices that promote ethical good in an untidy world perceived as shades of gray rather than tidy black-and-white. Many of those coming from fatherless homes or having few strong personal relationships in this social media age will find CT's emphasis on the possibility of real relationships horizontally and vertically attractive.

As for adult learners, in 1943 Rudoft Flesch perceptively wrote, "Adult education is, by definition, the education of people whose main business is *not learning, but living.*"[100] Like millennials and Gen Z, adult learners will want to participate in the lived experiences of others. This is because lived life educates participants holistically. CT fits the learning style of many in today's oral-digital-influenced world, including adult learners and the deaf.[101]

Furthermore, CT generates heart-changing dialogue that lends itself to positive character change. Real-life Bible case demonstrations propose actual challenges people face with God, the spirit and material worlds, other people, and themselves. Such case demonstrations create collective, contagious, continual conversations for potential life changes as "critical co-investigators in dialogue with the teacher" strive for "the emergence of consciousness and critical intervention in reality."[102] Bible characters easily enter our lives through familiar pedagogical paths and leave their footprints forever imprinted on our hearts.

The stories of people, which Ricoeur claims are "never ethically neutral,"[103] function as "a provocation to be and to act differently."[104] Mil-

---

99. Ryken, et al., *Dictionary of Biblical Imagery*, xiv.
100. Flesch, *Marks of a Readable Style*, 1 (emphasis added).
101. See Steffen, *Worldview-based Storying*, 94–95, and Collins, "Visual Bible."
102. Freire, *Pedagogy of the Oppressed*, 81.
103. Ricoeur, *Oneself as Another*, 140.
104. Ricoeur, *Time and Narrative*, 3:249.

lennials, Gen Z, and adult learners will appreciate this as they want to know if the experiences of Bible characters can actually become *their* experiences. The goal of CT in both testaments is to initiate dialogue, imagination, and emotions that actionize God's timeless truths, resulting in personal, collective, and social transformation that glorifies the Chief Character.

How will we know if transformation really happened? J. Peter McLain, President of T4 Global, answers this way: "oral cultures have built-in mechanisms to validate whether a project is successful. Simply ask: *Has it changed their everyday life experience?* If they are living differently, then the project has had impact."[105] If greed dissipates, gratitude gains opportunity to grow in a godly manner. The opposite will evidence itself if foolishness flourishes. Collective conversations about Bible characters offer opportunities to gain wisdom that constructs God-honoring character.

> "characters become images and archetypes of behavior that provide memorable, affect-laden references about the kind of person that members of the audience want to be (or conversely, would rather not be) and which roles they wish to play."[106]

In our often-misdirected desire to speedily grasp the meaning of a Bible story, i.e., biblical doctrines and life principles, we have too often left characters on the sideline. This easily leads to what Dorothy Sayers called "dull dogma,"[107] and therefore turned-off audiences, including those who have a good grasp of cognitive biblical facts.

Hauerwas offers an alternative: "Doctrines . . . are not the upshot of the stories; they are not the meaning or heart of the stories, rather they are tools . . . meant to help us tell the story better."[108]

Stories provide concrete-relational, cumulative case-based demonstrations that convey clothed characters that lead to coded core categories (often systemized). When this happens, dull dogma gives way to dynamic drama.

Enframed in OH, CT raises its own set of significant questions:

105. McLain, "Evaluations and Oral Cultures," 122 (emphasis original).

106. Jagerson, "Hermeneutics and the Methods of Oral Bible Storytelling," 205.

107. "We are constantly assured that the churches are empty because preachers insist too much upon doctrine—'dull dogma,' as people call it. The fact is the precise opposite. It is the neglect of dogma that makes for dullness. The Christian faith is the most exciting drama that ever staggered the imagination of man—and the dogma is the drama" (Sayers, *Greatest Drama Ever Staged*, para. 1).

108. Hauerwas, *Peaceable Kingdom*, 26.

> Could character theology not exclude, but take us beyond biblical theology (diachronic), systematic theology (synchronic), and narrative theology (literary)? Could it help integrate all of these? .... Character theology moves from the concrete (Adam) to the abstract (sin), and back to the concrete (Adam), which should work well with much of the majority world, not to mention the minority world. Observations and reflections on each character, however, should make God the hero of the story. The Adam story, e.g., should take the listener beyond Adam to the second Adam and Genesis to the second Adam, the King of Kings.[109]

Ryken and Longman note what has had some success globally, "Literary critics have generally seen their task as taking the Bible out of specialists' study and returning it to what one of them called the common reader."[110] Perhaps CT's greatest contribution is that it opens the door to the average person to discern the meaning of any Bible story, and to do so naturally.

The authors conclude that for oral or oral-preference audiences at home or abroad, CT offers the most natural, human, relational, personal, entertaining, memorable, communal place to start analysis, thereby presenting high potential for transformed lives, communities, and nations. And, it opens the door for *all* to interpret Bible stories, not just those formally trained in biblical and theological studies!

Whether in the grand narrative or the individual Bible stories who comprise her, CT relies on metaphorical muscle to bring meaning, enlightenment, retention, and replication; it relies on characters to telegraph theology, values, and morals in arresting, amusing, ambiguous, apparent, and abiding ways! Theology discovered through OH, driven by narrative logic, character thinking, and analysis, results in CT that will long be repeated and remembered.

> *How well does your hermeneutic laser in on abstract theology? Conversations? Clashes between characters? Someone's internal conflicts?*
>
> *How well does it focus on emotive, actionized behavior of characters?*
>
> *How well does it spark the imagination and emotions?*
>
> *How well does it tie symbols and rituals to conversations and stories?*

---

109. Steffen, "Pedagogical Conversions," 155–56.
110. Ryken and Longman III, *Complete Literary Guide to the Bible*, 22.

How well does it integrate the concrete and abstract into a seamless event?

Which type of theologizing best promotes the emotive rerobing of naked propositions for millennials? Gen Z? Adult learners?

Which hermeneutic model best matches their pedagogical preference?

What type of questions should be asked in character analysis?

It is to character-centric questions that unlock the door to OH that we now turn our attention.

7

Questioning Our Questions

"This is how humans are: we question all our beliefs, except for the ones we *really* believe, and those we never think to question."

—Orson Scott Card

"No dramatically better solution is possible without a better question."

—Hal Gregersen

"Questions are places in your mind where answers fit. If you haven't asked the question, the answer has nowhere to go. It hits your mind and bounces right off."

—Clayton Christensen

"If Jesus is the Answer, what is the Question?"

—from a bumper sticker in a Jewish area of Los Angeles

Engaging a new type of theology requires a new set of handles for how we grasp Scripture. The authors suggest that these handles come in the form of character-centric questions. We all grew up asking questions. That is how we learned. "Mommy, what's that?" "Daddy, are we there yet?" Our questions began simple, but gained sophistication over time. We soon intuitively learned that the more questions we asked, the more we learned, even if our incessant asking eventually led an exacerbated parent to exclaim, "Enough already!"

We also intuitively learned that asking questions can get one into trouble. Fear and shame began to influence our use of questions. Even so, asking questions became as intuitive as telling and interpreting stories. Growing up asking questions carried over naturally into interpreting Scripture. To ask was to hear, to discuss, to interpret, to remember, to stay the course, to modify, to reject, or to totally change direction. Asking questions cleared the clutter.

The greatest teacher ever to walk this earth began asking attention-grabbing questions publicly at the tender age of twelve (Luke 2:46–47). Eyewitnesses and narrators later captured some 399 of his sharply shaped questions, many of which were rhetorical.[1] The Master Storyteller understood the power of questions to stop allies and opponents in their tracks by obliterating deeply held assumptions, creating curiosity and conflict, building a hunger for truth and trust, initiating relationships, inviting the inquisitive, driving away and hiding the truth from the arrogant, enlivening and continuing conversations, and sharpening his own questions, thereby enhancing his social capital, showing gaps in arguments, raising new questions thereby reframing the issue, and causing people to "not only think but to rethink."[2]

Jesus' teaching was tied strongly to the use of questions, providing all teachers a model to master, requiring that the audience *discover* the meaning rather than *tell* them. Ask, don't tell. Jesus' use of questions may just be one of the most unheralded modes of interpretation, even as it encompasses one of the strongest features for promoting learning and transformation individually, collectively, institutionally, or nationally. Often forgotten is the Master Storyteller was also the Master Questioner!

Arguably the greatest classical philosopher, Socrates, would certainly concur, backed by his philosophy of teaching through in-depth dialogue conducted through asking probing questions (the Socratic method). *But which carefully crafted questions does the storyteller ask when Bible storying?*[3] *To review a previous Bible story, introduce a new one, and interpret and apply it, all in a way that contributes to a more robust character theology (CT), what*

---

1. See Tiede, "339 Questions Jesus Asked." John Dear identified 307 questions Jesus asked based on the NIV (Dear, *Questions of Jesus*, 2).

2. Wiseman, *Multipliers*, 116.

3. See Zuck, *Teaching as Jesus Taught*.

types of questions should the storyteller ask? The centerpiece of this chapter focuses on character-centric questions concentrated around conversations, actions,[4] and the interactions of characters in time and place.

To continue answering the central question of this book—*Why is it important to know and practice OH in order to ascertain and communicate biblical meaning?*—this chapter begins by identifying broad, foundational literary- or text-based questions scholars ask when conducting textual analysis. The authors then create a character explicitness scale to enhance textual analysis. The discussion then considers some of the benefits that character-centric questions offer. Two distinctives follow—character thinking and cultural influences.

The authors conclude by questioning the questions generally used in Bible storying today. The origins of those questions are briefly discussed, which raise a host of new questions that demand reflection. The authors then suggest and illustrate an alternative type of question. Our goal is *not* to provide a new list of questions to memorize or a specific sequence to follow, but rather identify an alternative type of question to internalize—character-centric—that can strengthen all questions used in the total storying process (figure 7.3).

Foundational Text-Based Questions

All approaches of interpreting Scripture begin with questions. For the Greeks it was, *what is God (what is the essence of divinity)?* For the Hebrews it was, *who is God (what is his name)?* As noted in chapter 3 in relation to Paul's use of questions in the construction of his Epistles, his questions focused on conversations rather than philosophical concepts. "Rather than a prosaic, philosophical 'What shall we think/reason/suggest/propose about this?' Paul poses the dialectical question: 'What then shall we say?' Note this is in the plural. Such collective oral engagement continues as the 'writers' use verbs of speaking rather than verbs or writing."[5]

Dean Flemming, Professor of New Testament and Mission at MidAmerica Nazarene University, tells us why: "Paul's writings are less a collection of doctrinal studies than a series of theological conversations between the apostle and his diverse audiences with their life circumstances."[6]

---

4. Alter, *Art of Biblical Narrative*, 42.
5. Winger, "Orality as the Key," 226.
6. Flemming, *Contextualization in the New Testament*, 105. Dunn adds, "One cannot hope to write a theology of Paul except by listening to his letters as dialogue, overhearing, as it were, a great theological mind and spirit as it grappled with diversely

Thorough theological conversations call for character-centric questions that generate individual-in-community oral engagement that encourages spiritual formation.

> "It is clear that the structure of the question is implicit in all experience. We cannot have experiences without asking questions.... Discourse that is intended to reveal something requires that the thing be broken open by the question.... deciding the question is the path to knowledge.... The art of questioning is the art of questioning ever further—i.e., the art of thinking.... Questions always bring out the undetermined possibilities of a thing."[7]

In relation to the literary sections[8] of Scripture, literary (or narrative) critics prefer to use questions focused on people's experiences with the spirit world, other humans, themselves, the animal world, or the environment, to name a few. As you read through the questions, note how few of the questions focus on "who." Ryken and Longman offer this broad range of questions:

> What human experiences have been embodied in this text? To what genre(s) does this text belong, and how does an awareness of the relevant generic conventions guide our encounter with the text? What are the unifying patterns and structure of the text? What artistry does the text exhibit? What devices of disclosure has the author encoded in the text to guide our interpretation of its religious and other meanings?[9]

Resseguie proposes a narrower set of abstract-focused questions, beginning with the shape and structure of the narrative. He asks: "How does the narrative begin? How does it end? What patterns develop within a narrative? Are there repeated words or phrases that alert the listener/

---

challenging situations and questions ... Rather, in the letters we see and are privileged to overhear *theology in the making,* theology coming to expression, Paul theologizing" (Dunn, *New Testament Theology,* 15–16; emphasis original).

7. Gadamer, *Truth and Method,* 362, 363, 364, 367, 375.

8. Ryken and Longman III divide Scripture into three forms of literature: theological, historical, and literary (Ryken and Longman III, *Complete Literary Guide to the Bible,* 16).

9. Ryken and Longman III, *Complete Literary Guide to the Bible,* 19.

reader/viewer to a narrative structure? Are repeated scenes used to develop a theme or motif?"[10]

From shape and structure Resseguie moves to rhetoric (techniques of persuasion):

> Does the narrator use irony to emphasize a particular point of view, or to heighten a discrepancy between a familiar way and a new way of seeing the world? . . . What images, symbols, paradoxes, or metaphors are present in the text? How do the ambiguities of words . . . complicate the nuances of a narrative? How can we know the narrative point of view and how is it expressed?[11]

Resseguie then focuses on characters and characterization, of special interest for our purposes in this book. Our focus is on discovery learning through character-thinking in the field of oral hermeneutics. That is because "Characters, like us, reveal who they are in what they say and do. Their speech and actions are open windows to their biases, privileges, norms, concerns, values, and worldview."[12] Characters also experience physical and spiritual changes. Resseguie asks:

> What events, conflicts, and encounters contribute to the change? At what point in the narrative does a character develop? Is a recognition scene present in which a character develops? Is a recognition scene present in which a character awakens to his or her circumstances and averts disaster? . . . What do characters say and do? . . . How do they say it? . . . How do the characters speak about each other, or react to others? What tone is implied in their speech? . . . is the character lifelike?[13]

A recognition scene is a pivotal moment in a storyline when a character makes a discovery, has an aha moment, an epiphany that changes him or her where the character "comes to himself" (to use the idiom in the Prodigal Son story of Luke 15). Narrative critics are also interested in how the narrator paints a character so listeners/readers/viewers can see and experience what he wants them to internalize. The narrator "makes choices, provides options, and offers alternatives in the selection of scenes,

---

10. Resseguie, *Narrative Criticism of the New Testament*, 19–20. See also Alter, *Art of Biblical Narrative*, 62, 180–83, 227 for insightful foundational textual questions.
11. Resseguie, *Narrative Criticism of the New Testament*, 20.
12. Resseguie, *Narrative Criticism of the New Testament*, 20.
13. Resseguie, *Narrative Criticism of the New Testament*, 20.

in what characters say, in the settings elaborated, and in the interaction with other characters."[14]

Character-related questions could include: "What titles or epithets (descriptive phrases) does the narrator use for characters? What judgments or evaluations does the narrator make concerning characters and events? What beliefs, norms, values, and identity does the narrator want the reader to adopt?"[15] Narrators paint lasting pictures in our minds of characters who create curiosity about the validity of how we lean into life.

The narrator's questions related to the setting of the story—mountaintop, housetop, synagogue, seaside, battlefield, sports arena[16]—are also of significance to narrative critics. Did any Bible characters flash before your mind when you heard the various settings? Questions could include: "Are the settings symbolic? Do they recall events from Israel's past?"[17]

Narrative critics also focus strongly on how conflict is understood from the perspective of each character involved, e.g., Jesus and the Pharisees, Judas and the other disciples, or the creditor and the widow. Characters who disrupt, demean, distrust, dissuade, or defile others should demand the listeners'/readers'/viewers' immediate attention as such actions signal the significant in the story. Questions could include, "What conflicts develop

---

14. Resseguie, *Narrative Criticism of the New Testament*, 21.

15. Resseguie, *Narrative Criticism of the New Testament*, 21.

16. A biblical example is the setting of Gilgal. This camping place was the first beachhead of the people of Israel after crossing the Jordan River into the promised land of Canaan, becoming their base of operations for the conquest of the land. It is where they renewed the covenant through circumcision of those men that had not been while wandering in the wilderness, and where they celebrated the Passover again after a long hiatus (Josh 5). So this place had emotional and spiritual significance to the Israelites—it was a place rich with memories and meaning for Israel, where they experienced affirmation of their identity as an elect people of God.

Thus, when Samuel the prophet was operating, the first leader since Joshua to be recognized throughout all Israel, he made Gilgal one of his circuit cities from which he judged Israel (1 Sam 7:15–17). Gilgal was where Saul was confirmed as the first king of Israel. Samuel called to the people, "Let us go to Gilgal and renew the kingdom there" (1 Sam 11:14–15 NKJV). Samuel was astute as to the symbolic significance of Gilgal as a place of covenant transactions and renewal for Israel, and so used it wisely. It is the place where twice Saul ignored God's commands and where Samuel judged he would lose the kingdom (1 Sam 13:1–15; 15). It is where David was reaffirmed as king after the revolt of Absalom had been defeated (2 Sam 19:9–15, 40). Gilgal was where Elijah was taken up to heaven in a whirlwind and one of the places where Elisha established himself as a great prophet (2 Kgs 2:1–14; 4:38–41).

So if a Bible storyteller-teacher's audience knows the Bible well, he/she might ask after telling a story with Gilgal as the setting (or part of it), "Did any Bible characters flash before your mind when you heard the setting was Gilgal?"

17. Resseguie, *Narrative Criticism of the New Testament*, 21.

in a narrative and how are they resolved? . . . What is the outcome of the conflict?"[18] See figure 7.1.

Philosopher, theologian, and New Testament scholar Vern Poythress proposes questions related to three analysis foci, the: (1) speaker, (2) discourse, and (3) situation:

> Speaker analysis asks, 'What did the speaker want to say? What did he intend to say? What did he think he was saying? What did he mean?' Discourse analysis asks, 'What did the speaker in fact say, and what does it in fact mean?' Situational analysis asks, 'How did the situation alter in response to the speaker's discourse?' Typically, the most important part of the situation is the speaker's actual audience, those who hear him. As the principal subdivision of situational analysis we have therefore audience analysis, which asks, 'What did the audience understand by the discourse? What did they think the speaker meant? How did they react to it?'[19]

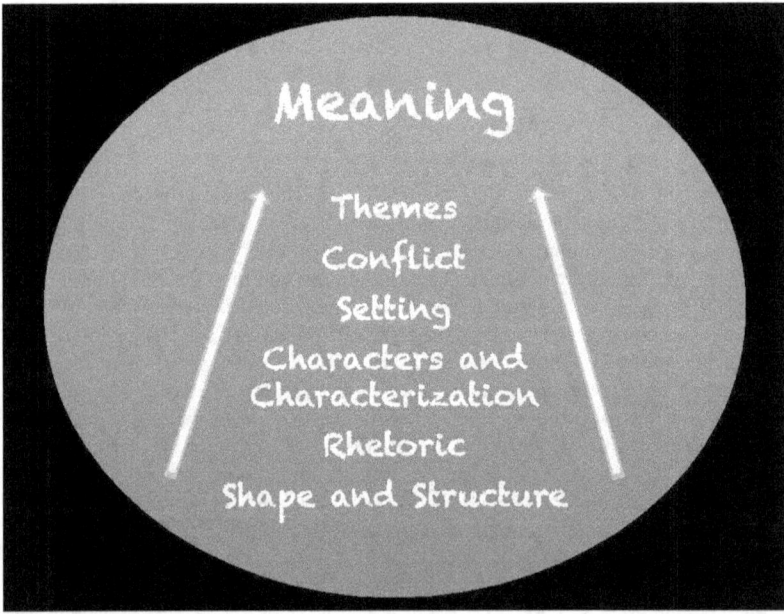

Figure 7.1. Discovering Meaning through Literary-based Questions

---

18. Resseguie, *Narrative Criticism of the New Testament*, 21. Lim notes the focus on Chinese confrontation styles that enhance harmony because these "focus on actions that will promote a relationship" that hopefully results in "feelings of closeness, unity, and trust" (Lim, "Influence of Harmony Motives," 403, 401). Mended relationships also address the face-shame issue.

19. Poythress, "Analyzing a Biblical text," 120–21.

OH centers on the characters portrayed in the text that results in CT. Questions therefore concentrate on who, on characters, e.g., Elisha, the widow, Naaman.

> *In what setting do the characters find themselves?*
>
> *In what era did the character live?*
>
> *What are the character's social status and role?*
>
> *What name did the narrator assign him/her?*
>
> *Who is involved in what happened?*
>
> *Whose comments stand out?*
>
> *Whose actions?*
>
> *With whom do they clash?*
>
> *What changes do they/others make?*

Like John Petersen, our questions focus on the function of characters because, "Characters become a quick means of identifying with a story, a focus of relationships and events, and the center of plotting activity."[20] OH concentrates on the concerns and conflicts within and between characters driven by character-centric questions. Characters reflect and express meaning.

The authors will move beyond questions related to revealing meaning. We are also interested in how the meaning of Bible stories are reviewed and applied in the lives of listeners.

Creating a Character Explicitness Scale

Biblical narrators of the Hebrew Bible tend to be skimpy when it comes to "analysis and assessment of character."[21] While there is strife and struggle between brothers, political and family tensions, and illegitimate unions, the narrators often leave it up to the imaginations of the listeners/readers/viewers to insert the details. *Why did Elisha tell the widow to shut the door?*

Berkeley Professor of Hebrew and Comparative Literature Robert Alter, who is Jewish, writes, "The narrator's extreme reticence in telling us what we should think about all these conflicts and questions is extraordinary, and, more than any other single feature, it may explain the greatness of these narratives."[22] *Why?* Because while there is bound to be levels of

---

20. Petersen, *Reading Women's Stories*, 23–24.

21. Alter, *World of Biblical Literature*, 65.

22. Alter, *World of Biblical Literature*, 65. See Appendix C for Robert Alter's questions related to his oral-textual parameters.

disagreements among the listeners/readers/viewers, "the writer draws us into a process of intricate, tentative judgment by forcing us to negotiate on our own among such terms, making whatever use we can of the narrative data he has provided."[23]

Narrative minimalism requires exegetes to dig deep into a story to discover the narrator's meaning intentionally assigned to each character. Even with such literary limitations, *are there better ways to grasp what a character conveys?*

In *The Art of Biblical Narrative*, Alter concludes that characters convey the narrator's message not only for the ancients, but also for us today:

> Characters can be revealed through the report of actions; through appearance, gestures, posture, costume; through one character's comments on another; through direct speech by the character; through inward speech, either summarized or quoted as interior monologue; or through statements by the narrator about the attitudes and intentions of the personages, which may come either as flat assertions or motivated explanations.[24]

Alter then offers an ascending scale to decipher a character's motives, attitudes, and moral nature. On the lower level of the scale, which is only suggestive, he references a character's actions *and appearance*. The middle level identifies inward or outward direct speech by the character or other characters about someone. On the top level, the most reliable, Alter identifies the narrator's statement(s) about a character's feelings, intentions, and desires.[25]

The authors now build on Alter (and Sternberg) to develop a rhetorical guide to aid in the exploration of individual Bible stories and story sets (see table 7.1). While totally integrated, the categories morph from, using Sternberg's terms, "explicit" to "covert."[26] After the more explicit background provided by the narrator identifies areas of conflict and changes within and among characters (plot), the more covert follows.

---

23. Alter, *World of Biblical Literature*, 65.
24. Alter, *Art of Biblical Narrative*, 116–17.
25. Alter, *Art of Biblical Narrative*, 116–17. Sternberg offers a "rhetorical repertoire" comprised of "fifteen rhetorical devises, ranging from the most explicit to the most covert, through which the Bible shapes our response to character and event" (Sternberg, *Poetics of Biblical Narrative*, 475).
26. Sternberg, *Poetics of Biblical Narrative*, 475.

> **Most explicit**
>
>   Narrator's comments about a character, setting, time
>
>   Conflict and changes within or between characters
>
>   Character's repeated comments and actions
>
>   Other character's repeated comments and actions
>
>   Appearance
>
>   Metaphors, symbols, and rituals
>
> **Most covert**

Table 7.1: Character Explicitness Scale

Petersen points out why Alter's tool would include the explicit: "Analysis begins with the basic tensions that drive the plot."[27] Plot, driven by conflict, can by extension be expected to generate conflict among those who hear the story. Explicit and repeated conflictive comments and actions by characters, like those of the narrator, do much to signal the significant within the story.

The same is true when other characters make repetitious comments or actions in relation to other characters in the story. Appearance—looks, expressions, clothing, hair, health, deformities—also provides listeners/readers/viewers clues about the truths within of the story. We conclude that the rhetorical tool that includes covert metaphors, symbols, and rituals, requires concrete characters and events to unpack their dense, hidden, suggestive, significant contributions.

To illustrate from the "Elisha and the Widow's Oil" story (2 Kgs 4:1–7) the narrator makes two explicit statements about the participating characters. First, the widow is the wife of one of the prophet's disciples (4:1). The narrator later adds some detail about Elisha—he is "the man of God" (4:7 VOICE).

Dropping down one notch from the top (see table 7.1) the widow lays out the setting—her husband, who greatly feared the eternal, is dead, leaving her with significant debt, which the prophet knew. She goes on to define and detail the conflict (plot)—a creditor is about to make slaves of her only two sons because of her deceased husband's debt!

Neither Elisha nor the widow make repetitious comments or mention appearance. The widow does mention she has a house. We later learn the

27. Petersen, *Reading Women's Stories*, 29.

house has several rooms (4:4). The jars and oil could serve as symbols, but their meanings remain vague. Much of the material provided by the narrator in this story is closer to "most explicit" than "most covert."

The authors will now build off of these broad, generic, literary-based questions previously discussed and begin to narrow their focus for use in story sets and individual Bible stories by crafting them to be more character-centric. Before doing so, we highlight some benefits and distinctives of character-centric questions.

Benefits and Distinctives of Character-Centric Questions

Character-centric questions related to OH and CT are designed to illicit answers that describe, demonstrate, display, encounter, experience, illustrate, represent, paint pictures, embody, and encounter. They rely on character thinking rather than critical thinking, they focus on experiential apologetics rather than evidential apologetics, and they analyze individuals and audiences rather than propositions and ideas. They prefer oral analysis over textual analysis, they require subjective participation with the actors on the lighted stage rather than objective observation from distant seats in a darkened room, and they prefer character-chasing questions over content-chasing questions.

Questions exploring characters (speakers and nonspeakers) within a story will help guide listeners/readers/viewers to the narrator's perspective because they demonstrate rather than define lived relationships in ways not unlike our own. Dialogue among participants in the storytelling event enhances the discovery of the narrator's purpose even as it is fundamental to spiritual formation in collectivist (and individualist) communities.

> "Who is this *Jesus*? How can it be
> that He has power over the wind and the waves?
> .... And who do you say I am?"
> (Mark 4:41; 8:29 VOICE)

Asking character-centric questions to discern comprehension, implementation, or accountability possibilities may take more time in the short run than just asking six to eight prepackaged questions. But the rewards are well worth the time and effort required. For example, the use of character-centric questions broadcasts publicly to all participants their voices are important. *How do y'all perceive this person? This group?*

Asking character-centric questions encourages relational-building dialogue that encourages the use of narrative logic, which in turn inspires application, memory, and reproducibility. Character-centric questions invite participation, something revered by many millennials, members of Gen Z, and adult learners, among others.

Character-centric questions help begin the journey toward individual, societal, and national transformation as "participants examine society, their local community, and their personal stories in a manner that rearticulates the concepts imbedded in Scripture for their meaning for the world today."[28] And all this happens in a very natural, normal, human way. That is because "Its [narrative and poetry] most pervasive influence is not informational but formational."[29]

Character-centric questions facilitate memory,[30] meditation, maturation, and multiplication. They do so by helping participants advance—in natural ways—beyond reflection to action; beyond titillation to transformation; beyond fictional faith to vibrant formidable faith. They fulfill Jesus' words to "Go and do likewise" (Luke 10:37 NIV).

While character-centric questions zero in on the complex, sometimes dicey relationships between characters, and require artful insightfulness to read and unpack, they encourage genuine responses from listeners that are fundamental to spiritual formation. Listening to the voices of the people at the micro level serves as a bridge to faith in God's willingness to interact with all his creation on the macro level. Character-dissecting questions help keep compromising weeds out of the CT garden, all the while developing character thinkers who instinctively and intuitively rely on narrative logic as they search for life's meaning. Not all questions are created equal. Character-centric questions not only offer significant benefits to tellers and interpreters, they also come with distinctives, two of which follow.

Character-Centric Questions Call for Character Thinking

Character-centric questions require something different than critical thinking. Rather than critical thinking—those who can analyze, conceptualize, synthesize, codify, and categorize the intricacies of a text—character-centric questions call for character thinking, i.e., those who can read, discern, and decipher people and relationships.

28. Jagerson, "Transformation through Narrative," 129.
29. Colijn, *Images of Salvation*, 40.
30. Bediako, *Christianity in Africa*, 51.

Character thinking takes into consideration the concerns of literary critics—characters, their surroundings, dress, the event, the location, the season, and so forth—but does so from a very different perspective. Character thinking reads people—their responses (verbal and nonverbal) and relationships. And it does so without stripping away the context or fragmenting the individual parts into minutia.[31]

The skill to discern and decipher characters, like all skills, develops over time. It should be no surprise that relational-oriented communities around the globe have a huge advantage over most Western Bible communicators. They tend to be experts in deciphering people and relationships vertically and horizontally, fantastic at deciphering facial feedback, and experts at intuitively reading people's body language.[32] Carol Goman, founder of Kinsey Consulting Services, defines body language as "the management of time, space, appearance, posture, gesture, vocal prosody, touch, smell, facial expression, and eye contact."[33]

An African captured it this way: "You know, you Americans read books; we read people."[34] Many societies socialize their citizens to read people and their web of relationships instinctively and intuitively. Reading people's verbal and nonverbal behavior, therefore, soon becomes second nature; a well-honed reflex to decipher the meaning of the moment.

Character thinking is the mindset that deconstructs the bundle of values characters promote within a story so as to discern the moral quality of their conversations, actions, relationships, and the Creator's perspective of those

---

31. All mentally healthy humans are endowed the ability to do what we are calling "character-thinking." The right brain capacities include the nonverbal, emotional, and relational attachment aptitudes in four levels of perception by parts of the right brain. These were aptly termed by neurotheologian Jim Wilder as: *attachment, assessment, attunement, and action* (see ch. 2). But the problem for many Westerners who are highly trained academically is that the left brain functions of logic, reason, conceptualizing, and analysis are the most habituated neural pathways, sometimes almost the default ones. Right brain "character-thinking" has, for some, not been as well developed. Thus, the skills needed for reading people must be intentionally exercised to recover, like muscles that have atrophied or at least become weak through minimal use.

32. Among the Arabs (and other shame-based societies), losing face or being shamed help keep sharp one's ability to read people: "Between the poles of honor and shame stretches an uncharted field where everyone walks perilously all the time, trying as best he can to interpret the actions and words of others, on the watch for any incipient power-challenging response that might throw up winners and losers, honor and shame" (Pryce-Jones, *Closed Circle*, 35).

33. Goman, *Silent Language of Leaders*, 3. Goman asks, "Did you know that your ability to accurately read and respond to the body language of others is fundamental to building empathy and rapport" (2)?

34. We are indebted to Doug Dorman for this comment.

interactions.[35] Character thinking also aids in helping people reconstruct their lives by ascertaining which character's words and/or works should be modeled, modified, or muted. Respondents can choose to make God the Hero of all their life stories, thereby locating their chapter in his eternal story. Character thinkers not only provide a different perspective of the Bible story, they offer a fuller, more comprehensive understanding of the story.

Culture Influences Our Character-Centric Questions

The authors assume that those within various cultures use and answer questions differently.[36] Following are a few cross-cultural challenges that will impact how character-centric questions are asked and answered when used in Bible stories and sets. For example, in the numerous shame-based cultures across the globe some will be reluctant to risk giving a wrong answer, thereby shaming themselves, their family, and/or their teacher, or appearing to their peers to be showing off intellectually. That does not mean the use of questions are unvalued or unused. Some reminders and routines can minimize possible perceived risks.

One of the magnificent things about stories is that the characters can serve as third-party mediators negotiating between two factions. Being somewhat distant relationally to the listeners/readers/viewers, characters can make comments or take actions that challenge them without being seen as socially dangerous or personally damaging, thereby saving face for the recipients even as the status quo is challenged. While family members and friends have to be extremely careful when challenging or criticizing each other, outsiders can say things insiders could never say, and get away with it.

Even the story itself becomes like a third-party mediator. When respondents answer questions, whether correctly or incorrectly, appropriately or inappropriately, rather than making a judgment statement, teachers return to the specific story (or previous stories) in the script to confirm conversations and/or actions. The script serves as a mediator rather than the facilitative storyteller, thereby once again minimizing social risk to participants.

Reminding the locals that their culture is much closer to the contours of biblical cultures than Western culture helps make them an authority

---

35. In Don Richardson's classic *Peace Child,* the Sawi eventually understood Judas was not the hero of story, rather Jesus was the Peace Child.

36. We encourage readers to conduct extensive research as to how locals use questions, e.g., *Who can ask them? Who can answer them? Which type of questions can be asked where? When? How do they use rhetorical questions?*

on the topic, thereby providing responders opportunity to actually build face, particularly when conducted in community. Breaking them into small groups before coming back to the main group to express group thoughts also minimizes individual social risk.

Sagacious storyteller-teachers who seek clear communication in shame-based societies will investigate early the locals' expectations in the use of questions, particularly in group settings.[37] For example, James Robinson discovered among Korean EFL (English as a Foreign Language) students that if they liked their teachers they would protect their *ch'emyon* (social face) by answering the teacher's questions, thereby verifying that the teachers knew their materials.[38]

The research should also reveal who can answer a question, which may be based on age, gender, formal education, social ranking, or asking a question for the benefit of another in the group. How questions will be answered, e.g., through a parallel local story or song, a chant, a drama, a metaphor, a symbol, or silence,[39] and so forth,[40] should also be investigated.

Research could also reveal when a question should be answered—prestory, during the story,[41] poststory, or any combination of the above. In regard to poststory, sometimes the story comes across so powerfully that the listeners/viewers remain silent for a while as they try to internalize what they have just vicariously experienced. Deep dialogue in a shame-based society can emerge through more than a series of questions asked poststory.

How the host audience prefers to connect objects that a character-centric question highlights may vary from context to context. For example, Nisbett discovered in his research of college students from the US and China that each tended to group objects differently. The University of Michigan professor concluded, "Westerners attend primarily to the focal objects or person and Asians attend more broadly to the field and to the relations between the object and the field. Westerners tend to assume that

---

37. Steffen, "Pedagogical Conversions," 147.

38. Robinson, "*Ch'emyon* in the EFL Classroom," 21.

39. Among the Antipolo-Amduntug Ifugao, silence from one party in a dispute or debate indicates defeat.

40. A missionary ministering in India told my (Tom) class how a Hindu she knew told a story. He moved from telling the story, to singing a sad or triumphal song to help it sink in emotionally, to dance (sometimes), to becoming a fiery preacher/prophet to lay out the moral lesson, then back to telling the story.

41. Alonzo Tayaban, a stalwart Ifugao church leader and powerful Bible teacher, once told me (Tom), "If straight story, we don't learn. We need discussion."

events are caused by the object while Asians are inclined to assign greater importance to the context."[42]

The Chinese tended to group objects according to thematic relationships (monkey and bananas because monkeys eat bananas) while the Westerners tended to group according to "common category membership"[43] (panda and monkey are both animals). Expect and be prepared for different responses when using the same question to illicit understanding of objects within a single Bible story. Relationship logic differs across cultures and subcultures.

Keith Chen's TED Talk, "Could Your Language Affect Your Ability to Save Money?,"[44] discussed the perception of time. He noted that the linguistic Chinese view of time (futureless languages) are events that describe and include all tenses while the English focused on featured languages (past, present, future). The former placed strong emphasis on the long-term while the latter, because the future seemed so distant, focused strongly on present consumption rather than possible future benefits. Due to shame, relationship differences, how and when to answer questions, colors, numbers, time orientation, or a host of other things, character-centric questions will elicit different responses based on cultural perceptions.

Character-centric questions offer a number of benefits to the storytellers and interpreters. They also come with distinctive features, two of which are character thinking and cultural expression. *Is there anything else the storyteller should be cognizant about?*

Questioning Our Questions

This section critiques the questions currently used in many inductive Bible studies conducted by those associated with the modern-day orality movement. The initial questions, seemingly initiated by members of the International Mission Board (Southern Baptist), have been modified by many. We will challenge some, suggesting a different type of question that covers the entire storying process (figure 7.3) that is more character-centric, culturally sensitive, free-flowing, numerous, and layered. We begin by looking briefly at the origin of the questions used in Bible storying.

---

42. Nisbett, *Geography of Thought*, 127.
43. Nisbett, *Geography of Thought*, 141.
44. Chen, "Could Your Language Affect Your Ability to Save Money?"

Origins of Questions for Bible Storying

While many of the question sets were initially designed for evangelism, the authors will expand them to incorporate ongoing spiritual meditation and maturation. The type of question introduced will also be applicable when adapted for social services such as TESOL (Teaching English to Speakers of Other Languages), BAM (Business as Mission), human trafficking, trauma counseling, and community development, among others.

A similar grand tour question to the one that follows was no doubt in the minds of the early curriculum developers of the Chronological Bible Storying model: *How can the questions be simply designed so that most participants in an evangelistic Bible study not only can discover God's spiritual treasures and make good applications to life, but also easily reproduce them in future Bible discussions?*

The answer to that question required questions be few in number, surface the key content, promote obedience, and be easily reproducible by attendees. The initial question set has since been modified by, among others, T4T (Training for Trainers), S-T4T (Storying Training for Trainers), OT4T (Orality Training for Trainers), DBS (Discovery Bible Study), STS (Simply the Story), DMM (Disciple Making Movements), Any3, and Simple Church. Following are representative inductive questions found in Discovery Bible Study (DBS) used often by Disciple Making Movements (DMM) and others:

> From the past week, what is something you're thankful for?
>
> From this past week, what was challenging for you?
>
> How did it go?
>
> ———
>
> What does this passage say about God?
>
> What does this passage say about people?
>
> What does this passage say about obedience?
>
> In light of what we now know about this passage, what is God calling you to do this week?
>
> ———
>
> How will I live this out loud this week?
>
> Who needs to hear this?
>
> In this upcoming week, what is going to be a challenge?[45]

---

45. It should be noted DBS has multiple versions. https://www.lipscomb.edu/

S-T4T adds a few questions to the familiar list:

What did you like about this story?

What confused you or bothered you in this story?

What did you learn about God?

What did you learn about people?

What should you obey from this story?

How will you remember this story?

To whom will you tell this story?[46]

New Questions Arise

The above question sets raise their own questions.

Do the questions focus more on cognitive content than characters?

Concepts than concreteness?

Propositions than personalities?

Ideas than actions?

Definitions than demonstrations?

Reasons than relationships?

Grammar than conversations?

Facts than emotional responses?

Ideas than incidents?

Individualism (individual self) than collectivism (social self)?

Egalitarianism than hierarchy?

On what happened rather than who was involved?

Would any of these questions require follow-up questions?

Which social values-morals (innocence-guilt, honor-shame, power-fear, purity-pollution)[47] drive the questions?[48]

---

missions/upload/file/65178/discovery%20bible%20study.pdf.

46. Stringer, *S-T4T*, 15.

47. Which social values-morals are dominant in said audience? Do these receive the attention they should?

48. See Steffen, *Worldview-based Storying*, 245–46.

How well do these questions match the audience's value-moral system?

Are the questions designed to deconstruct the false aspects of the audience's worldview so that a superior, rival, replacement grand narrative can begin (or continue) to be constructed?

Do the questions echo back to former stories/characters so that the Bible becomes perceived as a unified whole, so that a broader grand narrative continues to unfurl?[49]

Do the questions help identify the hero(es) of the story? The Divine Hero of the story?

Do the questions challenge the hearers to model a different behavior evidenced in one or more of the characters?

While limiting the number of questions for multiplication purposes in many Bible discussions today, *does the small number of questions actually do a disservice to the story? To the recipients? Should the number of questions be increased? More free flowing? More conversational?*

Do story-listeners, many having exceptional people intuition and phenomenal memories, have difficulty handling more than six to eight questions, especially when focused on what people say and do? Or, is this something Westerners, coming from a highly textual society where memories tend to be weak (because they are print-dependent), project on their audiences? Should the questions be more culturally sensitive? Do the questions focus mostly on the cognitive? On characters? On actionizing godly wisdom?

Possible Alternatives

OH takes its cues from characters. Exegetes therefore deal with certain parts of Scripture (narrative, some poetry, some history, and even some parts of the Epistles) where characters are central to the text. All hermeneutic models have their implicit biases and limitations, including OH.

---

49. Referencing a literary unit, Fokkelman divides these links in the chain into three levels: "(a) a group of stories, usually about five or six, which may be called an act, (b) a cycle of stories, often consisting of three to five acts, and (c) rarely, an entire Bible book comprising several of these acts. Because of the fact that the single story forms part of these greater wholes, it need not always have a plot of its own, and discussing the theme will in that case only be possible if we go up one or two levels and read the entire act or cycle first" (Fokkelman, *Reading Biblical Narrative*, 156).

Like narrative theology ("discourse about God in the setting of story"[50]) and like biblical theology (God's progressive, cumulative history with a predetermined trajectory) character theology (CT) finds its roots burrowed deep into the recesses of history, community, events, and characters. Unlike some biblical theologies,[51] CT can address those sections of poetry (e.g., Psalms and Proverbs) where characters and events are found. And unlike systematic theology (dissected, naked, and categorized concepts extracted from their homes) CT offers clothing for the naked.

Whether the poetry section or historical books, such as Isaiah or Jeremiah or even parts of the Epistles, Bible characters provide models to emulate (Daniel, Ruth) or avoid (Cain, Potiphar's wife). OH addresses those sections of Scripture where characters converse and interact positively and/or negatively, thus helping the author demonstrate truth-claims of the ultimate Hero.

OH, with its strong ties to CT, along with dependence on the Holy Spirit, attempts to integrate at least four components of learning to discover, imagine, know, feel, live wisely, and etch the meaning of a storied text into collective memory. These include: (1) doctrine (orthodoxy), (2) practice (orthopraxis), (3) emotions/imagination (orthopathy), and (4) memory (orthoecho). See figure 7.2.

While certain denominations and/or mission agencies may emphasize one or more component (e.g., T4T [Training for Trainers] and close associates, who place strong emphasis on guilt-oriented obedience [Matt 28:20; orthopraxis]), all four are required to make God's message accurate, trustworthy, meaningful, memorable, multipliable, and missional. Incorporating these four components driven by character-centric questions will help make Christianity a total way of life.

Where does OH begin within the four components? Does one paint by the numbers (quadrant 1, 2, 3, 4) or intuitively (quadrant 3, 1, 4, 2)? Many from the East would prefer to paint intuitively. They may choose to begin by highlighting the emotional side enticed by imagination—those outside the ark saw the tree-lines disappearing as the water continued to rise. For them, the subjective should precede the objective, thereby making it trustworthy, flexible, contemporary, and even more memorable. *Can formulating doctrine emotionally purify and petrify it?*

---

50. Fackre, "Narrative Theology," 343.
51. See Klink and Lockett, *Understanding Biblical Theology*.

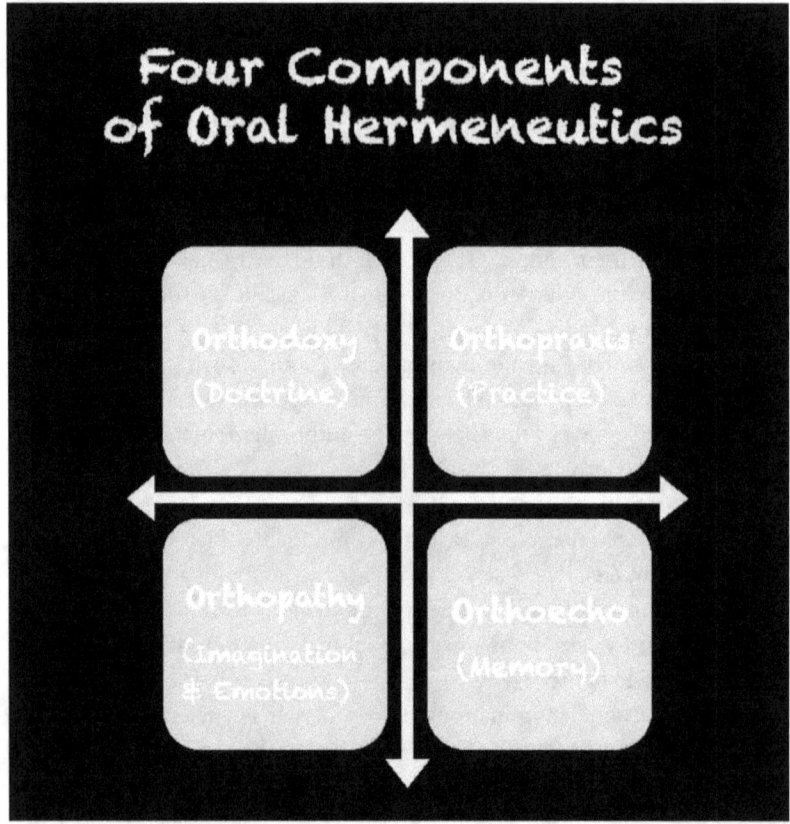

Figure 7.2. Four Components of Oral Hermeneutics

Many, especially from the West, would argue to begin with number 1—orthodoxy; paint by the numbers. People must first know what they believe—Noah's faith in God saved him and his family from the flood; it all begins with appropriate doctrine; the other components (except orthoecho) are secondary. Rational, objective truth precedes emotions and imagination, making it accurate, fixed, final, and hopefully memorable.

Audience preference rather than storyteller preference should determine which of the integrative hermeneutic components debuts first. That is because feelings lead to facts for some just as facts lead to feelings for others.

The starting point should influence the type of questions asked, and the sequence in which they progress, so should this be true of the four oral hermeneutic frames. Start points are just that—start points, not end points. Completing the cycle is the ultimate goal.

> "Truth unmoored from context and relationship becomes a commodity: cold, impersonal, dead, absolute. Coming to know the truth was no longer a shared endeavor of mutual discussion, discernment, and participation, the 'interplay of minds.'"[52]

Questions related to OH should center around certain components if Bible storytellers wish to capture the attention of story-listeners, not to mention discovering the truths within a story. Answers to the questions will be two-pronged: (1) they not only reveal what the participants discovered from the story, but possibly more importantly, (2) they will highlight aspects of their values, morals, and worldviews, providing Bible storytellers clues for contextualization and confrontation. These components could include:

Community

Relationships (human, spiritual, animal, nature)

Characters (human, spiritual, animal, nature, individual, group)

Events

Conversations

Symbols and Rituals

Values and Morals

Big Picture and Integration

Conflicts and Changes

Choices and Consequences

Consistencies and Inconsistencies

Contributions

If one runs these components through the questions proposed by DBS, S-T4T, and others previously highlighted, hits and misses occur.

---

52. Bradt, *Story as a Way of Knowing*, 33.

This is at least in part because the questions originate primarily from TH rather than OH.

The questions also typically emerge from a legal-based social value-moral system that until around 2000 dominated in the West—innocence-guilt.[53] This value-moral system naturally calls for obedience rather than loyalty (honor-shame), trust (power-fear), or cleanliness (purity-pollution). This is fine, of course, if innocence-guilt is a dominant value-moral system of the host culture. If not, one or more of the others will be required, making it/them much more culturally recognizable.

Note most of these methods focus on generalized, generic questions rather than character-specific conflictive relationships and conversations that help unveil the plotline. Observe also the strong focus on individuals rather than groups (e.g., Pharisees, community of faith, the crowd, Israelites)[54] and the minimal emphasis on who in the questions. Note also there is no connection made to summarizing symbols or proverbs or former Bible stories or the grand narrative. The good news is all this can easily be fixed.[55]

Changing the questions changes the focus, which alters possible answers and outcomes. As Hal Grefersen's book title suggests, *Questions are the Answer*.[56] The eminent management guru, Peter Drucker, would add, "the important and difficult job is never to find the right answer, it is to find the right question."[57] Character-centric questions challenge conclusions.

OH requires multiple, free-flowing, free-ranging, and layered character-centric questions to discover legitimate, comprehensive meaning of narrative texts. Cueing up question four to follow question three is a good way to abruptly close down a conversation or discover further truths in a story. It seems more advantageous to allow the conversation(s) and the activity(ies) of the character(s) in the text along with the ongoing dialogue between storyteller and listeners to determine the customized free flow and number of questions asked.

If the storyteller-questioner can learn to allow the voices and activities of the characters in the story, along with the ongoing dialogue between storyteller and listeners, and among listeners, to determine and dictate the line of questioning (rather than relying on a prescribed list of questions), at least three benefits emerge that are essential to spiritual formation. First, it

---

53. See Crouch, "Return of Shame."

54. "We almost always ask our Bible application questions as if the implications are just for individuals acting independently" (Paauw, *Saving the Bible from Ourselves*, 182).

55. While the focus is somewhat different, it would seem the use of character-centric questions would be applicable for checking Scripture videos as well in that performance of the spoken word is a significant part of the equation.

56. Gregersen, *Questions are the Answer*, 2018.

57. Drucker, *Practice of Management*, 353.

moves the listeners beyond their own world to the experiences of the lives, times, and places of the characters in the story, e.g., a destitute widow and the possible plight of her two sons. This can help reduce the sociocultural and emotional distance between the parties. Second, the ongoing dialogue between storyteller and listeners, and among listeners, provides instant and constant feedback as to which questions should follow. A third benefit is that character-centric questions will eventually cover all four components of OH (see figure 7.2) and do so in a natural manner!

These three benefits increase the possibility of discovering what the author wishes to communicate. Valid meaning can emerge out of socially constructed conversations through germane questions generated in the heat of the moment, all guided by the Spirit of truth. Discussion-driven questions lay a solid foundation for spiritual formation.

> "Scripture is incomplete in the sense that, as an authoritative script, it calls for appropriation on the part of the believing community—in a word, *performance*."[58]

Rather than the storyteller relying of a limited number of formulaic questions, the dialogue should determine the number, flow, and focus, how the storyteller should frame the questions (safe, closed, open ended, rhetorical), when questions are asked, and to whom they are directed. Generally, questions related to OH focus on characters, circumstances, conversations, controversies, changes, chances, conclusions, choices, and consequences of those choices within said story. All this comes naturally to many outside the West. The authors advocate the kind of natural, free-flowing, relational, discussion-driven questions that arise when asking what we learn from what the character(s) say and do (see Appendix E for an effective tool that customizes questions to the characters). *Should Westerners rethink how they use questions when storying the Bible at home and abroad?*

In relation to reviewing a *former* story within a story set, character-centric questions often begin by asking for testimonies (accountability) of what happened when they attempted to live out aspects of the last lesson (see figure 7.3). This helps to create emotional connections to the *current* story, and the questions set the table to alert listeners as to what happened to whom and what to anticipate (character-historical in contrast to grammatical-historical).[59]

---

58. Vanhoozer, *Drama of Doctrine*, 101 (emphasis original).

59. "To understand the life of Jesus, I must first give you some background history, events that occurred when Herod ruled Judea for the Roman Empire" (Luke 1:5 VOICE).

Character-centric questions then narrow the focus as they dig out pertinent details about relationships, discussions, decisions, and actions of the characters in the story. They then expand the focus to discover connections to former stories[60] even as they unfurl a growing understanding of the grand narrative[61] of Scripture.

Character-centric application questions follow as participants attempt to find their place *in* the story (not the sidelines) and now seek to demonstrate loyal allegiance to the Divine Hero behind the story. In the total questioning process, the storyteller-questioner seeks spiritual guidance from the Holy Spirit, the Master Interpreter/Clarifier.

The following list of questions is not meant to be memorized or followed in a specific sequence. Rather, it provides different examples of character-centric questions that focus on who as they follow the total storytelling process (see figure 7.3). The goal is for the storyteller to internalize the character-centric concept through concrete examples so that asking questions centered on characters (in contrast to content) becomes second nature for the entire storying event.

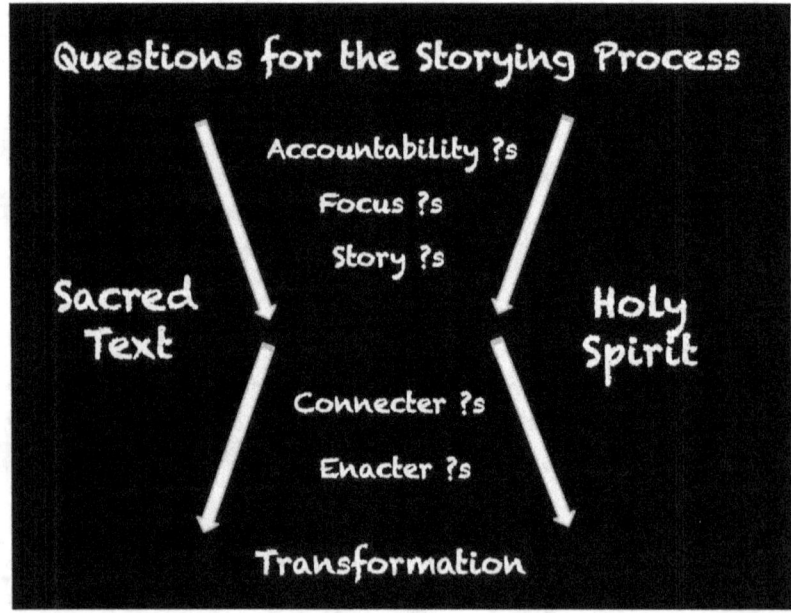

Figure 7.3. Questions for the Storying Process

60. Duvall and Hays astutely note, "It is important to keep relating the parts to the whole" (Duvall and Hays, *Grasping God's Word*, 345).

61. "We have to study not only the spiders, or the Bible characters; it is equally important to study the web, or the meta-narrative... because God has chosen to weave his grand story with the smaller stories of particular people" (Steffen, *Facilitator Era*, 148).

Character-centric questioning does not necessarily follow sequential steps in a linear path or in a circle or in a spiral.[62] Rather, it is much more free-flowing—more like lily pad-hopping. Sequence varies. Directional questions may be necessary at any time to refocus the dialogue, as modeled in the widow's story when the storyteller redirects a misguided discussion. Accountability and application questions may be required at any time during the story. Character-centric questioning recognizes that as oral listeners discern the characters and event(s) found in a story, they have their own way of processing from the known to the unknown,[63] just as we do.

Note those questions focused on value systems (innocence-guilt, honor-shame, power-fear, purity-pollution) and their relationship to heroes, heroines, rogues, and so forth. Note also the focus on action. Examine the use of groups as characters, such as Israel, the Pharisees, and the community of faith. Observe also in the review/application (enactor) questions the search for the more covert symbols and sayings that succinctly summarize the story for easy retrieval and reinforcing long-term memory. These could include proverbs or drawn Hebrew, Chinese, or Japanese letters/characters. Note also the questions are designed to creatively challenge perceptions through dialogue rather than test cognitive knowledge, which can be intimidating. Through dialogue, which enhances spiritual formation, the storyteller-questioner demonstrates mutual respect, thereby encouraging participation as equals.[64]

Welcome to the semispontaneous, asymmetrical oral world. Experience, time, alertness, intentional observation, questions, discussion, and most importantly, a desire to learn the host culture's worldview—which includes how they use questions—will provide cross-cultural storytellers insights into *their* legitimate, and yes, limited (not unlike our own), local pedagogies.[65]

62. Joas Adiprasetya, President of Jakarta Theological Seminary, makes this observation in relation to Paulo Freire's "circle of praxis" and Juan Luis Segundo's "hermeneutic spiral": "The popular illustration of a circle or spiral is merely the curving of four linear steps, starting from context (insertion and social analysis) to text (theological reflection) back to context (through pastoral planning and praxis). Thus, not only is the alleged language of 'circle' or 'spiral' inaccurate, the procedural rigidity that it employs can easily lead us into a 'methodological imperialism'" (Adiprasetya, "Towards an Asian Multitextual Theology," 127).

63. Those raised on the Internet also have been programmed to process information differently. "Nicholas Carr explains in *The Shallows: What the Internet Is Doing to Our Brains* that 'the linear mind is being pushed aside by a new kind of mind that wants and needs to take in and dole out information in short, disjointed, often overlapping bursts—the faster the better.' Our brains work one way when trained to read in logical, linear patterns, and another way when continually bouncing from tweet to tweet, picture to picture, and screen to screen" (Prior, *On Reading Well*, 16).

64. For an insightful discussion on this topic, see Lee-Thorp, *How to Ask Great Questions*.

65. While Bible storying to the Navajo, J. O. Terry discovered it was culturally

Some readers have no doubt concluded this approach is far too chaotic and confusing. They prefer a prescribed list of a small number of questions to cover. Simple. Straightforward. Done.

Well maybe not.

Problems associated with this shortcut and short stack include:

—little if any attention given to social value-moral systems outside of innocence-guilt, which has been long-favored in the West;

—questions tend to focus on reasons rather than relationships;

—the questions are too scripted, general, and minimal for the typical discussion or refocusing the dialogue;

—fails to tie back to former stories, thereby losing the grand narrative and perpetuating the fragmentation of Scripture so common in the West;

—they focus strongly on the individual rather than the group;

—gives little if any consideration to the role of summary symbols or parables.

Formulaic lists of questions can make one feel in control. After all, *who likes chaos in the classroom? But should control be the goal? Or, should the goal be to ask stop-you-in-your-tracks questions that challenge current worldviews? Should the goal be to continue asking questions until an aha moment is reached?* Character change should be the ultimate goal of one's questioning rather than classroom control.

Questions tied to conversations differ from those tied to texts. *And they should, even if chaos ensues for the storyteller-questioner!* One is tied to frozen texts while the other is tied to fluid conversations. Being oral in nature, conversations demand continual updating. Just as one's statements must be constantly updated to keep pace with an evolving conversation to be relevant, so must one's questions.

Dynamic questions are like wolves—they travel in packs, and observers are never quite sure where the lead wolf is headed. "What? So what?

---

improper to dissect or discuss a story *after* being told; stories are considered sacred. So, during the prestory dialogue he set up the story to trigger curiosity and sensitize listeners to what they were about to hear in the story through rhetorical questions. For example, he asked if anyone had ever been betrayed. As the story began all listeners were eagerly waiting for the betrayal event in the story. In Africa he found it was common to tell the truths or things to learn *before* telling the story (personal communication, Dec 30, 2017). Interestingly, in parts of Europe, the story *ends* with, "The moral of the story is . . ."

Now what?" does not always connect well with oralists. Expanding dialogue demands continual updating of the questions being asked. This requires careful listening to the comments and observations offered by participants, and responding well not just to the mind, but to the often unspoken questions of the longing heart.

Attention-grabbing, conversation-based questions emerge out of the emotion of the moment. They are dynamic, evolve out of the ongoing dialogue, are spontaneous, and therefore their number varies. They reject control; they demand sweeping comprehensiveness. *Why?* Because the spoken-written word was imparted not just for knowledge and wisdom but for emotional impact! In-the-moment arresting questions deliver impact that influences retention and replication!

> "Judge a man by his questions rather than by his answers."
> —Voltaire[66]

Dynamic conversations require dynamic questions, all of which demands the storyteller sage listen before asking questions. Listening can lead to those precise, probing questions to ask. Penetrating questions are conversationally controlled. Due to flashbacks, flashforwards, needs of the audience and the like, interpreting a story is rarely linear, therefore the questions should follow the dialogue. *How much attention should storytellers give to conversation-led questions rather than a prescribed short list?* OH is more about asking the right questions than knowing the precise answers! *Why?* Because right questions lead to right answers.

To sum up, if God-honoring, sustainable, actionized wisdom is to result more fully, the assistance of the Master Interpreter/Clarifier, the Holy Spirit, will be necessary. He will guide the storyteller-questioner as to which questions to ask, and the sequence in which they should follow. Only then will the streets of Samaria meet the streets of San Francisco; only then will the dialoguers be able to maximize discovery of memorable answers centered on the biblical text; only then is spiritual formation enhanced.

As you peruse the examples found in the storytelling process (figure 7.3), note, among others, the strong focus on who (characters and the Chief Character), different value-moral systems, groups, symbols and proverbs, and the ties to former stories to build a grand narrative. Note also how these compare to the OH (or TH) model you use:

---

66. Voltaire. https://www.brainyquote.com/quotes/quotes/v/voltaire100338.html.

Accountability Questions (for Previous Lesson Review):

1. Who (individual/group) would like to retell/sing[67] the last story?
2. Did anyone see someone in the faith community exemplify something learned from last week's story? How did the person/audience respond to him/her?
3. Who (individual or group) wants to tell us what happened when attempting to apply the behavior of various characters found in the last lesson? Tell someone beside you/the group what happened?
4. Who challenged you this week in how to apply the story?

Focus Questions (for Present Lesson):

1. Has <u>issue from text</u> happened to someone you know?
2. Are you familiar with the story of <u>Elisha and the widow</u>?
3. Would you like to hear some backstory about the <u>author</u> and the <u>characters</u> in the story? Where and when the <u>narrator</u> says it took place? To the <u>audience</u> he was writing?

Story Questions:

Character focused:

1. How did _____'s actions differ from _____'s actions?
2. How did the setting influence _____'s actions?
3. What did _____ wish to convey when s/he mentioned/used that particular symbol/ritual?
4. How did those in the crowd understand the symbol/ritual?

---

5. How does symbol/ritual relate to _____ comments/actions?

[67]. The Tala-andig of the Philippines composed over 400 "review songs" that have been placed on MP3 Saber players purchased from Global Recordings Network. Church leadership asked local gifted musicians to take on this task and train others. This has resulted in over 200 indigenous and 200 contemporary songs (Steffen, *Worldview-based Storying*, 56).

6. Who made wise choices?
7. Who was shamed? Honored? Polluted? Purified? Feared? Powerful? Guilty? Innocent?
8. Who took the greatest risk?

---

9. Who gave the best advice?
10. What other choices could _____ have made?
11. Who has power in the story? Who is marginalized? Whose voice is missing?
12. What is the meaning of _____'s name have to do with the story?

---

13. Who in the story is related? Any implications?
14. When _____ made the decision to _____, what were the consequences of his/her choice?
15. What did _____ mean to communicate when s/he said/did/wrote/drew?
16. What does it say when _____ treated _____ like s/he did? Who demonstrated wisdom?

---

17. How was _____'s relationship with _____ a good/bad thing?
18. Who changed for the best? Worst?
19. How did _____ overcome the obstacle of _____?
20. Who speaks the most? Who responds the most? What is the narrator trying to tell us about these individuals?

---

21. How does _____'s opinion differ from _____'s?
22. How would someone in the surrounding crowd (Pharisees/leper) have responded?

23. Who is different by the end of the story?
24. How should _____ have responded when s/he heard/saw what happened to _____?

---

25. Who is the hero/heroine of the story?
26. How is the community of faith portrayed in the story? Israel?
27. How is God portrayed in the story? The Holy Spirit? Jesus?
28. If the <u>author</u> of the book (e.g., Ruth/Esther/Daniel/Jonah was here, what would you like to ask him?

God/spirits focused:

1. Who experienced God's faithfulness?
2. Who experienced God's power?
3. Who experienced God's loyalty?
4. Who experienced God's justice?

---

5. How did God purify _____?
6. How did God protect _____?
7. What promise did God make to _____?
8. How does God challenge _____?

---

9. How did God bless/curse _____?
10. How did God react to _____'s choice to _____?
11. Who's the chief challenger of God in the story?
12. Who challenged God's authority?
13. Who is the honored hero/heroine/Divine Hero of the story?

Animal/nature focused:

1. How did God challenge _____?
2. What role did <u>animal</u> have in _____'s life?

Life-in-the-abstract connection:

1. What metaphor/letter/proverb/poem/song/artistic expression (e.g., dance or drums/symbol/ritual) would you use to capture this story? This story set? This book?
2. Would you/a group be willing to draw/sing/sculp/dance/dramatize/compose a song that reflects this story?

Connecter Questions (to Previous Stories):

1. What is the <u>author</u> of this book (e.g., Ruth/Esther/Daniel/Jonah) trying to tell us through the attitudes and allegiances of _____?
2. How does _____'s responses and/or actions in this story echo those found in previous stories in this book?
3. How does _____'s conversations/controversies in this story echo the previous stories in this book?

---

4. How does the <u>author's</u> message of the book echo other books we have heard/viewed?
5. Does _____'s actions remind you of someone else's actions in the Bible?
6. What is God trying to tell us through all the characters in this book? How do these characters relate to other characters we have previously heard about?

Enacter Questions:

1. Who was your favorite character in the story? Least favorite? Why?

2. Has what happened to _____ happened to some family member or friend? Can you tell us what happened to this person?

3. Which character's actions went against their/your culture? What happened/would happened if you/your family did this?

4. What was God trying to say to _____? Does this remind you of anyone?

---

5. Are there situations today like _____ experienced?

6. If you were _____, how would you/your family have reacted?

7. What would happen if we tried to live like _____?

8. What is God trying to tell your family through what _____ did/said?

---

9. Who do you know that demonstrates loyalty/allegiance to God?

10. Who in the story serves as a model to demonstrate our loyalty to God?

11. What can we as a group do to avoid living out what _____ did/said?

12. How can we make God the hero of our situation like _____ did?

---

13. Which character(s) does (do) the <u>narrator</u> want us to remember? Model? Why?

14. Which character(s) do(es) the <u>narrator</u> *not* want us to model? Why?

15. Who did you/your family side with in the story?

How can storytellers become more proficient in the use of character-centric questions that are conversational in nature and sequence? How could such questions turn Bible studies into impactful communal Bible discussions?

If the reader has time, review the questions the storyteller asked in chapter 1 and see how they demonstrate what is proposed in this chapter. Search for them again in the Bible story told in chapter 9.

Summarizing: OH centers on character theology (product) discerned through character-centric questions driven by narrative logic that analyzes the conversations and actions of the characters as they advance the plotline of the story in time and place (process). The demonstrated discoveries naturally, impactfully, and memorably telegraph theology, values, and morals to model, modify, or discard. The ultimate goal of this entire process (Prov 3:3) is to glorify the Creator by practicing godly wisdom that not only changes the listener, but communities and nations as well.

Fundamental for the above discussion to result in spiritual formation to its fullest are questions that focus on characters. Character-centric questions that highlight the value-moral system of the host audience, in contrast to cognitive-centered questions based on the value-moral system of the storyteller, serve as the most natural, powerful, and multipliable way to discern and communicate embodied truths in a Bible story. Questions (and theology) framed within relationships will prove the strongest in facilitating spiritual formation.

The authors will now provide some reflections on part 2.

8

Reflections

"If the ladder is not leaning against the right wall,
every step we take just gets us to the wrong place faster."
—Stephen Covey

"The indirect route is the straightest line to truth."
—Japanese Proverb

"The cave you fear to enter turns out to be the treasure you seek."
—Joseph Campbell

There are a number of questions in regard to hermeneutics that most, including the authors, have failed to ask. Many of these questions therefore were raised and touched on in chapters 3–7. For example,

> *Have we been sufficiently aware of how oral text influenced the construction and communication of the Hebrew Bible? The New Testament, including the speech letters (Epistles)?*
>
> *What implications does orality have for interpreting the Bible today?*
>
> *Was the spoken word Holy Spirit-inspired before it became the written word?*

REFLECTIONS

How has the European Enlightenment and Gutenberg Galaxy privileged TH?

What makes a hermeneutic paternalistic? A partner? A servant?

Why did the Holy Spirit, the Master Storywriter, choose to write Scripture in multiple genres (e.g., propositional, narrative, poetry)?

Why did the Holy Spirit choose to make narrative the predominant genre?

Why did the Holy Spirit include thousands in the cast of characters?

How do we determine the significant from the insignificant?

How do symbols and rituals influence interpretation?

How do imagination and emotions improve interpretation of Scripture?

Do we hear God speak when we read the Bible?

How do we make hermeneutics communal and concrete rather than private and abstract?

How could CT influence our hermeneutic to ascertain a fuller, richer, more memorable meaning?

How well does TH match the pedagogical preferences of Millennials? Gen Z? Adult learners? Oralists at home and abroad?

How well do the original languages, grammars, etymologies, word studies, Bible verse prooftexting, and propositional philosophy connect with most people around the globe?

Does God expect all people to be able to analyze grammar to grasp the meaning of the spoken-written word?

Does he expect some?

Is there more than propositional logic that carries equal significance and substance?

How does narrative logic access the emotions, imagination, and reason?

It is interesting to note that in *Exegetical Fallacies*, D. A. Carson[1] identified the top four exegetical fallacies as: (1) word-studies, (2) grammar, (3) logic, and (4) presuppositions and history. Westerners tend to be good at parsing; not so good at piecing things back together. *Is TH the West's ethnohermenutic?*

> *Is textual meaning limited to only one correct truth?*
>
> *How could asserting a single exclusive meaning of a text limit the mystery and majesty of God?*
>
> *How did orality influence the biblical text in antiquity?*
>
> *Does the fluidity between the fixed written text and the fluid oral text become the basis for, and necessity of, OH?*
>
> *How did honor and shame help ensure the sacredness of the text over time? How did memory? The faith community?*

> *Can exegetes move beyond turning first-century ancestors into us—textual analyzers searching for objective naked propositions?*
>
> *Can we also learn to experience relationships and conversations with characters in specific contexts to encounter meaning?*
>
> *How capable are we of differentiating modern readers from ancient hearers?*
>
> *Are these questions the answers?*

Professor emeritus of medieval history M. T. Clanchy correctly concluded, "The most difficult initial problem in the history of literacy is appreciating what preceded it."[2] And we would add, what *followed*—the oral-digital age (see appendix A). *What unlearning may be necessary for Bible communicators before new learning becomes possible?*

Loubser offers two reasons for the necessity of some unlearning: "Almost by default, most people living in modern literate cultures are 'media blind' . . . it [oral poetics] goes against the grain of our deep-seated literate inclinations."[3] C. S. Lewis, speaking of rhetoric, concurs that it is "the greatest barrier between us and our ancestors," which Wuellner goes on

---

1. See Carson, *Exegetical Fallacies*.
2. Clanchy, *Memory to Written Record*, 41.
3. Loubser, *Oral and Manuscript Culture*, 4, 74.

to define as "the categorical barrier between oral and literary structures."[4] The authors agree with Alter when he claims, "As modern readers of the Bible, we need to relearn something of this mode of perception that was second nature to the original audience."[5]

Challenges to Oral Hermeneutics

A number of cultural differences mitigate against embracing OH for Westerners raised on the print side of history, e.g., egalitarianism, individualism, dependence on the written text. Interpreters tend to forget or are unaware of how deeply collective and hierarchically oriented the ancients were, how most could not read; the existence of a professional class of readers; the limited access to scrolls; the high expense of a sheet of papyrus which usually only used one side[6]; and the rarity of libraries that required presence to use books (no loaners). We tend to forget or are unaware of the original text's absence of chapters, paragraphs, and verses, and of the need for people to hear the texts read in community, have the reading explained to them corporately,[7] dialogue about the various character-driven principles and practices, and how foreign it would have been to practice private devotions. In contrast, awareness of these things helps us modern literates to better relate to our ancestors in the faith and their intake of the word, and to appreciate and emphasize the importance of orality for our own intake of the word.

Bible communicators tend to forget or are unaware of how literacy relies strongly on the eye while orality relies on both ear and eye. Eyes speak and are heard. And multiplication rather than addition results when ear meets eye (cf. Paul's interdependent body parts metaphor in 1 Cor 12). Professor of political economy Harold Innis's summary is apropos, "In oral intercourse the eye, ear, and brain, the senses and the faculties acted

---

4. Lewis, quoted in Wuellner, "Where is Rhetorical Criticism Taking Us?," 457.

5. Alter, *Art of Biblical Narrative*, 62.

6. Harris concludes at least three sheets of papyrus would be needed for Paul's first letter to the Corinthians at a cost of "$30.00–35.00" a sheet (Harris, *Ancient Literacy*, 194–95).

7. We must never forget that there is a role for someone beyond the text—a Bible teacher. Recall the Ethiopian eunuch's need for an interpreter-teacher (Acts 8:31). It is only when humans engage the written texts that the texts fulfill their purpose. We believe that the best engagement is oral and collective (two or more). The Ethiopian asked a question, and "That began a conversation in which Philip used the passage to explain the good news of Jesus" (Acts 8:35 VOICE).

together in busy co-operation and rivalry each eliciting, stimulating, and supplementing the other."[8]

Literacy initiated TH, where words, phrases, and grammars prevail; it approved content (orthodoxy) as the starting point for interpretation. Detached objectivity superseded participational subjectivity. Exegetes tended to define objective meaning from the manuscript rather than communicate a narratable message that demonstrated truths. Application (orthopraxis), a call to action followed, and some interpretations became a part of the community's oral faith tradition (orthoecho).

> "In oral language, the form and meaning form an indissoluble pairing. When we don't understand a sentence/utterance we say, 'What do *you* mean?' not 'What does *it* mean?,' focusing upon the person doing the communicating, not on the utterance. In speech, then, form and meaning are indissolubly linked."[9]

Orality, on the other hand, serves as the bedrock for OH, where experiential, embodied, incarnated performance (action) prevailed, rather than print, making appropriate living (orthopraxy) and emotions (orthopathy)[10]

---

8. Innis, *Bias of Communication*, 105.

9. Olson, "Cognitive Consequences of Literacy," 113 (emphasis original).

10. Though he did not use the term "orthopathy," C. S. Lewis in his wisdom understood what we mean by this. His context was the highly cerebral mid-twentieth-century Oxford and Cambridge universities where he saw the modern debunking of emotions, sentiment, and sensibilities in the name of reason. In the first of his three essays in *The Abolition of Man*, Lewis critiques a particular contemporary textbook (which he refers to as "the green book") that asserted that emotions are *only* subjective and thus unimportant. Lewis argues that for traditional moral theorists, the purpose of education was to inculcate virtues by linking them to proper emotions (e.g., to feel admiration for the honorable, anger at injustice, shame for sin, sadness when others are hurt, disgust at what is vile, vulgar, and morally reprehensible, etc.). Lewis calls people who cultivate and practice these proper emotions, "men with chests." Those who would follow the "green book" and its kind would produce "men without chests." He gives us the following series of colorful, memorable analogies and similes: "In a sort of ghastly simplicity we remove the organ and demand the function. We make men without chests and expect of them virtue and enterprise. We laugh at honour and are shocked to find traitors in our midst. We castrate and bid the geldings be fruitful" (Lewis, *Abolition of Man*, 37). The characters of the Bible, when properly assessed, attuned to, and discussed by groups of friends who support each other's aspirations for their virtues (the role models) or repudiation of their lack of them (the anti-role models), can produce men with chests, and women with mature emotions properly lined to virtues. This is the goal of orthopathy.

the center of interpretation. Participants discovered meaning in the *message* rather than in the *manuscript*.

Diving deeper, rather than searching for cold, clammy facts in a Bible story through systematic analysis from off stage in a distant, dark auditorium, those using OH joined the actors on the brightly lit stage to read characters; they entered the story, lasering in on the emotive relationships between characters—from stormy to spurious to sensual, etc.; they sought out the significance of the experiences of the characters; they co-participated with the characters on stage, thereby experiencing in the present what the characters had experienced in the past. No time lapse seemed to exist between past and present.

Frothy facts found significance through memorable relational interchanges of experiences, i.e., entering the story-stage as co-participants and co-characters. Such co-participation was *not* to rewrite the script in any significant way! Rather it was to engage and experience the lives of the ancients physically, emotionally, mentally, and spiritually. Whether the ancients' attitudes and activities were accepted or dismissed, they were memorable![11]

The highly treasured discoveries identified through the conversations and interactions between characters therefore became worthy of praise or rejection, possible practice, retelling, and long-term collective memory (orthoecho); they discovered the Divine Hero behind the story (even if not explicitly named) in the midst of emotive relationships between heroes, heroines, hucksters, hacks, villains, and rogues (ethnodoxy).[12]

Startlingly from a human perspective, a relational, trinitarian God chose, in multiple case demonstrations in Scripture, to clarify the human-divine relationship through the relationships of others (orthodoxy). For example, the Word became human firstly through Jesus' birth as a human being, but also through Jesus' voice, actions, interactions, and through a cast of chosen characters with whom he interacted, as recorded in canonical Scripture.

Having a communal bent, Bible communicators have the ability to learn naturally through interacting as co-participants on the stages of the biblical stories. Through real (vicarious) relationships—which require listening, speaking, engaging, feeling, curiosity, imagination, and actions—Bible communicators learn about others, themselves, and most importantly, the Chief Character. We were naturally made for relationships through the relational-based Trinity. This brief summary discussion is not only the essence of OH, it is its genius.

---

11. For those readers who have viewed the "EE-Taow: The Moak Story" video I've (Tom) always wondered what was going through the mind of the Moak who played Jesus and was placed on a cross as he observed the story play out beneath him. What memories stayed with him? https://www.youtube.com/watch?v=hjRTBQcf-uc.

12. See Fig. 7.2.

> "Why does the Bible contain so many stories? Is it possible that stories reveal some truths and experiences in a way that no other literary form does—and if so, what are they? What are the differences in our picture of God, when we read stories in which God acts, as compared with theological statements about the nature of God?
>
> What does the Bible communicate through our imagination that it does not communicate through our reason? If the Bible uses the imagination as one way of communicating truth, should we not show an identical confidence in the power of the imagination to convey religious truth? If so, would a good startpoint be to respect the story quality of the Bible in our exposition of it?"[13]

Both hermeneutic models in all their variations attempt in their own ways (TH evidentially, and OH experientially) with different levels of success to make the unfamiliar familiar and the familiar unfamiliar. They creatively seek to make biblical truth understood, consistently practiced, and etched deep in collective memories for generations (orthoecho).

For many Bible teachers today there is no contest—TH *is* the hermeneutic king of the mountain. Therefore, strong resistance remains and sometimes resentment is felt toward any intruding competitor. Kelber, however, wisely waves a warning flag: "One should not underrate the role of print and the seductive perfection of the printed page in making us believe that the perfectly constructed print format is the carrier of a perfectly unified content."[14]

> *Is there, should there be, more than a single, superior standard to discern the truth-claims of the spoken-written word?*
>
> *If so, which exegetes have the credentials, credibility, and cultural experience to make such a decision?*
>
> *How would the questions differ? The expected answers?*
>
> *How detached and disengaged should exegetes be from the text?*
>
> *How unbiased is each hermeneutic model?*
>
> *What are the limits of each?*

---

13. Ryken, "Bible," 38.
14. Kelber, "Oral-Scribal-Memorial Arts of Communication," 249.

Do exegetes have sufficient skepticism for each?

Which model should be privileged when?

Who interprets for God?

How does Hebrew hermeneutics contribute to this discussion?

Another warning flag, not to throw OH under the bus, is found in Hebrew hermeneutics (ch. 5). Hebrew hermeneutics challenges late-modern Westerners to consider that the way most have been schooled in theological education (particularly hermeneutics and homiletics) was *not* the way it has always been done among God's people, nor was it necessarily the superior way. The tools of TH are valuable, useful, and necessary, but they are insufficient if Bible communicators wish to read the narrative sections of Scripture *for all their worth.*

> "The Christian faith is kaleidoscopic, and most of us are color-blind. It is multidimensional, and most of us manage to hold at most two dimensions in our heads at any one time. It is symphonic, and we can just about whistle one of the tunes."[15]

If exegetes use only the tools of TH as the gateway to gain meaning, they will have a reduced range of possibilities to experience the depths of the spoken-written word. Through the principles retrieved from the Hebrew and Jewish interpretive tradition, exegetes can transcend TH and once again meet the people behind the principles and hear the voices behind their written words.

Whether the bifurcation is between naked theology and clothing (chs. 5 and 6) or between the text and orality (ch. 3), each comes with its own contributions and confines. When Bible teachers separate doctrine from events, statements from stories, reasons from illustrations, explicitness from ambiguity, private from public, print from memory, and/or principles from participants, unnecessary things happen. The same occurs when there is a divorce between publication and performance,[16] immediateness and accumulation, proof and persuasion, reading and rhetoric, deductions and dialogue, documentation and relevance, and/or eye and ear; they do a great disservice to the Chief Character's message. Understanding of spoken writing will be limited.[17]

---

15. Wright, "Foreword," 11.
16. Some of these are adapted from Ong, *Orality and Literacy,* 37–57.
17. "In highly oral cultures, it was not sufficient for the reader simply to imagine

Bible communicators who recognize the hybridization of what the Author instructs in Revelation 2:1, "*Write down My words*" (VOICE) or in Luke 1:63, "he wrote saying" (Darby), will be able to present a more holistic picture of life to audiences. *Do we hear what the written text says? Do we recognize orality's robust role pretext, during textual construction, and post-text communication?* One-winged aircraft do not fly well.

Bible communicators must never forget OH has an important and instructive role in the interpretation of Scripture for multiple audiences today, most likely the majority! We must learn to appreciate story—a medium "that does not traffic in abstractions"[18]—on its own basis (characters, plot, setting, sequence, events) and its own merits (natural, imaginative, emotional, relational, personal, collective, mysterious, earthy, retainable, replicable). We must learn to hear, read, and view story *as* story, and appreciate the individual Bible stories as part of *the* Story (grand narrative). Bailey summarizes it well:

> A biblical story is not simply a 'delivery system' for an idea. Rather, the story first creates a world and then invites the listener to live in that world, to take on as part of who he or she is. Biblical stories invite the reader to accept them as *his or her* story. In . . . studying the Bible, ancient tales are not examined merely in order to extract a theological principle or ethical model. Instead, the Bible is read to rediscover who we are and what we must yet become, because the biblical story of sin and salvation, law and grace, is *our* story.[19]

Only if Bible communicators learn to welcome story as story will Bible communicators be able to discern and decipher the appropriate and robust contribution of OH.

Contributions of Oral Hermeneutics

The authors agree with Walton and Sandy when they assert "we will not interpret the New Testament correctly if we fail to grasp the oral dimensions

---

the sounds of the words being read. Books in such a culture do not 'contain' something called 'material.' They speak or say words . . . . Marcel Jousse, S. J., treats beautifully what he calls the 'eating of the word in oral cultures, its being passed from mouth to mouth' (45–54). This 'eating of the word' gives a new dimension and force to imaginary incidents such as the eating of the little scroll in Revelation 10:9–10, which otherwise may appear merely quaint or bizarre to technological man" (Ong, "*Maranatha*," 437).

18. Bradt, *Story as a Way of Knowing*, 102.

19. Bailey, *Jacob & the Prodigal*, 51–52 (emphasis original).

involved in its creation and transmission."[20] This does not mean there is no role for TH, or it is inferior or incorrect or dated. Nor do we advocate a hostile hermeneutic takeover. Rather, we believe both are necessary in their place because each provides a different and distinct toolset necessary to accomplish the singular task of Bible interpretation.

But the authors also believe a specific hermeneutic can be initially more appropriate than others when it comes to narrative sections of Scripture. In other words, hermeneutics is determined by genre. If God's book began interpretation through ways understandable to the original audience (ethnohermeneutics),[21] Bible communicators should make sure the same happens with their host audiences. For this to be achieved, however, many expatriate Bible teachers (and some locals trained under them) will have to undergo dehermeneutization so a new (actually an old) hermeneutic can emerge from the ashes of our forgotten Hebrew heritage.

Print can be imperialistic, but need not be, nor should it be. Frozen text can be thawed through communal dialogue as exemplified by authorized spokespersons, the "emissary-performer," (see ch. 3) sent by Paul in the past to read and explain the manuscripts, and present-day Bible storytellers. The grammatical-historical-literary requires the character-historical and the character-historical requires the grammatical-historical-literary. "Oral texts depended on writing for their survival while written texts were deeply dependent on those oral aspects for their legitimacy."[22]

---

20. Walton and Sandy, *Lost World of Scripture*, 86.

21. "We no longer have the luxury to assume that *our* way is the *best* way or the *only* way" (Caldwell, "Towards the New Discipline of Ethnohermeneutics," 24–25 [emphasis original]). Caldwell also posits, "I truly believe that God made His Word understandable to all who would seek to understand it. Consequently, we will learn how to do Bible interpretation using only the Bible" (Caldwell, *Doing Bible Interpretation!*, 12). We take exception with those "fellow evangelicals" who "sharply criticized" Caldwell for using the term "ethnohermeneutics," concluding that it opened the doors to "relativized hermeneutic approaches." What they seemed to have failed to observe is the ethnocentricism of their own hermeneutic approaches and the resulting multiple interpretations, and the internal and external guardrails orality provides within a Bible story to protect it from misinterpretation. Because of cultural biases, misinterpretation is possible in *any* hermeneutic model because *every* model, not just those models coming from outside the West, is an ethnohermeneutic (Moreau, *Contextualization in World Missions*, 91).

22. Botha, *Orality and Literacy in Early Christianity*, xvi.

> "Biblical texts circulate orally in both religious and nonreligious contexts through quotations and allusions in conversation, popular song, and widespread biblical imagery. The scriptures can be said to exist not just in formalized verbal text between hard covers, the dimension on which print-based scholars naturally fix their eyes, but also in an oral mode."[23]

But there is a preferred sequence in this integration. If the majority of the world is to begin to (re)appreciate the spoken-written Scripture, many Bible communicators coming from a print-dominant culture will have to learn to play the purist role poorly; they will need to learn to start with what may not seem so pure to them—OH. For many audiences today, likely the majority, OH (in all its variations) will be *their* ethnohermeneutic. They prefer a case book over a code book. We therefore attempted in this book to make Christ the center of the communal conversation by:

1. pointing out the incompleteness of a stand-alone TH (in all its variations) to ascertain meaning ("left-brain direction"[24]),
2. identifying a hermeneutic that can stand equally beside TH to fill a void—OH ("right-brain rising"[25] in all its variations),
3. suggesting a sequence to follow—OH to TH, i.e., sound that seeks sight. Then it can jump back and forth from one hermeneutic model to the other. Just as the "Great Divide" (ch. 3) between orality and literacy is now considered a continuum, so must the Great Divide between TH and OH (resulting in a "whole new mind"[26]), and

---

23. Finnegan, *Literacy and Orality*, 12.
24. See Pink, *Whole New Mind*, 3.
25. See Pink, *Whole New Mind*, 7.
26. Pink, *Whole New Mind*, 25. Daniel Pink has argued that our postmodern moment in Western history is a time of "right brain rising." To put very simply the argument of his book: "*Left brain direction*" (rational, scientific, analytic, text-oriented, logical, linear, sequential, detail-oriented) was dominant during modernity. "*Right brain direction*" (artistic, aesthetic, emotional and relational expression, literary, synthesis, nonlinear, context-oriented, big-picture, holistic, image, metaphor, and story-orientation) is rising in postmodernity out of human hunger for its lack during modernity. Right brain aptitudes are increasingly desired and needed. Left brain direction remains necessary, but it is not sufficient. We need a "whole new mind," a holistic mind (See Pink, *Whole New Mind*).

4. discovering author/Divine Author truths through the ongoing conversations between four interactive contributors: the word, the Holy Spirit, the community, and oral tradition (memory). The past speaks to the present through the power of the Holy Spirit, thereby providing hope for the future.

There is no singular, comprehensive, universal, culturally unbiased hermeneutic to interpret all of Scripture for all peoples of the world for all times. There is no hermeneutic model that can rightfully ascribe itself "most-favored nation" status. Our Creator is just too creative when it comes to how creation processes information, passes it on, and preserves it. No hermeneutic can guarantee specific comprehensive, exhaustive, universal truths because *all* methods evolved with cultural limitations and implicit biases. But there is a worthy hermeneutic mosaic. The questions become: *Which hermeneutic model works best for which genre? Which audience? Is there a best sequence?* Scripture construction and communication are not without clues as to the answers to these questions.

The answers to the above questions led the authors to begin Bible interpretation focused on OH for oralists through character theologizing using character-centric questions that results in character theology (CT), all driven by narrative logic. The authors defined CT as discussions about God's interaction with characters, characters' interaction with God, characters' interaction with themselves, with each other (and sometimes spirits, animals, nature), and possible life-lessons gleaned from those interactions. We highlighted CT because the "story-shapedness of Scripture corresponds to the story-shapedness of human experience."[27] Character clarity telegraphs the truths authors wish us to know and live out.

The lives of Bible characters speak to the lives of all peoples as they express slices of life—family feuds, sickness, sexual sins, deception, warfare, barrenness, birth, blessings, curses, deaths, power abuse, persecution, murder, poverty, executions, sports, fishing, building construction, making a living, making love, mishandling finances, dreams, play, and all else in human experience. A cast of biblical characters make it easy and natural for listeners/readers/viewers to identify with (or against) their choices, the resulting consequences, and the Creator's perspective of such. Bible characters provide a rich reservoir from which to draw a more complete, accurate picture of the face of God. But we do not leave the car parked permanently in the CT garage.

CT calls on *biblical theology* to identify the controlling characters and cumulative secrets surrounding the promised Savior and a present-future

27. Goldingay, "Biblical Story," 6.

kingdom. It does so as it traces the story through the Old Testament from creation to Israel (as nomads, pastorals, city state dwellers, exiled captives, and freed returnees) and through the New Testament where the mystery of the grand narrative reveals its God-ordained conclusions. CT calls on *narrative theology* to identify how characters relate to other characters in said story, and the larger story, e.g., the leper in Mark or Peter in Luke-Acts. CT calls on *systematic theology* to collect, identify, codify, categorize, construct, and confirm doctrines[28] from the words and phrases, actions, and interactions of the character(s) within *all* the individual stories so that the aggregate of the diverse truths of the Eternal One are collected from the complete canon. Each type of theology brings delicacies to the interpretive feast.

All theologies have a form or systemization (compressed categorized concepts), but not all make characters the starting point for discerning textual meaning. Making CT the center point for interpretation is a concrete, natural, human way that involves curiosity, imagination, emotions, reason, and the ability to read others. This makes meaning memorable, multipliable, and missional. But it does not stop there; it calls on other types of theologies to capture, codify, categorize, and classify (e.g., linearly, circularly) the entire canon, hopefully without severing the concrete events from their homes.

As noted in chapter 7, story-centric strategies call for character-centric questions that set the foundation for communal dialogue (which helps develop future storyteller-teachers). There the authors argued audience analysis requires the use of more than six to eight questions when it comes to discerning relationships. Rather, it is natural and expected to ask a host of related questions as the dialogue evolves, including questions to return the discussion to the story after someone digresses far from the topic as happened in the Elisha story (ch. 1). The authors also call for more elasticity in the order in which the questions are asked. Let the conversations and interactions of the biblical characters and audience discussion dictate the number of questions queried, the type of questions asked, and the sequence in which they are raised.

The authors go further, calling for the use of questions that respect the social value-moral systems of host audiences,[29] *and* those in Scripture. This will demand, in many cases, moving beyond the *legal language* of innocence and guilt, a preference of many from the West and those trained under her, to the *relational language* of honor and shame (preference among Asians, Middle

---

28. "Story is the ring that provides a setting for the precious gems of propositions" (Steffen, *Worldview-based Storying*, 138).

29. While all of these value-moral systems are present in any society, two will most likely be dominant.

Easterners, Africans, Latin Americans, and growing among Westerners), and/or the *control language* of power and fear (preference among animists and Catholics), and/or the *hygienic language* of purity and pollution (preference among Buddhists, Hindus, Muslims, First Nations).

Why make such adaptations? The incarnation of God as Jesus of Nazareth. Enculturated as a first-century Jew in a Roman-dominated world, the God-man adapted to those surrounding him, thereby setting the model for people of the Way. Jesus was not cultureless, nor were the Bible characters, nor are we, nor are our audiences. Adaptation rwas, and is, equired.

Having conversations and interactions between people, and then debating those discussions as co-participants, is a daily routine for many in multiple contexts. The same should be true of storytellers in the use of questions in a Bible story—the number asked, the sequence in which they proceed, and the inclusion of the audience's preferred social value-moral systems. Questions asked should come across as natural as they do in daily conversations. Driven by questions that encourage deliberation, debate, discussion, dissent, and divergent views, relationally-based OH focuses not just on *meaning*, but also on *emotional impact!* Such an approach enhances spiritual formation.

In sum, to discover a more comprehensive (in contrast to "the point is . . .") and complete meaning of a text and the Divine Author, and to do so in a more natural, concrete way that maximizes and mimics his mystery, magnificence, and majesty, OH becomes mandatory. OH, undergirded by narrative logic and driven by character-centric questions, results in CT that describes, demonstrates, displays, enacts, embodies, encounters, engages, illustrates, and incarnates, all of which we absorb through co-participation, if so desired. OH is a visually-based hermeneutic drawn through the words and works of Holy Spirit-chosen characters that result in a relational theology (CT) that expects witness and worship.

Sequentially,[30] OH begins the embodied meaning process by providing a necessary, vital, legitimate, authentic, significant contribution for the

---

30. We can draw a parallel between the sequence or priority in time of OH over TH from another angle in the history of philosophical theology. There are two major positions on the relationship between faith and reason in the establishing of knowledge of divine revelation: (1) "I understand (or know) in order to believe." This is the priority of reason to faith position. Truth must be demonstrated in propositions that satisfy the canons of (Aristotelian) logic before they are believed. Representatives include: Abelard, Descartes, John Locke, Carl Henry, Gordon Clark, and Norman Geisler. (2) "I believe in order to understand (or know)." This is the priority of faith to reason position. Faith may go beyond reason but not against it. Faith brings and continues to seek understanding. This is the most biblical position, as is especially evident in the Wisdom literature of the Old Testament and the Gospel of John. Representatives

majority of the world's people.³¹ It also meets their pedagogical preferences, particularly when incorporating the digital world. And OH, in relation to CT, moves seamlessly from evangelism to discipleship. Just as orality met the needs of premoderns, so OH is ideal (with digital extensions) to meet the needs of postmoderns, post-Christians, postliterates, postfactualists, the majority world, adult learners, and the deaf.³²

As our friend Ray Neu would ask, "Are we to think God did not account for oral learners? Are we to believe only we few literates who have this highly exalted slice of information are the only ones who have the potential to be correct? Would not God have foreseen all of this, and created space for various perceptions and preferences of the brilliant multifaceted diamond of his word?"³³ The authors would add, *is it time for some self-auditing? Is it time for the return of OH?*

It is again time to demonstrate what the authors have been discussing, this time with the reader having many more insights under her/his belt in relation to OH. To review, layer, and tie the book together, the authors turn to the story that follows closely after "Elisha and the Widow's Oil": "Elisha and General Naaman," found in 2 Kings 5.

---

include: Augustine, Anselm, Luther, Calvin, and Barth. Drawing the parallel, we would claim the priority of orality to textuality. Humans always hear before they ever read. And in terms of gaining or encountering the word of God, this seems confirmed by Romans 10:17: "So faith proceeds from hearing, as we listen to the message about God's Anointed" (VOICE).

Philosophers of science now increasingly realize, and are admitting, that all the work of science rests on faith commitments made by the scientists. Certain beliefs are presupposed as starting points which themselves cannot be proved by the scientific method. These faith-commitments are prior to logical reasoning and must be employed as premises in any attempted proof. Thus faith is prior to reasoning processes in science. And hearing is prior to reading.

31. Buddhist root texts (*'rtsa ba*) or scriptures (*bstan 'gyur*) have been taught for centuries by being read out loud, followed by explanation (*'grel ba*) by the lama or teacher (which could include partial rereadings of the text), followed by questions (*dris ba*) about the text. James Morrison, personal communication, April 25, 2019.

32. It is estimated 70 million deaf are scattered across the globe with over 130 different sign languages. Each sign language is heavily based in orality. Wycliffe and DOOR International, therefore, have partnered to provide the deaf with visual (signed) Bibles (Steffen, *Worldview-based Storying*, 80, 94).

33. Ray Neu, personal communication, December 22, 2017.

Part 3

Echoes

9

Elisha and General Naaman

"One story is good . . . till another be told."

—R. Greene, Mamilla II, 1593

This book is organized into three parts: Demonstrations, Proposals, and Echoes. An echo is a repeated or reverberated sound reflecting the original sound. So part 3, the following two chapters, will echo the ideas, images, and sounds of the first two parts, but with an expanded, elaborated, and amplified resonation of meaning. This chapter echoes the storytelling event of chapter 1, but with a different story and at a different time. The authors encourage the reader to bear in mind insights you gleaned from parts 1 and 2 and try to recognize them resonating here.

This chapter describes the storytelling session one week after the one described in chapter 1. It occurred at the same weekly Jewish Seeker's Bible study group described there. About one-third of the participants were Jewish. The story occurs in chronological sequence in the narrative flow of book of 2 Kings 3–5, with three shorter stories intervening between "Elisha and the Widow's Oil" and this story—"Elisha and General Naaman."

What follows, like chapter 1, is a printed version of an oral event. The three elements of the "storytelling triangle" are constant in every storytelling event: the storyteller, the story, the audience.[1] In this case the storyteller is the same person, the story is different, and the audience is virtually the same, minus a few absentees or a few attending who were not present the previous week. Thus, though those elements are constant, it is a unique event with its unique chemistry, part of which is the dynamic of the Holy

---

1. Lipman, *Improving Your Storytelling*, 17–18.

Spirit attending to and applying the word of God to people's hearts as the inspired story is made fresh in the telling and discussing.

The storyteller will lead and facilitate the discussion. He or she could also be called the storyteller-teacher because this role is a style of teaching.

Opening: From Last Week's Story Session to Applications to Life Today

STORYTELLER: Welcome everyone! Ready for a little review? We learned last week that the story of "Elisha and the Widow's Oil" happened about 900 years before the birth of the Messiah, back when kings reigned in ancient Israel. It was the time just after the great prophet Elijah had ministered in the Northern Kingdom of Israel. Elijah had renewed a school of prophets from earlier days. Elisha was Elijah's successor as leader of the sons of the prophets, a school of prophetic ministry, inheriting Elijah's mantle of authority and spirit. Elisha was the leading man of God at the time, performing many miracles. Our story was about "Elisha and the Widow's Oil."

Remember some of the spiritual observations we saw in the story last week? And some applications to life we drew from the story of "Elisha and the Widow's Oil?" What were some of those? What truth-treasures did we find from observing and questioning the characters in this story?

JESSE: From the widow's experience, God provides, miraculously, but that can require participation and obedience from the people he provides for. Javier's story was a great current-day application—about the woman in his congregation that had been through a divorce and was down and out and felt helpless, but the church members reached out and gave her work and formed relationships with her, helping her regain a sense of self-worth and purpose.

JAVIER: Yes, and Linda's story about her friend when she lived in the Bronx in New York.

LINDA: Yes, that the faith community's involvement was part of the solution, like the widow's neighbors from whom she borrowed all the empty jars.

LISA: Yes, and that the character of Elisha as the man of God used wisdom that helped this widow, who thought she had nothing, to realize she did have something, and when she used it, in faith obedience, she saw it multiply and saw God bless and prosper her.

JAVIER: Right, and how the woman's needs were met, and likely her self-respect and honor were affirmed through that, through the decisions she made with the little she had . . . she was not just a helpless victim. And the stories from today, from me and Linda; the widow's oil story happens today too!

LISA: And Jesse telling about how American handout aid and sending loads of clothes to Kenya didn't really help people there because it undercut the local cotton and garment-making jobs the people had. Pretty revealing about what kind of mercy ministry and humanitarian aid really helps and what doesn't help people.

ROSE: And the wisdom of Elisha in not just performing an isolated miracle but involving the neighborhood for maximum witness or influence. Think of the impact on those neighbors when they heard what happened!

STORYTELLER: Good. That's a great summary. During this last week, did any of us see any of these truths lived out in the lives of others or were able to apply them ourselves? If so, will you share with the group?

ABE: That proverb, "Give a man a fish, you feed him for day. Teach him how to fish, and you feed him for a lifetime" took on new meaning for me. It's not that God taught the widow how to fish, but that through Elisha's strategy of meeting her need, which was the wisdom of God, of course, the widow learned how God prefers to meet people's needs through our offering what little we have, involving the community, and in a way that maximizes witness to others about God's work. The woman did not just get a fish that day, her immediate need met, but learned God's ways, with her sons and neighbors in ways that stayed with them for life, I'm sure—that using what little you have in faith, God will multiply and that God wants to involve the community in meeting human needs. They would still need to depend on God's provision, but they learned how to better cooperate with him.

So this week I wasn't able to personally apply it, as such, but I did think of another current application or outworking of these principles. A good friend of mine supports this orphanage in Rwanda. The leader was trusting primarily on donations from the United States to supply for the sixty or so children. Instead of just continuing to have American donations as the only source, he was able to arrange for the young leader to buy several laying hens. The leader was able to teach the children how to care for the chickens, pick eggs, and eventually breed for more eggs. Some of the eggs were allowed to hatch chicks. So some were eventually sold for meat, as well as selling the eggs. They also ate some of the eggs. They were able to learn to generate income this way, and were less dependent on American money, and are now looking for other ways to be self-sustaining.

STORYTELLER: Good example, Abe.

Oral Introduction to the New Story

(*Storyteller stands up from having been seated, with a closed Bible*). Okay, we have the backstory to it so let's hear this week's story. We know the backstory now from last week. For this story we need to know a little background on, next to Elisha, the main character of this story—Naaman and his people. The Arameans were a Semitic people. *Aram* was the Hebrew and Aramaic name for Syria, the land to the north of the land of Israel, but often translated Syria in our English Bibles. The Syrians were the greatest military threat to the Northern Kingdom of Israel at the time. The Northern Kingdom was also called Samaria, which was also its capital city. There was a similar hostility then between Israel and Syria as there is today; a state of cold war, which could flare up any time.

Damascus was the major city then and is considered the oldest continuously inhabited city in the world. It is still the capital of modern Syria today. Rimmon was a high deity of the Syrians. It is the Semitic word for "pomegranate," and so is associated with fertility (its many seeds).

(*Pointing to a map*) The Abana River began in the snows of the Lebanon mountains and flowed to Damascus. It's clear waters irrigated the beautiful orchards and gardens. The Pharpar River flowed from Mount Hermon to the south of Damascus. Both were superior rivers to the muddy little River Jordan, where something of striking significance is about to happen.

For this story, one of the main characters has a skin disease, probably leprosy. We should know that leprosy was very painful, debilitating as the skin rotted, hair fell out, fingernails and toenails fell out, gums begin to shrink and could not hold the teeth any longer. The Law of Moses prescribed rituals for those with the disease. They were considered unclean and were exiled from the community. It would be a source of shame, and for an Israelite, it meant rejection by the community.

Also we should know that part of the worldview of the peoples in the ancient Near East was the notion of territorial gods. It was assumed that there are gods over every territory and those gods only had power over their own territory—your god is operative in your territory; our god is operative in ours.

Okay, let's pray first—Father in heaven, thank you that you have transmitted your word to us faithfully over the millennia, through prophets and the written Scripture. We ask you to illumine and give us insight, by your Holy Spirit, through this inspired story today. In Jesus' name, Amen.

Telling the Story

As you read below, imagine the storyteller standing and orally telling the story, and how his/her body language—eye behavior, facial expression, voice tone, emotions—might be appropriate to the plotline and character dialogue. Take note of the pauses in the speech and the affect they might have on the impact and meaning of the story.

The storyteller opens the Bible, begins to read the story, but then lays the Bible down on a nearby table. Looking at the audience, the storyteller continues telling the story . . . he is not reading the story, but telling it as if he had been there as an eyewitness reporter:

STORYTELLER: The king of Syria had great esteem for Naaman, the commander of his army, because through him the Lord had given Syria great victories. Naaman was a mighty warrior, but he was a leper.[2]

At this time Syrian raiders had invaded the land of Israel, and among their captives was a young Israeli girl who had been given to Naaman's wife as a servant. One day the girl said to her mistress, "I wish my master would go to see the prophet in Samaria. He would heal him of his leprosy."

So Naaman told the king what the young girl from Israel had said. The king of Syria told him, "Go and visit the prophet. I will send a letter of introduction for you to take to the king of Israel." So Naaman prepared and started out, with an entourage of servants and chariots and wagons carrying as gifts 750 pounds of silver, 150 pounds of gold, and ten sets of clothing. The letter to the king of Israel said: "With this letter I present to you my servant Naaman. I ask you to heal him of his leprosy."

When the king of Israel read the letter, he tore his clothes in dismay and said, "What!? Who does he think I am?! Am I God, that I can give life and take it away? Why is this man asking me to heal someone with leprosy? I can see that he's just trying to pick a fight with me."

But when Elisha, the man of God, heard that the king of Israel had torn his clothes in shock and dismay, he sent this message to him: "Why are you so upset? Send him to me, and he will see there is a prophet in Israel."

---

2. The text of this story is 2 Kgs 5: 1–19. It is my own selective hybrid of both the *New Living Translation*, *The Message,* and my own translation from the Hebrew.

So Naaman went with his horses and chariots; his entourage arrived in style and waited at the door of Elisha's house. But Elisha only sent a messenger out to him with this message: "Go and wash yourself seven times in the Jordan River. Then your skin will be restored, and you will be healed of your leprosy."

But Naaman was incensed and stalked away. "I thought he would certainly come out to meet me!" he said. "I expected him to wave his hand over the leprosy and call on the name of the Lord his God and heal me! Aren't the rivers of Damascus, the Abana and the Pharpar, better than any of the rivers of Israel? Why shouldn't I wash in them and be healed?" So Naaman turned and went away in a rage.

But his officers tried to reason with him and said, "Father, if the prophet had told you to do something very difficult and heroic, wouldn't you have done it? So you should certainly obey him when he says simply, 'Go and wash and be cured!'" Naaman contemplated it for some time, and then decided to go down to the Jordan River and dipped himself seven times, as Elisha had instructed him. And his skin became as healthy as the skin of a young child, and he was cleansed and healed!

Then Naaman and his entire party went back to find Elisha. This time Elisha came out to meet him and his party. They stood before him, and Naaman said, "Now I know that there is no God in all the world except in Israel. So please accept a gift from your servant."

But Elisha replied, "As surely as the Lord lives, whom I serve, I will not accept any gifts." And though Naaman urged him again to take the gift, Elisha refused.

Then Naaman said, "All right, but please allow me to take two mule loads of earth from this place, and I will take it back home with me. From now on I will never again offer burnt offerings or sacrifices to any other god except the Lord. And, may the Lord pardon me in this one thing: I am my master the king's first officer. When my master the king goes into the temple of his god Rimmon to worship there and he leans on my arm, may the Lord pardon me when I too must bow."

"Go in *shalom*," Elisha said. So Naaman started home again.

Retelling the Story

The group needs to hear the story at least twice to grasp it enough to imagine the whole storyline. Three times is better. As well, it is very effective for learning to engage the group orally in telling the story as soon as possible.

A common way is to ask for one volunteer to stand and retell the story from the best of their recall. The advantage of this way is that it gives one person the affirmation for her/his courage to stand and perform the story before the group. Always applaud the volunteer no matter how well he or she does.[3]

STORYTELLER: Okay. Do we have a volunteer to retell the story? It's okay, you won't recall it all, you will miss some . . . but it's okay, because we will all tell it together soon. Start with, "The king of Syria had great admiration for Naaman, the commander of his army." Anyone? (*Seconds of silence*) . . . Jesse! Okay, great! Stand and tell the story to us.

After Jesse stands and tells the story (he achieves about 85 percent accuracy), the storyteller leads in applause.

STORYTELLER: Great job, Jesse! I liked the passion and dramatic actions you showed when you told the part about Naaman coming up out of the water after the seventh dip, and seeing his clean, young skin, the emotion in his face, your face. Great job!

Okay . . . Great! Now you have engaged the story by hearing it told by me, and hearing it again from our volunteer, Jesse.

Lead through the Story

The storyteller leads the group through the story for the third time, accurately for the second time (the volunteer achieved about 80 percent accuracy). The storyteller asks the group to help him or her tell the story again. The volunteer begins telling and waits for the group to respond in unison. Often the storyteller begins a sentence and the group finishes it. The storyteller leads but hands off the telling to the group as much as they are able. So the telling proceeds in this responsive interactive way until the end of the story. The group is urged to keep telling as much of it as they can recall, and as accurately as they can. The storytelling ensures accuracy by naturally chiming into the group's telling, correcting any errors or omissions as the telling proceeds.

---

3. A second way is to ask people to turn in pairs and to have one tell the story to the other. This is the method I used for the "Elisha and the Widow's Oil" story of chapter 1 above. If you have enough time, have both members of the pair tell it to each other. The advantage of turning in pairs is that it gives more people an opportunity to engage the story orally. Also, it solves an uncomfortable situation if there is actually no one who wants to volunteer to retell the story before a group.

STORYTELLER: Okay, now let's go through it for a third time. We will tell it together. I will begin and you continue with me and fill in, okay? . . . So, the king of Syria had great admiration for Naaman . . . who was?

GROUP IN UNISON: . . . the commander of his army . . .

STORYTELLER: He was a mighty . . . ?

STORYTELLER AND GROUP IN UNISON: . . . Warrior, but he was a . . . leper.

STORYTELLER: Well one day, the Syrian army raiders had invaded . . .

STORYTELLER AND GROUP IN UNISON: The land of Israel . . . and they took captive an Israeli girl and she was given to Naaman's wife as a servant.

STORYTELLER: Well one day, the Israeli girl said to her mistress, "May you all be cursed of the Lord for taking me captive!"

FEW IN THE GROUP: No, no . . . she said, "I wish my master would go to see the prophet in Samaria. He would heal him of his leprosy."

> *(The storyteller throws in this obvious error both to keep the participants alert and to draw attention to an aspect of the Israeli girl's character that is highlighted by the error).*

STORYTELLER: Right, so then Naaman told . . .

GROUP IN UNISON: . . . Tell the king what the young girl from Israel had said. The king of Syria told him, "Go and visit the prophet . . . And the king says he will send a letter of introduction to the king of Israel." *(This telling together led by the storyteller continues until the story is finished.)*

STORYTELLER: Okay, great! Now we have been through the story three times. I told it. You heard the volunteer retell it. And now we just told it again together. Do you think we know it now well enough to discuss it?

GROUP IN UNISON: Yes . . . Yes, I think so.

STORYTELLER: Okay, let's discuss it and unpack what truths are in this story through questions and discussion.

Observations: Digging for Truth-Treasures

STORYTELLER: First of all, might someone briefly explain the situation in this story? . . . Just in a few words or a sentence or two? What was Naaman's dilemma in this story? . . . What is the point of tension he faces? (*Storyteller pauses for several seconds.*) . . .

Another way to get at this this basic problem is to ask: What makes the characters seem real? What makes you feel connected emotionally to the people in this story? (*Seconds of silence*) . . .

GARRET: I think the real tension is within Naaman himself, between how important his sense of honor was to him and his desperation to be healed of a painful and debilitating disease. What is most important to him? His honor and saving face or his healing?

STORYTELLER: Hmm, very good observation, Garret. Good, let's go through the story scene by scene and ask questions about each character and see what we can observe about God's ways and our own human nature and relationship to him.

The storyteller intermittently repeats parts of the story, scene by scene, to help the group focus its observations there.

> The king of Syria had great admiration for Naaman, the commander of his army, because through him the Lord had given Syria great victories. Naaman was a mighty warrior, but he was a leper.

In the opening part of the story, who are the featured characters?

DIANA: First off, it is Naaman and the king of Syria.

STORYTELLER: And what might we learn about Naaman from what he does or says or what is said about him? (*Seconds of silence*) . . .

DIANA: Well, he was a man of prominence in his society—a distinguished general, a dignitary—esteemed and honored by his king.

STORYTELLER: I'm wondering how important that honor was to him?

JESSE: I was struck by how the story says that through Naaman, "the Lord had given victories to Syria." These are Israel's enemies! I thought the Lord was on our side.

SAM: Very interesting . . . but we know, don't we, that other times in Israel's history God allowed her enemies to defeat them, to chastise them—like Babylon. So I suppose that is what is going on here. So, it shows that God is the sovereign, universal God over all peoples, not just his chosen people Israel.

STORYTELLER: Interesting that we get this view of God already in the story—that God is not just the God of Israel but the God of all nations. What else might we learn about this general?

LISA: *But* he was a leper! That's a huge *but*! Here is this successful, powerful military hero, but he has this debilitating disease. We have to imagine how horrible it was . . . as you said in the introduction the hair and nails and skin are falling off. Horrible! It must have been a struggle and a shame to him. Can you imagine him putting on his uniform or armor with parts of his skin falling off?

DIANA: Quite graphic . . . I'm thinking that often he did not care how successful and how much military honor he had . . . he would give it up in a moment if he could just get cleansed or healed.

STORYTELLER: Well, let's move to the next scene. Recall this part:

> At this time Syrian raiders had invaded the land of Israel, and among their captives was a young Israeli girl who had been given to Naaman's wife as a servant. One day the girl said to her mistress, "I wish my master would go to see the prophet in Samaria. He would heal him of his leprosy."

What might we learn about the character of this Israeli girl from what she says and does . . . and the choices she makes? (*Seconds of silence*) . . .

ABE: To me, it is striking that that she is so friendly to her captors. These are the enemies of Israel who have taken her away from her family and homeland. You would think she would be bitter and hateful toward them and not want to help them . . . curse them, not bless them. But she has a heart of goodwill and compassion toward her master.

STORYTELLER: Right, because let's think—what other choices did she have in that situation?

ABE: Many captives, taken into slavery would have said, "I hope his leprosy gets worse and he dies in agony!"

LISA: She could have just kept quiet, kept to herself.

STORYTELLER: Sure, she could have. So when we see she had other choices, it highlights the remarkable choice she did make.

SAM: I would think it is due to her faith. She is aware of the prophet Elisha and believes God heals through him. Her faith in her people's God, the God of Israel must have been strong.

ABE: And I think it says a lot about Naaman and his wife too. They must have treated her well. She seems to really care about her master Naaman's health.

STORYTELLER: Hmm, I'm thinking—is there something we can see about the ways of God already here? (*Several seconds of silence*) . . . I am thinking of the missional ways of God, his redemptive ways . . . seeking the lost. Might there be ways God had already been working on Naaman's behalf? (*Seconds of silence*) . . .

GARRET: Ah! The fact that an Israeli girl with this kind of character just happened to become the servant girl of his wife! By chance, right? . . . Hmm . . . it could have been a captive who was bitter to them. God placed her there! This girl becomes a link to a chain of events that eventually results in Naaman's healing.

STORYTELLER: So you think maybe it was not just chance that this girl ended up in Naaman's home?

TAL: No, it's like God sent her as a prophet to them.

STORYTELLER: Interesting! Or an emissary.

GARRET: So she was like an involuntary missionary. In the providence of God, he uses the results of a wartime raid and the evil of slavery—to reach people outside the land of Israel.

STORYTELLER: Great insight! Hmm. So she was like a little light to the gentiles, fulfilling Israel's calling, to be a light to the gentiles! I wonder about the role of choice here.

TAL: Yes, because even though this girl had this helpful goodwill toward them, why should they choose to believe her? Mr. and Mrs. Naaman were gentiles, pagans; they did not believe in the Jewish religion; Israel was their enemy. Why should they believe anything she said about one of their enemies' prophets . . . right? This show's Naaman had some humility.

STORYTELLER: Right. And this girl's character is becoming clearer. I hope we come back to her in this discussion. But let's move on to the next scene now. The story relates:

> So Naaman told the king what the young girl from Israel had said. The king of Syria told him. "Go and visit the prophet. I will send a letter of introduction for you to take to the king of Israel."

What more might we learn about Naaman from what he says and does in this part?

JAVIER: He made the decision to go. He believes the girl enough to plan to go down there into enemy territory to visit the prophet. Even the king apparently believes her . . . or he just has that kind of close relationship with Naaman . . . his commander-in-chief.

STORYTELLER: What other choices did Naaman have when he heard the girl's offer?

JAVIER: He could have just disregarded her. But this would be a very different story then . . . actually there would be no story.

LINDA: Naaman respects protocol and power, because he goes first to the king.

TAL: And the king. Wow! He is also staking a lot on this girl's word.

STORYTELLER: Yes, and all seems to be negotiated at the highest levels of power here. For these ancients, real power was held by the kings, perhaps even over their prophets? At least this king of Syria thought the king of Israel had such power. So Naaman gets approval, support, and a letter of introduction from his king to go to Samaria, requesting a cure from the king of Israel. Well, let's move to the next scene. The story continues:

> Naaman prepared and started out, with an entourage of servants and chariots and wagons carrying as gifts 750 pounds of silver, 150 pounds of gold, and ten sets of clothing. The letter to the king of Israel said: "With this letter I present to you my servant Naaman. I want you to heal him of his leprosy."

So he sets out with his panoply of chariots and servants to go down to Israel. How else are we getting to know Naaman from what he does next? (*Several seconds of silence*) . . .

ABE: Well, he wants to make a good impression. This is a man of status and social standing; he is not a beggar! (*Seconds of silence*) . . . And he has high expectations, and he is prepared to give gifts fitting with his status.

VALERIE: Or maybe Naaman's view was that he needed to pay to get cleansed or healed. He was ready to pay a hefty amount. He was desperate, with that horrible leprosy. He would pay anything. I remember a friend of my mother's got a very bad cancer back in the seventies. The doctors said it was terminal and they could do nothing for her. So she and her family went to Mexico to find a laetrile treatment, vitamin B-17. They would grasp at any straw of shred of hope. She died shortly after that.

ABE: Yeah . . . I can feel that kind of desperation.

STORYTELLER: Hmm . . . Okay, we move on to the next scene. The story continues:

> When the king of Israel read the letter, he tore his clothes in dismay and said, "What!? Who does he think I am?! Am I God, that I can give life and take it away? Why is this man asking me to heal someone with leprosy? I can see that he's just trying to pick a fight with me." But when Elisha, the man of God, heard that the king of Israel had torn his clothes in dismay, he sent this message to him: "Why are you so upset? Send Naaman to me, and he will see there is a prophet in Israel."

STORYTELLER: Would you have expected this response? What are we learning here?

TAL: I recall how "rending your garments" expresses deep grief or lament for a disaster. This guy is upset! He has no trust in an enemy king. And talking about power—he realizes he has no power to heal diseases.

STORYTELLER: Word seems to get to Elisha pretty fast. He has a residence close by in Samaria.

GARRET: It's interesting how much faith and certainty Elisha has in God; that God will act supernaturally toward this enemy gentile general . . . "he will see there is a prophet in Israel!" I love that faith in the God of Israel and the close relationship Elisha obviously has with him. Elisha meets this challenge fearlessly.

SEVERAL IN THE GROUP: Yeah . . . Really cool . . . Yeah, I like it.

STORYTELLER: And then this:

> So Naaman, with his horses and chariots and entourage, arrived in style and waited at the door of Elisha's house. But Elisha only sent a messenger out to him with this message: "Go and wash yourself seven times in the Jordan River. Then your skin will be restored, and you will be healed of your leprosy."
>
> But Naaman was incensed and stalked away. "I thought he would certainly come out to meet me!" he said. "I expected him to wave his hand over the leprosy and call on the name of the Lord his God and heal me! Aren't the rivers of Damascus, the Abana and the Pharpar, better than any of the rivers of Israel? Why shouldn't I wash in them and be healed?" So Naaman turned and went away in a rage.

STORYTELLER: Let's discuss our insights into Elisha's ways here and the encounter between these two. Was anyone surprised by Elisha's approach here?

LISA: I was surprised. Naaman is a visiting dignitary coming with all his trappings and expecting a proper and honorary reception. Elisha does not even come out to greet him. I mean he is really snubbing an important dignitary here. You wonder why he does this . . . but knowing Elisha's dramatic kind of prophetic acts, it also seems kind of in character for him. What is he up to here?

DIANA: But what a hopeful message! He can be healed! Yet he does not receive it!

VALERIE: He is too arrogant. He thinks he is so important that he deserves all kinds of ritual and fawning and honor.

A FEW IN THE GROUP: Yeah . . . Yes.

SAM: He thinks he is just being told to wash or bathe in the river and that will heal him. "You know," he says, "What is this!? Our rivers in Damascus are better and cleaner than this little muddy creek!" So he does not expect a miracle, really.

STORYTELLER: I want to pick up on the notion of honor you mentioned, Valerie. In the ancient Near East, as in Middle Eastern and Asian cultures today, honor and shame were much more of a cultural value and functional awareness than [they are] today in most of the modern West. We think and function more by guilt and innocence than by honor and shame. Let's dig into the honor theme here a bit more.

VALERIE: Can you define honor and shame?

STORYTELLER: Sure. Honor and shame are very relational. Innocence and guilt are more an individual awareness of having done something wrong or broke a law or rule. Honor is the sense of respect and esteem between people. It is the value and worth persons hold both in their own eyes and in the eyes of their community. So it involves the public reputation a person holds. It is a relationship that evokes loyalty, allegiance, love, and deference. Love of honor was a foremost value and could motivate the best and the worst behaviors.

Honor is when two people look into each other's eyes and feel mutual esteem, regard, admiration for each other. The terms "face" and "saving face" reflect this. One has a public "face" by which he or she is known. When people are shamed, they lose face. Shame then is the painful feeling caused by a break in the relationship through dishonor, disrespect, rejection, disloyalty, betrayal. It is when one's weaknesses are exposed. Shame makes a person feel unworthy, and bad about themselves. Thus, shame is losing face. Remember how Adam and Eve were naked and not ashamed. But when they broke relationship with God—were disloyal to him—they felt shame and covered themselves . . . to protect their weak and now shameful selves from further pain of rejection.

VALERIE: Wow . . . Okay . . . (*Seconds of silence*) . . .

GARRET: Hmm, Well, Naaman is all about honor. He was honored by his king. He had achieved honor in his own society. He expects now to be honored in Israel. All the expensive gifts he brought would show that he is an honorable man, a man of magnanimity and means . . . giving such gifts would maintain his honor.

JAVIER: So, I'm sure he felt dishonored and insulted that Elisha did not even come out to personally greet him. He said he expected the prophet to come out and go through some elaborate abracadabra and perform his healing arts.

DIANA: Wouldn't you feel insulted, if you were him? . . . To be snubbed like that? He felt shamed, I'm sure. Why would Elisha dishonor him like this?

GARRET: But he wanted a show. And to be told by a servant or messenger just to go wash in the river! Not what he expected.

JESSE: I see God's ways coming through Elisha here. It was a test. Naaman's sense of honor was based on pride. What decision would Naaman make? Would he hang on to his pride, his wounded honor? Or would he humble himself and obey this command?

GARRET: And he is about ready to go away in a huff, or a rage . . . "Why should I suffer this insult? I don't have to put up with this!" He was about to lose it here.

STORYTELLER: Yes. And then there is this:

> But his officers tried to reason with him and said, "Father, if the prophet had told you to do something very difficult and heroic, wouldn't you have done it? So you should certainly obey him when he says simply, 'Go and wash and be cured!'" So Naaman went down to the Jordan River and dipped himself seven times, as Elisha had instructed him. And his skin became as healthy as the skin of a young child, and he was cleansed and healed!

STORYTELLER: I am impressed with how he is persuaded by his servants here, to reconsider following this humiliating command. What insights might we gain here into the character of Naaman?

TAL: They called him "Father." They had good relationships. They honored and cared about their master, and he listened to and trusted them.

SAM: I am thinking of the Israeli servant girl whose tip he listened to, and that set things in motion for this whole trip. He listened to her. He listens to these servants. I think it shows he has some humility as a human being, even though he is such an honored general. He is not a total arrogant egoist.

TAL: Yes, amazing! So, though he has this proud persona of a powerful general, inside he has some humility.

STORYTELLER: And Naaman had other choices at this pivotal juncture, right? How else could he have chosen to act?

SAM: Well, he could have refused to submit to this humiliation and just marched back home to Syria. But then he would not have been healed. He would have chosen wounded pride and saving face over healing.

JESSE: Right. Yes, this was the test. Yeshua said, "He who exalts himself will be humbled and he who humbles himself will be exalted." This principle is playing out in Naaman's life. So it would cost him—not money, but it would cost him.

DIANA: In his honor-shame culture, this would have been very hard for him . . . harder than for us. But God does honor him. When he finally gives in, swallows his pride, he is healed of the leprosy. After his healing, he no longer needs to live with the shame of his leprosy.

JESSE: So there was a reversal or change in Naaman's view of honor. God's way of honor required he be willing to be humiliated by his own old standards of saving face before others—and be willing to do a humbling thing that showed faith in the God of Elisha.

STORYTELLER: Hmm, very interesting. I'm wondering what wisdom or meaning we might see in the instructions of the prophet to dip seven times in the Jordan River. (*Storyteller looks at Rose, who has not yet said anything*).

ROSE: Well, I did sort of wonder whether this was some sort of baptism he was commanded to do. There were various washings and ritual cleansings commanded in the Torah.

STORYTELLER: That's really an interesting observation, Rose. Thank you! What do some of you think?

VALERIE: I don't think it was a baptism. There is nothing in the story that gives that idea.

ROSE: I'm not so sure. Isn't he being initiated into a new relationship with God? Isn't baptism a sign of that? It is today with the New Testament messianic immersion, or Christian baptism.

ABE: Wow, I hadn't thought of that. When Naaman comes up out of the water, he is changed. He testifies to a relationship with the God of Israel. "Now I know there is no god in all the earth except the God of Israel!" Don't we have new believers, after we immerse them, testify to their commitment and allegiance to Yeshua as Messiah and Lord?

LINDA: But nothing is stated by Elisha or the narrator of the story that this is baptism. It is just a simple command to test his obedience, like Jesse was saying.

ABE: Couldn't it be both an obedience of faith test and a kind of ritual immersion . . . even though Naaman perhaps did not see it that way?

LINDA: Well, I suppose . . . but that begs the question doesn't it—is there meaning here for us hearers or readers that was not known to Naaman himself?

ABE: And does it have to be explicitly stated in the story for it to be there and be rightly understood as such?

STORYTELLER: *Really* fascinating, you guys . . . that is an important question, Abe. Maybe the author wants to expand our thinking. Might there be other ways Naaman is transformed or converted? Let's probe here a little more.

ROSE: Well, think of it. He is converted from being an idolater and polytheist, worshipping the Syrian gods, to becoming a monotheist, with allegiance to Yahweh, the God of Israel. His mind is changed. So it is a conversion of heart and head. Part of the change of mind was the change in his values as to what constitutes true honor. I think he must have come to feel that true honor was to honor the God who cleansed him, regardless of what the people in Syria might think.

And he was "cleansed," which is the word I heard used dealing with the leprosy, not "healed."

One of the apostles of Yeshua talks about the cleansing of baptism, I think . . . from sin. And it was the dipping, the washing in the Jordan that was key to that here . . . it was the outward expression of the change of heart in Naaman. That's what water baptism is, right? An outward sign of an inward spiritual transformation? Is there any other story in the Hebrew Bible that is as holistic and dramatic a conversion as this? So much for the view that God did not come to gentiles in the Old Testament era with grace and convert them! Surely this guy, who so radically believed in Yahweh, the true God of Israel, was saved, no!?

ABE: You argue a good case, Rose! Wow, if people today would all experience as holistic a conversion as this! Heart, mind, body, allegiance, social standing. Remarkable!

ROSE: And this was before Messiah, before regeneration through new birth in Messiah. And what does this say about the character of God? So much for the view of a harsh distant Old Testament God!

SAM: God is the same then as now in his desire for people to come to know him and thus find healing and blessing and shalom.

STORYTELLER: Rose, you have been silent until now. But when you speak, it is of great value! Worth the wait!

ROSE: Thanks.

ABE: On this baptism note I want to share an experience that might highlight how difficult this decision may have been for Naaman. When we lived in Israel, I will never forget a day we were going to immerse a few new Jewish believers in Messiah. This was in the eighties, so we still called it "baptism" . . . we would call it "messianic immersion," or "messianic *mikveh*" today. We baptized two of them, but the third one was full of anxiety and trepidation. When she came to us to lead her down into the swimming pool, she looked anguished. As we accompanied her, she stopped and just froze. Then she broke away and ran away and back to her car and left. To her, baptism was like the final step, the point of no return. To her it meant a breaking, perhaps finally with her religious Jewish family, which is how Christian baptism has often been perceived by Jewish people. It was a pivotal, monumental decision for her. A costly one. She was not ready. Since those days, I think the messianic Jewish movement has done a better job of communicating that baptism is a very Jewish thing, there were always immersions and *mikvehs* in Judaism. And that messianic Jewish believers don't have to leave their Jewish identity to follow Yeshua.

STORYTELLER: Well, we need to finish soon. Some of us have to leave in about fifteen minutes. So, let's observe this last scene of the story. It is essentially an exchange between Naaman and Elisha after his cleansing:

> So then Naaman and his entire party went back to find Elisha. They stood before him, and Naaman said, "Now I know that there is no God in all the world except in Israel. So please accept a gift from your servant."
>
> But Elisha replied, "As surely as the Lord lives, whom I serve, I will not accept any gifts." And though Naaman urged him to take the gift, Elisha refused.
>
> Then Naaman said, "All right, but please allow your servant to take two mule loads of earth from this place, and I will take it back home with me. From now on I will never again offer burnt offerings or sacrifices to any other god except the Lord. And, may the Lord pardon me in this one thing: I am my master the king's first officer. When my master the king goes into the temple of his god Rimmon to worship there and he leans on my arm, may the Lord pardon me when I too must bow."
>
> "Go in *shalom*," Elisha said. So Naaman started home *again*.

STORYTELLER: What further are we learning about Naaman here? We've talked about his cleansing and conversion. What about his response and choices after the miraculous cure? (*Seconds of silence*) . . .

VALERIE: He wants to give to Elisha the expensive gifts he brought. Is he just expressing appreciation here? Or does he think he has to pay for his healing?

LINDA: It is a gift of appreciation. He says, "Please accept this gift from your servant."

GARRET: The powerful warrior Naaman, who expected pomp and circumstance, now claims to be a servant. Amazing change!

VALERIE: Yes, but he is associating money with getting healed.

ABE: I'm thinking had Elisha accepted the gifts, Naaman would have gone home knowing that because he brought expensive gifts, he got healed. He paid a good price. Now he is leaving, cleansed, but without the silver and gold.

VALERIE: Yes. That is kind of my point, Abe. Naaman would have felt it was a transaction, or a commodity for which he paid well. Willing to pay . . . he was desperate . . . and pay he did, nonetheless.

STORYTELLER: These are valuable observations. We are getting at something here. Let's probe deeper here. What affect would feeling like he paid for his healing have on Naaman?

ABE: Well, it would reinforce or work against his humility . . . He would feel the old pride in himself . . . He was self-sufficient. He got this by his own means.

ROSE: Right. So there would not be the sense that this healing was freely given by the grace of God. He paid a professional healer or shaman for it.

STORYTELLER: Yes, grace! Okay, what about Elisha's response?

GARRET: We see the wisdom of God in him, don't we? A charlatan would have accepted the money. But not this true prophet of God. Elisha knows it would give the wrong message to Naaman, and would not be good for his newfound faith.

STORYTELLER: Let's move to Naaman's last curious requests of Elisha, and Elisha's response.

ABE: Seems odd, almost superstitious to us that he wanted some of the dirt from the land of Israel to take home. But you said in the introduction to the story that this was the belief of the "territorial gods." If he is going to worship the God of Israel, he needs some of the land of Israel to worship him from. Build an altar to the Lord on the soil of Israel.

STORYTELLER: Yes. Does Elisha deny this request?

SEVERAL IN UNISON: No . . . Don't think so . . . He doesn't.

ABE: I guess it expresses his devotion to the God of Israel to have some of the land of Israel to worship him on.

STORYTELLER: And Naaman asks for forgiveness in advance for he knows as the king's adjutant, he must accompany his king, and could not excuse himself from all the state functions. Even going to the god Rimmon's temple and helping his master bow to his god, since he leans on his arm, apparently even Naaman would need to bow too.

ROSE: This to me is really astonishing too. Elisha is a guardian of the Torah, for sure, as Yahweh's prophet. This would have been his opportunity to exhort Naaman in no uncertain terms that of course he could *not* defile himself by going into a pagan temple. He must now stay in the holy land of Israel. He must join God's people, become circumcised, observe all the commandments of the Law of Moses, and become a full proselyte to Judaism, live a Jewish life. Elisha had this option, but instead says, "Go in *shalom*." He apparently grants him permission to go back to his people and his way of life.

SEVERAL ALMOST SIMULTANEOUSLY: Yes . . . Elisha was known as a no-compromise, zero-tolerance-to-idolatry kind of prophet, right? So . . . Yeah. . . Surprising . . . What do we make of that?

STORYTELLER: Okay, Elisha is God's true prophet. So what might we learn about God, his character and ways, through this? (*Several seconds of silence*) . . .

JESSE: Well, Naaman was a gentile, not a Jew. So it seems God would not expect him to become a Jew and keep all the Jewish traditions.

ROSE: Well, that is how we think of it today, but for Israelites back then, they would have expected him to become a full convert, circumcision, all that.

JAVIER: Yes, but even the New Testament says, "Come out from among them and be separate," doesn't it? Believers can be corrupted and stumble when subjected to the kind of atmosphere Naaman would have been in back at his post in Syria. You'd think Elisha would have been concerned about that.

STORYTELLER: What indications do we have from what is in the story that might argue for a different view?

JESSE: Elisha heard his passionate testimony, "Now I know there is no god but Yahweh, the God of Israel." Elisha could discern his heart and spirit. I think Elisha had seen a deep and sincere enough conversion in Naaman that he could trust him to go back to his life situation and still be true to Yahweh.

JAVIER: Okay, I can see that. So I think believer's separation should be a separation from sin and idolatry, a spiritual separation, not a social or cultural or geographical separation.

ROSE: Sounds right, Javier.

ABE: Evidently, Elisha believed that Naaman could participate in the culture and even the religion of his home country, but remain faithful in his heart to the true God. He could accompany his king as his king bowed to and worshipped his god, Rimmon, without Naaman himself worshipping. He would go through the motions of the pagan religion, but his heart was devoted to Yahweh. So he could practice some of the forms of the religious tradition of his people, while his heart-faith and allegiance were to Yahweh, the God of Israel.

Focus on Application

The storyteller calculates that the group only has another five to ten minutes remaining for the storytelling session until they must formally close, so he transitions the focus to helping the group identify applications of the story to their lives today. So the questioning shifts focus from character analysis to how they speak into our life situations today. The key word he uses for this transition is "today." Given that this was a Jewish seekers Bible study group, the storyteller and group are oriented to Jewish culture.

STORYTELLER: Fascinating. Today, how might this story apply to challenges we face in helping Jewish people come to faith and follow the Lord? How might Naaman's encounter with the God of Israel, and Elisha's approach to his discipling inform and guide us today? (*Seconds of silence*)...

ROSE: Well, this does not really apply to Jewish people because Naaman was not Jewish.

STORYTELLER: Hmmm...

ABE: It might some. Some expressions of the messianic movement today are quite intent on making sure new Jewish believers in Yeshua practice the Jewish religion and the Jewish life cycle and holidays, etc., as part of their discipleship. Could an application of this story be that such is not so important? What was important was the inner spiritual conversion. After that, Elisha left it up to Naaman how he would live out his faith culturally. So, the application would be, we should let new Jewish believers determine how they will live out their Jewish identity and faith practices.

ROSE: Perhaps, but this story of Naaman and Elisha is such a different context. This was in Israel before the coming of Yeshua. Normally gentiles who came to believe in the God of Israel had to join the people of Israel, think of Rahab and Ruth. The peoplehood of Israel had a whole way of life and culture, observing the Torah. Naaman appears to be an exception to that.

ABE: But Elisha approves of him going back to his own people and culture. He apparently trusted that Naaman's newfound faith would sustain him as he lived it out in his own society and culture.

ROSE: I think a closer parallel today would be if a non-Jewish person, who was not a believer, were to come to faith in Jesus through a messianic Jewish congregation, and the leadership of the congregation told him he was free to go and live out his faith according to his own conscience and identity. He did not have to practice messianic Judaism.

STORYTELLER: So, I'm wondering, what if Naaman had been an Israelite general with leprosy? How might it have turned out differently?

ROSE: Well, he would have carried on practicing his own Jewish or Israelite identity, perhaps been more diligent in observing the Torah with its laws and statutes.

STORYTELLER: So I'm wondering what might be a more general application for today of Naaman's conversion and Elisha's trusting him to go back to his people in *shalom*?

JESSE: I have been thinking about this as you have been talking. I think it is that each person, whether Jewish or non-Jewish, when they come to faith in Yeshua, are free to live out their faith from their own cultural identity. Conversion is spiritual and moral, not cultural.

ABE: But gentile Christians are also free to identify with the Jewish people, and worship with messianic Jews and practice messianic Judaism. Like many of you in this group do, who are not Jewish.

ROSE: Yes. I think, though, with one qualification or difference for Jewish people. One is not born as a true Christian; you must be born-again. But one is born Jewish, and so it is a calling and destiny. Have you heard the saying, "Christianity is faith; Judaism is fate?" So for Jewish people, they do not convert to another religion, they just affirm the fulfillment of their own Jewish religion, embracing the Jewish Messiah. So, I do think that leaders of the messianic Jewish movement should disciple and teach Jewish believers to affirm their Jewish identity . . . not just assimilate into a Christian church and become a Christian culturally.

JESSE: OK, I guess. But it should not be coerced. Or legalistic.

ABE: I want to say—I see another application. We can often be ethnocentric and think our religious traditions are the only right ones. But let me share what I think is another application from this story, for gentile Christians. Being a Jewish believer and involved with the messianic Jewish movement, I often hope more Christians would see the importance of Israel and the Jewish people to the whole worldwide body of Christ.

Naaman, a gentile military leader and a powerful man, must go to the land of Israel, and to Israel's prophet to be healed, not to healers in his own country or tradition. It is the waters of the Jordan alone that were instrumental in his healing, his coming to the true knowledge of God, and to his *shalom*. He had to seriously humble himself to wash in the little Jordan, when he knew the rivers in Syria were superior.

So application—all Christians need to acknowledge that the source of all their most precious realities, their healing, cleansing, their salvation, their Bible, and their Savior, is the God of Israel. The gospel is "to the Jew first" as Paul said in Romans, because it came from them and is addressed first to them. We need to listen to Israel's prophets, embrace Israel's Scriptures, and believe in the Jewish Messiah. It is the God of Israel alone, Yahweh, supremely revealed in Jesus the Messiah, that all the church must embrace, not merely "God" . . . Nearly every religion has a "god." But ours is the God of Israel. Like Naaman, many Christians need to humble themselves and acknowledge this. They have to be willing to go dip in the muddy little Jordan River, as it were. There is still a long legacy of anti-Judaism and antisemitism in the church, and a lack of appreciation of the Jewish matrix and cradle of the church. The church was birthed out of Israel; the children should be grateful! They . . . we . . . should all remember what the apostle Paul said to the gentile believers in Rome about Israel, "you don't support the root, but the root supports you!"[4]

STORYTELLER: Wow! Well said, Abe. Thank you. Might we come back for a moment to the servants of Naaman? Remember the Israeli servant girl of Naaman's wife? She was the key link in the chain of events for Naaman's healing. Was she a follower of Yahweh?

SEVERAL ALMOST SIMULTANEOULY: Yes . . . For sure . . . She must have been.

STORYTELLER: And I am thinking about the servants in Naaman's party. What impact might this transformation of Naaman have had on them?

GARRET: Wow, just seeing the amazing supernatural healing, and hearing Naaman testify to the God of Israel as the healer and the only true God, surely must have convinced them to become believers in Yahweh too?

LINDA: Ya think, Garret?! . . . Yeah, I do. So I wonder, did these servants who were with Naaman in Israel know the Israeli servant girl? I'm thinking they probably did, because they were all in Naaman's circle or household, right? I can picture the reunion when they returned to Israel—rejoicing together about his healing.

TAL: And what might have the reunion been like between Naaman and the Israeli servant girl in his household when he returned? It was because of her that he is now healed. Imagine his gratitude. And now they are both believers in the God of Israel. And Naaman's wife likely believed too!

STORYTELLER: How might we see God's missional footprint in all this?

ABE: By not staying in Israel and becoming a Jewish proselyte, he was able to go back into his community as a believer and thus be a witness. With the Israeli girl, the other servants and his wife joining in the like faith in Yahweh, and given Naaman's influence, I can imagine a large household and clan of people now following the true God in Syria. Amazing!

GARRET: So Naaman's clan and household could have become like a church there in Damascus.

---

4. Rom 11:18 NKJV.

ROSE: I wish we had more information about what happened next in this regard.

STORYTELLER: But we don't. Though I can imagine a witness to the God of Israel there for a generation or more, and that may have touched many lives; we don't know and must speculate. Could there have been some God-fearers yet in Damascus when the apostle Paul arrived there, and a church was formed several centuries later? Perhaps we will meet some of them in heaven. It is certainly possible. But bottom line, what might we learn about God from this?

DIANA: God loves so much, he seeks people out, even pagan enemies of his chosen people. He is a seeking, missional God. So much for the notion of a harsh Old Testament God!

STORYTELLER: Yes, amen. Okay, this has been great! We always like to find a saying or proverb that captures the story. Does one come to mind for anyone about this story?

LINDA: You know I read children's literature to teach my fifth-grade class. One author I read is Madeleine L'Engle who sagely said, "Humility is throwing oneself away in complete concentration on something or someone else."[5] I think it applies to Naaman's experience, and I would think to many of ours too.

STORYTELLER: Good one, Linda. Any others? (*Several seconds of silence*) . . . Well, we need to close because of time. But think about these questions for next week: Today, does God still send "little Israeli girls" who are vulnerable, unassuming believers as involuntary missionaries into dangerous places where they become the mouth of God to reach powerful and sinful people whom God is seeking to redeem? What does that look like today? Does God still require powerful people to humble themselves and simply obey before they find *shalom* and healing?

This story is from 2 Kings 5:1–19 in case you want to locate it. Sam, would you close in prayer?

SAM: Sure. Father, thank you for this amazing story. Thank you for how your heart of love comes through this for people we would probably not have love for. Thank you for the message against prejudice toward people coming to faith and living it out in very different cultures than our own.

---

5. Goodreads. https://www.goodreads.com/quotes/43351-humility-is-throwing-oneself-away-in-complete-concentration-on-something.

Thank you for the message that when we humble ourselves before you, you exalt us. In Jesus' name, amen.

STORYTELLER: Okay, folks. Tell this story to someone this week. You know it now. Practice telling it. The more you tell it, the more you will own it. See if you can find a situation where it applies. We will all share about what happened next week. See you then. *Shalom.*

10

Reflections on the Elisha Story

> "The Christian life is a life of paradoxes. We must give to receive, realize we are blind to see, become simple to be wise, suffer for gain, and die to live."
>
> —Unknown

> "God sends no one away empty except those who are full of themselves."
>
> —Dwight L. Moody

> "Lovers are the ones who know most about God; the theologians must listen to them."
>
> —Hans Urs von Balthasar

In chapter one the authors told the story of "Elisha and the Widow's Oil" to demonstrate OH in practice. In chapter 2 we discussed the incarnational model, full-brain engagement, oral language, adult learning, group learning, the issue of who is in control in the storytelling session, how character-centric questions evoke discovery learning, and how storytelling is teaching but in a very different style. We also looked at symbols and proverbs, and ambiguity and multiple truths in a given story.

In this chapter, the authors offer reflections on the Elisha and General Naaman story, echoing by way of review and reverberation some of the OH principles and factors discussed throughout the book. These include story as a way of knowing, *four* theological truths drawn from the story, *four* missiological applications, as well as how all *four* of the components in OH have been at work in our discussion. We conclude with some questions related to formative (individual lessons) and summative (story set) evaluation to help improve storying.

Story as a Way of Knowing

In the "Hebrew Hermeneutics" chapter (5) the authors described how, in contrast to Enlightenment epistemology, Hebraic epistemology is narrative epistemology; it embraces story as *a way of knowing*. Hebrew logic is narrative logic and relational logic more than syllogistic logic. The Enlightenment has been so dominant that *story as a way of knowing* seems to many as premodern and thus inferior. But for Israel, story is the bottom line; her identity is based on her story. Her founding story (the exodus from slavery in Egypt) cannot be cashed out for some deeper theological substance and still retain credibility and meaning.

There are truths embedded in the Naaman story that embody doctrines and concepts that are often taught in a conceptual and analytic manner in works of philosophical and systematic theology and missiological theory, but that are here in story made concrete through characters. The authors will demonstrate *character theologizing* by drawing out four theological truths that are conveyed in the story of Naaman.

Often these truths are stated as doctrines in conceptual theology, and part of a Bible story may or may not be used to illustrate the stated doctrine. The authors believe the best starting point for stating these truths is story. It is pertinent here to recall the C. S. Lewis dictum, "Reason is the organ of truth, but imagination is the organ of meaning . . ." and "Imagination is not the cause of truth, but its condition."[1] Imagining this story is the foundation for grasping the truths drawn from it. Theology is inherent in the story, and therefore must be drawn from the story, without ever really leaving the story.

Here then is how and why story is the deepest way of knowing. Biblically, the deepest kind of knowledge is personal knowledge experienced in relationship, as seen in the use of the Hebrew word for knowing, *yada*. "Now Adam knew (*yada*) his wife Eve and she conceived and bore Cain" (Gen

---

1. Hooper, *C. S. Lewis*, 570.

4:1 NKJV). God is a person. We know him through relational knowledge, through encountering him. The living Word of God is a person (John 1:1-2). The Word expresses his mind to humans through the written word.

As humans we know other people primarily through right-brain operations of the prefrontal cortex—attachment, assessment, attunement, action (see ch. 2). To know the Divine Person, we need encounter with the person of the Holy Spirit, and this is primarily experienced through our relational right-brain capacities (what Scripture mostly calls heart, spirit, conscience). Theological reasoning (left brain) follows this experience. Left-brain cognition (a register of facts, or mental assent to facts) is not the deepest way of knowing.

Theology as reasoning about God is second in sequence to relational encounter with him. True knowledge is relationship more than reason. This is why the hermeneutical sequence should be story first, theologizing second. True theology will have an inherently relational character.[2]

How something is known affects *what* is known. Blaise Pascal interprets this well, "Human beings must be known to be loved; but Divine beings must be loved to be known."[3] There is a moral and relational condition or requirement in coming to know God.

How then shall we understand story as the vehicle or medium for the deepest way of knowing? Story represents the series of events and interactions in a trajectory of relationship(s). So the Bible represents the words and acts of God in his relationship with Israel. This developing story gave Israel an "alternative imagination" to the oppression they experienced in Egypt. As Bradt put it, "By hoping in the imagined future of her stories, Israel could marshal her powers to act in her own interest in the present while finding new meanings in her past."[4]

---

2. A few Johannine verses teach this, "Now by this we know that we know Him, if we keep His commandments" (1 John 2:3 NKJV). From this we see there is *relational* human action and response (human will or choice) needed in order to know that we know God. "But whoever keeps His word, truly the love of God is perfected in him. By this we know that we are in Him" (1 John 2: 5 NKJV). From this we see love is involved (the heart, affections, the will) in knowing God. And Pauline verses, "The coming of the *lawless one* is according to the working of Satan, with all power, signs, and lying wonders, and with all unrighteous deception among those who perish, because they did not receive the love of the truth, that they might be saved" (2 Thess 2:9-10 NKJV). From this we see that there will be those deceived by Satan and perish, not because they did not *know* the truth (cognitive), but because they did not *love* the truth (whole person, relational).

3. Brainyquote. https://www.brainyquote.com/quotes/blaise_pascal_100862.

4. Bradt, *Story as a Way of Knowing*, 236.

The *oral-aural interplay* of oral storytelling, especially in a group, is relational. Participants engage with people in relational knowledge—relating to both the characters in the story, including God, the Chief Character who is in every Bible story (even if not explicitly, as is the case in the Scroll of Esther), and relating to other learners in the group discussion. Relational knowledge is created (constructed). Right-brain assessment and attunement functions in relating to other persons are thus engaged by story. Storying is a way of structuring thought that is not reductive to left-brain reasoning but engages the whole mind.

The characters we encounter and relate to in storying the Bible help form our identity as story partners with God, and give us an alternative imagination for God's future purposes for us; they give us the strength to act in the present in our own best interests and find meaning in our past, as part of our life story in partnership with God. Just as each individual's identity is formed through the significant relational attachments in their lives (parents, family, friends, teachers, mentors), so Israel's identity was formed "as the story partner with YHWH."[5]

We are changed more by who and what we love, than by what we believe. This is Paul's theological assessment of what happens when we relate to God, as partners in his story, through storying the stories that make up the Master Story, the Grand Narrative. By engaging his story, we *behold* him, and in beholding him, we can *become* like him.

Four Theological Truths within the Naaman Story

The purpose of stating these truths as the authors do here is to demonstrate that doctrines normally appearing as categories in systematic theology texts can be drawn from a Bible story in a way that they remain clothed, and thus more easily remembered and applied in real life. TH and OH supplement each other; but we think the best sequence is OH prior to TH.

The four theological truths discussed below emerged in the group discussion (ch. 9), but here the authors state them in more reasoned and summarized prose, using more current Christian language. In doing so we started with the story of Naaman and never left the story. This is character theologizing yielding truths that focus on application, that remain in touch with earth. The truths are: (1) grace: prevenient and saving, (2) conversion as holistic transformation, (3) the immutability of God, and (4) the messianic (or Christian) paradox.

---

5. Bradt, *Story as a Way of Knowing*, 236.

Grace: Prevenient and Saving

Two aspects of God's grace are seen herein. First, *prevenient grace*. In the Naaman story, the Israeli girl taken captive by General Naaman's raiding party and made to be his wife's servant had faith in the God of Israel to heal through his prophet in Israel. She had good will toward Naaman and his wife. This was the divine contact which set in motion the chain of events resulting in Naaman's healing and conversion. The group participants in the storytelling event (ch. 9) learned this through character theologizing about the relationship between the servant girl and General Naaman and his wife.

God was seeking out Naaman in grace before he ever had a clue about it. Most prevalent in the Reformed theological tradition, the theological term "prevenient grace" captures the notion of God graciously seeking out, encountering, and extending favor to a person *before* conversion; it is grace that precedes human decision. Jesus spoke of it when he said, "No one can come to Me unless the Father who sent Me draws him . . ." (John 6:44a NKJV). God was seeking out and already at work in Naaman's life by providentially having just the right Israeli girl come into his life. It could be said she was a divine contact or had a divine appointment with General Naaman. It could be said she was sent as an involuntary missionary to Naaman. Prevenient grace did its work and brought Naaman to saving faith. So it is seeing this embodied example of prevenient grace, in the character of Naaman, and God's providing the contact through the captive Israeli girl, that we learn this doctrine.

The second aspect of grace seen here in *saving grace*. Often considered strictly a New Testament doctrine, the truth is that God has always saved people by grace through faith (it did not originate with Luther, or even with Paul). In this story it is evident that Naaman did not merit the grace that both healed him and brought him to faith in the true God. He was not part of the elect people of Israel. He was a pagan, a polytheistic military man whose soldiers took captives and enslaved them. Yet God graciously encountered him and transformed him inside and out. He could not buy, nor was he allowed to pay for, his salvation (Eph 2:8–9).

The overtones or implication (רֶמֶז remez, or "hint," to use the rabbinic hermeneutics [see ch. 5]), discovered by the group in discussion was that perhaps his ritual dipping in the Jordan River was a baptism lends weight to this interpretation that Naaman experienced salvation. The story demonstrates that a gentile sinner, before the coming of Messiah, was converted and transformed by unmerited favor—grace. Surely, he experienced the same or maybe greater grace than did those often called "the Old Testament saints," the God-fearing, Torah-observant people of Israel. Reading about this doctrine abstractly stated would be rather ho hum or even unconvincing. Seeing it demonstrated in Naaman is a memorable way of knowing!

Conversion as Holistic Transformation

Generally thought of as a New Testament reality via a new birth experience of regeneration, and the ongoing process of sanctification by the Holy Spirit, holistic transformation is seen in Naaman. He was healed of his skin disease, but it was more than skin deep. He had encountered the living God and thus underwent a change of beliefs and behavior, a change of attitude and allegiance (sought God's forgiveness; aspired to offer sacrifice only to Yahweh), and passed from sickness to health. Apparently, Elisha thought it a deep enough conversion that he trusted him to go back to his pagan, polytheistic culture without fearing that his faith would be compromised or destroyed. Seeing all the changes that comprise holistic transformation embodied in Naaman helps us to identify, to relate to, to aspire, and to believe for the same, and does so in a concrete manner.

The Immutability of God

Eras of biblical history are sometimes demarcated as the "Dispensation of Law" (Old Testament) and the "Dispensation of Grace" (New Testament). The Naaman story shows God's gracious working in Naaman's life is very similar (if not the same) as his working in lives after the coming of Christ (healing, inner transformation), thus expressing the same unchanging God. He is invariable and consistent in his character; he will keep his covenant promises and purposes.[6] He is the same in character under every era recorded in Scripture—prior to and after those.

Participants in the group discussion of this story need not have known anything about theological systems. Do Jewish believers, or new believers among the post-Christian millennial generation, need to get bogged down and perhaps confused by the academic controversies about covenant theology vs. dispensationalism? The participants in this storytelling session saw Yahweh's love and compassion for Naaman revealed in ways very similar to how Jesus showed compassion to lepers in his day. By relating to Naaman,

---

6. "The Westminster Shorter Catechism says, 'God is a spirit, whose being, wisdom, power, holiness, justice, goodness, and truth are infinite, eternal, and unchangeable.' Those things do not change. A number of Scriptures attest to this idea (e.g. Num. 23:19; 1 Sam. 15:29; Ps. 102:26; Mal. 3:6; 2 Tim. 2:13; Heb. 6:17–18; Jam. 1:17)." https://www.theopedia.com/immutability-of-god.

hearing his story, seeing his transformation, and recalling the ministry of Jesus, Bible learners come to know something of the immutable character of God, bypassing the left-brain theological controversies.

The Messianic (or Christian) Paradox

General Naaman had to lose his pride, his false sense of honor and social status, his old gods and allegiances, and surrender all in order to gain his healing and wonderful transformation. Had he not listened to his servants, but instead returned back home in a huff and rage, nursing his wounded pride, he would have remained a miserable lost leper. Here is where the D. L. Moody quote at the beginning of this chapter applies so well, "God sends no one away empty except those who are full of themselves."[7] Had Naaman chosen to remain full of himself (prideful), he would have gone away empty. He gave up his diseased, broken life to gain true life and wholeness.

Naaman graphically fleshes out a truth, a principle taught by Jesus, we call "the Christian (or messianic) paradox"—i.e., when a goal, or object, or good is sought autonomously from (or inconsistently with) the given forms within which it is obtainable in God's moral universe, it eludes the seeker.[8]

This is a principle of unintended consequences based on the dictum of Jesus the Messiah as recorded in all four Gospels (Matt 10:39; Mark 8:35; Luke 17:33; John 12:25). Jesus states it thus, "For whoever desires to save his life will lose it, but whoever loses his life for my sake and the gospel's will save it" (Mark 8:35 NKJV). Thus, there is a paradox involved in self-fulfillment, sought so ardently by many late-modern Westerners. It is that in seeking self-fulfillment, self-realization, self-satisfaction as an end in itself, humans find it is illusive and unattainable. In grasping selfishly, for selfish gain, we lose self. Like Lucifer, in overreaching we lose that for which we reach. This principle is counterintuitive and inherently ironic to humans in their natural condition. C. S. Lewis grasped this principle well:

> Until you have given up yourself to Him you will not have a real self . . . Your real, new self (which is Christ's and also yours, and yours just because it is His) will not come as long as you are looking for it. It will come when you are looking for Him. Does that sound strange? The same principle holds, you know, for more everyday matters. Even in social life, you will never make a good impression on other people until you stop thinking about

---

7. "Quotes by Dwight Lyman Moody (1837–1899)." http://www.jesus-is-savior.com/Great%20Men%20of%20God/dwight_moody-quotes.htm.

8. Bjoraker, "Faith, Freedom and Radical Individualism," 374–75.

what sort of impression you are making . . . The principle runs through all of life from the top to bottom . . . Nothing that you have not given away will be really yours. . . . Look for yourself, and you will find in the long run only hatred, loneliness, despair, rage, ruin and decay. But look for Christ, and you will find Him, and with Him, everything else thrown in.[9]

And finally, stated so memorably by missionary martyr Jim Eliot, killed in Ecuador in 1956, fulfilling his own restatement of the Christian paradox, "He is no fool who gives what he cannot keep, to gain what he cannot lose."[10]

The Christian paradox principle is demonstrated in the story of Elisha and General Naaman, embodied in Naaman's choices (the anguish which we can feel as we engage the story), can be discovered in discussion, and more easily remembered and passed on to others. This is how story is a way of knowing.

Summarizing, every theological doctrine is embedded somewhere within the whole corpus stories in the Bible. Telling and discussing these stories in groups, also called oral inductive Bible study, makes these doctrines accessible and understandable to myriads more people, most notably the approximately 80 percent of the world who are oral learners.[11] When seen concretely through character theology, people of any education level can grasp them. They can discuss them in their own vocabulary without having to learn the academic jargon used in the academies. Story is a potent way of knowing.

Four Missiological Implications within the Naaman Story

A discussion of four missiological concepts in use in contemporary mission practice, drawn from the Naaman story, follows, with a specific focus on the Jewish ministry context where applicable.

---

9. Lewis, *Mere Christianity*, 226–27.

10. https://www2.wheaton.edu/bgc/archives/faq/20.htm. The best sources for quotes by Jim Elliot are found in his biography by his wife Elisabeth Elliot in *Shadow of the Almighty*, which contains extensive quotes from his personal journals. The second source is an abridged version of the journals themselves, *The Journals of Jim Elliot*, edited by Elisabeth Elliot.

11. Lausanne Movement, "Orality."

Indigenization

Anthropologists use the term *indigenization* to describe what happens when locals take a practice or belief from outside their culture and adapt it, making it their own. Harvie Conn offers this definition: "The 'translatability' of the universal Christian faith into the forms and symbols of the particular cultures of the world . . . the word validates all human languages and cultures before God as legitimate paths for understanding his divine meaning."[12]

General Naaman practiced indigenization when he made faith in the God of Israel his own and went back to his life and position in Syria. If he led other Syrians to the faith that he and his wife's Israeli servant girl shared, they would have expressed that faith in a Syrian way, as did Naaman. This is how it should be—Yahweh-faith indigenized.

This is why biblical faith is the most transcultural and translatable religion of all time, because ideally it is not a transmission of religion (which is largely cultural), but a transmission of faith. This has always been God's heart and intent—to reach people where they are and allow them to maintain their cultural identity and express their faith in him from within that identity.

Along with Naaman the Syrian, consider Abel, Enoch, Noah, Melchizedek, Abimelech, Job, Jethro (a priest of Midian), Rahab, the Queen of Sheba, and others. None of these men and women were part of the elect covenant people of Israel (neither Hebrew, Israelite nor Jewish),[13] yet they

---

12. Conn, quoted in Moreau, *Evangelical Dictionary of World Missions*, 481. While groundbreaking and greatly needed to address colonialism's impact on the mission world, the authors recognize the inefficiencies of Venn and Anderson's "three-selfs"—self-governing, self-propagating, self-supporting—and Tippett's additional three selfs to rectify the problem—self-image, self-functioning, self-giving. While the term "contextualization" was to take us beyond "indigenization," indigenization remains a noble goal and valuable missions term. See Steffen, "Theories Drive Our Ministries."

13. The Jewish people were known as "Hebrews" from the time of the patriarchs (Gen 14:13), and "sons of Israel" (Jacob's new name) or "Israelites" dating from the time of the sojourn in Egypt, and the exodus. Later those who returned from the Babylonian exile were from the Southern Kingdom, dominated by the tribe of Judah. They then came to be called "Jews," a derivative of the name "Judah." Since then it has been customary to call the whole peoplehood descending from Abraham, Isaac, and Jacob and his twelve sons "the Jewish people." We retrospectively call Abraham the father of the Jewish people. They are one continuous peoplehood since the call of Abraham. Though the name "Israel" also refers to the "land of Israel," it generally refers to the "people of Israel" (the Jewish people), including in the New Testament. The term "Judaism" refers to the religion or way of life of the Jewish people but does not occur in the Hebrew Bible, and did not emerge until postexilic times or later, perhaps even as late as the early Christian centuries when there was a gradual formulation of the concept of "religions" by which to categorize different peoples. See https://www.bibleodyssey.org/en/people/related-articles/emergence-of-judaism.

were in a favorable relationship with God, at his initiative. Whatever the faith expression of these men and women was, they expressed it out of their own cultural identity indigenously.

In Old Testament times, there were *proselyte* conversions of gentiles to the Israelite faith and community (i.e., formal conversion to the people and religion of the Israelites/the Jewish people [e.g., Rahab and Ruth]) and later there were conversions to Judaism. These were people of other nations adopting the Jewish faith and religion. But there were also *nonproselyte conversions* of which Naaman is a model, i.e., conversion to faith in Yahweh, but not to the religion of Judaism. This would be an indigenization of Yahweh-faith by the people of those societies into their own cultures.

Critical Contextualization

Indigenization requires not just contextualization, but "critical contextualization,"[14] lest the little mustard seed of faith be choked out, as Jesus taught in his parable of the sower. Some seed "fell by the wayside and birds came and devoured them . . . some fell on stony places . . . where they were scorched by the sun." Others "fell among thorns and the thorns sprang up and choked them" (Matt 13: 4–7 NKJV). Cross-cultural storytellers who bring the gospel to peoples, allowing and helping indigenization of the faith to happen, are contextualizing the gospel. But they need to critique the culture collectively, because every culture is fallen, all having some sin and false beliefs.[15]

To illustrate, Naaman could have gone back to Syria and fell among the thorns, his newfound faith in Yahweh lost. But he asked Elisha, the man of God, for provisions to worship and for forgiveness in advance should he

---

14. Much has been written on contextualization in the evangelical missions world since the 1970s. The term "critical contextualization" came to prominence in the missions world through Christian anthropologist Paul Hiebert in the early 1990s. Hiebert articulated it well, but credits the work of Jacob Loewen and John Geertz among the Wanana in Panama for developing the field practice. See Hiebert, *Anthropological Reflections on Missiological Issues*, 75–92. For an insightful more contemporary text, see Moreau, *Contextualization in World Missions*.

15. "Earlier generations of scholars tended to think of Paul chiefly as a dogmatic theologian, the originator of a grand system of belief . . . today . . . the man from Tarsus was not a systematic theologian, at least not in the modern sense of someone who wrote treatments of different theological topics. Recent interpreters of Paul have viewed him as a pastoral theologian, a task theologian, a missionary theologian, a hermeneutical theologian, and the like. These different portraits all support the understanding that Paul is a *contextual theologian*—his letters, case studies in the contextualizing of the gospel in ways that intersect the concrete lives and cultures of his hearers" (Flemming, *Contextualization in the New Testament*, 89; emphasis original).

lapse into syncretism (a conscious or unconscious mixing of two religious systems that compromises each). Critical contextualization addresses syncretism which is always crouching at the door.

Naaman's very request shows his awakened conscience was active. In cross-cultural storying today, as indigenization of the faith is affirmed, so must new believers also be helped to critique those aspects of their culture that are sinful. This can be done by the cross-cultural storytellers asking strategic questions related to compromising beliefs and behaviors and telling related Bible stories that address syncretism and its consequences.

Syncretism

Uncritical contextualization encourages syncretism,[16] which Scott Moreau defines as "the replacement or dilution of the essential truths of the gospel through the incorporation of non-Christian elements."[17] Many evangelicals therefore rightfully fear that affirming indigenous movements to Jesus may be affirming *syncretism*. It is helpful to recall that the Creator accommodated to Abraham and the patriarchs' subbiblical beliefs and practices (like polygamy); God began where they were, leading them on a journey into increasing light and holiness.

If their Yeshua-faith is strong, many new Jewish believers today would do well to continue to participate in traditional (Reformed, Conservative, Orthodox) synagogues, where in the course of their community relationships they will inevitably witness to their faith in Yeshua the Messiah. Many of the practices of Judaism are *not* syncretistic and can remain the religious practice of messianic Jews, though some are mixed with folk religion and Eastern mystical beliefs. However, many of the beliefs of Rabbinic Judaism are false, especially about the identity of the Messiah, and must be corrected by New Testament teaching.

Many new Jewish believers in Jesus have faced family and/or rabbis who argue forcefully with them against the messiahship of Jesus. If the pressure on them to doubt and renounce Jesus-faith is too strong, they need to choose fellowship with other believers over their traditional synagogue.

Like Naaman the gentile, so for many of those today in the Muslim, Buddhist, and Hindu communities who embrace Jesus the Messiah as Lord, their current identities and some of their religious practices may be the starting point on their way to recognizing that the definitive revelation of

---

16. For a brief overview of early missions literature on syncretism, see Yamamori and Taber, *Christopaganism or Indigenous Christianity?*, 16–17.

17. Moreau, *Evangelical Dictionary of World Missions*, 924.

God is found in the story of Israel, climaxing in the story of Jesus. They may have mere baby faith, saving faith now, but over time—if they keep hearing the Bible together and following the Holy Spirit by responding to the critique brought from within the hermeneutical community of fellow believers—their theology will become clearer and their religious practices purer while still expressing their faith from within their culture.

Where genuine conversion to Jesus Christ occurs, *can we trust this promise of God to them,* "He who began a good work in you, will carry it on to completion until the Day of Christ Jesus" (Phil 1:6 NIV)? Apparently, Elisha trusted the new believer Naaman to God's continued work in him. Surely there is also messy syncretism with failures and defeats as well. Consider that birth, life, and growth are messy. Better the active yet imperfect efforts in the arena, than sitting on the sidelines or the benches in mission.

The implications for cross-cultural storytellers are that there must be the courage of faith and willingness to take risks—risks of failure, risks of being rejected and misunderstood. The goal of planting seeds that take root and bear fruit is worth the inherent risks.

Levels of Life Experience

It is helpful to delineate three levels of life experience in relation to God that can be depicted thus:

Culture

———

Religion

———

Faith

The seed of the gospel takes root at the *faith* level (encounter and personal-collective response, heart level), and then that faith is worked out in the *religion* and *culture* levels in which it was planted. As new believers remain in their communities, as Naaman did, they may retain any forms or practices at the *religion* and *culture* levels that are compatible with the Bible; while those elements that contradict the Bible are rejected.

Naaman had the prophet Elisha's blessing to go back to his pagan culture and even to accompany his master the king as he went to worship in the temple of fertility god Rimmon. Naaman surely maintained certain cultural and religious practices after his conversion that he practiced before his conversion. *Religion* is largely a part of *culture*; in fact, it can be said that religion is the "cult" in culture. Religion does not save—not even Israel's religion, nor the religion of Christianity—only God saves by grace through faith in Messiah Jesus. It is this *faith* level (personal knowledge through a relational encounter) that is key to people's salvation. Believers in Jesus may reinterpret *forms*. Certain cultural and even religious *forms* may remain the same before and after conversion, but infused with new *meaning*.

For example, because Jewish culture has its source in the Hebrew Bible, the Jewish feasts are easy to messianize—the Passover (the lamb of God), Shavuot (giving of Law, and of the Holy Spirit), the Feast of Tabernacles (harvest of souls of the ages), Hanukkah (Feast of Lights, Yeshua as Light of the world). The Jewish rites of passage—circumcision, Bar/Bat Mitzvah, Jewish weddings, Jewish funeral and mourning practice—are all also easily infused with messianic meaning.

For religions whose source is further from the biblical tradition, more critical contextualization of *form* and *meaning* is required. For example, in Islam the form of praying five times a day bowing face-down to Allah on a rug facing Mecca must take on different meaning for Muslim background believers—praying to the God and Father of our Lord Jesus the Messiah, rather than to Allah as understood in Islam. Or, Muslim followers of Jesus may still fast during Ramadan, but not to earn merit with Allah as understood by Islam, but to intercede in prayer in the name of *Isa al-Masih* (Jesus the Messiah) for the salvation of their community.

Practices that are dark, demonic, immoral, or sinful demand repentance. False beliefs contrary to biblical truth must be rejected, and biblical teaching must correct them. Even in religions with greater distance from biblical truth (Hinduism, Buddhism, aspects of animism) some *forms* of reinterpretation are possible but require more rigorous critical contextualization.[18]

---

18. A now-classic case of contextualization is the work of missionaries Don and Carol Richardson, who in the 1960s worked among the native animistic and cannibalistic Sawi tribe in Dutch New Guinea. The tribes of the region made deceptive friendships with men of other tribes with the intention of killing and eating them. Then the victim's tribe would plot revenge and the cycle of violence continued. The Richardsons were able to begin telling the story of the gospel of Jesus to the people, but because they valued treachery, Judas Iscariot became a hero to them! (This argues for the need to tell the biblical stories in a chronological manner, and as much of the master story of the Bible as possible, and for tethers and controls in oral hermeneutics). However, the tribes devised a "peace child" ceremony, in which a village presents the enemy with an infant as a peace child. As long as the child lives, the village lives at peace. In the case of an offense, someone may plead the peace child and hostility will cease. Richardson saw this as an analogy to Jesus as God's peace child. He tells the tribe as long as they accept God's peace child, they never need to offer a human peace child again. Through some additional experiences the tribe began to accept Jesus as their "peace child." There was eventually a people movement to Christ among the Sawi, and a strong church exists

The reader has just observed theologizing and missiological applications in the conceptual and analytic genre, and this is valuable knowledge. As noted, story is also a way of knowing, and offers the deepest way of knowing. It is the richest, most productive form of communication because it offers cases studies and role models, easy to imagine, and from which multiple truths and applications can be drawn.

How many people in our world of 80 percent oral learners will be able or willing to pursue systematic theology courses at the undergraduate or graduate levels, where they can learn propositional doctrines distilled by earlier scholars? Due to lack of interest, access, ability, or finances, the answer is: a relatively small number. In contrast, oral strategies of Bible learning and communication that embrace *story as a way of knowing*—the approaches of OH—is far more accessible to far more people.

Using story as a way of learning automatically advantages it as a communication tool in comprehension, retention, and repetition. Group participants will therefore comprehend these principles better and retain them longer than they would have had they learned them in an academic form from a textbook.[19] As well, they have the story in the Bible to which they can refer back, and which they can tell to others, who can in turn tell others. The Bible study group (ch. 9) discovered these truths and applications by discussing the concrete and memorable characters in the story. Character theologizing about the people in the story generated these insights!

When questionable beliefs and behaviors arise, the storyteller can aid the discussion process surrounding critical contextualization, syncretism, and form and meaning by using story as a way of knowing. Questions that could be asked of the present situation under discussion could include: *What are the traditional components and function of this behavior? What areas are biblically compatible? What areas demand change?* Once these questions are answered, it is time to implement the decision. Later, the group participants should review the outcomes and make needed adjustments.[20]

Another help storytellers can provide the group is a set of Bible stories that address these crucial issues. Some of the key stories the group should be familiar with that address syncretism could include: Joshua's speeches to the people about idolatry (Josh 24); Elijah and the prophets of Baal (1 Kgs 18);

---

among them today. Richardson seized upon this preexisting *form* in this culture and was able to infuse it with new *meaning*. This is called making a redemptive analogy between an existing form and the gospel, or a biblical teaching. The story is chronicled in Richardson, *Peace Child*.

19. See Klem, *Oral Communication of the Scripture,* and Koehler, *Telling God's Stories with Power.*

20. Steffen, *Passing the Baton*, 196.

the Mary stories;[21] the Council at Jerusalem (Acts 15); Paul among the polytheists in Lystra and Derbe (Acts 14:8–18);[22] Paul among the philosophers in Athens (Acts 17:16–34); Paul and the false exorcists, the Sons of Sceva (Acts 19:11–20). Some key Bible characters the participants should become familiar with are those who challenged or caved to syncretism. These could include: Joshua, Elijah, Manasseh, King Josiah, King Hezekiah, Mary, and the apostle Paul. Bible stories and characters as a way of knowing do not overlook biblical truths related to contextualization, syncretism, and form and meaning; rather they bring them to life.

The Four Components of Oral Hermeneutics

The authors now show how all four of the components in OH (depicted in figure 7.2) have been at work in our discussion and reflections upon the Elisha and General Naaman story.

Orthodoxy (Doctrine)

As the authors conducted character theology and spelled out theological truths, we purposely strove to be faithful to what the Bible teaches. We also noted legitimate different perspectives of doctrines may be identified by those in other cultures because our hermeneutic is not cultureless. Multiple truths within a single story can enhance biblical faith as a total way of life for Christ-followers in any society or subculture. Character-centric questions unearth embedded theology found in controlling characters that results in relational theology rather than rational theology. Though both TH and OH are needed, the authors have argued in this book that TH without the practices of OH is inadequate to deliver the fullness of biblical truth.

Orthopraxy (Practice)

True Christianity ("biblical faith") goes beyond principles to practices; beyond the cognitive to the character-forming; it is lived out in daily life (Jas 2:14). If OH is anything, it is praxis, practice, practical.

---

21. For those serving in Catholic countries see The Mary Stories from the Bible available from J. O. Terry <jot2@sbcglobal.net>.

22. The Ebenezer Stories are helpful in discipling new believers among Muslim women who focus on praying to the Father in the name of Jesus for their personal and family needs instead of following their traditional cultural <jot2@sbcglobal.net>.

As the authors made missiological applications to today's world, and to some of the frontiers of mission such as reaching and winning devotees of the world's oldest and most established religions, we endeavored to align our practice in faithful discipleship to Jesus. Critical contextualization is a challenging endeavor, and controversial for the church. And though the term is new, the practice is not. The authors think the risk of trying new experimental approaches (where earlier different approaches have failed) in the interest of reaching huge blocks of unreached people is worth the risks. We trust biblical storytelling (using story sets that address worldview themes of our audiences), being soft-confrontation (indirect), as the best practice for reaching hearts and minds (see the Nathan Principle in ch. 5).

We trust God to guide and correct as needed. Here is where an awareness of global theologies can serve as a corrective. Here is where the global body of Christ can function as a hermeneutical community. Here is where telling God's stories many times, in many circles, in many venues, in many languages will help us advance in faithful practice.

Orthopathy (Imagination and Emotion)

Narrative logic calls for the participation of one's imagination and emotions. OH, unlike TH, is comfortable with ambiguity (as noted in ch. 2) when referencing oral language. In the Naaman story of healing and transformation, oral language was used in the storytelling and discussion to elicit appropriate emotions and stir the imagination to help bring the story to life without compromising it. *Story as a way of knowing* naturally engages the whole mind (right and left brain), because when listeners are relating to the characters in the stories—identifying with them (or not), aspiring to be like them (or not), clicking their tongues, shaking their heads, giving thumbs up or high-fives (or the culture specific equivalents of these expressions)—they are fully engaged.

When participants continue to talk and speculate about what may have happened when Naaman went home and sing the praises of the courage and faith of the Israeli slave girl, surely their imagination, emotions, and whole person are engaged.

Orthoecho (Memory)

Repetition—the three tellings of the story, i.e., the storyteller's first presentation, the telling by the volunteer, and the lead-through when the storyteller led the group to tell the story again together helps ensure memory. The same is true when the new lesson (storytelling session) begins by reviewing application of last week's lesson. The oral language that impressed the imagination, the discussion, the enjoyment of discovery learning with friends, finding a proverb, symbol, or saying that captures at least part of the story's truth, the encouragement to retell it, the excitement to see what will happen when they tell this story at their own water wells or water coolers—all of this aids in retention, reiteration, and replication so the learners can make this story their own so as to naturally retell it to others.

Improving Our Storying

After every story it is good for storytellers to ask themselves how the story could be improved in relation to the four components of OH: doctrine, practice, imagination and emotion, and memory. The same holds true when reviewing a story set. *All* storytelling models and methods, and *every* story and story set told, *can be improved.* The review could begin by asking,

> *Which questions did the listeners find difficult to answer?*
>
> *What other questions should have been asked?*
>
> *How character-centric were the questions in each aspect of the storying process (figure 7.3)?*
>
> *Did the Chief Character become the hero of the story?*
>
> *How was the story tied to the grand narrative?*
>
> *How much of the backstory could be incorporated into the story itself?*
>
> *How did the story challenge current worldviews?*
>
> *Did the application aspect call for drawings or other artwork, performing a drama, composing a song?*
>
> *What symbols could strengthen retention and reiteration of the story?*
>
> *Which Hebrew letter(s) could accompany the title to visually summarize or signal the story?*[23]

---

23. A Chinese character that represents and reminds the storytellers and listeners

What did I learn from this telling? From this story set?

What percentage of the stories told are from the Old Testament? New Testament?[24]

How intensely storytellers review each lesson (formative evaluation) and a story set (summative evaluation) will determine to a great extent how the next story and story set will be improved and strengthened. "To change lives, curricula must touch lives."[25] *How well did the story and story set touch lives?*

The authors will now wrap up the book with concluding reflections.

---

of the "Elisha and the Widow's Oil" story could be 油 (oil, pronounced "yo"). It means refuel, oil, lubricate, make an all-out effort. For the "Elisha and General Naaman" story, 洗 (wash, pronounced "she") could signal the story. It means to wash, bathe, baptize, and in combination to purge. Such symbols aid in the recall of the story and the characters within it. We are indebted to Anne Alexander for these mental visualizations that summarize and signal the two stories.

24. For Jewish ministry a very high percentage of Bible stories should be from the Hebrew Bible; nearly every story points toward the Messiah in some way, and skilled questioning by the storyteller-teacher who knows the Messiah can draw out awareness of the Messiah.

25. Steffen, *Passing the Baton*, 202.

Concluding Reflections

"He who thinks he knows, doesn't know.
He who knows that he doesn't know, knows."

—Joseph Campbell

"Without reflection, we go blindly on our way,
creating more unintended consequences."

—Margaret J. Wheatley

WHY THE FERVENT INTEREST in first-century Christianity in the last three decades in the Americas? Why have so many evangelicals switched to Orthodoxy? And this includes the Bible Answer Man, Hank Hanegraaff, and Frank Schaeffer, son of Francis and Edith Schaeffer! *What did they miss in their churches that they discovered in older church traditions?* The same could be asked of evangelicals who transferred to Catholicism. *What attracted them?*

Why do African-Americans with a rich Christian heritage[1] convert to the Black Hebrew Israelites? Why do many highly educated African-American

---

1. J. Deotis Roberts, an African American pioneer of black theology, makes these observations relevant to oral hermeneutics: "Where he [Tillich] was greatly concerned about the dialogue between philosophy and theology, the black theologian may find the dialogue between the humanities, behavioral sciences, and the 'live' black religious tradition more helpful ... The black Christian is concerned about the relation between faith and life. His or her 'ultimate concern' has to do with life-and-death decisions. His or her 'situation' is the racism that affects the total life and the experiences of his or her loved ones ... The existence of God does not, therefore, need to be established through the several 'proofs' ... Much of the raw material of Black Theology will be intuitive. We

millennials, First Nation' people,[2] *people of India,*[3] *Asians, among others, perceive Christianity as a white man's religion? Why do so many baby boomers take issue with the numerous inconsistencies and contradictions found in the Bible, thereby declaring it a defective book? Why do so many Western millennials and other generations believe the Bible to be irrelevant? Why has church attendance continued to drop? Why are 54 percent of American adults disengaged from or indifferent to the Bible even as 66 percent of the total population expresses some interest in learning more about the Bible?*[4]

Whether transfers, traditionalists, inbetweeners, or dropouts, could aspects of orality related to OH be part of the solution? Could the abstractness of doctrines, in contrast to character theology (CT), be part of the solution?[5] *How does a growing posttext, postfact, oral-preference Western world challenge current hermeneutics? How does an oral-preference Eastern world challenge current hermeneutics?* The authors believe oral hermeneutics (OH), driven by narrative logic and character-centric questions that give the text a voice so that CT results, can at least partially provide the answers to these questions.

Whether coming from an expert-centric or user-centric perspective, as you read the concluding reflections of the book that focuses on the narrative sections of Scripture, listen for the echoes heard from the preceding chapters that help make the case for the return of OH. The echo summaries that follow in this chapter attempt to answer the central question of this

---

have to do to a great extent with an 'unwritten' body of doctrine. For much of its history, the black church was 'an invisible institution . . . The history of the black church and of black worship is largely an oral tradition'" (Roberts, *Liberation and Reconciliation*, 3–4).

2. See Smith, *Whiteman's Gospel*.

3. A female Indian student wrote this on her final exam, "Most of the missionaries who came to India in the past tried to teach people based on Western cultural values. This made a deep wound and separation in the society between East and West. Christians and Bible are considered completely foreign" (Mischke, personal correspondence, August 31, 2015). Chia paints the picture this way, "In Biblical terms, unless Asian Christianity is baptized in the 'Jordan' of Asian religions and confirmed by the 'Calvary' of Asian poverty, it will remain foreign and unacceptable by the majority of the people of Asia" (Chia, "Asian Christianity," 12–13). Tite Tiénou calls for de-Westernized Christianity: "If Christianity is de-Westernized, Christians in Africa, Asia, and Latin America will be able to defend themselves when accused of being agents of Westernization and puppets in the hands of foreigners whose intention is the destruction of local cultures and religions" (Tiénou, "Christianity Theology," 42).

4. American Bible Society, "State of the Bible 2018," 6, 12.

5. In *For the Life of the World*, Volf and Croasmun conclude something is totally amiss in academic theology. Focus has shifted from answering the fundamental questions of life faced by the average churchgoer to in-house theological debates surrounding esoteric topics and teachers of the past, all based on individualism and the "great edifices of science" (Volf and Croasmun, *For the Life of the World*, 4, 13).

introductory book on the topic of OH: *Why is it important to know and practice OH in order to ascertain and communicate biblical meaning?*

For those already using some version of OH, investigate how the echoes could improve usage. For those using some variation of textual hermeneutics (TH), note how these echoes could possibly complement it. Premises come with promises and possibilities. *How well are they working out?*

Echoes of Orality

Relationally based orality takes us back in time, in this book, back to the beginning of the oral traditions of the Israelites, to the first church, to the emerging canon, and back to how we all first learned—orally through communal relationships. While letter-based literacy tends to instinctively restrict meaning, speech-based orality tends to instinctively expand it.

This distinctive is because orality engages through sight and sound; it prefers group inclusion and immersion, the visual (an unfolding theater), the spoken word, the sensory; it calls for the immediacy, spontaneity, and repetition of lived experience in all its practical fulsomeness; it calls for emotional curiosity and imagination in an ambiguous world of symbols and rituals; it welcomes alliterations, echoes, and mystery, even as it relies on memory to maintain its oral tradition. The holistic, integrative nature of orality is its distinction and genius. Part of that distinction and genius is grounded in OH, and by extension, CT.

Have Western exegetes turned an Eastern book into a Western one? Has our fondness for a fixed, printed text, capable of being analyzed with precision and exactitude, blinded us to other hermeneutic possibilities? Does God require all people to be able to analyze grammar to interpret Scripture? Does God assume all people can interpret Scripture through oral means?

In *The Return to Oral Hermeneutics* the authors recognize the effects of centuries of literacy socialization that produced a blind spot in the Western Christian world—the neglect by most in the academies, agencies, and assemblies of the foundational and forceful role *orality* had on the text and teaching. From the inspired, spoken word of the prophets, including Jesus (pretext), to the elite literate scribes who painstakingly hand printed the sacred text to posttext interpretation and teaching, the footprint of orality throughout the entire process is acutely visible to those having the oral-aural-influenced eyes and ears of the Mediterranean ancients.

The oral-aural-toned worldview of the biblical authors and recipients demanded an oral-based text because, among other things, the human mind then (and presently) requires mental visualization. Reflecting on the

Epistles, Asbury Seminary's Ben Witherington identifies these writings as "simply necessary surrogates for oral communication." Referencing Paul's letters specifically, he asserts "they were surrogates for the speeches Paul would have made could he have been present with this audience."[6]

The oral-aural influenced the design of every aspect of the canon, and how it was communicated. It called for the text to be read collectively *with* the participants (not *to* them); it called for dynamic, collective interpretation. And because of the integrative nature of the oral process, application became immediate and often corporate. For the Bible to be grasped to its fullest, therefore, it must be deliberately read, taught, interpreted, and implemented as oral-aural as the authors intentioned it.

The foundational and forceful role *orality* had in the canon is also evident in its sheer *volume* of narrative (55 to 65 percent of Scripture) and poetry (25 to 35 percent of Scripture). The communal *dialogue* that ensued over the oral *delivered*[7] manuscript centered on the whole document[8] so that recipients could understand and live it. Recipients used OH to interpret it, and collective *memory* to retain and replicate it (see ch. 3 and figure 6.1). If one cannot enter the oral-influenced Mediterranean world of biblical times, this book and much of Scripture will make little sense.

Orality's influence on and interfacing with Scripture is one reason why the authors believe Samford professor of Christian ministry J. D. Payne is on target when he identifies "orality" as one of the twelve "pressure points" facing the global Christian church today. He correctly concludes, "We will have to learn to function as translators—filtering the biblical truths through our literate framework and into the world of the oral learner."[9] Charles Madinger tells us why, "The framework for our communication strategies must take on everything you think of when 'oral' comes to mind . . . Every message, lesson, curriculum program and strategy will succeed partly to the degree it takes the orality framework into account."[10]

---

6. Witherington, "Sacred Texts in an Oral Culture," paras. 3, 18. See also Witherington, *What's in the Word*, and Witherington, *New Testament Rhetoric*.

7. Referencing the gospel writers, Flemming observes, "In the culture of the day, oral delivery would have been quite dramatic and spirited, emphasizing the emotional impact of the Gospel on the hearers. This enables the Gospel to become not just a story but an event which directly involves the listeners" (Flemming, *Contextualization and the New Testament*, 239).

8. Birger Gerhardsson's observation about oral texts no doubt has implications across the entire canon: "There was however a somewhat different way of learning an oral text collection. It was first learned as a whole; analysis and interpretation was undertaken later" (Gerhardsson, *Memory and Manuscript*, 117).

9. Payne, *Pressure Points*, 140.

10. Madinger, "Applied Orality," 6.

To help right the ship the authors have attempted to move beyond the bifurcation of orality and literacy, of OH and TH, of character theology and systematic theology, and beyond anointing one hermeneutic model as superior to another. But the authors do call for a sequential order when interpreting the narrative sections of Scripture.[11] Central to this sequence are the distinctives found in the oral-literacy continuum.

To illustrate, just as moderns use numerous discourse features (bolding, italicizing, spacing) in books to signal meaning, so did the writers of antiquity (gestures, posture, voice inflection). They were, however, different, yet with some overlap. Near Eastern specialist H. Van Dyke Parunak summarizes it this way: "Where we use signals specially tailored to the printed page, they employ a system of indicators that can function in either oral or written presentations."[12] Parunak captures this ancient blended process in the article's title as "oral typesetting."

Rather than spotlight only the dangers and deficiencies of OH and TH, the authors preferred to highlight their riches and resourcefulness. The authors illustrated (chs. 1 and 9) calling for an interfacing that follows a sequence—the cycle from concrete to concepts. To gain textual meaning that is fuller, broader, and more trustworthy, OH (with its multiple versions embedded in orality) followed by TH (with its multiple versions embedded in textuality) both serve as gateways and guardrails to Bible interpretation.

The apostle John captures the integration of the spoken and written this way: "Blessings come to those who *read* and proclaim these words aloud; blessings come to those who *listen* closely" (Rev 1:3 VOICE). A two-winged hermeneutic airplane flies better than a one-winged aircraft.

Echoes of Oral Hermeneutics

OH begins the cycle from concrete to concepts through audience analysis; it critiques characters in search of God-pleasing beliefs and behaviors for individuals, families, communities, and nations. Rather than diagrammed grammatical analysis and word studies, OH relies on the characters in the story to embody and demonstrate the truths found in the whole passage. Bible characters serve as summarizing codes for lifestyles that evidence distinctions between godly wisdom and foolishness; Bible characters give life

---

11. Interestingly, Witherington makes a similar call for the Pauline, Petrine, and Johannine letters: "the NT documents . . . should in the first instance *mainly be analyzed by ancient rhetorical conventions*, and only secondarily by epistolary ones" (Witherington, "Sacred Texts in an Oral Culture," para. 20; emphasis original).

12. Parunak, "Oral Typesetting," 154.

to cold abstract ideas. OH lays the foundation for the possibility of absorbed godly choices through character analysis (ch. 6).

OH is designed to transfer the experiences of one person to another through imagination and emotions, as well as ideas. Such emotive imaging lifts the recipient out of his/her current reality into the Bible character's reality, thereby providing a possible onramp (or offramp) to new, more God-honoring realities. From triumphs to tragedies the ancients in all their cultural variants pull us into their lives—and our own—revealing the universality of the human heart's need for something or someone *beyond* ourselves, for someone *bigger and better* than ourselves.

OH allows for multiple truths within the literary "boundaries of acceptability"[13] of a story, a possibility which increases when an author includes multiple plots. While definitions must be precise to be valid, demonstrations reflect some ambiguity yet remain equally valid as they tease out multiple possible embedded truths (values, morals, theology, and so forth). While TH searches for a single truth, OH allows for multiple truths.

Much of this broadness of truths and transfer of experience is subjective in nature, thereby making it difficult to develop a matrix to measure or reach "conclusions of certainty."[14] A significant part of this elasticity of meaning derives from the characters themselves. By design, author-chosen real or fictive characters enliven our imaginations, emotions, and minds, serving as legitimate entry points to discern the truth(s) being communicated within a story.

OH refuses to accept the eighteenth-century European Enlightenment premise that championed human reason alone as leading to a single, spot-on solution that is universal to any political, scientific, economic, or moral issue, among others. And it does so best when entirely independent of tradition or experience.

So that Christianity could remain relevant in the public square to this new reality, some consciously, others unconsciously, bought into this limiting philosophy, thereby influencing the theological world in the process. A text or Bible story, it was therefore concluded, had a single, author-intended meaning that is discernible independent of tradition or experience. This is insufficient, argues OH. Humans are much more than a brain. The experiential is also a required companion. The interpretive process requires both reason and the experiential, which could result in multiple truths within a single story.

No Bible story, however, is open to *any* interpretation. Rather, all interpretation is internally corralled by literary boundaries (e.g., chiasm, verbal

---

13. Klein, *Introduction to Biblical Interpretation*, 201.
14. Polkinghorne, *Narrative Knowing and the Human Sciences*, 175.

echoes, parallelism) and externally protected through the individual shame of the Bible storyteller, the collective shame of the local hermeneutic faith community, the international hermeneutic faith community through all ages,[15] and the guiding hand of the Holy Spirit (ch. 3). The circumference of biblical truth, concludes Ivon Poobalan, "must be both rooted [in the Word] and responsive [culturally contextual]."[16] OH operates within the confines of literary boundaries, individual and collective shame, and the universal priesthood of the believers so that minimal interpretive distortion occurs.

Not all of life is to be measured based on scientific instruments. Science, like narrative, has its limitations. In contrast, OH focuses on intuitive evaluation centered on characters. *Do the characters jump off the pages and grab us, making it difficult to shake off their clutching grasp? Do listeners initiate actions that change reality based on the observed experiences and behaviors of characters in the text?* To discern truth, OH relies on what characters describe (ear) and display (eye) rather than detailed definitions and elaborate explanations.

OH is *not* a rival to TH, rather it is its *source spring of living water*. OH is *not* a substitute hermeneutic, rather it has a *signature shared role in a specific sequence*. OH is *not* a supplemental hermeneutic, rather it serves as a *catalyst*. OH is *not* just an addition to TH, rather it is its indispensable *bedrock and cornerstone*. OH is *not* a simplistic hermeneutic, rather it is as *complex as TH*. OH is *not* an inferior hermeneutic, rather it is a *different type of hermeneutic that fills in missing gaps found in TH*.

The Bible is God's great spoken-written word—it is reason revealed, the abstract described, the principle personified. In most cases in antiquity, hearing about characters in action preceded reading about them. God's highest creation, therefore, were people of the voice *before* they were people of the book (ch. 5). Spoken Scripture gives voice to written Scripture.

In the midst of complementing the oral with the written,[17] there was, and remains, a hermeneutic sequence. Sequence matters because the

---

15. "To remember was to live, to forget was to die. Memory became the essential link to the past. There emerged a never-ending struggle to protect it from distortion and to prevent the treat of distortion . . . The rhetoricians made memory into a matter of honor and shame" (Byrskog, "Introduction," 2). Hiebert adds, "Out of the exercise of the priesthood of believers within an international hermeneutical community should come a growing understanding, if not agreement, on key theological issues that can help us test the contextualization of cultural practices as well as theologies" (Hiebert, *Anthropological Reflections on Missiological Issues*, 91–92).

16. Poobalan, "Christology in Asia," 84. Just as Bible authors borrowed and adapted relevant elements from various cultures outside of Israel (covenants, circumcision, kingship), so must today's Bible communicators.

17. Referencing the gospels, Holly Hearon concludes, "[W]e need to view these

spoken-written Scripture did not arrive initially to humanity as the *written*-spoken word of God. Interestingly, and instructively, God cultivated a relationship with people by walking and talking in a garden and on a road (Emmaus) even as the God of Israel wrote on stones and the Anointed One in the sand. Such communication sequences signal a hermeneutic sequence. While OH is *not the final word* for the narrative sections of Scripture, it should be *the first*.

Echoes of Logic and Pedagogy

OH, driven by narrative logic and character-centric theologizing, eventually faced centuries of challenge it could no longer repel. Alphabets, literacy, writing, paper, the printing press, and the European Enlightenment *slowly* changed first-century OH into what became perceived by many as an inconsequential, inappropriate, inadequate, primitive, subjective, simplistic, and a feared model for its relativization.

TH, using a different form of logic (propositional in contrast to narrative) and asking different types of questions (content-chasing rather than character-chasing), catapulted to the catbird seat. Centuries later, the written text, generally speaking, became more valued than the spoken voice (ch. 3). Critical thinking eclipsed character thinking. Content objectiveness overwhelmed character subjectiveness. Conceptual logic bested character logic.[18] Concepts divorced their contexts.

The homiletical big idea sunk the big character. Grammatical-historical overawed character-historical. Individualism replaced collectivism. Honor and shame gave way to innocence and guilt. Silence smothered sound.[19]

---

written texts as being closely intertwined with spoken word. They reflect, on the one hand, the engagement of the Hebrew Scriptures (written word) as words read aloud and remembered, and as spoken that is taught, proclaimed, and debated. They also reflect spoken word (proclamation and teaching) that finds its basis in experience recounted as spoken word; that is, spoken word that is independent of written word. Nonetheless, it is possible that this spoken word engages themes or images recoded in written word (the Hebrew Scriptures) that are encountered and employed primarily, if not exclusively, as spoken word, depending on the social context. Second, they suggest that these written texts would have been perceived as in some way an extension of spoken word" (Hearon, "Interplay between Written and Spoken Word," 71).

18. Hoefer correctly surmises, "Clearly, our Western form of logic may not be suitable for doing theology and apologetics in different cultures. It may not even be the best form of logic for religious discourse at all" (Hoefer, "Rooted or Uprooted," 135).

19. Scott and Dean call for "sound mapping," concluding that for speakers in oral settings, "sound creates structure, sound trains the ear, and sound balances the importance of signifier and signified" (Scott and Dean, "Sound Map of the Sermon on the

Individual textual analysis bettered collective character analysis. Evidential apologetics superseded experiential apologetics. Definitions outshined demonstrations. Statements surpassed the sensory. Fulsomeness surrendered to isolated facts. Fragmentation disintegrated the integrity of the grand narrative of Scripture.[20] Propositional ideas prevailed over performative action. Doctrinal collections dominated character collections. Curricular titles highlighted abstract topics rather than concrete characters. A single textual truth dethroned the possibility of multiple truths. Academic professional forms replaced populistic forms. The quickly revealed torpedoed the mystery of discovery over time. Analytical knowledge rewarded in the classroom depreciated wisdom aggregatively accumulated through life experience. Systematic theology outclassed biblical theology, narrative theology, and her close cousin—character theology. Books and libraries replaced collective oral tradition (generational memory). Categorical theology supplanted relational theology. Western individualism replaced Eastern collectivism. The eye (sight) dominated the ear (sound)—"Read O Israel!" replaced "Hear O Israel!" Minority degreed professional interpreters outclassed the majority rank-and-file interpreters. Theoretical theology distanced itself from practical theology. Proof-chants (of sections of Scripture) gave way to prooftexts. Textbooks substituted for stained glass art and song.

In summation, the head hermeneutic, TH, unseated the heart hermeneutic, OH, to determine *all* biblical meaning for *all* times in *all* genres, cultures, and countries; OH became obsolete.

We who grew up under such sweeping and powerful influences that set in motion hermeneutical changes were often totally unaware of the literary biases that accompanied them (not unlike our oral predecessors when print arrived or our contemporaries when radio, television, and the internet debuted). Too often these changes resulted in an unperceived

---

Mount," 680).

While Lee and Scott overstate their case surrounding semantics and sound, some truth remains, "Because the New Testament compositions were spoken aloud and processed in real time through listening, sound necessarily served as their primary organizing device.... An audience cannot afford to rely primarily on semantic meaning to make sense of a written composition.... [sound] organizes speech into comprehensible units and is therefore the most reliable guide to compositional structure" (Lee and Scott, *Sound Mapping the New Testament*, 385, 135, 175).

20. Rarely today do authors of New Testament survey textbooks reference or build upon the grand narrative of the Old Testament. Nor is a grand narrative of the New Testament called for or discussed at the conclusion of such textbooks. This tendency perpetuates a fragmented understanding of Scripture rather than an understanding of an unfolding single story; two separate books rather than one book with unfurling chapters; and the superiority of the last third of the Bible over the first two-thirds. *The Story Retold*, by Beale and Gladd, serves as a helpful reversal to this trend.

and/or unchallenged superiority based on the evolving enhancement of the printed page.

Often lost in what Ong called the "Great Divide" was the recognition of any limitations or biases the European Enlightenment (the Age of Reason) and the fixed-print legacy of Gutenberg may have had on Bible interpretation and transmission. Many exegetes have long missed the diagnosis of how the cultural biases that surround their propositional logic have privileged a specific hermeneutic—TH.

If the insufficiencies of TH to provide a fuller understanding of the narrative sections of Scripture are to be addressed, they must first be identified. Contrasting the oral scaffolding that long preceded and underpinned it can aid in this cause (ch. 4). This should also include investigation of the oral residue that remained behind once literacy began its reign.

> *What if OH is already contextualized for honor-shame cultures around the globe?*
>
> *For posttext and postfact audiences?*
>
> *What if OH, like TH, is a preference rather than a limitation?*
>
> *What if OH is a more natural learning tool for audiences at home and abroad today (as TH driven by science was initially for moderns)?*
>
> *What if the interplay between OH and TH actually strengthens Bible interpretation?*

Answering these questions may require *new eyes and ears!*

In relation to eyes, *both* must be wide open for a more complete interpretation to result! Michael Novelli, the founder of Echo the Story, tells us why:

> We must begin to come to the Bible with both eyes open—with stereoscopic vision. This means moving beyond (but not leaving behind) the myopic lens of modernity that analyzes with a microscope and gets lost in the minutia. To create balance, our other eye—the eye that gives us a sense of Scripture's mystery and multivalence—may need to become dominant for a while. This eye gives us an imaginative lens to discover another dimension of the Bible and experience it as our own story.[21]

The analytic requires the imaginative and vice versa. A parallel is discernible here between how left-brain functions were dominant in

---

21. Novelli, *Shaped By the Story*, 91.

modernity, but right-brain functions come to the fore to fill the vacuum in postmodernity. Entering the lives of others with both eyes open provides greater opportunity for a more comprehensive interpretation, and therefore godly choices that bring honor to the liberating King.

Echoes of Naturalness

When do hermeneutics harm? Bible communicators from the West have a tendency to make the simple complex, punctuated with jarring jargon, e.g., "hypostatic union" or "penal substitutionary atonement." *Have we done that with TH in relation to narrative texts? Has our prevailing single focus of atomized analysis of words and diagrammed grammar of a text actually discouraged visualizing it as cinema of the mind, as was designed? Has TH obscured the truths of Scripture for many at home and abroad?* The authors have concluded that visually, image-driven generations at home and abroad do *not* naturally or normally gravitate to grammar analysis.

Again, *does God expect and demand all interpreters to be able to analyze grammar, to be able to grasp the meaning of his spoken-written word?* No! *Does he expect some to do so?* We hope so. Character clarification provides an initial natural hermeneutic to interpret the spoken-written word. Rather than harm, OH offers a necessary balm to hermeneutic healing.

Common to many in collectivist communities is a member's uncanny ability to naturally read people and relationships. This competence in such communities, unlike for many of us growing up in an individualistic society, is one learned intuitively from a very early age. Its vitalness to interpretation in OH should not be underestimated or overlooked.

OH finds its roots in spiritual and human relationality molded and modeled after the Holy Trinity (who exists in original and fundamental relationality) as it seeks to discover truths in narrative texts through natural social connections, conversations, and the actions of characters. Sometimes the most valuable things in life are those that take place naturally. OH, a long-buried treasure again being *unearthed and rediscovered* (ch. 5), is one of those valuable treasures.

TH harms character-driven narrative texts when it distances itself from the simple naturalness of relationships. Thankfully, God does not require everyone to learn the complexities of grammar (original languages or local) to grasp the meaning of the spoken-written Scripture. Truths are most easily and naturally discovered in narrative texts when portrayed as a movie played out in acts in time and place; where characters are visualized in the mind.

The saying, "The main things are the plain things; and the plain things are the main things" works here. Those main, plain things that we absorb into our lives are the embodiments and demonstrations of beliefs and behaviors of a cast of author-selected characters. Paraphrasing Hannah Arendt,[22] "OH reveals meaning without committing the error of defining it." And it does so brilliantly for those in the East and West, and North and South.

Echoes of Integration

The authors do not call for the *enthroning* of a new hermeneutic king—OH in any of its multiple variations. Nor does it call for the *annihilation* of a former hermeneutic—TH in its multiple versions. Neither do we wish just to add OH to TH. Rather, we attempted to make the case for *the return of OH* so the Great Divide becomes a well-traversed bridge spanning the strengths and weaknesses of both oral and textual hermeneutics; so each complements the other; so the mind is utilized to its fullest capacity cognitively, imaginatively, intuitively, conscientiously, emotionally, and spiritually. Like the Alter-Sternberg Character Explicitness Scale (see table 7.1), the authors call for a continuum between the most explicit and most covert.

Such a hermeneutic wedding unites imagination and reason, voices and monographs, events and facts, people and pages, dialogue and dictation, stories and slogans, demonstration and description, mystery and meticulousness. It fuses action to ideas, encounters to explanations, actions to attitudes, aggregates to parts, character to characters, participation to perception, performance to propositions, formation to information; it clothes naked theology.

Just as orality preceded literacy, so OH preceded TH. Just as the spoken and the written word were eventually perceived as a continuum, so must OH and TH. Why? Because TH keeps OH on target through fragments while OH keeps TH full of life without sacrificing the grand narrative.

Echoes of Change

In the beginning was TH; and then a suspicious stranger, a perceived competitor, abruptly arrived in the same community, stirring still waters. This unplanned engagement was the result of some dissatisfied, frustrated Western

---

22. "Storytelling reveals meaning without committing the error of defining it" (Arendt, *The Quotation Page*, www.quotationspage.com/quote/4861.html).

exegetes (the authors included) in search of a hermeneutic for the narrative sections of Scripture that could unearth a more relational theology.

Influenced by the modern-day orality movement,[23] the researchers eventually ascertained that "Before time itself was measured, the Voice was speaking" (John 1:1 VOICE). They had discovered the role of the speaking, living voice in the written text; they had discovered OH. Actually, they had rediscovered an old Hebrew hermeneutic (ch. 5). Far from introducing a suspicious competitor onto the hermeneutic community, they had proposed a crucial complementor. They had rediscovered that in the beginning was actually OH.

The authors hope they did more than just provoke the reader by proposing another Bible hermeneutic. They hope you were at least made curious, if not convinced. The authors hope they advanced a coherent, cogent, and compelling case for OH through scholars and personal case demonstrations from rural and urban settings, thereby offering the reader a cup of confidence. They hope the two Elisha Bible stories (chs. 1 and 9) along with theoretical foundations helped draw the reader onto the OH stage along with a growing number of other interactive participant-performers.

The authors hope they have been disruptive in a positive manner by proposing what *only* the gift of OH can provide Bible exegetes. They hope, figuratively speaking, that those present-day Apollos' out there who teach Scripture boldly yet lack "full understanding" of the role of orality in the text and teaching will now be able to teach Scripture "more accurately and fully."[24]

Speaking of the two Bible stories the authors included to clothe naked theology by demonstrating how OH differs from TH, did you notice:

> The Bible story titles focused on characters?
>
> The use of a map to enhance visualization of geography?
>
> The storyteller served as a facilitator-teacher?
>
> The participants dialogued with each other, not just the leader?
>
> The backstory centered on characters?
>
> The storying experience was an unfolding experience rather than a scripted outline?
>
> The storyteller's questions focused strongly on characters, including the Chief Character?
>
> The free-flowing nature and the numerous questions asked?

---

23. See chs. 1–4 in Steffen, *Worldview-based Storying*.
24. Acts 18:26 VOICE.

Questions highlighted the audience's preferred values-morals, e.g., honor and shame?

The narrative logic that drove the questions?

How the questions engaged emotions, imagination, the whole brain-mind, to bring out values and morals?

How the questions focused on groups as well as individuals?

The overall great emphasis on who-related questions?

How characters telegraphed (rather than defined) values, morals, and theology?

The focus on relationships to demonstrate who God is, including his missional nature?

The possibility of multiple truths within one story?

The individual *and* communal role in discerning and protecting meaning?

How dialoguers corrected each other?

How the storyteller corrected error?

How the storyteller deconstructed the present worldview so a better one could replace it?

How the conversations and actions of characters clothed naked truth?

The call for a summarizing symbol and/or proverb?

How individuals or groups were asked to draw/sing/sculp/dramatize the story?

How individual stories added small, essential increments to build the grand narrative?

Can we who compose the assemblies, academies, and agencies move beyond a grammatical, text-preference hermeneutic? Can we stop turning the ancients into us—textual grammatists and diagrammers? Can our communication, interpretation, instruction, retention, and replication become more oral sensitive? Only when these questions receive affirmative answers will:

- oral-preference audiences have greater opportunity to advance beyond "cold, creedal, and cerebral Christianity;"[25]

---

25. Archer, "Pentecostal Way of Doing Theology," 311.

- a more comprehensive composite of the face of God be drawn more distinctively;
- the oral and written, sound and sight, emotions and facts, imagination and reason, participants and principles converge;
- naked doctrine be appropriately clothed;
- free-flowing questions take precedent over prescribed question sets;
- the learning styles and communication preferences of all peoples of the world be addressed;
- spiritual formation be able to reach greater heights.

Those who grasp the potential of using *both* OH and TH to interpret the spoken-written sacred storybook will do much to enhance understanding, spiritual meditation and maturation, individual and collective musings and memory, kingdom expansion, and most importantly, the glorification of the Chief Character. While OH educates the heart, TH educates the head. Both are required and needed, even if a necessary sequence remains (See the continuum summary in table 11.1).

For those in Western churches, seminaries, Bible colleges, and institutes to move beyond a single-focused textual hermeneutic, humble learning at the feet of the ancients and lots of listening to present-day oralists at home and abroad will be required. This is what it took for the authors to gain currency when working among the tribal Ifugao in the Philippines and modern/postmodern Jewish people in Pasadena (and greater Los Angeles).

OH is required presently in North America because today's world is not your daddy's world. Nor is it any longer the same world into which many readers were born. *How much more so for immigrants or posttext, postfacts audiences here or abroad? Can Bible exegetes look in the mirror to see the reflections of the preferences of oralists rather than reflections of our modern grammatical, textual-diagrammed selves? Can we learn to hear the questions of others rather than echoes of our own?* Lord, give us *new* eyes and ears!

Table 11.1. Oral Hermeneutic-Textual Hermeneutic Continuum

Bible is a case book	—	Bible is a code book
Bible discussions	—	Bible studies
Narrative logic	—	Propositional logic
Meaning is central	—	Words are central
Whole	—	Fragments
Heart hermeneutic	—	Head hermeneutic
Experiential apologetics	—	Evidential apologetics
Character thinking	—	Critical thinking
Character-centric questions	—	Content-centric questions
Character analysis	—	Textual analysis
Character-historical	—	Grammatical-historical
Character-centric meaning	—	Text-centric meaning
Demonstrations	—	Definitions
Relational	—	Rational
Character theology	—	Categorical theology
Relational theology	—	Abstract theology
Big character	—	Big idea
Multiple truths	—	One main point
Proof chants	—	Proof texts

The world is much more oral than most recognize, and the same is true of the voiced word, including the Epistles.[26] This means the spoken word leans heavily on the concrete. Winger wisely writes, "'Orality' . . . is a characteristic of the Scriptures both in their origin and in their function which simply must be accounted for in the exegetical enterprise."[27]

---

26. "Societies with writing often have an intricate interplay of orality and textuality, where written texts are intensely oral, while even exclusively oral texts are deeply affected by written culture" (Carr, *Writing on the Tablet of the Heart*, 7).

27. Winger, "Orality as the Key," 315.

Echoes of the Future

Given that most Global North[28] Bible communicators of the past who went to the Global South[29] did not pack OH to take with them, and since it still remains mostly a suspicious, unopened package in the Global North today, this time-tested, Hebrew-based hermeneutic offers an attractive global alternative (ch. 5). OH advances a meaningful construct for a global audience who will appreciate it as they discover from the spoken-written sacred storybook the demonstrated rather than the defined, a relational Hero rather than an abstract Idea. *Could OH be the mother of relational theology?*

Could the incorporation of OH that has such strong ties to relationships between characters be a weighty way to connect with those oralists who orbit in a posttext, postfacts world? Will the use of their preferred learning style—the intuitive-imaginative-emotive within a communal process that reads audiences and characters—result in relational-based theology that demonstrates rather than defines biblically based beliefs and behaviors? Could OH strengthen Bible interpretation and communication for today's pastors? Small group leaders? Evangelists? Disciplers? Church planters? Bible translators?[30] Short-termers? Long-termers? Bible teachers? Theologians? Western Bible curricula developers exporting materials to non-Western audiences around the globe? Prison workers? Therapists? ESL[31]/TESOL teachers? Community developers? Medical and business personnel? Refugee and immigrant workers? Sex and slave trafficking workers?

How might Bible communicators influence the present generation in Bible interpretation, preaching, and teaching in ways that would help guarantee its failure? Leighton Ford's concern is apropos: "My greatest fear for you is not that you will fail but that you will succeed in doing the wrong thing."[32] *How might Bible communicators influence the present generation in Bible interpretation, preaching, and teaching in ways that would help guarantee its success in doing the right things?*

Does OH offer the potential to unleash Scripture to the majority of God's people and future Jesus-followers around the world? While TH hopefully will continue to succeed in what it is scientifically designed to do, the authors

---

28. Includes North America, Europe, Australasia, and developed areas of East Asia.

29. Includes Asia, much of the Middle East, Africa, Latin America, and the Caribbean.

30. See Maxey and Wendland, *Translating Scripture for Sound and Performance*, where various authors persuasively argue that Bible translation is much more comprehensive than simply translating one language to another linguistically. An oral-aural framework is also required in the translation process so that the subjective human relational aspect interfaces with objective accuracy and clarity.

31. See languageolympics.com.

32. Ford, *Power of Story*, 79.

believe Bible communicators will fail to get people into the Bible and get the Bible into people to the greater extent we would all hope for if we fail to invite OH to the banquet table.

Wrapping Up

A metaphorical wagon wheel could summarize this book. The hub, which connects the entire wheel to the axle, constitutes symbolically the breadth and depth of orality that drives OH. The axle that turns the entire wheel (often unseen and assumed) symbolizes narrative logic that guides and galvanizes OH. The multiple spokes that connect the hub to the rim represent the controlling characters within said story, including the Chief Character. Guided by text discussion-driven, character-centric questions, character-theologizing begins, eventually emerging into character theology. The truths discerned are then displayed on the outer rim where abstract values, morals, and theology are constantly in touch with terra firma in life's journey (or where the rubber [steel] meets the road).[33]

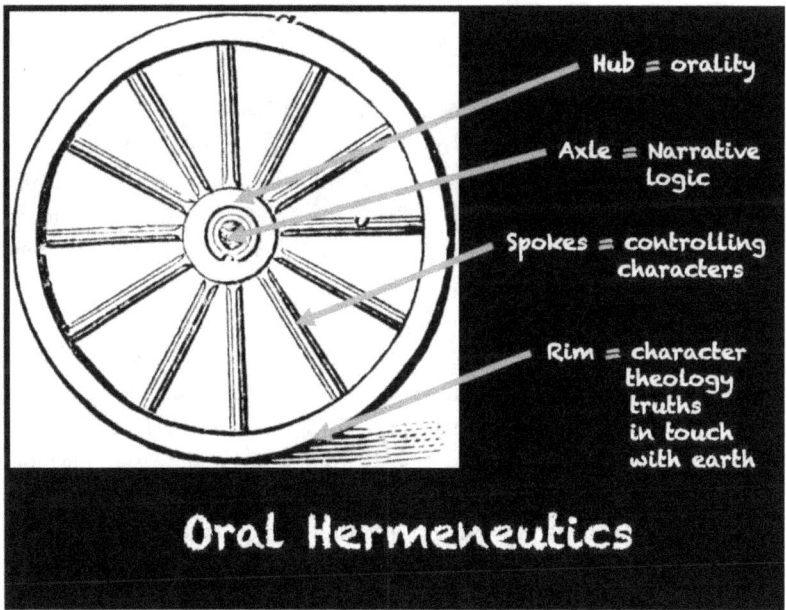

Figure 11.1. Oral Hermeneutics Summarized in a Wagon Wheel

"The very voice" (*ipsissima vox*), the captured truths of Jesus' teaching heard by eyewitnesses, rather than "the very words" (*ipsissima verba*), was, and should remain, central to interpreting and communicating God's

33. See Figure 11.1. Attribution goes to cliparts.co/ for the use of this clipart.

written voice. OH begins this "aesthetic experience"[34] by focusing on the truths characters portray in the text rather than their precise words.

How an exegete or teacher seeks meaning governs to a great extent what is discovered. One's hermeneutic approaches influence one's understanding of Scripture, which influences storying-teaching methods, which influences how recipients will understand the text, which influences the resulting depth of godly wisdom and worship. The resulting wisdom and worship, however, will not be what it most likely could be—godly, genuine, germane to life—if it fails to take seriously a foundational component of the text in construction, diffusion, reception, and retention—orality.

It had never dawned on me (Tom) how literacy biased I was while living among the Ifugao. The translation of parts of the New Testament was growing annually through the capable efforts of SIL Bible translators Dick and Lou Hohulin. Afterall, *how could the Ifugao Jesus followers mature in their new-found Christian faith without written Scripture?* Literacy classes followed. A songbook was composed as well as Bible commentaries with an Ifugao team. They loved the songs, learning much theology through them (and some bad theology). Seminars carried a strong literacy component; the blackboard playing a huge role in outlining the topics under discussion. The expatriate and Ifugao team would produce a variety of written documents, including the entire Bible.

I never gave special thought or attention to the public reading of Scripture—to putting the page on the stage (1 Tim 4:13).[35] *Isn't that what Bible teachers do to get to the most important thing in a service—teaching Bible truths? Hermeneutics?* My Dallas days of the grammatical-historical learning came through strong even if only a few could follow it. I assumed the written was helpful to the spoken; I did *not* assume the spoken was helpful to the written.

While I would never forfeit the written materials left behind, nor my Dallas days, I do regret not giving the oral-aural side of the equation equal status or attention. I do regret not recognizing that Saul's armor doesn't fit everyone. Kelber was correct when he identified "the tendency among biblical scholars to think predominantly, or even exclusively, in literary, linear, and visual terms."[36] He was also correct when he implored, "If [only] we can wean ourselves from the notion that texts constitute the center of gravity in tradition."[37] Hopefully, my story can serve as a cautionary tale to those serv-

---

34. Prior, *On Reading Well*, 21.
35. See Arthurs, *Devote Yourself*.
36. Kelber, "Jesus and Tradition," 2. See also Botha, "Mute Manuscripts."
37. Kelber, "Jesus and Tradition," 163.

ing among people like the Ifugao or any oral-preference audiences around the globe, whether in rural or urban settings: *Do not neglect the riches* of the oral-aural in ministry!

> *Is it time to investigate this underexplored, undervalued, natural hermeneutic?*
>
> *Is it time to make OH generational again (ch. 5)?*
>
> *Is it time to return OH to its rightful, rich, and resourceful role in interpreting, preaching, and teaching the spoken-written word?*
>
> *Is it time to introduce or increase the role of OH in homiletics courses in our seminaries?*
>
> *Is it time to adopt and adapt OH for each specific context, thereby celebrating worldview complexity in the search for Divine truth?*
>
> *Is it time to unearth and repurpose this long-buried hermeneutic treasure and share its valuable contents broadly, at home and around the globe?*
>
> *Is a perceived conflict actually a contribution?*
>
> *Will a bottom-up movement seat OH at the hermeneutical table?*

Recall from the introduction, Setting the Stage, pastor Dinanath's story of discouragement and confusion because his theological training made it unnecessarily difficult for those in his village to understand the gospel. Thankfully the Indian pastor's story took a positive turn:

> In 1999 I attended a seminar where I learnt how to communicate the gospel using different oral methods. I understood the problem in my communication as I was mostly using a lecture method with printed books, which I learnt in the Bible school. After the seminar I went to the village but this time I changed my way of communication. I started using a storytelling method in my native language. I used gospel songs and the traditional music of my people. This time the people in the villages began to understand the gospel in a better way . . . There was one church with few baptized members in 1999 when I attended the seminar. But now in 2004, in six years we have 75 churches with 1350 baptized members and 100 more people are ready for baptism.[38]

Recall also from the Setting the Stage the expatriate president of a seminary in Thailand who was frustrated because the Asian students were

---

38. Lausanne Occasional Paper, *Making Disciples of Oral Learners*, 2–3.

just not getting it. A couple of years later, I (Tom) had dinner with him and a few of the faculty. Like for pastor Dinanath, things had changed dramatically once the narrative component was added. I listened with enthusiasm as the Epistle to the Romans professor told how he added narrative to his teaching approach and the student response—they get it! They have since added a strong focus on face and honor-shame—value-morals which are vital to Thai culture *and* grasping Scripture.

Like Ella, contemptuously called Cinderella, has OH been neglected, undervalued, and excluded from the Hermeneutic Palace? Can a female scullery maid and cinder cleaner (in the minds of her stepmother and stepsisters) become a sought-out, beautiful princess at the Hermeneutic Palace Ball? Will Prince Charming ever be able to find someone who perfectly fits the lost glass slipper, marry her, and live happily ever after in the Hermeneutic Palace? The authors hope so.

Only when OH assumes its rightful robust role will exegetes and Bible teachers have a stronger chance to learn to read with both eyes *and* ears; only then will they have a stronger chance to not only learn the landscape of the text, but also its soundscape; only then will they have a stronger chance to experience sound interpretation of Bible stories, symbols, and rituals as they speak to recipients. Only then through interconnectedness will listeners have a stronger chance to identify with biblical characters as they describe and train through telegraphed theology, values, and morals. Only then will purification of past practices have a stronger chance to happen as interpreters discover their individual and collective place and role in God's grand narrative. Only then will what Dorothy Sayers labeled "dull dogma" be given a strong chance to become "dynamic drama" that produces godly wisdom; only then will the face of God have a stronger chance to be drawn with added specificity, making it possible for the Hero of the story to receive fuller honor.

Hear any echoes? Whether the ancients before the sacred biblical text existed or the growing numbers of posttext, postfacts people of the world's population today, each of these communities represent the need for and give legitimacy and integrity to visually based, image-based, sensory-based, relationally based OH. Today's Bible communicators can ill afford to ignore the oral tradition of the past or its modern-day counterparts any more than scholars could when the Enlightenment's exaltation of reason appeared on the horizon. OH is the most natural cultural currency for today's oralists around the globe, which comprises around 80 percent of the world.[39] What

---

39. Lausanne Movement, "Orality."

does OH add that TH misses? Let the discussions begin between those in the academies, agencies and assemblies.

For most, our hermeneutic is something that seldom receives conscious self-reflection theoretically or methodologically. It is time for *in-depth reflection and discussion* on hermeneutics between professors, pastors, and practitioners; it is time to evaluate the *strengths and weaknesses* of the OH and TH models presently in use. It is time to wade into the warming waters and *challenge our certainties.* It is time to question some of our *standard answers.* It is time for the *oral-preference recipients* of Bible storying to teach *the textual-oriented teachers.* It is time to reimagine the *scope and sequence* of hermeneutics. It is time to *welcome* the unfamiliar, the unacknowledged, the undervalued, the unexplored, the excluded, the feared. It is time to make lost paths *well-worn pathways again.* It is time to make the *ancient modern again.* It is time to awake a *sleeping partner* to enrich TH. It is time to recover, reinstate, and revitalize a *long-lost friend.* It is time to add the *heart hermeneutic* to the *head hermeneutic.* It is time *for the return of oral hermeneutics!*

Glossary

Character Theology: To avoid reducing the narrative sections of Scripture to less than all their worth, and minimizing life-applications, character theology calls for a theologizing process that concentrates on how characters (human, spiritual, individuals, groups) challenge us positively or negatively. Author-selected characters demonstrate attitudes and actions through their context, circumstances, challenges, conversations, choices, consequences of those choices, inconsistencies, changes, chances taken, challenging how we lean into life. Their contributions also help unfurl the Bible's master story or grand narrative that guides and guards all the individual stories.

Character theology analyzes audiences, i.e., it investigates (intuitively and formally) the conversations and actions of the character(s) in the story. From their concrete actions and interactions, abstract concepts, doctrines, values, ethics, morals, and worldview emerge, offering the hearer choices to make. At the same time they reveal imaged characteristics of the Chief Character of the Bible. Character theology centers on characterization and choices.

Controlling Characters: Human or spiritual entities, real or fictional, individuals or groups, protagonists (Job) or antagonists (his friends), who drive and determine a story's direction (plotline) as they review and reveal the "manysidedness of real life."[1] "Literary characters have a lot to teach us about *character*"[2] and the Chief Character.

Metanarrative/Grand/Master Narrative: Anthropologically, a metanarrative succinctly summarizes a specific people group or culture's anchor and master stories, thereby informally validating how life should be lived, and often drives the momentum of a society, creating its worldview. By so doing,

---

1. Ryken and Longman, *Complete Literary Guide to the Bible*, 22.
2. Prior, *On Reading Well*, 18 (emphasis original).

it tacitly creates strongly held beliefs and behaviors that determine distinctiveness and offer continuity over time. These internals often cause sharp divisions between those within the culture (insiders) and those without (outsiders), as well as between subcultures within a society. From a literary biblical perspective, the metanarrative connects the smaller individual stories into a coherent, larger arc. It is like the string connecting pearls into a lovely pearl necklace. And it takes its time doing so, building suspense along the arduous journey, like a flowing river, never seemingly in a hurry to reach the climax being built. A metanarrative is the story that shapes all other stories, and all other stories shape the metanarrative. Some prefer the term "grand narrative" or "arch-narrative" or "master story." And of course, the Bible has a master story and is *the* Master Story.

Narrative: A succinct summary of a series of events/stories; the "sequential and retrospective representation of experience."[3]

Oral Hermeneutics: An experiential interpretation method to understand more fully the narrative genre in Scripture. It accomplishes this by focusing on the conversations, actions, and interactions of characters found in a biblical text. This ancient-modern art ponders passages of Scripture characterologically, considers the era, event(s), setting and surroundings, plot, attire, gestures, posture, direct and inward speech, symbols, rituals, conduct, conflicts, choices, and consequences of choices, among other things, as characters embody and demonstrate (rather than define and explain) meaning. To discover author-intended meaning it conducts character analysis through primarily character-centric questions. Multiple versions are presently in use. The word "oral" tips readers off that its operational mode uses oral skills and is relational, i.e., reading out loud, vocal telling that is always accompanied by body language, group discussion, and the sharing insights. The dynamic of relational chemistry always produces a surplus of meaning. The mutual honing of observations and applications as group members discuss, complement and correct each other facilitates relevance, accuracy, and application to life. This is in contrast to a hermeneutic that can be done alone by an individual sitting in a library, or a study carrel with a stack of books.

Oral Interpretation: The "art and science of communicating faith literature to an audience in its intellectual (content), faith (spiritual), pathetic (emotional) and aesthetic (artistically attractive) entirety through the medium of the human voice in a manner that impacts people."[4] The authors would add that this

---

3. Landa, "Narrating Narrating," 422.
4. Berger, *Oral Interpretation of the Bible*, 11.

often involves more than one voice. Rather than from a monologue, meaning often emerges through group interaction and participation.

Orality: A preferred way to hear, process, remember, and communicate with the human voice as the primary medium. This multi-sensory mode of communication weds the ear (sound) and eye (symbols). Orality includes multiple media, such as storytelling, poetry, music, visual art, drama and dance. Often orations are transcribed into print, but the form is still recognizably oral. For an example, the book of Deuteronomy is called *Devarim* (literally, "Words") in Hebrew; this is a fitting title in that Deuteronomy is "the most sustained deployment of rhetoric in the Bible."[5] It is a transcription of oral speeches and sermons (mostly by Moses), such that they are best understood when they are oralized, i.e., brought back to living speech.

Plot: Levels of conflict, chaos, or confusion created between and/or within characters through an often calculated and causal scripted sequence of events and episodes creating anticipation for, and in search of, a determined resolution that demands the hearers/readers/viewers make a judgment of some type (e.g., moral, ethical, religious).

Primary Orality: A descriptor that refers to those who cannot read or have very limited reading abilities; they therefore self-identify[6] as relational (connected) learners through integrative, holistic (e.g., use of body movements, power, the five senses, space, time) verbal, and visual means of communication.

Ritual: Refers to collective or individual memories of a series of sacred and/or secular wordings, meaningful events, and actions reenacted routinely in a familiar way to rehearse, recall, reinvigorate events considered important to preserve over time. It may be initiated by an unforeseen event or follow a prescribed annual calendar. Rituals are performative acts designed to enhance long-term memory, e.g., the annual feast cycle of Israel.

Ritual Hermeneutics: Those who learn experientially through oral means or media require an experiential hermeneutic that results in an experiential theology. As part of oral hermeneutics, ritual hermeneutics spotlight the interpretation of rituals that represent individual and societal (including the community of faith) worldviews. A ritual is a memorable metaphor often based on symbols that tell stories. Rituals reinforce, reframe, reclaim, revise, or resist past or present reality. Such parades of abstractness are susceptible

5. Alter, *Hebrew Bible,* 609.
6. See Thigpen, "Connected Learning," 194.

to multiple interpretations and therefore require constant reiteration of their meaning from a biblical perspective. Visual ritual theology requires a hermeneutic that addresses the particular distinctives of the elements used in the ritual and their intended meaning.

Secondary Orality: A descriptor that refers to those who can read yet prefer and practice a more visual-oral-digital-social means of integrative, holistic (e.g., use of body movements, social power, the five senses, space, time) communication such as YouTube, Facebook, or smartphones.

Story: An account given of a sequence of events of experiences that takes place in some setting(s) and time(s) in which competing characters (human or spiritual, real or fictitious, individual or group) advance toward a mysterious resolution that solves a conflict-driven plot(s). Stories include characters who make choices resulting in consequences, creating plot in a setting and time that advances toward a resolution that reveals values, morals, and theology.

Symbol: May consist of letters, words, numbers, places, people, colors, clothes, trees, animals, water, food/a meal (bread and wine), feathers, smoke, smells, sounds, gestures, movements, and the like that represent other realities; they convey more than conventional meaning. Symbols may be memorable metaphors that tell stories that (de/re)construct worldviews.[7] They "serve as a kind of external scaffolding for interior experience;"[8] they serve as shorthand for complex lives and events. Like stories, symbols embody a surplus of meaning.

Symbol Hermeneutics: As part of oral hermeneutics, symbolic hermeneutics spotlights the interpretation of symbols that represent individual and societal (including the community of faith) worldviews. A symbol is a memorable metaphor that tells a story and is rehearsed in ritual, if significant. Such objects of abstractness are susceptible to multiple interpretations and therefore require constant Scripture-soaked interpretation. Visual symbolic theology requires a hermeneutic that addresses symbol distinctives.

Textual Hermeneutics: An intellectually based analytical hermeneutic model (in contrast to a more holistic, relational, communally based oral hermeneutic) to identify a purportedly objective, original, granular, singular, author-intended meaning of a specific text. The conventional academic tools for this task are nearly all cognitive—linguistic analysis (word studies

---

7. See Steffen, *Worldview-based Storying*, ch. 5.
8. Morgan, *Sacred Gaze*, 50.

in the original languages, semantic theory, lexical and syntactical analysis using grammars, concordances, lexicons, dictionaries, and encyclopedias), archaeological studies, and historical and literary context studies.

In the modern Western historical-critical or higher critical schools of thought, there were various methods used such as source criticism and redaction criticism. In modernity, these tools and methods are generally deemed necessary to extract the true meaning of a text. It is characterized by a *deductive* method (rather than inductive); it uses logical analysis (Aristotelian, not narrative logic) to deduce propositions. For example, look at the approach in any standard modern critical commentary series (there are several). The well-known historical-grammatical method is a modest and popular expression of textual hermeneutics. Multiple versions are in use.

Worldview: Cultural worldview is one's filtered perceptions/assumptions of reality through which all of life is interpreted. This privileged perspective by a given society emerges through collective socialization of certain cultural concepts situated in and/or expressed by a symbol/story/ritual framework. From these a community establishes prioritized principles and practices to constantly and consistently evaluate themselves and others as they lean into life.

Worldview Transformation: Transforming one's worldview requires deconstruction so that formerly held symbols, stories, and rituals can be replaced in part or whole with rival ones. This resymboling, restorying, and reritualing results in much more than changed observable behavior, it also includes deep-level alteration of heart values, motivations, and allegiances. Such a life shift results in a new life script. Such transformation generally includes a change in beliefs, behavior, and belonging; it has life-altering and identity-forming/reforming implications.

Appendix A

Three Communication Eras

Orality Era	Textuality Era	Digitorality Era
Invention of the alphabet and writing (circa. 2000 BC)	Invention of movable type printing (Gutenberg, 1437)	Invention of personal computers and the Internet (1980s)
Pre-literate	Print literacy	Digital literacy
Ancient	Modern	Post- or Late-Modern
Events, Stories	Words, Ideas	Images, Stories, Ideas
Oral communication by all, storytellers, oral tradition.	Books, newspapers, libraries, printed matter.	Television, personal computers, plethora of electronic devices, etc.
Right-Brain Dominant	Left-Brain Dominant	Left and Right Brain Needed
Oral Galaxy	Gutenberg Galaxy	Digitoral Galaxy

Appendix B

The Continuum between Reading and Listening

Reading	Listening
Eyes	Ears
Read marks on a page	Attend to the sound of a voice
A lone person with a book, written by someone miles away, or dead, or both	An interpersonal, relational act
The book is at the reader's mercy. The book does not know if I am paying attention or not	Listener is required to be attentive to the speaker, at speaker's mercy. The speaker knows if I am paying attention or not
The reader initiates the process; the reader is in charge	The speaker initiates the process; the speaker is in charge
Images in life: The stereotype of the husband buried in the morning newspaper at breakfast, preferring to read scores of yesterday's sports events, and opinions of columnists he will never meet, than to listen to the voice of the person who has just shared his bed, poured his coffee, and fried his eggs, even though listening to that live voice promises love and hope, emotional depth and intellectual exploration far more than what he can gather informationally from the *New York Times*.	Images in life: All Israel assembled at the foot of Mt. Sinai as Moses addresses them.... A first-century Pauline congregation gathered to hear the oral reading of a letter from the apostle Paul... A soldier standing at attention, listening to the commands of his drill sergeant.... Boy Scouts around a campfire listening in rapt attention to a storyteller tell a ghost story... A family Passover Seder dinner, in which the father animatedly tells, once again, the great story of our freedom, the children ask questions, the symbolic foods are eaten, and the songs are sung.

(Adapted from Peterson, *Working the Angles*, 88–89)

Appendix C
Alter's Oral-Textual Parameters

THE RETELLING OF A Bible story was *not* without external oral parameters or internal literary signals to protect it over time. But recognizing such oral parameters is often difficult for those who grew up in the print world. Robert Alter, Berkeley professor of Hebrew and Comparative Literature, who is Jewish, calls for some changes, "As modern readers of the Bible, we need to relearn something of this mode of perception that was second nature to the original audience."[1]

What required relearning is necessary for today's Bible interpreters? Alter becomes more specific, calling for new lenses for sharper focus on what the readers anticipated and the authors provided. These would include, "pronounced patterns at certain narrative junctures . . . words, motifs, themes, personages, and actions" all of which formed "an elaborate dance of significant innovation."[2]

The authors will now elaborate on four foundational oral components that have implications to protect biblical meaning.

First, Alter identified *single words and brief phrases* because they "carry forward narrative motifs."[3] Words could be not only those included, but also those excluded. Brief phrases, e.g., relational descriptions, especially when repeated by the speakers (interlocutors), help develop narrative motifs as well. In the Widow and Elisha story, the word "widow" and phrase "sons of the prophets" immediately set the stage for the necessity of a miracle to keep creditors from making slaves out of her two sons.

Second, a further necessity is identifying the role of *action*. Alter looks for recurrence, e.g., "large themes over a series of occurrences" and repeated events "with different characters,"[4] for parallels, for analogies,

1. Alter, *Art of Biblical Narrative*, 62.
2. Alter, *Art of Biblical Narrative*, 62.
3. Alter, *Art of Biblical Narrative*, 180.
4. Alter, *Art of Biblical Narrative*, 180.

i.e., "where one part of the story provides a commentary on or a foil to another."[5] The cycle of sin and deliverance in Judges comes to mind. Here we see Israel's persistence to forget her Lord but his faithfulness to discipline and deliver her. Such become the "hallmarks of reported action in the biblical tale."[6] Contrasting actions, words and phrases, and scenes also assist in theme development.

Third, Alter focuses on *dialogue* because "Everything in the world of biblical narrative ultimately gravitates towards dialogue."[7] In the Widow and Elijah story, the conversation went from "I have nothing at all!" to "Bring me another jar" to "There aren't any more!" And the oil stopped flowing.

When Bible authors consider something essential to communicate, they often move to extended dialogue between characters where they reveal themselves, often through contrasts (preferred by Hebrew writers). For example, Job's extended conversations with his three friends reveal strong differences about each, including their view of God. "Extended dialogue should signal the need for special attentiveness."[8]

Some questions to ask as to how the dialogue emerged and developed could include:

> Is this the first reported speech for either or both of the two interlocutors? If so, why did the writer choose this particular narrative juncture to make the character reveal himself through speech? How does the kind of speech assigned to the character—its syntax, tone, imagery, brevity or lengthiness—serve to delineate the character and his relation to the other party to the dialogue?[9]

Biblical authors often used the exchange of contrasting conversations to convey their message explicitly or through subtle hints oral learners would intuitively identify.

To *words, actions,* and *dialogue,* Alter concludes with *narration.* He notes readers must trust that the biblical authors are conveying God's message through the words, dialogue, and actions of selective characters, and they can discern their intended meaning *without* the author stepping out of the story to explain it to them. One does not have to wonder how Peter felt when Paul "got in his face and exposed him *in front of everyone*" (Gal 2:11 VOICE). Characters highlighted by biblical authors take listeners/readers/viewers into *their own* world and have to explain nothing.

5. Alter, *Art of Biblical Narrative*, 180.
6. Alter, *Art of Biblical Narrative*, 180.
7. Alter, *Art of Biblical Narrative*, 182.
8. Alter, *Art of Biblical Narrative*, 182.
9. Alter, *Art of Biblical Narrative*, 182–83.

To help discern what is happening, Alter asks, "When do characters ostensibly answer one another without truly responding to what the other person has said? When does the dialogue break off sharply, withholding from us the rejoinder we might have anticipated from one of the two speakers?"[10] What did Barnabas really want to say to Paul about taking John Mark with him (Luke 17:36-40)? What did Paul want to say to Barnabas? We are left in the dark at this point.

By answering Alter's questions we begin to see their humanness, *and our own*. All four of Alter's foundational oral components argue for what we are calling "character theologizing" that leads to "character theology."

---

10. Alter, *Art of Biblical Narrative*, 227.

Appendix D

The Quintessential Characters, Stories, and Texts of the Old Testament

Jennifer Jagerson (used with permission)

The Quintessential Characters:

- These are the central protagonists of the narratives in each respective book of the Bible that played critical roles for understanding how the metanarrative of Scripture moves along.
- It may be assumed that at every point along all narratives of Scripture, God is the most important character, even when silent. This is such a pervasive reality that it was deemed unnecessary to identify him as a Quintessential Character in each story.
- While there are always many other characters in a given narrative, their relationship to the story gathers around the goals and purposes of the primary protagonist, either as antagonists, allies, and/or foils.
  - By putting a razor focus on the protagonist(s), we properly understand the roles of all the other characters.
  - We can begin to identify the meaning of the story according to how the consequences of their choices develop along the plotline and how the problem of the story resolves.
  - The consequences of the choices of each character and what happened to them provides the audience with a description to help them process the *kinds* of things that happen in real life and the *kinds* of dynamics and choices that contribute to them. In Scripture, this always relates to the degree to which humans are living in right relationship with God, which includes their ethical choices and how they relate to other humans. Stories do not usually explicitly explain right relationship with God through propositional

statements, but by revealing it through the interactions of the characters and the outcomes of their choices.

List 1: The Quintessential Stories:

- These stories provide the barebones continuity of God's purposes across the metanarrative, creating connecting points that show God's major movements in His salvation plan for Israel and the world.
- These stories also demonstrate the author's main purpose for writing each book. If this is understood, then all of the other stories in the book that can be interpreted through the paradigm/purpose illustrated by the quintessential story.
  - For example, in Genesis 12, God initiates His covenant with Abraham. All the stories in the rest of Genesis (and indeed, the Old Testament) flow from an understanding of that covenant promise.
  - The drama of Judah and Tamar, of Joseph's slavery and rise in Egypt, and the final blessings of Jacob are interpreted properly only when understood in light of God's covenant with Abraham.
- Most books will require only one such story, however, some will require two or three. For example, Genesis establishes a number of important foundational theological concepts that are critical to understanding the rest of Scripture such as: creation, humanity made in God's image (and as husband and wife), and the fall.

List 2: Secondary Stories:

- While there are quintessential stories that highlight the driving point of each book, there are many important developments in the storyline of Scripture that are not contained in those essential stories.
  - Stories that contribute significantly to the ongoing plot itself or
  - Stories that teach theological concepts that are major contributions of the biblical book to the metanarrative.
    - o For example, Exodus 19:4–6 provides the hermeneutical key to the entire book, and perhaps the entire Torah.
    - o However, another major theme of Exodus (and indeed, the rest of the Old Testament) will become the rebellion of Israel in spite

of God's gracious covenantal promises. The initial archetypal story for this ongoing and ultimately devastating tendency of God's people comes in Exodus 32 with the story of the Golden Calf. Even as the Lord was articulating the stipulations of the covenant to Moses on Mount Sinai, the people were violating it with Aaron in the lead. The stories that collect around this stage of history contribute to an important understanding of a major theme of Scripture that will help rightly interpret God's responses for much of the rest of the Old Testament.

- At other times, a story will produce an archetype that takes on typological value that resonates through the rest of Scripture such as the bronze snake or the lion of Judah. These might also be considered important for an oral learner's ability to interpret much of Scripture.

- Sometimes there are concepts for which one story won't do. There are times when there is a collection of stories that developed in a way that they are meant to be taken together. The subtraction of any one of the stories will significantly diminish a proper understanding of the whole. By providing those stories on the graph, practitioners can consider how to honor what they collectively illustrate. Two potential ways this can be done are:
  o Taking time to go through the whole group of stories
  o Providing an introduction to one of the stories that explains the import of the other stories to the meaning of the one being addressed.

List 3: Quintessential Texts Outside the Narrative Genre

- There are important distinctions between the different genres of Scripture and how the author conveyed meaning through them. It is important to teach the literary conventions of narrative for the reading of stories, such as by focusing on the conversations and actions of the characters and the development of the plot. However, poetry and prophecy utilize a different set of literary conventions that should also be honored. Since there are a number of places where important theological concepts of particular books (even books that are primarily narrative) are conveyed in non-narrative form, a third list was developed to address this.

- For example, in the book of Job, the quintessential passage is the theophany. The passages of God's epic self-revelation are the key to the entire book and establish major theological principles about humanity's relationship to him but written poetically.
- Another example is the case of Jacob's blessings at the end of Genesis. These passages bring closure to the saga of the patriarchal family and set the stage for the rest of Israel's history, but it comes in the form of a sort of poetic blessing.

Old Testament Texts

Book Title	List 1 Quintessential Stories	List 2 Secondary Stories	List 3 Non-narrative Quintessential or Secondary Passages
Genesis Quintessential Character(s): Adam and Eve Abraham and Sarah	*Gen 1* Creation *Gen 2* Man made in God's image/marriage/stewardship *Gen 3:1–16* The Fall *Gen 12:1–8* The Abrahamic Covenant	*Gen 4* Cain and Abel–the escalation of sin *Gen 6:1–22; 8:1–22* Noah *Gen 11* Babel *Abraham's Story of Faith* *Gen 15:1–21* covenant; *14* Melchizedek; *16:1–15* Sarai and Hagar; *17* covenant and circumcision; *19:1–26* Sodom and Gomorrah; *Gen 22:1–18* The sacrifice of Isaac	*Gen 48:8–22; 49:22–26* The blessings of Joseph *Gen 49:8–12* The blessings of Judah
Exodus Quintessential Character(s): Moses	*Exod 19:1–7* Israel as God's Treasured Possession	*Exod 3:1–9* The Call of Moses *Exod 32:1–20* The Golden Calf	*Exod 20:1–12* The Ten Commandments/summary of the Law *Exod 25:10–22* The Ark of the Covenant

Old Testament Texts

Leviticus Quintessential Character(s): Moses	*Lev 16:1–17* The Day of Atonement	*Lev 10:1–10* Distinguishing between the holy and the profane—the importance of purity *Lev 26:1–26* Covenant blessings and curses for the nation of Israel	
Numbers Quintessential Character(s): Moses	*Num 14:1–25* The Israelites refuse to enter the land	*Num 9:15–23* Setting up the Tabernacle: The cloud of God leads them out *Num 20:1–13* Moses and the rock: No entering the land *Num 21:1–9* The Brass Serpent	
Deuteronomy Quintessential Character(s): Moses and Joshua	*Deut 1:1–8* Moses preaches the Law at Moab to prepare the 2nd generation to enter the land.	*Deut 34:1–12* The death of Moses and the assumption of Joshua	*Deut 4:32–40* Covenant renewal-the great God who intervened in history to call out a people—uniqueness of situation and calling—promises *Deut 6:1–18* The Shema *Deut 18:1–14* (blessings) and *18:15–37* (curses) for keeping or breaking covenant promises
Joshua Quintessential Character(s): Joshua	*Josh 1:1–9* Be strong and courageous in taking the land	*Josh 3:1–17* The Ark and Crossing the Jordan *Josh 6:1–21* Jericho *Josh 7:1–16* Ai	*Josh 24:1–28* Speech: once established in the land-review of national history and renewal of the covenant: "Choose this day whom you will serve" in the Land of Promise.

Old Testament Texts

Judges Quintessential Character(s): Multiple possibilities, (Ehud and Deborah)	*Judg 2:6–23* Summary of the whole book	*Judg 3:12–30* Ehud (demonstrates all the stages of the cycle of sin in Judges: sin, judgment, crying out, deliverance) *Judg 4:1 23* Deborah	*Judg 21:25* There is no king in Israel, and so everyone did what was right in their own eyes.
Ruth Quintessential Character(s): Ruth	*Ruth 4:1–22* Boaz and Ruth get married	*Ruth 1:1–22* Ruth's loyalty *Ruth 3:1–13* Ruth appeals to her kinsman-redeemer	*Ruth 4:16–22* The line of David
1 Samuel Quintessential Character(s): Samuel, David	*1 Sam 16:1–11* The Anointing of David	*1 Sam 1:1–18; 19–28* Hannah and Samuel's dedication *1 Sam 15:1–9* Saul rebels; vv. 10–23 Samuel rebukes Saul—Saul loses kingship *1 Sam 16:1–13* Samuel anoints David *1 Sam 17:20–30; 41–58* David and Goliath	
2 Samuel Quintessential Character(s): David	*2 Sam 7:1–17* God's Covenant with David	*2 Sam 6:12–23* The Ark is brought to Jerusalem *2 Sam 9:1–13* King David's greatness—Mephibosheth and *hesed* covenant love[1] *2 Sam 11:1–22* Uriah	*2 Sam 22:1–20* (Ps 18:1–19) Psalm of Deliverance *Ps 51* David's Repentance

---

1. *Hesed* is the Hebrew term for God's overwhelming, lavish, unending, gracious love, as demonstrated by King David's kindness towards Saul's family once he arrived on the throne. David's first act was to search out Saul's one remaining descendent—Jonathon's son Mephibosheth—restore Saul's land to him, and elevate him to be as a member of the royal family. David was honoring the covenant he made with Jonathon to protect his family, which exemplified God's covenantal love for Israel.

APPENDIX D: THE QUINTESSENTIAL OLD TESTAMENT

Old Testament Texts

1 Kings Quintessential Character(s): Solomon	*1 Kgs 8:1–11* The Ark is brought into the Temple and the glory of the Lord comes down.	*1 Kgs 3:1–14* The kingdom is consolidated and Solomon asks for wisdom *1 Kgs 12:1–20* The Kingdom divides *Sin of North Kingdom* *2 Kgs 12:25–33* Jeroboam institutes new worship in Shechem *2 Kgs 12:1–10* Prophet denounces Jeroboam—future King Josiah will purify *1 Kgs 18:20–39* Yahweh or Baal on Mount Carmel	*1 Kgs 11:1–14* The sin of Solomon leads to the division of the Kingdom and its ultimate demise (Speech of the Lord)
2 Kings Quintessential Character(s): Isaiah, Hezekiah	*2 Kgs 25:1–12* The Fall of Jerusalem and the destruction of the Temple	*2 Kgs 23:21–27* Josiah's godly reign, but God's impending judgment *2 Kgs 19:8–18* Hezekiah's prayer of covenant faithfulness	*2 Kgs 17:7–23* Why the Northern Kingdom fell (Summary)
1 Chronicles Quintessential Character(s): David	*1 Chr 11:1–9* David made king—Jerusalem made capital		*1 Chr 17:16–27* David prays in response to covenant: Temple plans are from the Lord.

Old Testament Texts

2 Chronicles Quintessential Character(s): Solomon	*2 Chr 5:1–14* Solomon done building, ark brought in, *Shekinah* glory on the Temple	*2 Chr 1:1–12* Solomon becomes king and asks for wisdom—God promises him prosperity *2 Chr 9:1–24* Queen Sheba and others from around the world stream to Solomon because of his wisdom and wealth-God's promises realized and His glory magnified *2 Chr 36:15–23* Final description of how God directed Babylon to conquer Israel and would also direct Cyrus to initiate the return	*2 Chr 6:12–42* Solomon's prayers dedicating the Temple
Ezra Quintessential Character(s): Ezra	*Ezra 1:1–11* King Cyrus proclaims the return of the Jews to Jerusalem with the instruments from the Temple	*Ezra 3:1–12* The rebuilding of the Altar and the foundation of the Temple *Ezra 10:1–6* The remnant deal with the sin of taking foreign wives	
Nehemiah Quintessential Character(s): Nehemiah	*Neh 1:1–11* Nehemiah prays to return to Jerusalem	*Neh 2:11–20* Opposition to the kingdom *Neh 10:28–11:2* The people recommit to covenant behavior with some moving into Jerusalem *Neh 13:6–31* The book ends with Nehemiah's second return from Babylon to find the people violating the covenant promises at the close of the story	

APPENDIX D: THE QUINTESSENTIAL OLD TESTAMENT

Old Testament Texts

Esther Quintessential Character(s): Esther	*Esth 4:1–12* Esther puts her life in jeopardy for the deliverance of the diaspora Jews in Persia	*Esth 7* Vindication for Esther and Mordecai *Esth 8* Vindication for the Jewish People	
Job Quintessential Character(s): Job	*Job 42:1–17* Job repents after seeing God	*Job 1:1–12* Establishes Job's character and the deal between Satan and God	*Job 38:1–7* God's first challenge to Job
Psalms Quintessential Character(s): David			*Ps 1–2* The likely introduction to the Psalter that sets the themes.
Isaiah Quintessential Character(s): Isaiah	*Isa 6:1–13* Isaiah is commissioned at God's throne	*Isa 7:1–17* King Ahaz refuses to trust God and so judgment is on its way *Isa 36–39* Hezekiah from Assyria to Babylon—culminating section of all that precedes	*Isa 53* Suffering Servant
Jeremiah Quintessential Character(s): Jeremiah	*Jer 52:1–16* Nebuchadnezzar takes Jerusalem		*Jer 11:1–17* God explains why he is going to judge *Jer 31:31–34* The New Covenant
Lamentations Quintessential Character(s):			*Lam 3:1–33* Grief over exile and redemption

Old Testament Texts

Ezekiel Quintessential Character(s): Ezekiel	*Ezek 24:1–24* As with Ezekiel, the people are not to grieve over the impending judgment of Babylonian exile	*Ezek 37:1–14* The Valley of the Dry Bones—the restoration of Israel	*Ezek 36:24–38* Restoration through the sprinkling of blood and the giving of a new heart
Daniel Quintessential Character(s): Daniel	*Dan 1:1–21* The exile in Babylon and the faithful sons of Israel		*Dan 7:13–14* "One coming like a Son of Man"
Jonah Quintessential Character(s): Jonah	*Jonah 3–4* God's second direction to go to Nineveh and Jonah's sour response to God's grace		

Appendix E

The Wise Counselor Story

Simply the Story (used by permission)

SIMPLY THE STORY (STS)[1] uses this story as a tool for forming perceptive, natural, character-centric, discussion-driven questions to mine the treasures of truth in any Bible story. The storyteller internalizes this story and then asks the participants in a storytelling event questions about the characters in the story, just as (analogously) the wise counsellor asked of the characters in the village. The storyteller asks what might be learned about each character from what they say, do, the choices they made (or did not make), the consequences of those choices, who was impacted, and what is learned about God.

When the story is internalized, the storyteller can draw upon it in the midst of discussion to form questions. He/she pictures in the mind's eye what the wise counsellor would ask the villagers, and so asks similar questions of the characters in the story at hand. The responses to the questions are thus unique to those specific characters, flowing out of a particular character (this is "narrative logic" and "character-thinking" in process).

As the storyteller listens intently to participants, responds appropriately, and guides the discussion, he/she (as well as other discussion participants) will be prompted to ask questions that evoke deeper meaning of the character in relation to today's listeners. Depending on time, the group can deepen the discussion of the truths in the Bible story.

Toward the conclusion of the storytelling event, after the story's treasures have been unearthed, the storyteller asks application questions to help participants see how and where these truths can be utilized—to correct, comfort, encourage, guide, and impart faith and hope in their own life situations. Do people today, say, do, and make choices like the characters in this story spoke/acted/decided? What does that look like? Have you, or

---

1. See http://simplythestory.org.

anyone you know, ever experienced something like this? Would you like to share this with the group?

Here is the story:

Some villagers had been disputing over a well and water rights for a long time, so they went to a wise counsellor to get good advice. This counsellor was known to ask many questions, because he wanted to thoroughly understand the people and the problem so that he could give wise advice. Before asking for the story, the counsellor asked, "Can you briefly explain the situation? In just a few words, what's going on?"

After the villagers told the counsellor about their problem in just a few words, he then wisely asked: "Did anything happen before this problem started that could help me better understand it?"

The villagers shared what had led up to the dispute. Then the counsellor said, "Now tell me the whole story, but please tell it to me slowly and don't leave out any of the details." So the people began to tell their story.

As soon as the villagers told part of their story, the counsellor stopped them and asked, "Now tell me, at this point, did any of you say anything or maybe did you do something? Because that will help me to better understand what happened." At that moment, an old woman said, "From the very beginning, I've been telling my neighbor that she is taking too much water!" The counselor listened and then asked if anyone else said or did anything up to that point in their story. As the counsellor listened carefully, he thought to himself, *what might I learn about the people from what they said and did?*

The wise counsellor then asked the other villagers, "Did anyone make any choices? And if you made a choice—were there any other choices you could have made?" A strong young man stepped forward and said, "When I saw what was going on, I decided to guard the well. But now I'm wondering if maybe I could have done something different." The counsellor thanked the young man and asked if anyone else made a choice—or could have made other choices. The counsellor again thought to himself, *what might I learn about the people from the choices they actually made?*

After hearing about the choices that were made, the wise counsellor said, "I'm wondering, from the choices that were mentioned, were there any results or might anyone else have been impacted?" Soon, a mother came forward with her small daughter, who was limping. She told him, "My daughter was injured in the fights over the well on the very first day." The counsellor replied, "Thank you for sharing that." One by one the villagers shared the results of their choices and how they had been impacted.

So the counsellor continued in this manner. He said to the villagers, "Please tell more of your story." Then after they told a little more, he said, "Do stop there," and he asked the same questions about what the villagers may have said and done, about choices they made or could have made, and about the results and ongoing impact of their choices. *From their answers, the wise counsellor was learning more and more about the people.*

Finally, they finished telling their story. Then, because the wise counsellor had listened carefully to the villagers' answers, he learned a lot about the people and truly understood their dispute. He was then able to give them good advice.

STS desires to discover the valuable information that every Bible story contains. To locate these treasures, just like the wise counsellor, storytellers listen carefully to the Bible story and ask many strategic questions. This allows them to go deeper than just what happened in the story. Storytellers want to discover spiritual lessons.

Remember how that wise counsellor asked two questions *before* the villagers began telling the story slowly in sections? The counsellor asked the villagers to "briefly explain the situation." STS does the same with the Bible story. Most Bible stories have something that draws listeners emotionally into the story—a tension, problem or joy. STS calls that *the situation*. Before the storyteller begins to go slowly through the Bible story and ask questions, he/she looks for its situation. Are those in the story hungry or in danger? Are they scared or confused or maybe experiencing something positive?

Knowing the situation causes the people in the story to become more real. Listeners are emotionally drawn into the story as they realize what it must be like for people to experience that kind of situation.

The counsellor also asked the villagers to tell what happened before they experienced their problem. STS models the wise counsellor. When looking for treasures inside a Bible story, storytellers look for the *setting*, also called the *context*.

Notice this. Although the historical context of any story is helpful, STS goes beyond what the wise counsellor did. Storytellers also look for the *spiritual context*. They look for ways God has been working in these people's lives before the story, and how they have or have not responded. Storytellers might attempt to find how they found themselves in their situation, or how long they had been struggling, or if they had been serving God. Discovering the spiritual context helps storytellers better understand the spiritual content of the story being explored.

Remember how the wise counsellor had the villagers tell their story slowly, and after each section he told them to stop? Then he asked the *same questions in each section* about what the people said and did because he wanted to learn about the people from their words and actions. STS does the same, starting at the beginning of the story and slowly and carefully listening to the story one section at a time. Storytellers ask themselves: "What might we learn spiritually from the actions and words of each person in this section of the Bible story?"

Also in every section, even when God's name is not mentioned, storytellers always ask, how was God working in people's lives in this section? What might we learn about God? STS continues this process for each section until the end of the story. The answers to all of these questions reveal what STS calls "Spiritual Observations."

This slow and careful hunt for treasures helps the storyteller to experience what living people in the Bible, like ourselves, said and did in real-life encounters. Storytellers can learn a great deal when considering the results of the choices that were made or could have been made. Finally, after asking many questions and listening carefully to the Bible story, just as the wise counsellor offered good advice, the storyteller is ready to make "Spiritual Applications."[2]

---

2. The wise counsellor story is part of a larger training program offered by *Simply the Story*. To download a free full training manual, wherein the wise counsellor is embedded, go to http://simplythestory.org/oralbiblestories/ and search under "Resources" tab. Check the "Training Info" tab for workshop opportunities regularly offered in various countries.

Bibliography

Adiprasetya, Joas. "Towards an Asian Multitextual Theology." *Exchange* 43 (2014) 119–31.
Alexander, T. Desmond. *From Eden to the New Jerusalem: An Introduction to Biblical Theology*. Grand Rapids: Kregel, 2008.
Alter, Robert. *The Art of Biblical Narrative*. New York: Basic, 1981.
———. *The Hebrew Bible: A Translation with Commentary, Volume 1*. New York: Norton, 2019.
———. *The World of Biblical Literature*. New York: Basic, 1992.
American Bible Society. "State of the Bible 2018: Bible Engagement Segmentation," https://1s712.americanbible.org/cdn-www-ws03/uploads/content/state-of-the-bible-2018.pdf.
Anderson, Bernhard. *Out of the Depths: The Psalms Speak for Us Today*. Philadelphia: Westminster, 1983.
Anderson, Francis I. *Job: An Introduction and Commentary*. Downers Grove, IL: InterVarsity, 1976.
Archer, Kenneth J. *A Pentecostal Hermeneutic for the Twenty-first Century: Spirit, Scripture and Community*. New York: Bloomsbury, 2004.
———. "Pentecostal Story: The Hermeneutical Filter for the Making of Meaning." *PNEUMA* 26 (2004) 36–59.
———. "A Pentecostal Way of Doing Theology: Method and Manner." *International Journal of Systematic Theology* 9 (2007) 301–14.
Archer, Margaret S. *Structure, Agency and the Internal Conversation*. Cambridge: Cambridge University Press, 2003.
Arndt, William F., and F. Wilbur Gingrich. *A Greek-English Lexicon of the New Testament and Other Early Christian Literature*. Chicago: University of Chicago Press, 1957.
Arrington, Aminta. *Songs of the Lisu Hills: Practicing Christianity in Southwest China*. University Park, PA: Penn State University Press, 2020.
Arthurs, Jeffrey. *Devote Yourself to the Public Reading of Scripture: The Transforming Power of the Well-Spoken Word*. Grand Rapids: Kregel Academic, 2012.
Autry, Arden C. "Dimensions of Hermeneutics in Pentecostal Focus." *Journal of Pentecostal Theology* 3 (1993) 29–50.
Bailey, Kenneth F. "Informal Controlled Oral Tradition and the Synoptic Gospels." *Asia Journal of Theology* 5 (1991) 34–54.

———. *Jacob & the Prodigal: How Jesus Retold Israel's Story*. Downers Grove, IL: IVP Academic, 2003.

———. *Jesus Through Middle Eastern Eyes: Cultural Studies in the Gospels*. Downers Grove, IL: IVP Academic, 2008.

———. *Poet & Peasant and Through Peasant Eyes: A Literary-Cultural Approach to the Parables in Luke*. Grand Rapids: Eerdmans, 2000.

Barber, Karin. *Anthropology of Texts, Persons and Publics: Oral and Written Culture in Africa and Beyond*. Cambridge: Cambridge University Press, 2007.

Barclay, William. *The Revelation of John*, Vol. 1. Edinburgh: Saint Andrew, 1975.

Bartholomew, Craig G., and Michael W. Goheen. *The Drama of Scripture: Finding Our Place in the Biblical Story*. Grand Rapids: Baker Academic, 2004.

Bates, Matthew W. *Salvation by Allegiance Alone: Rethinking Faith, Works, and the Gospel of Jesus the King*. Grand Rapids: BakerAcademic, 2017.

Bauckham, Richard. *Jesus and the Eyewitnesses: The Gospels as Eyewitness Testimony*. Grand Rapids: Eerdmans, 2006.

Bauer, Walter, et al., eds., *A Greek-English Lexicon of the New Testament and Other Early Christian Literature*. Chicago: University of Chicago Press, 2000.

Baxter, J. Sidlow. *The Master Theme of the Bible: A Comprehensive Study of the Lamb of God*. Grand Rapids: Kregel, 1997.

B. B. "Genealogical Storying in A Nomadic Context." Unpublished paper, 1999.

Beale, G. K., and Benjamin L. Gladd. *The Story Retold: A Biblical-Theological Introduction to the New Testament*. Downers Grove, IL: IVP Academic, 2020.

Bediako, Kwame. "Biblical Exegesis in Africa: The Significance of the Translated Scriptures." In *African Theology on the Way*, edited by Diane B. Stinton, 12–20. London: SPCK, 2010.

———. *Christianity in Africa: The Renewal of a Non-Western Religion*. Maryknoll, NY: Orbis, 1995.

Berger, Daniel R. *Oral Interpretation of the Bible*. Eugene, OR: Wipf & Stock, 2003.

Bjoraker, William D. "Faith, Freedom and Radical Individualism in Late Modern America: A Missiological Evaluation." PhD diss., Fuller Theological Seminary, 2007.

———. "The Place of Story in Messianic Jewish Ministry." *Kesher* 32 (2018) 3–37.

Black, Stephanie L. "Key Hermeneutical Questions for African Evangelicals Today." *Africa Journal of Evangelical Theology* 34 (2015) 3–33.

Blomberg, Craig L. *Interpreting the Parables*. Downers Grove, IL: InterVarsity, 1990.

Bochner, Arthur P. "Narrative Virtues." *Qualitative Inquiry* 15 (2001) 131–57.

Bock, Darrell L. *Jesus According to Scripture: Restoring the Portrait from the Gospels*. Grand Rapids: Baker Academic, 2002.

———. "The Words of Jesus in the Gospels: Live, Jive, or Memorex." In *Jesus Under Fire*, edited by Michael J. Wilkins and J. P. Moreland, 73–99. Grand Rapids: Zondervan, 1995.

Bock, Darrell, and Daniel Carroll-Rodas, "How Does Narrative Teach Theology and Ethics?" *The Table Podcast*, February 25, 2014. https://voice.dts.edu/tablepodcast/old-testament-ethics-1/.

Boomershine, Thomas E. "Biblical Megatrends: Towards a Paradigm for the Interpretation of the Bible in Electronic Media." In *Society for Biblical Literature 1987 Seminar Papers*, edited by Kent Harold Richards, 144–57. Atlanta: Scholars, 1987.

Boring, M. Eugene. "The Voice of Jesus in the Apocalypse of John." *Novum Testamentum* 34 (1992) 334–59.

Bosch, David J. *Transforming Mission: Paradigm Shifts in Theology of Mission.* Maryknoll, NY: Orbis, 1991.
Botha, Pieter J. J. "Mute Manuscripts: Analyzing a Neglected Aspect of Ancient Communication." *Theologia Evangelica* 23 (1990) 39–42.
———. *Orality and Literacy in Early Christianity.* Eugene, OR: Cascade, 2012.
Bowman, James. "Finding My Real Father: My Journey with God to the Ends of the World." Unpublished manuscript, 2020. PDF file.
Boyer, Steven, and Christopher Hall, *The Mystery of God: Theology for Knowing the Unknowable.* Grand Rapids: Baker Academic, 2012.
Boynton, Susan, and Diane Reilly, eds. *The Practice of the Bible in the Middle Ages: Production, Reception, and Performance in Western Christianity.* New York: Columbia University Press, 2011.
Bradt, Kevin M. *Story as a Way of Knowing.* Kansas City: Sheed & Ward, 1997.
Brewster, E. Thomas, and Elizabeth S. Brewster, *Language Learning Made Practical: Field Methods for Language Learners.* Colorado Springs: Lingua House, 1976.
Brown, Adam Stewart. "Spiritual Lessons from the Land of Israel, or Why You Should Visit the Holy Land." *The Gospel Coalition*, June 22, 2019. https://www.thegospelcoalition.org/article/spiritual-lessons-land-israel/.
Brown, Francis, et al. *The New Brown-Driver-Briggs Hebrew and English Lexicon.* Peabody, MA: Hendrickson, 1996.
Brueggemann, Walter. *Hopeful Imagination: Prophetic Voices in Exile.* Minneapolis: Fortress, 1986.
Bruner, Jerome S. *Acts of Meaning.* Cambridge: Harvard University Press, 1990.
———. *Actual Minds, Possible Worlds.* Cambridge: Harvard University Press, 1986.
———. *The Culture of Education.* Cambridge: Harvard University Press, 1996.
Brunn, Dave. *One Bible, Many Versions: Are All Translations Created Equal?* Downers Grove, IL: IVP Academic, 2013.
Buber, Martin. *I and Thou.* Translated by Walter Kaufmann. New York: Touchstone, 1970.
Burger, Daniel R. *Oral Interpretation of the Bible.* Eugene, OR: Wipf & Stock, 2003.
Bush, Ryan. "Synthesizing the Orality Debate." In *Orality and Literacies: Implications for Communication and Education*, edited by Charles Madinger, 1–13. Richmond, VA: International Orality Network, 2016. https://orality.net/content/oralities-literacies-chapter-1-synthesizing-the-orality-debate/.
Byrskog, Samuel. "Introduction." In *Jesus in Memory: Traditions in Oral and Scribal Perspectives*, edited by Werner H. Kelber and Samuel Byrskog, 1–20. Waco, TX: Baylor University Press, 2009.
Caine, Renate N., and Geoffrey Caine. *Making Connections: Teaching and the Human Brain.* Alexandria, VA: Association for Supervision and Curriculum Development, 1991.
Caldwell, Larry W. *Doing Bible Interpretation!* Sioux Falls, SD: Lazy Oaks, 2016.
———. "Third Horizon Ethnohermeneutics: Reevaluating New Testament Hermeneutical Models for Intercultural Bible Interpreters Today." *Asia Journal of Theology* 1 (1987) 314–33.
———. "Towards an Ethnohermeneutical Model for a Lowland Filipino Context." *Journal of Asian Mission* 7 (2005) 169–93.
———. "Towards the New Discipline of Ethnohermeneutics: Questioning the Relevancy of Western Hermeneutical Methods in the Asian Context." *Journal of Asian Mission* 1 (1999) 21–43.

Calvin, John. *John Calvin's Bible Commentaries on the Psalms 1–35*. North Charleston, SC: Createspace, 2016.

Carr, David M. *Writing on the Tablet of the Heart: Origins of Scripture and Literature*. Oxford: Oxford University Press, 2005.

Carr, Nicholas. *The Shallows: What the Internet is Doing to Our Brains*. New York: Norton, 2011.

Carson, D. A. *Christ and Culture Revisited*. Grand Rapids: Eerdmans, 2008.

———. *Exegetical Fallacies*. Grand Rapids: Baker Academic, 1996.

Cates, Georgia. *Beauty from Pain*. Beauty Series, Volume 1. Virginia Beach, VA: CreateSpace, 2013.

Cawley, *The Myth of the Non-Christian: Engaging Atheists, Nominal Christians and the Spiritual but Not Religious*. Downers Grove, IL: InterVarsity, 2016.

Chan, Sam. *Evangelism in a Skeptical World: How to Make the Unbelievable News about Jesus More Believable*. Grand Rapids: Zondervan, 2018.

Chen, Keith. "Could Your Language Affect Your Ability to Save Money?" TedGlobal, June 2012. https://www.ted.com/talks/keith_chen_could_your_language_affect_your_ability_to_save_money.

Chia, Kee Fook (Edmund). "Asian Christianity: The Postcolonial Challenge of Identity and Theology." *Compass* 46 (2012) 9–13.

Chifungo, Davidson Kamayaya. "An Oral Hermeneutics within the Lay Preaching Context of the Nkhoma Synod of the Church of Central Africa Presbyterian (CCAP): A Critical Evaluation." PhD diss., University of Stellenbosch, 2013.

Clanchy, Michael T. *Memory to Written Record: England 1066–1307*. Malden, MA: Blackwell, 1993.

Clear, James. "Why Facts Don't Change Our Minds." https://jamesclear.com/why-facts-dont-change-minds.

Colijn, Brenda B. *Images of Salvation in the New Testament*. Downers Grove, IL: InterVarsity, 2010.

Collins, Dee. "A Visual Bible for Each of Their Visual Sign Languages." *International Orality Network*, n.d. https://orality.net/content/a-new-day-dawns-for-the-deaf/.

Collins, John J. *Introduction to the Hebrew Bible*. Minneapolis: Fortress, 2018.

Conn, Harvie M. "Indigenization." In *Evangelical Dictionary of World Missions*, edited by A. Scott Moreau, 481–82. Grand Rapids: Baker, 2000.

Cooke, Phil. "The Insight that Changed the Way I Share My Faith." https://www.philcooke.com/the-insight-that-changed-the-way-i-share-my-faith/.

Cordi, Kevin. "How Storytelling Serves as Actors and What We Can Learn from Each Other (Part 1)." https://storynet.org/how-storytellers-serve-as-actors/.

Crapanzano, Vincent. "Hermes' Dilemma and Hamlet's Desire: On the Epistemology of Interpretation." *Rocky Mountain Review of Language and Literature* 47 (1993) 74–77.

———. "Must We Be Bad Epistemologists? Illusions of Transparency, the Opaque Other, and Interpretive Foibles." In *The Ground Between: Anthropologists Engage Philosophy*, edited by Veena Das et al., 254–79. Durham, NC: Duke University Press, 2014.

Crites, Stephen. "The Narrative Quality of Experience." *JAAR* (1971) 290–307.

Crouch, Andy. "The Return of Shame." *Christianity Today* 59 (2015) 32–41.

Dear, John, ed. *The Questions or Jesus: Challenging Ourselves to Discover Life's Great Answers*. New York: Doubleday, 2004. Kindle edition.

Descartes, René. *A Discourse on the Method of Correctly Conducting One's Reason and Seeking Truth in the Sciences*. Oxford: Oxford University Press, 2006.

deSilva, David A. *The Hope of Glory: Honor Discourse and New Testament Interpretation.* Eugene, OR: Wipf & Stock, 2009.

Dewey, Joanna. "The Gospel of Mark as Oral Hermeneutic." In *Jesus the Voice and the Text,* edited by Tom Thatcher, 71–87. Waco, TX: Baylor University Press, 2008.

———. "The Survival of Mark's Gospel: A Good Story?" *Journal of Biblical Literature* 123 (2004) 495–507.

Dillard, Annie. *Pilgrim at Tinker Creek.* New York: HarperCollins, 1974.

Dockery, David S. *Christian Scripture: An Evangelical Perspective on Inspiration, Authority, and Interpretation.* Nashville: Broadman & Holmes, 1994.

Dossey, Larry. "Our Identity Crisis and a Solution: The One Mind." *EXPLORE* 12 (2016) 393–400.

Draper, Johnathan A. "Vice Catalogues as Oral-Mnemonic Cues: A Comparative Study of the Two-Ways Tradition in the *Didache* and Parallels from the Perspective of Oral Tradition." In *Jesus the Voice and the Text,* edited by Tom Thatcher, 111–33. Waco, TX: Baylor University Press, 2008.

Drucker, Peter F. *The Practice of Management.* New York: HarperBusiness, 2006.

Dunn, James D. G. *Jesus According to the New Testament.* Grand Rapids: Eerdmans, 2019.

———. *New Testament Theology: An Introduction.* Nashville: Abingdon, 2009.

———. *The Oral Gospel Tradition.* Grand Rapids: Eerdmans, 2013.

Duvall, J. Scott, and J. Daniel Hays. *Grasping God's Word: A Hands-on Approach to Reading, Interpreting, and Applying the Bible.* Grand Rapids: Zondervan, 2012.

Editors of GQ. "21 Books You Don't Have to Read." *GQ* 4 (2018) 17. https://www.gq.com/story/21-books-you-dont-have-to-read.

Edwards, Jonathan. "The Distinguishing Marks of a Work of the Spirit of God (Part 2)." http://www1.cbn.com/churchandministry/the-distinguishing-marks-of-a-work-of-the-spirit-of-god-part-2.

Ekeka, Emeka C. "Oral Expression of African Christianity in Songs and Choruses (A Case Study of African Independent Churches in Calabar-Nigeria)." *Research on Humanities and Social Sciences* 2 (2012) 154–63.

Ekman, Paul. *Emotions Revealed: Recognizing Faces and Feelings to Improve Communication and Emotional Life.* New York: Holt, 2003.

Erickson, Millard. *The Evangelical Left: Encountering Post-Conservative Evangelical Theology.* Grand Rapids: Baker, 1997.

Fackre, Gabriel. "Narrative Theology: An Overview." *Interpretation* 37 (1983) 340–53.

Fee, Gordon D., and Douglas Stuart. *How to Read the Bible for All its Worth: A Guide to Understanding the Bible.* Grand Rapids: Zondervan, 1993.

Fentress, James J., and Chris Wickham. *Social Memory: New Perspectives on the Past.* Oxford: Blackwell, 1992.

Finnegan, Ruth. *Literacy and Orality: Studies in the Technology of Communication.* Oxford: Blackwell, 1988.

———. *Oral Literature in Africa.* Cambridge, UK: Open Book, 2012.

Fisher, Walter W. *Human Communication as Narration: Toward a Philosophy of Reason, Values, and Action.* Columbia: University of South Carolina, 1987.

———. "Narrative, Reason, and Community in Memory, Identity, Community: The Idea of Narrative." In *The Human Sciences,* edited by Lewis P. Hinchman and Sandra K. Hinchman, 307–27. Albany: State University of New York, 1997.

Fitzgerald, Frances. *The Evangelicals: The Struggle to Shape America.* New York: Simon & Schuster, 2017.

Flanders, Christopher L. *About Face: Rethinking Face for 21st Century Mission*. Eugene, OR: Pickwick, 2011.

Flemming, Dean. *Contextualization in the New Testament: Patterns for Theology and Mission*. Downers Grove, IL: InterVarsity, 2005.

Flesch, Rudolf. *Marks of a Readable Style: A Study in Adult Education*. New York: Teachers College, Columbia University, 1943.

Fokkelman, J. P. *Reading Biblical Narrative: An Introductory Guide*. Louisville: Westminster John Knox, 1999.

Foley, John Miles. *Oral Tradition in Literature: Interpretation in Context*. Columbia: University of Missouri, 1986.

———. "The Riddle of Q: Oral Ancestor, Textual Precedent, or Ideological Creation?" In *Oral Performance, Popular Tradition, and Hidden Transcript in Q*, edited by Richard A. Horsley, 123–40. Semeia Studies. Atlanta: Society of Biblical Literature, 2006.

Ford, Leighton. *The Power of Story: Rediscovering the Oldest, Most Natural Way to Reach People for Christ*. Colorado Springs: NavPress, 1991.

Forest, Heather. *Wisdom Tales from Around the Word*. Little Rock, AR: August House, 1996.

Frame, John M. *A History of Western Philosophy and Theology*. Phillipsburg, NJ: R & R, 2015.

Frei, Hans W. *The Eclipse of Biblical Narrative*. New Haven: Yale University Press, 1974.

Freire, Pablo. *The Pedagogy of the Oppressed*. 4th ed. New York: Bloomsbury, 2018.

Frye, Northorp. "Literary Criticism." In *The Aims and Methods of Scholarship in Modern Languages and Literatures*, edited by James Thrope, 68–81. New York: Modern Language Association, 1970.

Furniss, Graham. *Orality: The Power of the Spoken Word*. New York: Palgrave Macmillan, 2004.

Gadamer, Hans-Georg. *Truth and Method*. New York: Crossroad, 1985.

Gaille, Brandon. "15 US Literacy Rate and Illiteracy Statistics." https://brandongaille.com/us-literacy-rate-and-illiteracy-statistics/.

Gallagher, Shaun. *Hermeneutics and Education*. Albany: State University of New York, 1992.

Geertz, Clifford *The Interpretations of Cultures: Selected Essays*. New York: Basic, 1973.

Georges, Jayson, and Mark D. Baker. *Ministering in Honor-Shame Cultures: Biblical Foundations and Practical Essentials*. Downers Grove, IL: IVP Academic, 2016.

Gerhardsson, Biger. "The Gospel Tradition." In *The Interrelationships of the Gospels*, edited by David L. Dungan, 495–545. Leuven: Belgium, 1986.

———. *Memory and Manuscript: Oral Tradition and Written Transmission in Rabbinic Judaism and Early Christianity*. Grand Rapids: Eerdmans, 1998.

Gilmore, David G., ed. *Honor and Shame and the Unity of the Mediterranean*. Arlington, VA: American Anthropological Association, 1987.

Goldberg, Michael. *Jews and Christians: Getting Our Stories Straight: The Exodus and the Passion-Resurrection*. Eugene, OR: Wipf & Stock, 1991.

Goldingay, John. "Biblical Story and the Way it Shapes Our Story." *The Journal of the European Pentecostal Theological Association* 27 (1997) 5–15.

Goman, Carol Kinsey. *The Silent Language of Leaders: How Body Language Can Help—Or Hurt—How You Lead*. San Francisco: Jossey-Bass, 2011.

Goody, Jack. *The Domestication of the Savage Mind*. Cambridge: Cambridge University Press, 1977.

Graham, William A. *Beyond the Written Word: Oral Aspects of Scripture in the History of Religion*. New York: Cambridge University Press, 1993.

Green, Donald E. "Evangelicals and *Ipsissima Vox*." *TMSJ* 12 (2001) 49–68.

Gregersen, Hal. *Questions are the Answer: A Breakthrough Approach to Your Most Vexing Problems at Work and in Life*. New York: HarperBusiness, 2018.

Grenz, Stanley J., and John R. Franke. *Beyond Foundationalism: Shaping Theology in a Postmodern Context*. Louisville: Westminster John Knox, 2001.

Groothuis, Douglas. *Truth Decay: Defending Christianity against the Challenges of Postmodernism*. Downers Grove, IL: InterVarsity, 2000.

Grossberg, Lawrence, and Clifford G. Christians. "Hermeneutics and the Study of Communication." A paper presented at the Annual Meeting of the Association for Education in Journalism, Seattle, Washington, August 13–16, 1978, 1–41.

Haidt, Jonathan. *The Righteous Mind: Why Good People are Divided by Politics and Religion*. New York: Vintage, 2012.

Halliday, E. M. "Hemingway's Iceberg Theory." https://english101490.files.wordpress.com/2017/06/hemingways-iceberg-principle.pdf.

Hamilton, James M., Jr. *What is Biblical Theology?: A Guide to the Bible's Story, Symbolism, and Patterns*. Wheaton, IL: Crossway, 2014.

Hapgood, Fred. "Simulations Help Make Better Businesses." *CIO*, June 15, 2001. https://www.cio.com/article/2441483/simulations-help-make-better-businesses.html.

Harris, William V. *Ancient Literacy*. Cambridge: Harvard University Press, 1989.

Harvey, John. "Orality and its Implications for Biblical Studies: Recapturing an Ancient Paradigm." *JETS* 45 (2002) 99–109.

Hauerwas, Stanley. *The Peaceable Kingdom: A Primer in Christian Ethics*. Notre Dame: University of Notre Dame Press, 1983.

Hauerwas, Stanley, and David Burrell. "From System to Story: An Alternative Pattern for Rationality in Ethics." In *Why Narrative?: Readings in Narrative Theology*, edited by Stanley Hauerwas and L. Gregory Jones, 158–90. Grand Rapids: Eerdmans, 1989.

Havelock, Eric. "The Oral-Literate Equation: A Formula for the Modern Mind." In *Literacy and Orality*, edited by David R. Olson and Nancy Torrance, 11–27. Cambridge: Cambridge University Press, 1991.

———. *Preface to Plato*. Cambridge: Belknap Press of Harvard University Press, 1982.

Hays, Richard B. *The Conversion of the Imagination: Paul as Interpreter of Israel*. Grand Rapids: Eerdmans, 2005.

———. *Echoes of Scripture in the Letter of Paul*. New Haven: Yale University Press, 1989.

———. *The Faith of Jesus Christ: The Narrative Subculture of Galatians 3:1—4:11*. Grand Rapids: Eerdmans, 2002.

Hearon, Holly. "The Interplay between Written and Spoken Word in the Second Testament as Background to the Emergence of Written Gospels." *Oral Tradition Journal* 25 (2010) 57–74.

———. "Storytelling in Oral and Written Media Contexts." In *Jesus the Voice and the Text*, edited by Tom Thatcher, 89–110. Waco, TX: Baylor University Press, 2008.

Hemingway, Ernest. *Death in the Afternoon*. New York: Charles Scribner's Sons, 1932.

Henry, Carl F. H. *God, Revelation, and Authority, Volume III: God Who Speaks and Shows: Fifteen Theses, Part Two*. Waco, TX: Word, 1979.

Hesselgrave, David J., and Edward Rommen. *Contextualization: Meanings, Methods, and Models*. Grand Rapids: Baker, 1989.

Hiebert, Paul G. *Anthropological Reflections on Missiological Issues*. Grand Rapids: Baker, 1994.

———. *Transforming Worldviews: An Anthropological Understanding of How People Change*. Grand Rapids: BakerAcademic, 2008.

Hoefer, Herbert E. "Rooted or Uprooted: The Necessity of Contextualization in Missions." *International Journal of Frontier Missions* 24 (2007) 3, 131–38.

Hood, Jason B., and Matthew Y. Emerson. "Summaries of Israel's Story: Reviewing a Compositional Category." *CBR* 11 (2013) 328–48.

Hooper, Walter. *C. S. Lewis: A Companion & Guide*. New York: HarperCollins, 1996.

Horsley, Richard A. "Oral Performance and Mark: Some Implications of the Oral and the Written Gospel, Twenty-Five Years Later." In *Jesus the Voice and the Text*, edited by Tom Thatcher, 45–70. Waco, TX: Baylor University Press, 2008.

———. *Whoever Hears You Hears Me: Prophets, Performance, and Tradition in Q*. Harrisburg, PA: Trinity, 1999.

Howell, Brian. "Mystery: To Know and Be Known in Ethnography." In *On Knowing Humanity: Insights from Theology for Anthropology*, edited by Eloise Meneses and David Bronkema, 33–53. New York: Routledge, 2017.

Hunter, George. "Emotional Relevance in Outreach Ministry." *Great Commission Research Journal* 9 (2018) 192–200.

Idema, Wilt, and Lloyd Halt, trans. *A Guide to Chinese Literature*. Michigan Monographs In Chinese Studies. Ann Arbor: University of Michigan Center for Chinese Studies, 1997.

Innis, Harold A. *The Bias of Communication*. Buffalo, NY: University of Toronto Press, 1999.

International Council on Biblical Inerrancy. "The Chicago Statement on Biblical Inerrancy." https://www.sbcreformed.org/hp_wordpress/wp-content/uploads/2012/06/Chicago-Statement-Inerrancy-Hermeneutics-Application.pdf.

Iverson, Kelly R. "Orality and the Gospels: A Survey of Recent Research." *CBR* 8 (2009) 71–106.

Jagerson, Jennifer. "Hermeneutics and the Methods of Oral Bible Storytelling for the Evangelization and Discipleship of Oral Learners." *Great Commission Research Journal* 4 (2013) 251–61.

———. "Transformation through Narrative: Exploring the Power of Sacred Stories among Oral Learners in Ethiopia." PhD diss., Talbot School of Theology, Biola University, 2016.

James, Steven. *Story: Recapture the Mystery*. Grand Rapids: Revell, 2006.

Jardine, David. "Reflections on Education, Hermeneutics, and Ambiguity: Hermeneutics as a Restoring of Life to its Original Difficulty." In *Understanding Curriculum as Phenomenological and Deconstructed Text*, edited by William Pinar and William M. Reynolds, 116–27. New York: Teachers College Press, 2015.

Jersak, Brad. "Noah: Who are the Watchers and Why the Panic?" *Clarion*. March 31, 2014. http://www.clarion-journal.com/clarion_journal_of_spirit/2014/03/noah-who-are-the-watchers-and-why-the-panic-by-brad-jersak.html.

Jewish Virtual Library. "Encyclopedia Judaica: Aggadah or Haggadah." https://www.jewishvirtuallibrary.org/aggadah-or-haggadah-jewish-virtual-library.

Johnston, Robert K. "Orthodoxy and Heresy: A Problem for Modern Evangelicalism." *Evangelical Quarterly* 69 (1997) 7–38.

Justarius. "What is Philosophy?" https://philoscifi.com/2007/02/15/what-is-philosophy/.

Kaiser, Walter C. "Narrative." In *Cracking Old Testament Codes: A Guide to Interpreting the Literary Genres of the Old Testament,* edited by Brent D. Sandy and Ronald L. Giese Jr., 69–88. Nashville: B & H, 1995.
Kant, Immanuel. "What is the Enlightenment?" http://www.columbia.edu/acis/ets/CCREAD/etscc/kant.html.
Keener, Craig S. *Spirit Hermeneutics: Reading Scripture in Light of Pentecost.* Grand Rapids: Eerdmans, 2016.
Keener, Craig S., and M. Daniel Carroll R., eds. *Global Voices: Reading the Bible in the Majority World.* Peabody, MA: Hendrickson, 2013.
Kelber, Werner H. "In the Beginning were the Words: The Apotheosis and Narrative Displacement of the Logos." *Journal of the American Academy of Religion* 58 (1990) 69–98.
———. "Jesus and Tradition: Words in Time, Words in Space." In *Orality and Textuality in Early Christian Literature,* edited by Joanna Dewey, 139–67. Semeia Studies. Atlanta: Scholars, 1995.
———. "Modalities of Communication, Cognition, and Physiology of Perception: Orality, Rhetoric, Scribality." *Semeia* 65 (1994) 193–216.
———. *The Oral and Written Gospel: The Hermeneutics of Speaking and Writing in the Synoptic Tradition, Mark, Paul, and Q.* Minneapolis: Fortress, 1983.
———. "The Oral-Scribal-Memorial Arts of Communication." In *Jesus the Voice and the Text,* edited by Tom Thatcher, 235–62. Waco, TX: Baylor University Press, 2008.
———. "The Works of Memory: Christian Origins and Mnemo-history—A Response." In *Memory, Tradition, and Text: Uses of the Past in Early Christianity,* edited by Alan Kirk and Tom Thatcher, 221–48. Semeia Studies. Atlanta: Society of Biblical Literature, 2005.
Keller, Timothy. *Jesus the King: Understanding the Life and Death of the Son of God.* New York: Penguin, 2016.
Kennedy, George. *New Testament Interpretation through Rhetorical Criticism.* Chapel Hill: The University of North Carolina Press, 1984.
King, Alison. "From Sage on the Stage to Guide at the Side." *College Teaching* 41 (1993) 30–35.
King, Roberta R. *Global Arts and Christian Witness,* Grand Rapids: Baker Academic, 2019.
———. *Music in the Life of the African Church.* Waco, TX: Baylor University, 2008.
Kirk, Alan. "Manuscript Tradition as a *Tertium Quid*: Orality and Memory in Scribal Practices." In *Jesus the Voice and the Text,* edited by Tom Thatcher, 215–34. Waco, TX: Baylor University Press, 2008.
Kirk, Alan. *Memory and the Jesus Tradition.* New York: Bloomsbury, 2018.
Kirk, Geoffrey S. *The Songs of Homer.* Cambridge: Cambridge University Press, 1962.
Klein, William W., et al. *Introduction to Biblical Interpretation.* Nashville: Thomas Nelson, 2004.
Klem, Herbert V. *Oral Communication of the Scripture: Insights from African Oral Art.* Pasadena, CA: William Carey Library, 1982.
Klink, Edward W., and Darian R. Lockett. *Understanding Biblical Theology: A Comparison of Theory and Practice.* Grand Rapids: Zondervan, 2012.
Knighton, Ben. "Orality in the Service of Karamojong Autonomy: Polity and Performance." *Journal of African Cultural Studies* 18 (2006) 137–52.

Knowles, Malcolm S. *The Modern Practice of Adult Education*. Englewood Cliffs, NJ: Prentice Hall Regents. 1980.

Koehler, Paul F. *Telling God's Stories with Power: Biblical Storytelling in Oral Cultures*. Pasadena, CA: William Carey Library, 2010.

Koller, Charles W. *Sermons Preached without Notes*. Grand Rapids: Baker, 1964.

Koyama, Kosuke. "We had Rice with Jesus." In *Theology in Action: Papers and Extracts on Doing Theology in Today's World,* edited by Jae Shik Oh and John C. England, 19–32. Manila: East Asian Christian Conference, 1972.

Kuhn, Karl Allen. *Luke: The Elite Evangelist* (*Paul's Social Network: Brothers and Sisters in Faith*). Collegeville, MN: Liturgical, 2010.

Kumar, Anugrah. "Hollywood's 'Noah' Tops Box Office with $44M Debut." http://www.christianpost.com/news/hollywoods-noah-tops-box-office-with-44m-debut-117091/.

Landa, José Àngel Gracía. "Narrating Narrating: Twisting the Twice-Told Tale." In *Theorizing Narrativity,* edited by John Pier and José Àngel García Land, 419–52. New York: De Gruyter, 2008.

Lausanne Movement. "Orality: An Infographic." https://www.lausanne.org/content/orality-an-infographic.

Lausanne Occasional Paper No. 54. *Making Disciples of Oral Learners*. Pattaya, Thailand: Lausanne Committee for World Evangelization, 2005.

Lee, Margaret Ellen, and Bernard Brandon Scott. *Sound Mapping the New Testament*. Farmington, MN: Polebridge, 2009.

Lee, Morgan. "'Noah' Movie Sparks Massive Spike in Global Reading of the Bible's Book of Genesis." *The Christian Post*. April 4, 2014. http://www.christianpost.com/news/noah-movie-sparks-massive-spike-in-global-reading-of-bible-book-of-genesis-117334/.

Lee-Thorp, Karen. *How to Ask Great Questions: Guide Discussion, Build Relationships, Deepen Faith*. Colorado Springs: NavPress, 2018.

Lehman, Karl. *Outsmarting Yourself: Catching Your Past Invading the Present and What to Do about it*. Libertyville, IL: This Joy!, 2011.

Lewis, C. S. *The Abolition of Man*. New York: Touchstone, 1996.

———. *Collected Works of C. S. Lewis*. New York: Inspirational, 1996.

———. *Mere Christianity*. New York: HarperCollins, 2001.

Lewis, C. S., and Walter Hooper, ed. *C. S. Lewis: Selected Literary Essays*. New York: Cambridge University Press, 2013.

Lim, Lena L. "The Influence of Harmony Motives and Implicit Beliefs on Conflict Styles of the Collectivist." *Journal of Psychology* 44 (2009) 401–9.

Lipman, Doug. *Improving Your Storytelling: Beyond the Basics for All Who Tell Stories in Work or Play*. Little Rock, AR: August House. 1999.

Longenecker, Bruce W., ed. *Narrative Dynamics in Paul: A Critical Assessment*. Louisville: Westminster John Knox, 2002.

Longman III, Tremper. "Literary Approaches to Biblical Interpretation." In *Foundations of Contemporary Interpretation,* edited by Moises Silva, 90–192. Grand Rapids: Zondervan, 1987.

Lord, Albert B. *The Singer of Tales*. Cambridge: Harvard University Press, 1960.

———. *The Singer of Tales*. 2nd ed. Edited by Stephen Mitchell and Gregory Nagy. Harvard Studies in Comparative Literature. Cambridge: Harvard University Press, 2000.

Lotz, David W. "The Proclamation of the Word in Luther's Thought." *Word & World* 3 (1983) 344–54. http://wordandworld.luthersem.edu/content/pdfs/3-4_Luther/3-4_Lotz.pdf.

Loubser, J. A. *Oral and Manuscript Culture in the Bible: Studies on the Media Texture of the New Testament—Explorative Hermeneutics.* Eugene, OR: Cascade, 2013.

Lovejoy, Grant, "The Extent of Orality." *JBTM* 5 (2008) 121–33.

Maccoby, Hyam. *Early Rabbinic Writings, Cambridge Commentaries on Writings of the Jewish and Christian World 200 BC to AD 200, Vol. 3.* Cambridge: Cambridge University Press, 1988.

MacIntyre, Alasdair. *After Virtue: A Study in Moral Theory.* Notre Dame: University of Notre Dame Press, 1981.

MacKay, Anne, ed. *Signs of Orality: The Oral Tradition and its Influence in the Greek and Roman World.* Boston: Brill Academic, 1999.

Madinger, Charles. "Applied Orality: More than Method." *Mission Frontiers* 36 (2014) 201–13.

Matthews, Michael. *A Novel Approach: The Significance of Story in Interpreting and Communicating Reality.* Victoria, BC: TellWell, 2017.

Maxey, James A., and Ernst R. Wendland, eds. *Translating Scripture for Sound and Performance: New Directions in Biblical Studies.* Eugene, OR: Cascade, 2012.

Mays, Kelly J. *The Norton Introduction to Literature.* Shorter Twelfth Edition. New York: Norton, 2017.

McAdams, Dan P. "What Do We Know When We Know a Person?" *Journal of Personality* 3 (1995) 365–96.

McCauley, Robert N., and E. Thomas Lawson. *Bringing Ritual to Mind: Psychological Foundations of Cultural Forms.* New York: Cambridge University Press, 2002.

McClendon, James William, Jr. *Biography as Theology: How Life Stories Can Remake Today's Theology.* Eugene, OR: Wipf & Stock, 2002.

McFague, Sallie. *Speaking in Parables: A Study in Metaphor and Theology.* Minneapolis: Fortress, 2000.

McGilchrist, Iain. *The Master and His Emissary: The Divided Brain and the Making of the Modern World.* New Haven: Yale University Press, 2009.

McGrath, Alister E. "The Biography of God." *Christianity Today* 35 (1991) 22–24.

———. *Christian Theology: An Introduction.* Malden, MA: Wiley-Blackwell, 2011.

McHugh, Adam S. *The Listening Life: Embracing Attentiveness in a World of Distraction.* Downers Grove, IL: IVP, 2015.

McLain, J. Peter. "Evaluations and Oral Cultures." In *Orality Breakouts: Using Heart Language to Transform Hearts,* edited by Samuel Chiang and Avery T. Willis, 119–26. Hong Kong: International Orality Network, 2012.

McLuhan, Marshall. *Understanding Media: The Extensions of Man.* Cambridge, MA: MIT Press, 1994.

McLuhan, Marshall, and Quentin Fiore. *The Medium is the Message: An Inventory of Effects.* New York: Penguin, 1967.

McQuinn, Scott. "Basic Principles for Teaching a Second Language Based on SLA Research." Lecture at a Hebrew Pedagogy Workshop sponsored by the Biblical Language Center at Fresno Pacific University, June 3–7, 2019.

Miller, Dorothy A. *Simply the Story Handbook.* Hemet, CA: The God's Story Project, 2012.

Moody, Dwight Lyman. "Quotes by Dwight Lyman Moody (1837–1899)." http://www.jesus-is-savior.com/Great%20Men%20of%20God/dwight_moody-quotes.htm.

Moon, Jay. "Encouraging Ducks to Swim: Suggestions for Seminary Professors Teaching Oral Learners." *William Carey International Development Journal* 2 (2013) 3–10.

Mooney, Bill, and David Holt. *The Storyteller's Guide: Storytellers Share Advice for the Classroom, Boardroom, Showroom, Podium, Pulpit, and Center Stage.* Atlanta: August House, 1996.

Moreau, Scott A. *Contextualization in World Missions: Mapping and Assessing Evangelical Models.* Grand Rapids: Kregel, 2012.

———. *Evangelical Dictionary of World Missions.* Grand Rapids: Baker, 2000.

Morgan, David. *The Sacred Gaze: Religious Visual Culture in Theory and Practice.* Berkeley: University of California Press, 2005.

Motty, Bauta. "Spreading the Word to Know the Truth." *Mission Frontiers* 36 (2014) 9.

Murrin, Michael. *The Veil of Allegory: Some Notes Towards a Theory of Allegorical Rhetoric in the English Renaissance.* Chicago: University of Chicago Press, 1969.

Neyrey, Jerome H. *Honor and Shame in the Gospel of Matthew.* Louisville: Westminster John Knox, 1998.

Nida, Eugene A. (Interviewee), and David Neff (Interviewer). "Meaning-full Translations." *Christianity Today* 46 (2002) 46–49.

Niditch, Susan. *Oral World and Written Word: Ancient Israelite Literature.* Louisville: Westminster John Knox, 1996.

Niemi, Loren. *The Book of Plots.* Coral Springs, FL: Llumina, 2006.

Nisbett, Richard. *The Geography of Thought: How Asians and Westerners Think Different . . . and Why.* New York: Free Press, 2003.

Noth, Martin. "The 'Re-Presentation' of the Old Testament Proclamation." In *Essays on Old Testament Hermeneutics*, edited by Claus Westermann, 76–88. Louisville: Westminster John Knox, 1960.

Novelli, Michael. *Shaped By the Story: Discover the Art of Biblical Storying.* Minneapolis: Sparkhouse, 2013.

Okholm, Dennis. *Learning Theology through the Church's Worship.* Grand Rapids: Baker Academic, 2018.

Oliver, Charles M. *Ernest Hemingway A to Z: The Essential Reference to the Life and Work.* New York: Checkmark, 1999.

Olson, David R. "The Cognitive Consequences of Literacy." *Canadian Psychology/Psychologic Canadienne* 27 (1986) 109–21.

———. "From Utterance to Text: The Bias of Language Speech and Writing." *Harvard Educational Review* 47 (1977) 257–81.

———. *The World of Paper: The Conceptual and Cognitive Implications of Writing and Reading.* New York: Cambridge University Press, 1994.

Ong, Walter. "Before Textuality: Orality and Interpretation." *Oral Tradition* 3 (1988) 259–69.

———. "Hermeneutic Forever: Voice, Text, Digitization, and the 'I.'" *Oral Tradition* 10 (1995) 3–36.

———. "Literacy and Orality in Our Times." In *Composition and Literature: Bridging the Gap*, edited by Winfred Bryan, 126–40. Chicago: University of Chicago Press, 1983.

———. "*Maranatha*: Death and Life in the Text of a Book." *Journal of the American Academy of Religion* 45 (1977) 419–49.

———. *Orality and Literacy: The Technologizing of the Word*. New York: Methuen & Co., 1982.

———. "Oral Remembering and Narrative Structures." In *Georgetown University Round Table on Languages and Linguistics 1981*, edited by Deborah Tannen, 12–24. Washington DC: Georgetown University Press, 1982.

———. *Rhetoric, Romance, and Technology: Studies in the Interaction of Expression and Culture*. Ithaca, NY: Cornell University Press, 1971.

Opler, Morris E. "Themes as Dynamic Forces in Culture." *American Journal of Sociology* 51 (1945) 198–206.

Orum, Anthony M., and Xiangming Chen. *The World of Cities: Places in Comparative and Historical Perspective*. Oxford: Blackwell, 2003.

Osborne, Grant R. *The Hermeneutical Spiral: A Comprehensive Introduction to Biblical Interpretation*. Downers Grove, IL: InterVarsity, 2006.

———. "Historical Criticism and the Evangelical." *JETS* 42 (1999) 193–210.

———. "Historical Narrative and Truth in the Bible." *JETS* 48 (2005) 673–88.

Paauw, Glenn R. *Saving the Bible from Ourselves: Learning to Read & Live the Bible Well*. Downers Grove, IL: InterVarsity, 2016.

Papacharissi, Zizi. "The Unbearable Lightness of Information and the Impossible Gravitas of Knowledge: Big Data and the Makings of a Digital Orality." *Media, Culture, & Society* 37 (2015) 1–6.

Pardo-Kaplan, Deborah. "Bible Study's New School: How Bible Study Fellowship is Rewriting its Rulebook to Double its Under-40 Membership and Adapt for a New Generation." *Christianity Today* 61 (2017) 39–43.

Parker, David C. *The Living Text of the Gospels*. Cambridge: Cambridge University Press, 1997.

Parsons, John J. "Seventy Faces of Torah." https://hebrew4christians.com/Articles/Seventy_Faces/seventy_faces.html.

Parunak, H. Van Dyke. "Oral Typesetting: Some Uses of Biblical Structure." *Biblica* 62 (1981) 153–68.

Pascal, Blaise. "Manifest Propensity." https://manifestpropensity.wordpress.com/2013/03/23/the-heart-has-its-reasons-which-reason-does-not-know-blaise-pascal/.

Pastor, Paul J. "How the Bible Project Is Using Video to Get People into Scripture Again." *Christianity Today* March 15, 2019. https://www.christianitytoday.com/ct/2019/april/bible-project-tim-mackie-jon-collins-scripture.html.

Patterson, Kerry, et al. *Critical Conversations: Tools for Talking When Stakes are High*. Chicago: McGraw-Hill, 2012.

Payne, J. D. *Pressure Points: Twelve Global Issues Shaping the Face of the Church*. Nashville: Thomas Nelson, 2013.

Pelikan, Jaroslav. *The Christian Tradition: A History of the Development of Doctrine, Vol. 1: The Emergence of the Catholic Tradition (100-600)*. Chicago: University of Chicago Press, 1971.

Pellauer, David. "Paul Ricoeur." *Stanford Encyclopedia of Philosophy*, 2016. Edited by Edward N. Zalta. https://plato.stanford.edu/entries/ricoeur/.

Pennington, Jonathan T. *Reading the Gospels Wisely: A Narrative and Theological Introduction*. Grand Rapids: Baker Academic, 2012.

Peppiatt, Lucy. *Women and Worship at Corinth: Paul's Rhetorical Arguments in 1 Corinthians*. Eugene, OR: Wipf & Stock, 2015.

Petersen, John. *Reading Women's Stories: Female Characters in the Hebrew Bible*. Minneapolis: Fortress, 2004.
Peterson, Eugene H. *Leap Over a Wall: Earthy Spirituality for Everyday Christians*. New York: HarperCollins, 1997.
———. *Working the Angles: The Shape of Pastoral Integrity*. Grand Rapids: Eerdmans, 1987.
Pew Research Center. "Why America's 'Nones' Don't Identify with A Religion." *FacTank* (blog) August 8, 2018. https://www.pewresearch.org/fact-tank/2018/08/08/why-americas-nones-dont-identify-with-a-religion/.
Pink, Daniel H. *A Whole New Mind: Why Right-Brainers Will Rule the Future*. New York: Riverhead, 2005.
Pinnock, Clark. "The Work of the Holy Spirit in Hermeneutics." *Journal of Pentecostal Theology* 2 (1993) 3–23.
Piper, John. *Desiring God: Meditations of a Christian Hedonist*. Sisters, OR: Multnomah, 2011.
Plimpton, George. "Ernest Hemingway, The Art of Fiction No. 21." *The Paris Review* 21 (1958) 1–31. http://thresholds.chi.ac.uk/wp-content/uploads/2010/08/The-Art-of-Fiction-Hemingway.pdf.
Polkinghorne, Donald E. *Narrative Knowing and the Human Sciences*. Albany: State University of New York Press, 1988.
Poobalan, Ivor. "Christology in Asia: Rooted and Responsive." In *Asian Christian Theology: Evangelical Perspectives*, edited by Timoteo D. Gener and Stephen T. Pardue, 83–100. Cumbria, UK: Langham Global Library, 2019.
Porter, Stanley E., Jr., and Beth M. Stovell. *Biblical Hermeneutics: Five Views*. Downers Grove, IL: InterVarsity Academic, 2012.
Postman, Neil. *Amusing Ourselves to Death: Public Discourse in the Age of Show Business*. New York: Sifton, 1985.
Poythress, Vern. "Analyzing a Biblical Text: Some Important Linguistic Distinctions." *Scottish Journal of Theology* 32 (1979) 113–31.
Prior, Karen Shallow. *On Reading Well: Finding the Good Life through Great Books*. Grand Rapids: Brazos, 2018.
Pryce-Jones, David. *The Closed Circle: An Interpretation of the Arabs*. Chicago: Dee, 2009.
Pui-lan, Kwok. "Hearing and Talking: Oral Hermeneutics of Asian Women." In *New Directions in Mission & Evangelism 3: Faith and Culture*, edited by James A. Scherer and Stephen B. Bevans, 76–90. Maryknoll, NY: Orbis, 1999.
Ramm, Bernard. *The Christian View of Science and Scripture*. Grand Rapids: Eerdmans, 1954.
Rau, Andy. "'Noah' Generates a Flood of Bible Readers Over the Weekend." *Bible Gateway Blog*. April 2, 2014. https://www.biblegateway.com/blog/2014/04/noah-generates-a-flood-of-bible-readers-over-the-weekend/.
Ray, Blaine, and Contee Seely. *Fluency through TPR Storytelling: Achieving Real Language Acquisition in School*. 8th ed. Denver: Command Performance Language Institute, 2018.
Resseguie, James L. *Narrative Criticism of the New Testament: An Introduction*. Grand Rapids: Baker Academic, 2005.
Rhoads, David. "Performance Criticism: An Emerging Methodology in Second Testament Studies—Part II." *Biblical Theology Bulletin* 36 (2006) 164–84.

Richard, Ramesh. "Training Pastors: A High Priority for Global Ministry Strategy." *The Exchange* (blog) January 1, 2016. https://www.christianitytoday.com/edstetzer/2015/december/training-pastors-high-priority-for-global-ministry-strategy.html#_edn2.
Richardson, Don. *Peace Child*. Minneapolis: Bethany House, 2005.
Richardson, Rick. *Re-imaging Evangelism: Inviting Friends on a Spiritual Journey*. Downers Grove, IL: InterVarsity, 2006.
Ricoeur, Paul. *Essays of Biblical Interpretation*. Philadelphia: Fortress, 1980.
———. *Oneself as Another*. Chicago: University of Chicago Press, 1992.
———. *Paul Ricoeur Interpretation Theory*. Fort Worth: Texas Christian University Press, 1976.
———. *Time and Narrative, Vol. 1*. Chicago: University of Chicago Press, 1983.
———. *Time and Narrative, Vol. 3*. Chicago: University of Chicago Press, 1988.
Roberts, J. Deotis. *Liberation and Reconciliation: A Black Theology*. Louisville: Westminster John Knox, 2005.
Robinson, James H. "Ch'emyon in the EFL Classroom." *MinneTESOL/WITESOL Journal* 15 (1998) 13–28.
Ryken, Leland. "The Bible: God's Story-book." *Christianity Today* 23 (1979) 34–38.
———. *The Literature of the Bible*. Grand Rapids: Zondervan, 1974.
———. *Words of Delight: A Literary Introduction to the Bible*. Grand Rapids: Baker Academic, 1992.
Ryken, Leland, and Tremper Longman III, eds. *A Complete Literary Guide to the Bible*. Grand Rapids: Zondervan, 1993.
Ryken, Leland, et al., eds. *Dictionary of Biblical Imagery: An Encyclopedic Exploration of the Images, Symbols, Motifs, Metaphors, Figures of Speech and Literary Patterns of the Bible*. Downers Grove, IL: InterVarsity, 1998.
Sachs, Jonah. *Winning the Story Wars: Why Those Who Tell (and Live) the Best Stories Will Rule the Future*. Boston: Harvard Business Review, 2012.
Saenger, Paul. "Silent Reading: Its Impact on Late Medieval Script and Society." *Viator* 13 (1982) 367–14.
Sailhamer, John H. *The Pentateuch as Narrative: A Biblical-Theological Commentary*. Grand Rapids: Zondervan, 1992.
Sandy, D. Brent, and Ronald L. Giese Jr. *Cracking Old Testament Codes: A Guide to Interpreting the Literary Genres of the Old Testament*. Nashville: B & H, 1995.
Sayers, Dorothy. *The Greatest Drama Ever Staged*. London: Hodder and Stoughton, 1938. http://www.gutenberg.ca/ebooks/sayers-greatest/sayers-greatest-00-h.html#ch01greatest.
Schattner, Frank. *The Wheel Model: Catalyzing Sustainable Church Multiplication Movements*. Rocklin, CA: William Jessup University Press, 2014.
Schniedewind, William. *How the Bible Became a Book*, Cambridge: Cambridge University Press, 2004.
Schultze, Dell, and Rachel Sue Schultze. *God and Man*. Manila: Self-published, 1984.
Scott, Bernard Brandon, and Margaret Dean. "A Sound Map of the Sermon on the Mount." In *SBL Seminar Papers*, edited by Eugene H. Lovering, 672–25, Atlanta: Scholars, 1993.
Searle, John R. "Austin on Locutionary and Illocutionary Acts." *The Philosophical Review* 77 (1968) 405–25.

Senge, Peter M. *The Fifth Discipline: The Art & Practice of the Learning Organization.* New York: Doubleday, 2006.

Seymour, D. Bruce. *Creating Stories that Connect: A Pastor's Guide to Storytelling.* Grand Rapids: Kregel, 2007.

Shaw, Susan M. *Storytelling in Religious Education.* Birmingham, AL: Religious Education, 1999.

Shoemaker, H. Stephen. *Godstories: New Narratives from Sacred Texts.* Valley Forge, PA: Judson, 1998.

Siegel, Daniel J. *The Developing Mind: How Relationships and the Brain Interact to Shape Who We are.* New York: Guilford, 1999.

———. *Pocket Guide to Interpersonal Neurobiology: An Integrative Handbook of the Mind.* New York: Norton, 2012.

Sills, M. David. "Competing and Conflicting Mission." *Southwestern Journal of Theology* 57 (2014) 39–48.

Silva, Moises. *Foundations of Contemporary Interpretation.* Grand Rapids: Zondervan, 1996.

Slavsky, Alexander. "Gallup Poll: US Church Attendance Dropping." https://www.churchmilitant.com/news/article/gallup-poll-u.s.-church-attendance-dropping.

Smith, Craig Stephen. *Whiteman's Gospel.* Winnipeg, MB: Indian Life, 1997.

Smith, James K. A. *Desiring the Kingdom: Worship, Worldview, and Cultural Formation.* Grand Rapids: Baker Academic, 2009.

Smith, Steve, with Ying Kai. *T4T: A Discipleship ReRevolution.* Monument, CO: WIGTake Resources, 2011.

Snowden, Mark. *Orality in America.* Palm Desert, CA: Mission America Coalition, 2016.

Sontag, Susan, ed. *A Barthes Reader.* New York: Hill and Wang, 1982.

Sperber, Dan, and Deirdre Wilson, *Relevance: Communication and Cognition.* Malden, MA: Blackwell, 1995.

Stark, Rodney. *The Victory of Reason: How Christianity Led to Freedom, Capitalism, and Western Success.* New York: Random House, 2006.

Stearns, Maureen. *Conscious Courage: Turning Everyday Challenges into Opportunities.* Seminole, FL: Enrichment, 2004.

Steffen, Tom. "A Clothesline Theology for the World: How a Value-Driven Grand Narrative of Scripture Can Frame the Gospel." *Great Commission Research Journal* 9 (2018) 235–72.

———. "Discoveries Made While Reconnecting God's Story to Scripture and Service." *Christian Education Journal* 14 (2017) 160–83.

———. *The Facilitator Era: Beyond Pioneer Church Multiplication.* Eugene, OR: Wipf & Stock, 2011.

———. "Foundational Roles of Symbol and Narrative in the (Re)construction of Reality and Relationships." *Missiology* 26 (1998) 477–94.

———. "Minimizing Crosscultural Evangelism Noise." *Missiology* 43 (2015) 413–28.

———. *Passing the Baton: Church Planting that Empowers.* La Habra, CA: Center for Organizational & Ministry Development, 1997.

———. "Pedagogical Conversions: From Propositions to Story and Symbol." *Missiology* 38 (2010) 141–59.

———. *Reconnecting God's Story to Ministry: Cross-cultural Storytelling at Home and Abroad.* Waynesboro, GA: Authentic Media, 2005.

———. "Saving Locals from Our Theologies." Unpublished paper presented at the Evangelical Missiological Society Northwest, Spokane, WA, April 1, 2017.
———. "Saving the Locals from Our Theologies, Part 1." *JAM* 19 (2018) 3–33.
———. "Saving the Locals from Our Theologies, Part 2." *JAM* 19 (2018) 37–61.
———. "Theories Drive Our Ministries Whether We Know Them or Not." *Reformed Life Theology and Mission* 1 (2011) 191–39.
———. *Worldview-based Storying: The Integration of Symbol, Story, and Ritual in the Orality Movement*. Richmond, VA: Orality Resources International, 2018.
Steinbarg, Eliezer, ed., *The Jewish Book of Fables*. Coral Gables, FL: Dora Teitelboim Center for Yiddish Culture, 2003.
Sternberg, Meir. *The Poetics of Biblical Narrative: Ideological Literature and the Drama of Reading*. Bloomington: Indiana University Press, 1987.
———. "Time and Space in Biblical (Hi)story Telling: The Grand Chronology." In *The Book and the Text: The Bible and Literary Theory*, edited by Regina Schwartz, 81–145. Cambridge, MA: Blackwell, 1990.
Stevens, Mitchell. *The Rise of the Image, the Fall of the World*. New York: Oxford, 1998.
Stock, Brian. *The Implications of Literacy: Written Language and Models of Interpretation in the Eleventh and Twelfth Centuries*. Princeton: Princeton University Press, 1987.
Stout, Harry S. "Theological Commitment and American Religious History." *Theological Education* 25 (1989) 44–59.
Stringer, Stephen, ed. *S-T4T: Intentional Evangelism Utilizing Stories from God's Word Resulting in Multiplying House Churches*. Monument, CO: WigTake, 2008.
Strobel, Lee. *The Case for Christ: A Journalist's Personal Investigation of the Evidence for Jesus*. Grand Rapids: Zondervan, 1998.
Swearingen, C. Jan. "Oral Hermeneutics During Transition to Literacy: The Contemporary Debate." *Cultural Anthropology* 1 (1986) 138–56.
Sweet, Leonard. *The Bad Habits of Jesus: Showing Us the Way to Live Right in a World Gone Wrong*. Carol Stream, IL: Tyndale House. 2016.
Tannehill, Robert, C. "The Composition of Acts 3–5: Narrative Development and Echo Effect." In *Society of Biblical Literature 1984 Seminar Papers*, edited by Kent Harold Richards, 217–40. Chico, CA: Scholars, 1984.
Tedlock, Dennis. *Finding the Center: Narrative Poetry of the Zuni Indians*. New York: Dial, 1978.
Thatcher, Tom. "Beyond Texts and Traditions: Werner Kelber's Media History of Christian Origin." In *Jesus the Voice and the Text*, edited by Tom Thatcher, 1–26. Waco, TX: Baylor University Press, 2008.
Thatcher, Tom, ed., *Jesus, the Voice and the Text: Beyond the Oral and the Written Gospel*. Waco, TX: Baylor University Press, 2008.
Thigpen, Lynn L. "Connected Learning: A Grounded Theory Study of How Cambodian Adults with Limited Formal Education Learn." PhD diss., Cook School of Intercultural Studies, Biola University, 2016.
Third Millennium Ministries. *The Book of Revelation: The Background of Revelation Discussion Forum*. Casselberry, FL, Third Millennium Ministries, 2013. https://thirdmill.org/seminary/manuscripts/TheBookOfRevelation.Forum1.Manuscript.English.pdf.
Thomas, Rosalind. *Literacy and Orality in Ancient Greece*. Cambridge: Cambridge University Press, 1992.

Tiede, Bob. "339 Questions Jesus Asked." http://339questionsjesusasked.com/wp-content/downloads/eng-P8VoLUagOIjvyerRXfmATLRLDqIZ6qMG.pdf.
Tiénou, Tite. "Biblical Foundations for African Theology." *Missiology* 10 (1982) 435–48.
———. "Christianity Theology in an Era of World Christianity." In *Globalizing Theology: Belief and Practice in an Era of World Christianity*, edited by Craig Ott and Harold A. Netland, 37–51. Grand Rapids: Baker Academic, 2006.
Tozer, A. W. *The Attributes of God, Vol. 1: A Journey into the Father's Heart with Study Guide*. Chicago: Wing Spread, 2003.
Tucker, Ruth A. *The Biographical Bible: Exploring the Biblical Narrative from Adam and Eve to John of Patmos*. Grand Rapids: Baker, 2013.
Tverberg, Lois. *Reading the Bible with Rabbi Jesus: How A Jewish Perspective Can Transform Your Understanding*. Grand Rapids: Baker, 2017.
Vanhoozer, Kevin J. *The Drama of Doctrine: A Canonical Linguistic Approach to Christian Theology*. Louisville: Westminster John Knox, 2005.
———. *First Theology: God, Scripture & Hermeneutics*. Downers Grove, IL: IVP Academic, 2002.
———. "'One Rule to Rule Them All?' Theological Method in an Era of World Christianity." In *Globalizing Theology: Belief and Practice in an Era of World Christianity*, edited by Craig Ott and Harold A. Netland, 85–139. Grand Rapids: Baker Academic, 2006.
———. "The Semantics of Biblical Literature: Truth and Scripture's Diverse Literary Forms." In *Hermeneutics, Authority, and Canon*, edited by D. A. Carson and John D. Woodbridge, 49–104. Eugene, OR: Wipf & Stock, 2005.
Volf, Miroslav, and Matthew Croasmun. *For the Life of the World: Theology that Makes a Difference*. Grand Rapids: Brazos, 2019.
von Balthasar, Hans Urs. *A Theology of History*. New York: Sheed and Ward, 1963.
Wall, Robert W. "The Significance of a Canonical Perspective of the Church's Scripture." In *The Canon Debate*, edited by Lee Martin McDonald and James A. Sanders, 528–40. Peabody, MA: Hendrickson, 2008.
Walls, Andrew F. *The Missionary Movement in Christian History: Studies in the Transmission of Faith*. Maryknoll, NY: Orbis, 1996.
———. "Spirituality and Theological Education." *Ogbomoso Journal of Theology* 16 (2011) 1–12.
Walton, John H., and D. Brent Sandy. *The Lost World of Scripture: Ancient Literary Culture and Biblical Authority*, Downers Grove, IL: InterVarsity Academic, 2013.
Wan, Sze-kar. "Betwixt and Between: Toward a Hermeneutics of Hyphenation." In *Ways of Being, Ways of Reading: Asian American Biblical Interpretation*, edited by Mary F. Foskett and Jeffrey Kah-Jin Kuan, 137–51. St. Louis: Chalice, 2006.
Warner, Marcus, and Jim Wilder. *Rare Leadership: 4 Uncommon Habits for Increasing Trust, Joy, and Engagement in the People You Lead*. Chicago: Moody, 2016.
Warnke, Georgia. *Gadamer: Hermeneutics, Tradition and Reason*. Stanford: Stanford University Press, 1987.
Watson, David. *Honor among Christians: The Cultural Key to the Messianic Secret*. Minneapolis: Fortress, 2010.
Watson, Jill A. "Interpreting across the Abyss: A Hermeneutic Exploration of Initial Literacy Development by High School English-Language Learners with Limited Formal Schooling." PhD diss., University of Minnesota, 2010.
Weathers, Robert A. "Leland Ryken's Literary Approach." *JETS* 37 (1994) 115–24.
West, Gerald O. "Biblical Hermeneutics in Africa." In *African Theology on the Way*, edited by D. B. Stinton, 21–34. London: SPCK, 2010.

Wilder, James E., et. al. *Joy Starts Here: The Transformation Zone*. Lexington, KY: Shepherd's House, 2013.
Willimon, William H. *Conversations with Barth on Preaching*. Nashville: Abingdon, 2006.
Wilkins, Michael J., and J. P. Moreland, eds. *Jesus Under Fire: Modern Scholarship Reinvents the Historical Jesus*. Grand Rapids: Zondervan, 1995.
Wilson, Marvin R. *Our Father Abraham: Jewish Roots of the Christian Faith*. Grand Rapids: Eerdmans, 1989.
Winger, Thomas M. "Orality as the Key to Understanding Apostolic Proclamation in the Epistles." ThD diss., Concordia Seminary, St. Louis, 1997.
———. "The Spoken Word: What's Up with Orality?" *Concordia Journal* 27 (2003) 133–51.
Wiseman, Liz. *Multipliers: How the Best Leaders Make Everyone Smarter*. New York: HarperCollins, 2010.
Witherington III, Ben. *New Testament Rhetoric: An Introductory Guide to the Art of Persuasion in and of the New Testament*. Eugene, OR: Cascade, 2009.
———. *Paul's Narrative Thought World: The Tapestry of Tragedy and Triumph*. Louisville: Westminster/John Knox, 1994.
———. "Sacred Texts in an Oral Culture—How Did They Function?" https://benwitherington.blogspot.com/2007/10/sacred-texts-in-oral-culturehow-did.html.
———. *What's in the Word: Rethinking the Socio-Rhetorical Character of the New Testament*. Waco, TX: Baylor University Press, 2009.
Woodhull, Kenny. "The Art of Parabling: Leveraging the Narrative Parables of Jesus as Models of Missional Engagement." *Missiology* 41 (2013) 74–86.
Wright, G. Ernest. *God Who Acts: Biblical Theology as Recital*. London: SCM, 1960.
Wright, N. T. "Foreword." In *The King Jesus Gospel: The Original Good News Revisited*, edited by Scot McKnight, 11–13. Grand Rapids: Zondervan, 2011.
———. *The New Testament and the People of God*. Minneapolis: Fortress, 1992.
Wu, Jackson. "Chiasm, Oral Peoples, and the Grand Biblical Story." *Patheos*, July 26, 2017. https://www.patheos.com/blogs/jacksonwu/2017/07/26/chiasm-oral-peoples-grand-biblical-story/.
Wu, Joshua. "Desiring the Kingdom in Missions: An Application of James K. A. Smith's 'Liturgical Anthropology' in a Cross-cultural Context." *Global Missiology* 4 (2015) 1–27.
Wuellner, Wilhelm. "Where is Rhetorical Criticism Taking Us?" *Catholic Biblical Quarterly* 49 (1987) 448–63.
Yamamori, Tetsunao, and Charles R. Taber, eds. *Christopaganism or Indigenous Christianity?* Pasadena, CA: William Carey Library, 1975.
Yancey, Philip. *The Bible Jesus Read: Why the Old Testament Matters*. Grand Rapids: Zondervan, 1999.
Zion, Noam. "The Origins of Human Violence and the Crisis of the Biblical First Family: Cain and Abel in Torah, Commentary, Midrash, Art, Poetry, Movies, and Thought." Notes from a class taught at the Shalom Hartman Institute in Jerusalem, 2014.
Zuck, Roy B. "The Role of the Spirit in Hermeneutics." *Bibliotheca Sacra* 141 (1984) 120–29.
———. *Teaching as Jesus Taught*. Eugene, OR: Wipf & Stock, 2002.

www.ingramcontent.com/pod-product-compliance
Lightning Source LLC
Chambersburg PA
CBHW070837020526
44114CB00041B/1490